Bert Swart and André Klip (Eds.)
International Criminal Law in the Netherlands

Beiträge und Materialien aus dem Max-Planck-Institut
für ausländisches und internationales Strafrecht, Freiburg i.Br.

Herausgegeben von Professor Dr. Dr. h.c. Albin Eser, M.C.J.

Band S 66

International Criminal Law in the Netherlands

Edited by

Bert Swart and André Klip

Freiburg im Breisgau 1997

Professor Dr. Bert Swart
Dr. André Klip
Willem Pompe Instituut
voor Strafrechtswetenschappen
Janskerkhof
3512 BM Utrecht
The Netherlands

Die Deutsche Bibliothek - CIP-Einheitsaufnahme

International criminal law in the netherlands / ed. by Bert Swart
and André Klip. - Freiburg im Breisgau : Ed. iuscrim, Max-Planck-
Inst. für Ausländisches und Internat. Strafrecht, 1997
  (Beiträge und Materialien aus dem Max-Planck-Institut für
  Ausländisches und Internationales Strafrecht Freiburg i. Br. ; S 66)
  ISBN 3-86113-960-X

© 1997 edition iuscrim
Max-Planck-Institut für ausländisches
und internationales Strafrecht
Günterstalstraße 73, D - 79100 Freiburg i. Br.

Printed in Germany/Imprimé en Allemagne

Herstellung: Reprodienst GmbH • Gündlinger Str. 8
D - 79111 Freiburg i. Br.

ISBN 3-86113-960-X

Preface

This book is the product of a long-standing cooperation between the departments of criminal law of the University of Utrecht (Willem Pompe Institute) and the University of Amsterdam (Van Hamel Institute). All the contributors are, or have been, members of these departments, engaged in academic research in the field of international criminal law.

Why should we produce a book on international criminal law in the Netherlands? Our decision to do so was based on several motives.

Our first and most important goal is to make international criminal law in the Netherlands accessible to foreign scholars. From an academic point of view, it seems valuable to present a systematic and comprehensive overview of that part of the law in a given legal system. This may enable scholars in other countries to acquire a fuller and deeper understanding of an important area of the law in a different legal system, to become acquainted with its special features and peculiarities, and to study it against its historical background as well as economic, social and cultural factors shaping its contents. Moreover, studies like the one presented here may contribute to facilitating and stimulating comparative research in the field of international criminal law, which is all the more important now that international criminal law is itself in a process of rapid transition.

Our hope is that this book will also be of some value to practitioners in the field of international criminal law, both in the Netherlands and in other countries. It may, perhaps, help them in communicating with one another and in exchanging views in the day-to-day business of international cooperation in criminal matters. Diplomats and civil servants engaged in negotiations on new international instruments regarding international criminal law may be similarly benefitted.

Finally, some of us have been engaged in teaching international criminal law to foreign students visiting Dutch law faculties, whether within the framework of Erasmus and Socrates programmes or on another basis. This book may make Dutch law in this area more readily accessible to them.

These various aims explain why we did not limit ourselves to offering a collection of essays. Included as an Appendix to the text are also translations of the most important statutes with regard to international criminal law in the Netherlands. Moreover, another Appendix includes data on all international treaties that are, in a broad sense, relevant to the subject-matter and to which the Netherlands has become a party. In particular, it contains the full original or translated text of reservations and declarations made by the Netherlands to these instruments.

The editors would like to express their sincere gratitude to Wieneke Matthijsse who cheerfully produced the book. We are also indebted to Kitty Arambulo, Jeanne Dortu, Eveline Eckelboom, Irene Fros, Kathelijn Korver, Göran Sluiter and others who have assisted us in our work. The Ministry of Foreign Affairs of the Netherlands has kindly permitted us to update and revise translations of statutes made by the Ministry and to publish them. It would not have been possible to make this book without the generous financial support of the Willem Pompe Institute and the Van Hamel Institute. Finally, we are very grateful to the Max-Planck-Institut für ausländisches und internationales Strafrecht for having agreed to publish this collection of essays.

Amsterdam/Utrecht, March 1997

Bert Swart
André Klip

Table of Contents

Abbreviations

A	Aruba
AB	Administratiefrechtelijke Beslissingen
AIDP	Association Internationale de Droit Pénal
Bevans	Treaties and other International Agreements of the United States of America, 1776-1949 (C.F. Bevans ed., 1970, 13 vols.)
BRvC	Bijzondere Raad van Cassatie
CCNR	Central Commission for Navigation on the Rhine
DD	Delikt en Delinkwent
ECHR	European Court of Human Rights
ETS	European Treaty Series
EuGRZ	Europäische Grundrechte Zeitschrift
HR	Hoge Raad
ICJ	International Court of Justice
ILM	International Legal Materials
KG	Kort Geding
LNTS	League of Nations Treaty Series
Martens Nouveau Recueil	Nouveau Recueil Général des Traités
NA	Netherlands Antilles
NJ	Nederlandse Jurisprudentie
NJB	Nederlands Juristenblad
NL	Netherlands
NTIR	Nederlands Tijdschrift voor Internationaal Recht
NYIL	Netherlands Yearbook of International Law
OJ	Official Journal of the European Communities
PB	Publicatieblad van de Europese Gemeenschappen
PCIJ	Permanent Court of International Justice
RIDP	Revue Internationale de Droit Pénal
SEW	Sociaal-Economische Wetgeving
Stat.	United States Statutes at Large

Stb.	Staatsblad
Stc.	Staatscourant
StV	Strafverteidiger
TIAS	Treaties and Other International Acts Series (United States)
Trb.	Tractatenblad
TS	Treaty Series (United States)
UNTS	United Nations Treaty Series
UST	United States Treaty Series
W.	Weekblad van het Recht
ZStW	Zeitschrift für die gesamte Strafrechtswissenschaft

Glossary

Administratiefrechtelijke Beslissingen	Reports of Administrative Cases
Bijzondere Raad van Cassatie	Special Court of Cassation
Gerechtshof	Court of Appeal
Hoge Raad	Supreme Court
Kort Geding	Reports of Interim Injunction Proceedings
Nederlandse Jurisprudentie	Netherlands Law Reports
Raad van State	Council of State
Rechtbank	District Court
Staatsblad	Official Journal
Staatscourant	Official Gazette
Tractatenblad	Netherlands Treaty Series

Table of Cases

Cour d'Appel Liège

16 October 1991, 74 Revue de Droit Pénal et de Criminologie 1994, p. 111
   224

Germany

Bundesverfassungsgericht

6 March 1986, EuGRZ 1987, 92 and StV 1987, 137   *222*

Bundesgerichtshof

30 May 1985, EuGRZ 1987, 94   *222*
19 December 1986, StV 1987, 138   *221, 223*

Oberlandesgericht Düsseldorf

31 May 1983, NJW 1984, 2050   *222*

United Kingdom

House of Lords
Cheng v. Governor of Pentonville Prison [1973], 2 Weekly Law Reports,
   746-772   *103*

United States

Supreme Court

Alvarez Machain (112 S. Ct. 2188, 1992)   *220*

Table of Statutes and Orders

Wet identificatie bij financiële dienstverlening 1993 *(Act on the identification of clients of financial institutions 1993)*, 16 December 1993, Staatsblad 1993, 704   *45*

Wet melding ongebruikelijke transacties *(Act on the disclosure of unusual transactions)*, 16 December 1993, Staatsblad 1993, 705   *45, 161-162*

Wet houdende bepalingen verband houdende met de instelling van het Internationaal Tribunaal voor de vervolging van personen aansprakelijk voor ernstige schendingen van het internationale humanitaire recht, begaan op het grondgebied van het voormalige Joegoslavië sedert 1991 *(Act containing provisions relating to the establishment of the International Tribunal for the prosecution of persons responsible for serious violations of international humanitarian law committed in the territory of the former Yugoslavia since 1991)*, 21 April 1994, Staatsblad 1994, 308   *89-90, 125, 193*

Rijkswet goedkeuring en bekendmaking verdragen *(Kingdom Act on the approval and publication of treaties)*, 7 July 1994, Staatsblad 1994, 542   *89*

Wet voorkoming misbruik chemicaliën *(Act on prevention of misuse of chemical substances)*, 16 March 1995, Staatsblad 1995, 258   *41*

Uitvoeringswet verdrag chemische wapens *(Act implementing the Chemical Weapons Convention)*, 8 June 1995, Staatsblad 1995, 338   *33, 69*

Douanewet *(Customs Act)*, 2 November 1995, Staatsblad 1995, 553   *71, 232, 241, 246*

General Observations

Bert Swart

Introduction

This book offers a collection of ten essays dealing with specific aspects of international criminal law in the Netherlands. Taken together they intend to give a comprehensive analysis of that part of the law to the foreign reader. Some contributions deal with matters which, from a Dutch perspective, might be called matters of substantive criminal law (international offences, jurisdiction, foreign *res judicata*), others with matters of procedure (extradition, mutual assistance in criminal matters, transfer of proceedings and transfer of enforcement of criminal judgments, extraterritorial investigations), while still others deal with matters which, in a narrow definition, either do not entirely belong to the realm of international criminal law or closely border on it (police cooperation, cooperation in tax matters). Most contributions are concerned with traditional and familiar issues of international criminal law. Some, however, venture into fields which have attracted but little attention in the past and might at present be considered to be important 'growth areas' of the law (notably police cooperation and extraterritorial investigations).

The following observations aim to achieve two different purposes. The first is to discuss some general aspects of Dutch (criminal) law with a view to helping the reader in studying and appreciating the contents of other contributions. In this respect it may be useful to provide information on the constitutional structure of the Kingdom of the Netherlands, on the implementation of international law in the Dutch legal order and on the influence of the Council of Europe, the Benelux, the European Union and Schengen on international criminal law in the Netherlands. My second aim is to draw some conclusions from the other contributions to this book. I will try to answer the question of whether and in what respects a specific Dutch approach to matters of international criminal law does exist, and how that approach might be explained against the background of political, economic or cultural factors shaping the Netherlands and its place in the world.

The Kingdom of the Netherlands: its constitutional structure

In matters of international criminal law it is essential to take the constitutional structure of the Kingdom of the Netherlands into account. The Kingdom consists of three, largely autonomous, parts. On the one hand, there is the European part of the Kingdom, always referred to as the Netherlands in legal texts. On the other, there are the Netherlands Antilles (comprising the islands of Bonaire, Curaçao, Saba, St Eustatius and St Maarten) and Aruba, both located in the Caribbean. The constitutional relations between the three component parts of the Kingdom are governed by the 1954 Charter for the Kingdom of the Netherlands *(Statuut voor het Koninkrijk der Nederlanden)*, granting autonomy to the Netherlands Antilles and Aruba in domestic affairs. Criminal justice is one of the areas over which autonomy extends. As a consequence, the Netherlands, the Netherlands Antilles and Aruba each have their own systems of criminal justice. On the other hand, a few matters have remained matters of concern to the Kingdom as a whole. Article 3 of the Charter lists foreign affairs and extradition among them. In these few matters, legislation takes the form of a so-called Act of the Kingdom. The various provisions of the Charter have considerable consequences for cooperation in criminal matters between the three parts of the Kingdom as well as with third states. They will be briefly discussed here.

Articles 36 to 40 of the Charter are devoted to mutual assistance, consultation and cooperation between the Netherlands, the Netherlands Antilles and Aruba. In this respect the provisions use the expression 'interregional cooperation'. Article 36 enshrines the general principle that the three countries shall offer help and assistance to one another. Article 40 declares that judgments as well as other decisions of courts in one part of the Kingdom shall be enforceable in the other parts. Article 39 lays down the principle of 'concordance': in certain areas, among them criminal justice, legislation in the three countries should, as far as possible, be the same.

Since the Netherlands, the Netherlands Antilles and Aruba have their own criminal justice systems, the provisions of the Charter on interregional cooperation are of vital importance. They enable the authorities of the three countries to cooperate with each other in ways not too different from cooperation between national authorities among themselves.[1] However, difficulties and uncertainties sometimes arise. Proposals to enact an Act of the Kingdom on the

---

1 For a study of the subject see *Hofstee/Schalken*, Strafrecht binnen het Koninkrijk.

matter are currently under discussion.[2] Of course, international treaties to which the Kingdom is a party do not apply in the reciprocal relations between the three parts of the Kingdom. The same is true for legislation in the Netherlands, the Netherlands Antilles and Aruba on international cooperation in criminal matters.

The fact that the three parts of the Kingdom enjoy autonomy in the area of criminal justice has considerable consequences for international criminal law. Each country possesses its own legislation governing international cooperation with other states. While the principle of concordance of the Charter would make harmonized legislation desirable, in actual practice this is often not the case. Although, for instance, the regulations in the Netherlands Antilles and Aruba on extradition are modelled after the 1967 Extradition Act of the Netherlands, there are also considerable differences, notably in matters of procedure. A number of factors play a role here: differences in mentality and outlook, differences in the way criminal justice systems are organized, differences in the importance attached to international cooperation in criminal matters, and the difficulties for small communities such as the Netherlands Antilles and Aruba involved in keeping legislation of an often technical and complex nature up to date. The second major consequence of autonomy is that each part of the Kingdom will, as a rule, handle requests for assistance in criminal matters to and from foreign states directly, the main exception being cases in which the use of diplomatic channels is required.

Since foreign relations have remained the concern of the Kingdom as a whole, the ratification and denunciation of treaties touching on matters of international criminal law is also a matter that has to be decided at that level. With respect to each individual treaty a decision will have to be taken on whether it will be ratified (or denounced) for the whole of the Kingdom or for one or two parts only. Though not sacrosanct under the Charter, in actual practice the wishes of the Netherlands Antilles and Aruba are, as far as is known, always respected. Ratification or denunciation of a treaty for the whole of the Kingdom is, therefore, not an automatism. Usually, though, the treaties to which the Kingdom has become a party will apply to the Netherlands Antilles and Aruba as well. This is, to a considerable extent, even true for treaties adopted within regional organizations such as the Council of Europe and the European Union, examples being the 1957 European Convention on Extra-

---

2   Cf. the Voorontwerp van Rijkswet inzake de strafrechtelijke samenwerking tussen de landen van het Koninkrijk.

dition and the 1991 Convention between the Member States of the European Communities on the Enforcement of Foreign Criminal Sentences. One of the consequences of traditional policies is that the Netherlands Antilles and Aruba, though located in the Caribbean, are rather Europe-oriented in their treaty relations with the outside world. As yet, they maintain bilateral treaty relations with but a few other states in the western hemisphere.[3]

As far as the Netherlands Antilles and Aruba are concerned, it is not enough to ascertain that the Kingdom of the Netherlands has become a party to an international treaty. One always has to be aware of the possibility that a treaty does not apply to one or both of them. Moreover, there may also be differences with respect to the applicability of reservations and declarations made to a treaty by the Kingdom. Detailed information on these matters is provided in Appendix II to this book.

The foregoing explains why the contributions to this book are limited to the Netherlands and do not attempt to discuss the law of the Netherlands Antilles and Aruba. Trying to do so would have required us to write three different books in one.

The Constitution and international law

Since issues of international law crop up in several contributions to this book, some introductory remarks should be made on the implementation of international law in the Dutch legal order.

Article 93 of the 1815 Constitution for the Kingdom of the Netherlands *(Grondwet voor het Koninkrijk der Nederlanden)*, as it now reads, declares that provisions of treaties and of decisions of international organizations which are binding on all persons by virtue of their contents shall be binding after they have been promulgated. Here, as well as in other statutory provisions, the word 'treaty' refers to any international agreement concluded between states, whatever its designation.[4] Although Art. 93 is silent on customary international law, it must be assumed that customary law, too, may in certain cases be binding on

---

3 Treaties are in existence with Argentina, the Bahamas, Canada, Mexico, Suriname and the United States. The 1981 Inter-American Convention on Extradition has not yet been ratified by the Netherlands to the benefit of the Netherlands Antilles and Aruba since few member states of the Organization of American States have ratified it.
4 Cf. Art. 2 of the Vienna Convention on the law of treaties.

all persons. The absence of any mention in Art. 93 is explained by the fact that by its very nature customary law does not need to be promulgated.

Case law has given a broad meaning to the concept of 'binding on all persons'. Whether or not rules of international law can be applied directly by the courts or other state organs mainly depends on the degree of freedom they leave to the Netherlands to achieve their purpose. Treaty provisions will normally be considered self-executing unless their purpose can be achieved by different means, and choices have to be made at a national level as to how to implement them. Making these choices is a matter for the legislature.

Provisions conferring rights on individual persons will, as a rule, be considered self-executing. But the same may also be true for provisions granting certain powers to the authorities or necessitating that individual rights be infringed upon. As examples we may mention treaty provisions allowing Dutch officials to perform cross-border pursuits or requiring that a person be remanded in custody within the framework of extradition proceedings.[5] However, treaty provisions or customary law allowing or requiring the Netherlands to criminalize certain acts cannot, as a rule, be considered to be directly applicable since implementing them usually requires many choices to be made.[6]

According to Art. 94 of the Constitution, statutory regulations in force may not be applied if such application would conflict with provisions of treaties or of decisions of international organizations which are binding on all persons. Such conflicts easily arise in extradition law, notably in the case of older extradition treaties which deviate from the provisions of the 1967 Extradition Act.[7] But problems may also present themselves in other areas of international criminal law.[8] In the Constitution the supremacy of international law is proclaimed. But only partially so, since Art. 94, too, fails to mention customary law. However, in a number of statutes provisions can be found which provide the courts with the opportunity to test national laws or their application against customary international law. Article 8 of the Penal Code, for instance, states that the applicability of the provisions in the Code on jurisdiction is subject to the exceptions recognized in international law.[9] Another example is Art. 539a

---

5 Cf. HR 26 April 1988, NJ 1989, 186, and Rechtbank Haarlem 10 November 1988, NJ 1988, 523.
6 See infra p. 27.
7 See infra pp. 90-91.
8 See infra pp. 27, 67-68, 82-83, 239.
9 See infra pp. 67-68.

of the Code of Criminal Procedure, requiring Dutch officials to pay due respect to international law when carrying out investigations outside Dutch territory.[10]

International criminal law and regional cooperation

The Netherlands is a member of various international organizations, all to a greater or lesser extent active in the field of international criminal law. Special attention should be paid here to regional organizations and regional forms of cooperation in Europe, since their influence on (international) criminal law in the Netherlands easily surpasses that of other international organizations. Some remarks on the Council of Europe, the Benelux, the European Union and Schengen seem in order here.

Since its coming into existence in 1949, the Council of Europe has created some twenty conventions in the penal field. Fifteen of them have been ratified by the Netherlands, a sixteenth will be ratified in the near future.[11]

In particular, the impact on Dutch law of the numerous conventions of the Council of Europe with respect to interstate cooperation in criminal matters can hardly be overestimated. It is not exaggerated to state that Dutch legislation in this area has been profoundly influenced by them. The wish to ratify the 1957 European Convention on Extradition and the 1959 European Convention on Mutual Assistance in Criminal Matters led to the adoption of a new Extradition Act *(Uitleveringswet)* in 1967, as well as to the introduction of new provisions on mutual assistance in criminal matters in the 1921 Code of Criminal Procedure *(Wetboek van Strafvordering)* in the same year. The 1964 European Convention on the Supervision of Conditionally Sentenced or Conditionally Released Offenders, the 1970 European Convention on the International Validity of Criminal Judgments, the 1972 European Convention on the Transfer of Proceedings in Criminal Matters, and the 1983 Convention on the Transfer

---

10 For case law on the provision see e.g. HR 24 June 1984, NJ 1984, 538 (*Magda Maria*, seizure of goods on board a ship outside Dutch territorial waters). Cf. also infra pp. 225-226.

11 The Netherlands has not signed or ratified the 1964 European Convention on the Punishment of Road Traffic Offences, the 1970 European Convention on the Repatriation of Minors, the 1976 European Convention on the International Effects of Deprivation of the Right to Drive a Motor Vehicle, and the 1985 European Convention on Offences relating to Cultural Property. In all cases the wish not to become a party has to do with the belief that the subject-matter of a convention is sufficiently covered by other conventions to which the Netherlands became a party.

of Sentenced Persons have had similar consequences. Their ratification has been the occasion for introducing new general provisions on transfer of proceedings into the Code of Criminal Procedure in 1985 and for the adoption of the Act on the transfer of enforcement of criminal judgments *(Wet overdracht tenuit-voerlegging strafvonnissen)* in 1986. The contents of Dutch legislation on international cooperation in criminal matters is closely modelled after the European conventions. The philosophy inspiring that legislation is also profoundly influenced by ideas developed within the Council of Europe, a matter that will be discussed below in more detail. Finally, by having served as models for national legislation, the European conventions also exert an indirect influence on treaties and conventions concluded between the Netherlands and other states in later years.

The second, less important, framework for international cooperation is the Benelux. The Benelux is composed of Belgium, the Netherlands and Luxembourg, neighbouring countries with a long-standing tradition of cooperation. In 1958 they founded the Benelux Economic Union. Three conventions adopted to implement the purposes of the Union are of special significance here. The first is the 1960 Convention on transferring border checks of persons to the external frontiers of the Benelux, creating a free travel area. The second is the 1969 Convention on cooperation between administrative and judicial authorities in matters pertaining to the Benelux Economic Union, establishing a structure for combating infringements of Union law. The third is the 1970 Convention on arms and ammunition which, however, has not entered into force due to the fact that not all three states have ratified it.

Other treaties have been adopted outside the framework of the Union. The most important one is the 1962 Benelux Treaty on Extradition and Mutual Assistance in Criminal Matters, together with its 1974 Protocol. Theoretically no less important are the 1968 Treaty on the Enforcement of Criminal Judgments and the 1974 Treaty on Transfer of Proceedings in Criminal Matters. While both treaties have been ratified by the Netherlands, they have not yet entered into force, the first awaiting ratification by Luxembourg and the second ratification by Belgium or Luxembourg. Of the few model laws that have been adopted in the penal field, the 1964 model law on perjury before international courts deserves mention here.[12]

The three Benelux treaties on international cooperation in criminal matters closely resemble their European counterparts. Usually, though, they establish

---

12 See infra p. 22 (note 1) and p. 57.

more extensive obligations to cooperate and they are less afraid of limiting national sovereignty for the sake of cooperation.[13] After 1974 no new treaties or model laws have been adopted in the penal field. For a long time now the Benelux countries have abandoned the thought of further expanding cooperation and harmonization. Of the various reasons behind that development we may especially mention the fact that the European Community and the European Union have gradually offered the three countries more important frameworks for cooperation.

Finally, the European Union and Schengen must be mentioned.

Within the framework of European Political Cooperation, the predecessor of the European Union, six different conventions on cooperation in criminal matters have been adopted in the period between 1979 and 1993. Four of them have been ratified by the Netherlands.[14] From a Dutch perspective these conventions are valuable but modest supplements to the body of conventions already adopted by the Council of Europe. However, their significance partly also lies in the fact that they might be ratified by states not willing to ratify specific Council of Europe conventions.

In anticipation of the creation of a free travel area between the member states of what is now the European Union, France, the Federal Republic of Germany and the Benelux countries took the initiative to create such an area between themselves. To that end they concluded the 1985 Agreement on the gradual abolition of checks at their common borders at the Luxembourg town of Schengen. It was later followed by the 1990 Convention applying the Schengen Agreement of 1985. At present, ten member states of the European Union are parties to both instruments. From a Dutch perspective, the 1990 Convention is especially important in that it contains elaborate and innovative provisions on police cooperation and on a common information system called the Schengen Information System. Moreover, the provisions in the Convention

---

13 For a more detailed study of Benelux treaties see *De Schutter,* International Criminal Law in Evolution: Mutual Assistance between the Benelux Countries.

14 The 1979 Agreement concerning the Application of the European Convention on the Suppression of Terrorism, the 1987 Convention on Double Jeopardy, the 1989 Agreement on the Simplification and Modernization of Methods of Transmitting Extradition Requests, and the 1991 Convention on the Enforcement of Foreign Criminal Sentences. Not signed was the 1990 Convention on Transfer of Proceedings in Criminal Matters since it seemed to add nothing to the already existing convention of the Council of Europe. As far as the 1987 Agreement on the Application of the Convention on Transfer of Sentenced Persons is concerned, it was thought proper not to ratify it before Spain and the United Kingdom would have solved their dispute regarding the applicability of the Agreement to Gibraltar.

on harmonization of legislation and policies with respect to drugs, controversial at the time of their adoption, have proven to be a source of disagreement between some parties to the Convention.[15]

In 1993, the Maastricht Treaty creating the European Union was ratified by all signatories. Title VI of the Treaty on European Union, dealing with cooperation in the fields of justice and home affairs, now provides the most important regional framework for cooperation in criminal matters to the Netherlands.[16] Until the end of 1995 four different conventions touching on cooperation in criminal matters have been created within the framework of the Union and it is to be expected that all of them will be ratified by the Netherlands.[17] Moreover, a number of joint actions, recommendations and resolutions on penal matters have been adopted. The future of international criminal law in the Netherlands will certainly be profoundly influenced by the developments within the European Union.

Parameters of international criminal law

Inevitably, the approach taken in the Netherlands with respect to international criminal law is determined by many different factors. Among them one may mention the place of the Netherlands in the international society, its legal traditions and legal culture, existing concepts of citizenship and authority, or expectations of what a criminal justice system is supposed to achieve. It is, of course, quite impossible to analyse all relevant factors here and to show how they influence the approach taken to international criminal law. Nevertheless, some general observations can and should be made.

The Netherlands is a small and densely populated country located in a corner of the European continent, roughly between France, Germany and the United

---

15 See pp. 41-42. For an analysis of the provisions of the Convention see *O'Keeffe*, The Schengen Convention: A Suitable Model for European Integration?; *Schutte*, Schengen: Its Meaning for the Free Movement of Persons in Europe; *Swart*, Police and Security in the Schengen Agreement and the Schengen Convention.

16 Cf. *Hendry*, The Third Pillar of Maastricht: Cooperation in the Fields of Justice and Home Affairs.

17 The 1995 Convention on simplified extradition procedure; the 1995 Convention on the use of information technology for customs purposes; the 1995 Convention on the establishment of a European Police Office (Europol); the 1995 Convention on the protection of the European Communities' financial interests.

Kingdom. Being small and vulnerable it depends heavily on contacts with the outside world for its survival and prosperity. In a society shaped by merchants and sailors such contacts are a natural way of life.

Dependence on contacts with the outside world is also a feature of the criminal justice system, and increasingly so. In many criminal cases it needs the cooperation of other states in order to be able to enforce its laws. The reverse is also true. Statistics show that the Netherlands provides far more assistance in criminal matters to other states than it demands from them. Given its size and geographical location this is not surprising.

In a tradition going back to the time of Grotius, the promotion of international law has always been seen as a matter of self-interest. It is believed that international law may, to some extent, provide a shield to smaller states protecting them against the pressure and the whims of more powerful states. This may explain why the Netherlands has ratified so many international treaties and conventions touching on international criminal law when compared with most other states. It probably also partially explains one of the most striking features of legislation on international cooperation in criminal matters: the existence of a treaty as a requirement for providing assistance to other states. Treaties help to ensure equality in mutual relations.

Another characteristic of the law on international cooperation is the relative neglect of sovereignty as a motive for refusing assistance, one of the reasons probably being that to insist on sovereignty for sovereignty's sake is a course of action that smaller states can permit themselves less easily. In the area of judicial assistance, for instance, there is little resistance against foreign authorities being present at and participating in the execution of letters rogatory or, for that matter, against applying foreign law in proceedings.[18] Similarly, while unauthorized activities of foreign officials on Dutch territory are resisted, permission to carry out investigations is easily granted to them. There is, of course, no provision in the law making unauthorized investigations by foreign authorities a criminal offence.[19] As a final example, transfer of enforcement of criminal judgments may be mentioned. In legislation on that matter it is more or less accepted as a matter of course that the state willing to enforce a judgment at the request of another state must be able to adjust the sentence imposed elsewhere to local standards.[20]

---

18 See infra pp. 133-134, 164-165, 218-219.
19 See infra pp. 216-217.
20 See infra pp. 202-204.

The Netherlands has a civil law system of justice, introduced when Napoleon made the country a part of his empire at the beginning of the nineteenth century. The fact that criminal justice in the Netherlands operates along the lines of the civil law tradition is of basic importance to international criminal law in a number of respects.

One of the features of the civil law approach to criminal justice is that there is no strong connection between the place where an offence has been committed and the place where the accused has to stand trial. While common law systems of justice, at least in theory, still cling to the point of view that all crime is local, attachment to territoriality is traditionally less strong in civil law systems. As a consequence, jurisdiction over extraterritorial offences is more easily accepted in the Netherlands than in most common law systems. This is notably true where the so-called active nationality principle is concerned. Moreover, if there is a preference for a forum where the accused should stand trial and undergo his punishment, that preference, in the Netherlands as well as in other civil law jurisdictions, is often given to the community to which the offender belongs. Until recently the Netherlands did not extradite its own nationals. While a change in the 1967 Extradition Act has now made their extradition a possibility, it is subject to a number of restrictions and conditions which reveal that the traditional preference for the forum where the offender lives is far from having become irrelevant or obsolete.[21] Finally, transfer of proceedings in criminal matters as a mode of international cooperation fits far more easily with civil law conceptions of criminal justice than with those of common law systems. It is no coincidence that elaborate provisions on transfer of proceedings have been introduced in Dutch legislation in 1985 and that this form of cooperation is seen as potentially as important as extradition and mutual judicial assistance.

A second feature distinguishing civil law systems from common law systems, to some extent linked with the first, is that the former traditionally feel fewer inhibitions against the use of hearsay evidence in criminal cases. Especially in the Netherlands such inhibitions were, until recent years, rather weak indeed. A number of consequences derive from that with respect to the handling of requests for the hearing of witnesses from other states by the Netherlands and, conversely, with respect to requests from the Netherlands made to other states.[22] As far as transfer of proceedings in criminal matters

---

21 See infra pp. 107-109.
22 See infra pp. 135, 143, 226-227.

is concerned, it is obvious that the fewer inhibitions against the use of hearsay evidence exist, the easier it becomes to achieve transfer between states.

Among foreign observers criminal justice in the Netherlands has a reputation of being liberal, pragmatic and mild.[23] It attracts both praise and criticism for these characteristics, depending on the observer's preferences. Sometimes differences tend to be overemphasized or exaggerated. If, for instance, the rate of incarceration is used as a yardstick to measure a penal climate, it should be noted that the low rate in the Netherlands is largely a thing of the past; it is now rapidly approaching the European average. Nevertheless, there is truth in the judgment of foreign observers. Their impressions are shared by many in the Netherlands. Whatever the merits and the deficiencies of criminal justice in the Netherlands, they seem to suit the national character and there is little inclination to change them in order to please the outside world.[24]

Inevitably, though, in present times national policies in the area of criminal justice have effects on other states and may, therefore, become a source of friction. This is obviously the case with Dutch policies in the field of combating the traffic in and the use of drugs and psychotropic substances. These policies seem to differ from those of neighbouring countries in that they put a stronger emphasis on the protection of public health and the limitation of adverse social consequences of the use of drugs as the primary goals of law enforcement.[25] Moreover, although massive efforts are made to combat drug trafficking, partly explaining why the rate of incarceration has risen so rapidly, there is widespread dissatisfaction with and doubt over the usefulness and desirability of using the criminal law as the major instrument for solving a society's problems with drugs. Decriminalization is, however, not an option open to the Netherlands in view of its international obligations and its relations with other states. Drugs policies are the most important example of a situation in which a country is caught between the desire to follow its own traditions and preferences on the one hand, and its duties to and solidarity with other countries on the other. Perhaps similar dilemmas will present themselves more often in the near future. The attitude of the Netherlands towards harmonization of criminal law and criminal policies within the framework of the European

---

23 Cf. e.g. *Berghuis/Franke*, Foreign Views on Dutch Penal Policy; *Downes*, Contrasts in Tolerance; *Kommer*, Punitiveness in Europe – a comparison.
24 Cf. *Blankenburg/Bruinsma*, Dutch Legal Culture.
25 See infra pp. 41-42.

Union is marked by ambivalence. The prospect of harmonization is welcomed as well as feared.[26]

A second field in which differences in penal policies between states play a role is that of transfer of enforcement of criminal judgments. Conversion of sentences imposed abroad in order to adjust their severity to standards prevailing in the Netherlands may sometimes act as a barrier against requesting transfer of enforcement to the Netherlands.[27]

The last general observation on international criminal law in the Netherlands concerns the growing influence of human rights treaties, notably the European Convention on Human Rights, on cooperation in criminal matters. Most contributions to this book make that influence visible. Suffice it to mention two examples here. First, the case law of the European Court of Human Rights on extradition and human rights has forced the Dutch courts to change their approach in the matter.[28] Secondly, the case law of the Court on the right to a fair trial has provided important stimuli to make criminal proceedings in the Netherlands more adversarial than they used to be.[29] One of the side-effects of that development is a marked increase in the number of requests for the hearing of witnesses made by the Netherlands to other states.

International criminal law from a Dutch perspective

Reading the various contributions to this book, one may wonder whether, and to what extent, it is possible to discern a distinct Dutch approach to international criminal law. To give an answer to this question is not easy. The first thing to note here is that it would be exaggerated, or even wrong, to assume that the vast body of legislation covering international criminal law in the Netherlands is inspired by a coherent and consistent philosophy that has remained the same throughout the years. At most one can speak of certain recurrent features. It seems equally exaggerated to assume that the approach taken to international criminal law in the Netherlands is unique or very different from that chosen by other states. This being said, however, it is in my opinion possible to discern a number of characteristics which give international

---

26 Cf. *Swart*, De Nederlandse strafrechtspleging in een internationaal krachtenveld, pp. 127-131.
27 See infra p. 203.
28 See infra pp. 112-115.
29 Cf. *Swart/Young*, The European Convention on Human Rights in the Netherlands and the UK, pp. 67-73, 84-86.

criminal law in the Netherlands its own individuality and originality. In trying to analyse these characteristics I will focus on concepts with respect to the structure of the international society, on the division of burdens and responsibilities between states, and on the goals of international cooperation in criminal matters, all seen from the perspective of Dutch legislation.

As has already been noted, in its approach to international criminal law a state reveals its view of the international society and of its own place in it. Not surprisingly, the view reflected in Dutch law is predominantly traditional. The desire to cooperate with other states in order to cope with crime is not primarily inspired by a conception of the international community as a *civitas maxima* in which, to quote *Bassiouni* and *Wise*, 'states constitute only an intermediate level of political organization in what actually is a more general and genuine community comprising all humanity'.[30] Like the law of other states, Dutch law is still firmly rooted in the Westphalian tradition, according to which each state is free to pursue its own interests and to enter into cooperation with other states in order to protect mutual interests if it so desires. In this approach, the development of international criminal law mainly depends on the existence of common interests. What distinguishes Dutch law from that of many other states, especially those of civil law systems, is perhaps the relatively strong emphasis on reciprocity as a precondition for international solidarity.

As far as substantive criminal law is concerned, numerous provisions in the Penal Code and in other statutes protect the interests of other states and those of groups of states. What is remarkable, however, is that almost all of them derive their existence from a treaty or a decision of an international organization. Provisions unilaterally protecting foreign interests are virtually absent. Where they do exist, e.g. in the area of state security or that of protecting foreign heads of state, it is obvious that national interests are as much at stake as those of other countries.[31] Apart from these few exceptions, statutory provisions protecting collective interests only aim at protecting the interests of Dutch society, and there is no inclination in case law unilaterally to broaden their scope. Thus, for instance, to resist an officer in the legitimate exercise of his duties constitutes a criminal offence only in the case of a Dutch officer.[32]

---

30 *Bassiouni/Wise,* Aut Dedere Aut Judicare; The Duty to Extradite or Prosecute in International Law, p. 28.
31 Cf. Arts. 98 and 107a of the Penal Code on the one hand and Arts. 115-116, 118-119 on the other. See also infra p. 70 for military offences.
32 See HR 17 March 1987, NJ 1987, 887 *(Linquenda).* Cf. also pp. 61-62, 216-217.

Special provisions in the Code or in other statutes, criminalizing resistance against foreign authorities in specific situations, all serve to implement international obligations.

Similarly, there is virtually no inclination unilaterally to extend jurisdiction over extraterritorial offences for the sake of international solidarity. Apart from the offence of piracy, the universality principle has been adopted only where the obligation to do so derives from a treaty to which the Netherlands has become a party. This approach is even maintained where crimes under general international law are concerned; in the absence of treaty provisions, the universality principle does not apply to genocide or other crimes against humanity.[33] The importance attached to treaties also explains why, with the exception of piracy, the principle of *aut dedere aut punire* has been accepted in Dutch law only as a consequence of treaty obligations to that effect, and never unilaterally.

Finally, the treaty requirement is a central feature of the law on international cooperation in criminal matters. Extradition of persons to other states and enforcement of foreign judgments in the Netherlands may take place pursuant to a treaty only. The provision of mutual assistance to other states requires the existence of a treaty if, in order to satisfy a foreign request for assistance, the Dutch authorities would have to apply coercive measures. Where transfer of proceedings in criminal matters is concerned, it is only possible for the Dutch authorities to take over proceedings from those of another state with respect to offences over which the jurisdiction of Dutch courts does not already extend where the request of that state is based on a treaty.

At first sight, the Dutch approach to international criminal law may appear to be rather inward-looking, self-centred and indifferent to the legitimate interests of other states. Not surprisingly, it has been reproached for being 'intravert' and caring little about international solidarity, an attitude which may have been acceptable during the nineteenth century but hardly meets the needs of the international community in present day circumstances.[34] Although there may be some truth in this judgment, it seems to miss the main point about international criminal law in the Netherlands. That point is that international solidarity is best achieved on the basis of reciprocal relationships. As many contributions to this book show, this approach is accompanied by strong willingness to enter into treaty relations with other states. It is the reluctance to take unilateral steps that is characteristic rather than an inward-looking

---

33   Cf. *Swart*, De berechting van internationale misdrijven, pp. 37-43.
34   Cf. *Strijards*, Rechtsharmonie en wetsharmonie in het internationale strafrecht, pp. 378-385.

attitude. This reluctance is partly due to worries about equality between states. But it also has to do with the fear that unilateral steps intended to promote international solidarity may be counterproductive and produce more harm than good. In other words, a fear that they create chaos where order should reign. This requires a closer look at a second characteristic of international criminal law in the Netherlands: the underlying philosophy with respect to a proper division of labour between states.

Preoccupation with conflicts of jurisdiction is a remarkable aspect of the Dutch approach to international criminal law. To eliminate such conflicts as much as possible is traditionally seen as one of the major goals of this part of the law. In the Dutch view, the primary responsibility for adjudicating criminal offences lies with the state where the offence has been committed, followed by the state whose nationality the offender possesses. In this view, the exercise of jurisdiction on the basis of other jurisdictional principles should not be excluded but should preferably be limited to cases in which a request for instituting proceedings has been made by a state more directly affected by the offence, i.e. the state of the *locus delicti* or the state of nationality of the offender. A certain hierarchy of jurisdictional principles is desired since it puts the responsibility for reacting to an offence on the doorsteps of the states having the strongest jurisdictional claims, reduces the danger of conflicts between states and protects individual persons against double jeopardy.

The 1881 Penal Code clearly reflects this philosophy. In it, the territorial principle is the self-evident backbone of jurisdiction. It is supplemented by the active nationality principle as the second major principle. Although, throughout the years, other principles have gained in importance, it still remains true that sparing use has been made of them. This is especially the case for the principles of passive nationality and universality.[35] The desire to eliminate conflicts of jurisdiction is also evident in Art. 68 of the Code, the provision on foreign *res judicata*. From a comparative view the bar erected by this provision against renewed prosecutions as a consequence of a foreign judgment is exceptionally strong. Renewed prosecutions are ruled out completely unless the foreign judgment has not been completely enforced. This is the case even when the offence has been committed within the Netherlands or was directed against Dutch state interests.[36]

---

35 See infra pp. 58-59, 62-65.
36 See infra pp. 78-80.

In recent years, the traditional preference for jurisdictional rules which eliminate conflicts of jurisdiction as much as possible has manifested itself in two different ways. On the one hand, the Netherlands has made reservations to a number of multilateral treaties carrying the duty for the contracting parties either to prosecute the alleged offender themselves or to extradite him to another contracting party. The purpose of these reservations is to establish that international offences are, as a rule, prosecuted by contracting parties with a strong jurisdictional claim. Therefore, the Netherlands has not unrestrictedly accepted jurisdiction on the sole basis that the alleged offender is present on its territory. It is prepared to accept such jurisdiction only if a request for the extradition of the alleged offender has been made and has been refused.[37] On the other hand, the so-called 'representation principle' has recently been introduced in the Penal Code, enabling the Dutch authorities to institute criminal proceedings against a person in the interests of another state. It is typical for the Dutch approach to jurisdictional matters that jurisdiction on the basis of this principle may be exercised only at the request of the other state.[38]

From the foregoing it has become clear that a relatively high value is attached to a sharp and rational division of responsibilities and burdens between states where the repression of international offences and other offences is concerned. To assume extraterritorial jurisdiction for the sake of international solidarity is, as a rule, accepted only if coupled with measures apt to establish a proper division of labour, ruling out conflicts of jurisdiction. Rational division of labour is also a key concept behind the law on international cooperation in criminal matters, to which we must now turn.

Legislation in the Netherlands on international cooperation in criminal matters draws its inspiration and cohesion from the concept of a proper administration of justice. Provisions in various statutes use that concept as a criterion for granting or requesting assistance.[39] The idea of making a proper administration of justice the normative goal of international cooperation goes back to the 1960s and 1970s, when transfer of proceedings and transfer of the enforcement of criminal judgments were systematically developed as new and promising forms of cooperation within the framework of the Council of Europe and that of the Benelux.

---

37 See infra pp. 64-65, 186-187.
38 See infra pp. 65-67.
39 Cf. Art. 35 of the Extradition Act; Art. 552t of the Code of Criminal Procedure; Art. 51 of the Act on the transfer of enforcement of criminal judgments.

Applied to offences with an international element, the concept implies that, whatever forum is chosen to try the accused and to punish the convicted person, that choice should best serve the proper administration of justice. This choice is determined by the interests of the cooperating states and those of the individual person concerned. In this respect, the various modes of cooperation (extradition, mutual assistance, transfer of proceedings and transfer of enforcement of criminal judgments) are interrelated and indispensable instruments, enabling states to be flexible in the interest of a proper administration of justice.

Proper administration of justice as a concept has several dimensions. One of these is that by making flexible use of the various instruments of cooperation states may prevent or solve conflicts of jurisdiction. Another is that, taken together, the various modalities of cooperation are able to ensure that at least one state is in a position effectively to react to offences with an international element. Thirdly, a coherent set of interrelated instruments may result in promoting the interests of individual offenders and better ensure their social rehabilitation. Finally, it may enable states to achieve more equitable and efficient justice at lower costs.[40]

The general consequences of this set of ideas are twofold. The traditional presumption that an accused should preferably be tried by the state on whose territory he has committed an offence is no longer undisputed and self-evident. There may be many situations in which his trial by another state at the request of the state of the *locus delicti* offers more promising prospects from the perspective of a proper administration of justice. This is even more the case where the enforcement of sentences, custodial sentences in particular, is concerned. Moreover, in this approach to international cooperation, transfer of proceedings and transfer of enforcement of judgments are tools as important as extradition and mutual assistance.

The concept of a proper administration of justice has had considerable influence on legislation and policies in the Netherlands, as a few examples will show. That influence explains why the Extradition Act was amended in 1986 in order to allow the extradition of Dutch nationals. Their extradition is now permitted for the purpose of standing trial abroad, on the proviso, however, that they will be able to serve a custodial sentence in the Netherlands. On the other hand, extradition for the purpose of serving a sentence elsewhere is still ruled out, the reason being that transfer of enforcement of that sentence to the

---

40 For a more detailed analysis see *Swart,* Goede rechtsbedeling en internationale rechtshulp in strafzaken.

Netherlands should be preferred in the interest of a proper administration of justice.[41] As far as transfer of proceedings is concerned, it is the official policy of the Dutch authorities systematically to transfer proceedings against foreigners without fixed abode in the Netherlands to their state of origin, while, on the other hand, Art. 552y of the Code of Criminal Procedure rules out the taking over of proceedings from other states if they concern a foreign national without fixed abode in the Netherlands.[42] The influence of the concept is also visible in the law on transfer of enforcement of criminal judgments. Conversion of sentences as a mode of enforcement is preferred over continued enforcement, since the former offers greater opportunities for adapting a sentence imposed elsewhere with a view better to ensure the convicted person's social rehabilitation.[43] A step further along this path is set by Arts. 48 to 50 of the Act on the transfer of enforcement of criminal judgments, implementing the 1968 Benelux Treaty on the Enforcement of Criminal Judgments. On the basis of the Benelux Treaty, courts in the state where the offence has been committed may, after conviction, refrain from imposing punishment and leave that to the courts of the state where the convicted person resides.

Meanwhile, it is fair to say that the concept of a proper administration of criminal justice has had a smaller influence than had been expected. Part of the explanation is that the rehabilitative philosophy which used to inspire the makers of the relevant conventions of the Council of Europe and the Benelux so strongly in the past, has now lost much of its appeal. In present times, there is a stronger emphasis on retribution and general deterrence as the preferred goals of punishment, and this shift in preferences is not without consequences for international cooperation in criminal matters. On the other hand, the relevant conventions of the Council of Europe have been ratified by few states, while those of the Benelux have not even entered into force. However, one cannot rule out the possibility that a proper administration of justice as the overall goal of cooperation in criminal matters will gain new relevance within the framework of the European Union. Compared to their counterparts of the Council of Europe and the Benelux, the recent conventions of the European Union on transfer of proceedings and transfer of enforcement of criminal judgments offer at least the advantage of being far less technical and elaborate and they are, therefore, more likely to be ratified by a large number of states.

---

41 See infra pp. 107-108, 204.
42 See infra pp. 177, 183.
43 See infra pp. 203-204.

Substantive Criminal Law

Rijnhard Haentjens and Bert Swart

Introduction

States have numerous interests in common. They cooperate in repressing acts which harm their mutual interests or those of the international community at large. Environmental pollution, trade in human beings, arms and narcotic drugs, violations of rules of warfare and acts endangering international peace or human dignity are but some examples of human conduct which states seek to prevent and to punish in a common effort. An ever growing number of international instruments require states to criminalize and punish forms of human behaviour. At present, therefore, large parts of national criminal law have their roots in international law. The obligation to criminalize may derive from customary international law. It may also originate from multilateral or, very rarely, bilateral treaties. Or it may have decision-making by international organizations as its basis. Resolutions of the United Nations Security Council and regulations or directives of the European Community are examples that come to mind here.[1]

At present, numerous specific offences defined in the Dutch Penal Code *(Wetboek van Strafrecht)* derive their existence from international law. The present situation is in marked contrast with that of 1886, the year in which the Code entered into force. At that time it contained only three international offences: piracy, slave trade and interference with submarine cables. Even more prominent is the role of international law where offences are concerned which are covered by the 1950 Economic Offences Act *(Wet op de economische*

---

1   National legislation may also be based on model uniform laws. This is the case with Art. 207a of the Dutch Penal Code. The provision, making it a crime to commit perjury before an international court, is inspired by a 1964 Benelux model law. See also infra p. 57 and Klip, RIDP 67 (1996), pp. 267-295.

delicten). More recently, international law has also begun to influence the
domestic system of criminal penalties and measures. Examples here are the
implementation in Dutch law of two Council of Europe conventions: the 1983
European Convention on the Compensation of Victims of Violent Crimes and
the 1990 Convention on Laundering, Search, Seizure and Confiscation of the
Proceeds from Crime.

In this chapter we cannot discuss all provisions in Dutch law implementing
international obligations to criminalize forms of human behaviour or which
affect domestic law in other ways. The vastness and complexity of the subject
matter require us to make choices; a list of all relevant treaties to which the
Netherlands is a party can be found in Appendix II in this book. We will,
therefore, put the emphasis on developments in general international law after
1945. The law of the European Communities and that of the Benelux will, with
some exceptions, not be discussed.[2]

Implementing international obligations to criminalize human conduct in
domestic law always involves choices since international law usually leaves
states considerable freedom in the manner in which they fulfil their obligations.
Moreover, as a matter of course the effect of international rules is to a
considerable extent determined by the general characteristics of a national
criminal justice system. Before paying attention to specific offences we will,
therefore, briefly indicate some general characteristics of substantive criminal
law in the Netherlands and make a few remarks on policies adopted in
implementing international obligations.[3] We will concentrate on those aspects
of substantive law which are directly relevant to the implementation of
international rules.

General characteristics of substantive criminal law

Dutch law distinguishes between crimes *(misdrijven)* and misdemeanours
(overtredingen). Crimes constitute the more serious offences carrying more
severe penalties. They require either intent or negligence on the part of the

---

2   For a survey of the implementation of Community law in Dutch criminal law see *Guldenmund,*
     Strafrechtelijke handhaving van gemeenschapsrecht.
3   For more detailed discussions in the English language see *Hulsman/Nijboer,* Criminal justice
     system, pp. 309-358; *Van Kalmthout/Tak,* Sanction-Systems in the Member-States of the
     Council of Europe, Part II, pp. 663-907; *Tak,* Criminal Justice Systems in Europe: The
     Netherlands. For a systematic comparison between American and Dutch criminal law see
     Lensing, Amerikaans strafrecht; Een vergelijkende inleiding.

author. *Mens rea* is usually not required where misdemeanours are concerned. However, case law takes the view that a person cannot be convicted if he is able to show 'absence of all culpability'. The jurisdiction of the various courts is determined by the type of offence.

Persons below the age of twelve may not be prosecuted. To persons between the age of twelve and twenty-one special rules apply.

Pursuant to Art. 51 of the Penal Code, criminal responsibility is extended to legal persons. Criminal responsibility is also incurred by those persons within a legal person who ordered the offence or who did not prevent the offence from being committed while they were in a position and under a duty to do so.

A set of general rules applies to attempt and participation. However, attempt to commit misdemeanours and complicity in misdemeanours are not punishable.

An attempt to commit an offence is defined in case law as a conduct from which it clearly appears to the outside world that a person is determined to finish the offence and is only prevented from doing so by outside causes. In the case of an attempt the maximum punishment is reduced by a third. In 1994, new legislation was introduced criminalizing preparatory acts. It only applies to offences carrying a prison term of at least eight years. Special rules on preparatory acts are to be found in the 1928 Opium Act *(Opiumwet)*. Except for some offences against state security, conspiracy to commit crimes is not punishable. However, to some extent Art. 140 of the Penal Code acts as a replacement here. This makes it an offence to participate in an organization whose purpose it is to commit crimes. The concept of organization presupposes a certain continuity in the activities of persons joining each other for the purpose of committing crimes as well as a discernible organizational structure.[4] To participate in such an organization implies an individual contribution, whatever its nature, in the furtherance of its goals.

Dutch law distinguishes between various modes of participating in the commission of an offence. The main distinction is between principals and accessories. Article 47 of the Code considers as principals co-authors *(medeplegers)*, those who solicit others to commit offences *(uitlokkers)*, and those who use others as instruments in committing offences *(doen plegers)*. According to Art. 48, accessories *(medeplichtigen)* are persons who lend support to the committing of offences by others; in their case the maximum punishment is reduced by a third. Article 46a of the Code deals with the attempt to solicit another person to commit an offence. From a comparative viewpoint it is important to note that participation after the fact is not a general concept in

---

4   HR 16 October 1990, NJ 1991, 442. See also infra p. 99.

Dutch law. It has been made punishable in some situations only, usually in the form of a separate offence.

The basic distinction in the system of sanctions is that between penalties and measures. A general precondition for imposing penalties is that the accused can be held personally responsible for his acts so as to enable his conviction. The relationship between personal responsibility and measures varies from measure to measure and will be explained below. The primary aim of measures is to protect society or to restore the situation which existed before the committing of an offence. Courts may convict the accused without imposing punishment.

Penalties are divided into principal and accessory, or additional, penalties. The principal penalties are imprisonment, detention, community service and fines. A fine may always be imposed in addition to imprisonment. The death penalty was abolished for common crimes during the nineteenth century. Due to a revision of the Constitution in 1983 it has now been eliminated also where other crimes, notably military crimes and war crimes, are concerned. A second important feature of the system of penalties is that, while the maximum penalty is established for each offence individually, the same is not true for the minimum penalty. From a comparative point of view one of the striking aspects of Dutch criminal law is that it has adopted general minima for all offences. In the case of imprisonment, the general minimum amounts to one day, in that of a fine to five guilders. Obviously, this system puts its faith in the courts in meting out the most appropriate punishment.

The severest punishment is imprisonment. The Penal Code distinguishes between life-long imprisonment and temporary imprisonment. Life-long imprisonment may be commuted later into temporary imprisonment, as is almost always done in actual practice. Temporary imprisonment may not amount to more than fifteen years or, in some cases, twenty years. The convicted person may be granted early release, but only after having served two thirds of his sentence. As a rule, release must be granted and may not be revoked.

Accessory penalties include deprivation of specific rights, forfeiture of objects or rights, and publication of the verdict of the court. Other additional penalties may be found in special statutes. The system of forfeiture has been revised recently. We will have a closer look at it when discussing the impact of the 1988 United Nations Convention and the 1990 Council of Europe Convention on confiscation of proceeds in Dutch law.

Measures which a court may impose include the committal of the accused to a psychiatric institution, in-patient or out-patient hospital orders, the withdrawal of goods from circulation, the confiscation of the proceeds from crime, and the payment of compensation to the victim of an offence. Committal to a psychiatric institution may be ordered only if the accused cannot be considered responsible for his acts. Hospital order and withdrawal of goods from circulation can be pronounced regardless of whether the accused is criminally responsible. Confiscation and the payment of compensation may only be ordered in the case of conviction. The legal rules with respect to withdrawal of goods from circulation and confiscation, revised recently, will be discussed in more detail later when we look at the impact of the 1988 United Nations Convention and the 1990 Council of Europe Convention on domestic law.

While, obviously, the Penal Code is the most important statute where substantive criminal law is concerned, numerous other statutes create criminal offences. Some of them, like the 1928 Opium Act and the 1952 Act on criminal law in time of war *(Wet Oorlogsstrafrecht)*, are of great significance to the implementation of international law. Probably the most important statute in this respect is the 1950 Economic Offences Act. In actual practice, it is the preferred framework for giving effect to most of the innumerable regulations and directives of the European Communities. It also often serves as a vehicle for implementing other international instruments which, in some way or another, touch on economic or social matters.

The Economic Offences Act provides a common framework for repressing certain categories of offences, called economic offences. Originally, the emphasis lay on regulations aiming to secure the proper functioning of economic markets. Gradually, however, other laws having a bearing on economic and social conditions in society were brought within the ambit of the Act. They now include most statutes intended to protect the environment. At present, the Act provides a vehicle for enforcing more than a hundred different statutes. If it is still possible to detect a common denominator among them, it may be that most offences covered by the Act enable the author to obtain easy financial or economic advantages and that most offences are as likely to be committed by legal persons as by natural persons.

Like the Penal Code, the Economic Offences Act distinguishes between crimes and misdemeanours. However, this is partly done by declaring an offence to be a crime if committed intentionally, and a misdemeanour in other situations. The Act contains its own system of penalties and measures, geared to the special character of economic offences. Understandably, the emphasis is on penalties and measures of a financial nature as the most appropriate instruments for securing compliance with the Act. Another aspect of the Act which deserves mention here is that it has created a system for investigating and adjudicating economic offences which is different from the one of the Code of Criminal Procedure in a number of respects.

The implementation of international law

Having dealt with some basic characteristics of Dutch criminal law we may now turn to policies with respect to the implementation of customary international law and treaties in the domestic legal order. How are international legal norms interwoven in the fabric of Dutch law and what problems present themselves here?[5]

Before discussing these questions we may note that the basic decision preceding all others is whether or not the Netherlands should ratify a treaty. That decision, of course, depends on many considerations which may vary from treaty to treaty. It is, however, fair to say that the Netherlands has ratified most treaties concluded after 1945 which aimed to create international offences or affected domestic criminal law in other ways.[6] A few were not. The most important examples are the 1950 Convention for the Suppression of the Traffic in Persons, the 1968 Convention on the Non-Applicability of Statutory Limitations, the 1973 *Apartheid* Convention, and the 1989 International Convention against the Recruitment, Use, Financing and Training of Mercenaries. We will discuss the motives for not ratifying them later. On the other hand, denunciation of treaties is a rare occurrence indeed. One of the few examples that comes to mind is the denunciation of the 1923 International Convention for the Suppression of the Circulation of and Traffic in Obscene Publications and its 1947 Protocol in 1986 as a consequence of a major revision of domestic law in the matter of sexual offences.[7] An alternative for not ratifying a treaty is to enter one or more reservations. It is less rare for the Netherlands to enter a reservation to a treaty for the reason that specific provisions in it are considered to be irreconcilable with basic national conceptions of criminal justice. As an example we may refer to the Dutch reservation to Art. 3, paras. 6 to 8, of the 1988 United Nations Convention against Illicit Traffic in Narcotic Drugs and Psychotropic Substances.

Once the decision has been made to ratify a treaty, implementing legislation is usually needed in order to make the courts competent to try offences envisaged

---

5   Cf. *Orie/Rüter/Schutte/Swart*, RIDP 60 (1989), pp. 395-418.
6   See Appendix II, Treaties concluded by the Kingdom of the Netherlands.
7   For difficulties in enforcing treaties on narcotic drugs and psychotropic substances see infra p. 36.

in a treaty, the exception being the case in which the conduct prohibited by treaty is already fully covered by domestic criminal law.

Pursuant to Arts. 93 and 94 of the Dutch Constitution, international law may be directly binding on all persons. It may directly confer rights on individual persons and impose duties on them. Whether this is actually the case depends on the degree of freedom an international rule leaves a state to achieve its purpose. Treaty provisions will be considered self-executing unless it is obvious that their purpose can be achieved by different means and implementing measures are, therefore, needed.[8]

International obligations to criminalize specific forms of human conduct cannot, as a rule, in themselves be considered self-executing within the meaning of the constitutional provisions. This is not only true for treaties carrying an obligation to repress certain acts but for customary international law as well. There is almost always a need for a national statute indicating, among other things, the penalties which may be imposed, the authorities competent to investigate offences and the courts competent to adjudicate them. This is clearly illustrated by a judgment of the Special Court of Cassation rendered in a case involving the trial of a member of enemy forces for war crimes committed during the Second World War. While the court said that international law permitted the Netherlands to punish international crimes committed on its territory, it nevertheless held that Dutch courts could not adjudicate such cases since no domestic statute conferred jurisdiction on them.[9] Until now, one of the few exceptions accepted to the rule that provisions of treaties cannot be considered self-executing concerns Art. 34 of the 1962 Benelux Treaty on Extradition and Mutual Assistance in Criminal Matters, dealing with the duty of a witness to appear before a court of another Benelux country. For the purpose of applying Art. 192 of the Penal Code, dealing with the duties of witnesses, courts may rely directly on the provisions of that treaty.

However, this is not to say that the conduct proscribed by international law must have been defined in each and every detail by domestic law. On the contrary, once a statute has created a proper framework for repressing international offences it may very well refer back to international law where the definition of these offences is concerned. One of the most striking examples of this legislative technique is provided by Art. 8 of the 1952 Act on criminal law in time of war. It simply declares violations of the laws and customs of war to

---

8   See supra pp. 4-6.
9   BRvC 17 February 1947, NJ 1947, 87 *(Ahlbrecht)*. See also *Röling*, The Law of War and the National Jurisdiction since 1945, p. 339.

be punishable offences under Dutch law. The same technique has been used, for instance, in the Sanctions Act 1977.

Where the implementation of treaties is concerned, there is a certain preference for integrating new offences into existing statutes and giving them a place among provisions that proscribe similar conduct. However, this may not always be possible. For instance, special statutes have been adopted to make genocide, torture and the production of biological and chemical weapons crimes under domestic law. Whatever solution is chosen, incorporating treaty provisions into domestic law always involves important choices, whether they relate to the applicable penalties, statutes of limitation, rules with respect to attempt and participation or to other matters.

One of the most crucial aspects of implementing international law concerns the definition of the offence. As we have noted, the technique is sometimes used of not defining the prohibited conduct in a statute but referring back to international law. Usually, however, the offence will be defined in domestic law. This is especially important in cases in which treaty provisions contain rather loose or vague definitions of what conduct should be prohibited. In such situations, the legality principle may require more specific definitions in domestic law. There is, moreover, always a risk of discrepancies occurring between the definition of an offence at the international and the national level, however conscientiously a treaty may have been implemented. If need be, Dutch courts will look at international law in order to elucidate the meaning of domestic provisions.

Incorporating international offences in domestic law amounts to making a national system of criminal justice competent to deal with the offences. It will, of course, do so in a manner consistent with its own traditions and values. They may vary from contracting party to contracting party. For instance, incorporating an international offence into Dutch law has consequences different from incorporating the same offence into French or German law. It is equally unavoidable that concepts of criminal law employed in treaties are to some extent interpreted in conformity with the meaning which the same concepts have in domestic law. In such ways a process of osmosis between international law and domestic law develops. As long as the very purpose of a treaty is not frustrated no objection should be made against this.

Crimes against the peace and security of mankind

Like all states, the Netherlands is bound to prevent and repress violations of general international law which amount to international crimes. Moreover, the Netherlands has ratified most conventions adopted since 1945 in order to protect the peace and security of mankind. Among them we may mention in particular the 1948 Convention on the Prevention and Punishment of the Crime of Genocide, the 1949 Conventions of Geneva and their 1977 Additional Protocols, the 1954 Convention for the Protection of Cultural Property in the Event of Armed Conflict, the 1972 Convention on the Prohibition of the Development, Production and Stockpiling of Bacteriological (Biological) and Toxin Weapons and on their Destruction, the 1980 Convention on Prohibitions or Restrictions on the Use of Certain Conventional Weapons Which May Be Deemed to Be Excessively Injurious or to Have Indiscriminate Effects and its Protocols, and the 1993 Convention on the Prohibition on the Development, Production, Stockpiling and Use of Chemical Weapons and on their Destruction. Although it is debatable whether torture amounts to a crime under general international law we will also discuss the United Nations and Council of Europe conventions on the matter here.

Two United Nations conventions which the Netherlands refused to ratify are the 1968 Convention on the Non-Applicability of Statutory Limitations to War Crimes and Crimes Against Humanity and the 1973 Convention on the Suppression and Punishment of the Crime of *Apartheid*. The main reason for not ratifying the first convention was that it carries the obligation to eliminate statutory limitations also with respect to crimes for which time limits had already expired. The *Apartheid* Convention was rejected on two grounds. It was thought that criminalization of *apartheid* served no useful purpose given the fact that racial discrimination had already been made an offence under the 1966 International Convention on the Elimination of All Forms of Racial Discrimination. Moreover, extraterritorial jurisdiction over the crime of *apartheid* was objected to because of the vague definition of the crime.[10] Obviously, these arguments are in line with the point of view taken by most Western states at the time.

While aggression is the international crime *par excellence*, there is no provision in Dutch law making crimes against the peace criminal offences. The thought of making crimes against the peace criminal offences has probably never

---

10 See Jaarboek van het Departement van Buitenlandse Zaken 1972-1973, appendix I.

entered the mind of the legislature. One conceivable argument in favour of not taking action might have been that there is no definition of aggression sufficiently precise to be acceptable for the purpose of creating criminal responsibility. Another is that crimes against the peace are almost by definition committed by states and their organs, and there is no justification in international law for subjecting one state to the criminal jurisdiction of another for *acta jure imperii*.

Violations of the laws and customs of war are governed by two different statutes.

The oldest statute is the Decree on criminal law in exceptional circumstances *(Besluit Buitengewoon Strafrecht)*, adopted by the Dutch Government in exile in 1943. Originally, and in conformity with a tradition prevailing in continental Europe, it applied domestic criminal law to all those accused of war crimes, members of enemy forces not excluded. As Dutch courts took the view that members of enemy forces should be tried on the basis of international law rather than domestic law,[11] a new Article was added to the Decree in 1947. It does not itself define war crimes but directly refers to Art. 6(b) of the Charter of the Nuremberg International Military Tribunal. The Decree only applies to war crimes committed during the Second World War.[12]

The second statute is the 1952 Act on criminal law in time of war *(Wet Oorlogsstrafrecht)*. Article 8 of the Act is concerned with war crimes. Without attempting to define specific offences it simply declares all violations of the laws and customs of war to be crimes under Dutch law. Its open-ended character has frequently been criticized, although there is probably less reason for doing so now that Protocol I to the 1949 Geneva Conventions has been ratified by the Netherlands.[13] Depending on the circumstances, conduct amounting to a war crime is liable to maximum punishment of ten, fifteen or twenty years imprisonment. The categorization more or less corresponds to but does not wholly coincide with the distinction between grave breaches and other breaches in the Geneva Conventions and Protocol I. All breaches of the Conventions and the Protocol have been declared crimes. Moreover, Art. 8 also covers other violations of international humanitarian law, whether violations of customary international law or of treaties. Article 9 of the Act contains a special provision

---

11 BRvC 17 February 1947, NJ 1947, 87 *(Ahlbrecht)*, mentioned supra p. 27.

12 For an analysis of case law regarding war crimes see *Röling* (supra note 9), pp. 329-456.

13 Cf. e.g. *Keijzer*, Het oorlogsstrafrecht, Algemene aantekeningen 44-49; *Röling*, Enkele volken-rechtelijke aantekeningen bij de Wet Oorlogsstrafrecht, pp. 274-278.

creating criminal liability for superiors who have intentionally allowed their subordinates to commit a war crime. To intentionally allow is not identical with to order. It also covers failure to prevent others from committing a crime.

The repression of war crimes is not the only purpose pursued by the Act. It also contains provision criminalizing conduct which jeopardizes vital interests of the Dutch state in time of war or similar circumstances. Another purpose of the Act is to provide a special framework for investigating and adjudicating offences, which may replace the ordinary criminal justice system in extraordinary circumstances. This, for instance, explains why genocide and torture are among the offences which may be tried on the basis of its provisions.

The multi-purpose character of the Act has led to considerable confusion as to its scope. According to its Art. 1 the Act is applicable to crimes committed in time of war, including civil war. The Act may also be declared applicable with respect to offences committed during an armed conflict which does not amount to war, provided that the Netherlands has become involved in such a conflict and that additional requirements are met. The question has been raised whether the term 'war' refers to all wars or only to wars in which the Netherlands is involved.[14] The second interpretation would mean that violations of the laws and customs of war can be tried in the Netherlands in a rather limited number of situations only. This would hardly be reconcilable with obligations arising out of the four Geneva Conventions and Additional Protocol I for the Netherlands. Courts will have to decide the issue shortly.

Crimes against humanity have been criminalized by the Decree on criminal law in exceptional circumstances in the same manner as war crimes. The Decree refers to Art. 6(c) of the Charter of the Nuremberg International Military Tribunal. The Decree is limited to crimes against humanity committed during the Second World War.

There is no other statute criminalizing crimes against humanity as such. Article 8 of the Act on criminal law in time of war deals with crimes against humanity as circumstances aggravating war crimes. A war crime can be punished by imprisonment of twenty years' duration if it is a manifestation of a policy of systematic terror or illegal acts directed against the whole population or a group of the population.[15] The point of view taken here is that

---

14 Cf. *Röling* (supra note 12), pp. 271-273; *Mouton*, NTIR 7 (1960), pp. 65-67.
15 The definition is inspired by BRvC 11 April 1949, NJ 1949, 425, interpreting Art. 6(c) of the Nuremberg Charter. Cf. also HR 13 January 1981, NJ 1981, 79 *(Menten)*.

crimes against humanity can be committed only during wars or other armed conflicts.[16] This does not seem to be the correct view.

With respect to the most serious crime against humanity, genocide, the situation is more satisfactory. The Netherlands has become a party to the 1948 Convention on the Prevention and Punishment of the Crime of Genocide. The 1964 Act implementing the Genocide Convention *(Uitvoeringswet genocideverdrag)* has made genocide and conspiracy to commit genocide criminal offences carrying a maximum punishment of life-long or twenty years' imprisonment. The definition of genocide closely follows that of the Convention. It does not matter whether or not genocide has been committed in time of war. For a superior to allow subordinates to commit genocide is also a criminal offence.

While torture is prohibited by the Geneva Conventions as well as the International Covenant on Civil and Political Rights and the European Convention on the Protection of Human Rights and Fundamental Freedoms, none of these treaties contains a definition of the prohibited conduct. This is different for the 1984 United Nations Convention against Torture and Other Cruel, Inhuman or Degrading Treatment or Punishment, ratified by the Netherlands in 1988.

Article 1 of the 1988 Act implementing the Torture Convention *(Uitvoeringswet Folteringverdrag)* defines torture in wording closely following the language of the Convention but making use of some technical expressions in the Penal Code. The definition shows how difficult it may sometimes be to translate prohibitions of treaties into penal provisions in domestic law.[17] The maximum punishment for torture is fifteen years' imprisonment. Article 2 of the Act threatens the person who orders torture or allows its commission with the same punishment.

The Netherlands has also ratified the 1987 European Convention for the Prevention of Torture and Inhuman or Degrading Treatment or Punishment.

All statutes discussed here have in common that they prevent the accused from invoking Arts. 42 and 43 of the Penal Code. They thereby rule out the defence of superior order. However, the possibility remains of invoking the excuse that

---

16 Cf. *Rüter*, Enkele aspecten van de strafrechtelijke reactie op oorlogsmisdrijven en misdrijven tegen de menselijkheid, pp. 43-45.

17 For a comparative analysis of the two definitions see *Egter van Wissekerke*, NJB 63 (1988), pp. 115-116.

the accused did not and could not know the illegality of an order given to him.[18]

We have already mentioned that the Netherlands did not want to ratify the 1968 United Nations Convention on the Non-Applicability of Statutory Limitations to War Crimes and Crimes against Humanity, and explained why this step was taken. Nevertheless, the Convention has exerted a considerable influence on Dutch law in that it inspired the 1971 Act containing provisions on the elimination of statutory limitations with respect to war crimes and crimes against humanity *(Wet nadere regels betreffende de verjaring van het recht tot strafvordering en uitvoering van de straf terzake van oorlogsmisdrijven en misdrijven tegen de menselijkheid)*. The Act effected changes in the existing legislation concerning war crimes, crimes against humanity and genocide. Immunity from prosecution or punishment by reason of lapse of time is ruled out for offences carrying a maximum penalty of fifteen years' imprisonment or more. The Act is retroactive in the sense that it also applies to crimes committed before its entering into force. However, cases in which prosecution or punishment had already become barred by reason of lapse of time may not be reopened. The normal rules with respect to time limitations are applicable to the crime of torture.

The Netherlands has ratified the 1974 European Convention on the Non-Applicability of Statutory Limitations to Crimes Against Humanity and War Crimes.

Finally, we may mention the 1981 Act implementing the Biological Weapons Convention *(Uitvoeringswet verdrag biologische wapens)* and the 1995 Act implementing the Chemical Weapons Convention *(Uitvoeringswet verdrag chemische wapens)*. All offences against both statutes have been made economic offences within the meaning of the Economic Offences Act. They carry maximum penalties varying from six years' imprisonment to six months' detention.

International terrorism and violence

The upsurge of international terrorism and violence has led to the creation of a series of multilateral treaties aiming at their repression through international

---

18 Cf. *Keijzer* (supra note 13), Aantekeningen 3-7 op Art. 10. See also *Keijzer*, Military Obedience, pp. 195-205.

cooperation. These treaties include the 1970 Convention for the Suppression of Unlawful Seizure of Aircraft, the 1971 Convention for the Suppression of Unlawful Acts against the Safety of Civil Aviation and its 1988 Protocol, the 1973 Convention on the Prevention and Punishment of Crimes against Internationally Protected Persons, Including Diplomatic Agents, the 1979 International Convention against the Taking of Hostages, and the 1988 Convention for the Suppression of Unlawful Acts against the Safety of Maritime Navigation and its Protocol. We may mention here also the 1980 Convention on the Physical Protection of Nuclear Material. All treaties have been ratified by the Netherlands.

Implementing these treaties in domestic law has not been a simple matter. This is partly due to the fact that there is no such offence as terrorism in Dutch law.[19] There are only acts of violence. Moreover, the existing provisions of the Penal Code hardly distinguished between the various motives for using violence and the targets chosen. It has, therefore, been necessary to rewrite large parts of the law. Where prohibitions contained in various treaties were not yet covered by existing provisions, several techniques were used to incorporate them. Sometimes existing provisions were rewritten, at other times the international offences were made into aggravated forms of already existing common offences, in yet other situations entirely new provisions have been introduced.[20]

It is hardly possible to discuss all new and rewritten provisions here. We must limit ourself to mentioning some aspects of particular interest from a comparative point of view. It is characteristic of the provisions on hostage-taking that they require the offender to detain another person in order to compel a third party.[21] As far as crimes against internationally protected persons are concerned, the applicable provisions require the offender to know the international status of the victim and to commit the offence for that purpose. This reveals a restrictive interpretation of the 1973 Convention. As far as the scope of the 1988 Protocol to the 1971 Montreal Convention is concerned, we may refer to the declaration made by the Netherlands at the time of its signature.[22]

---

19 For an attempt to define terrorism for the purpose of criminal law see *Keijzer*, Het Europees verdrag tot bestrijding van terrorisme, p. 5.
20 New provisions in the Code include Arts. 117a to 117b, 161quater, 162a, 282a, 284a, 385a to 385d.
21 Cf. Art. 1 of the Hostages Convention.
22 See Appendix II p. 389.

Arms and ammunition

The 1986 Act on weapons and ammunition *(Wet wapens en munitie)*, replacing three different older statutes, was largely inspired by the 1970 Benelux Convention on weapons and ammunition. The aim of this treaty was to harmonize legislation in the three Benelux countries. In that it has failed. As Belgium has not yet ratified the convention, it has not entered into force. The 1986 Act follows the Benelux Convention in dividing weapons and ammunition into three different categories according to the degree of danger they (may) create. The most serious offences in the Act carry a maximum punishment of imprisonment of four years' duration.[23]

The Netherlands is a party to the 1978 European Convention on the control of the acquisition and possession of firearms by individuals. The purpose of this convention, however, is not to harmonize national legislation. This is different in the 1990 Convention applying the Schengen Agreement, ratified by the Netherlands in 1993. Articles 77 to 91 of this convention deal with firearms and ammunition. Article 87 obliges the contracting parties to take appropriate measures, including seizure of firearms and withdrawal of permits, and to punish in an appropriate way infringements of the laws and administrative provisions applicable to firearms. The provisions of the convention are clearly a compromise between states with more liberal and those with more stringent legislation in the matter. As the Netherlands has perhaps the most stringent laws of all parties to the convention, its ratification has not led to changes in the Act. In 1994 the Act was amended in order to make its system compatible with the 1991 EC Directive 91/477 on the control of the acquisition and possession of weapons.[24] The main significance of the two conventions and the directive for the Netherlands is that they create a framework for exchanging information on the production, sale and possession of arms and ammunition.

Violations of human rights and fundamental freedoms

The oldest example in the Penal Code of the influence of treaties aiming to protect human rights is to be found in Arts. 274 to 277, criminalizing slave trade. Articles 274 to 277 replace the 1818 Act containing penal provisions for

---

23 For a discussion on the international aspects of the Act see *Poelman*, Wat aan de Wet Wapens en Munitie is voorafgegaan, pp. 22-25.

24 1991 OJ L 256/51.

the repression and prevention of slave trade *(Wet houdende strafbepalingen om den Slavenhandel te keer te gaan en te beteugelen)*. The provisions of that Act implemented the 1818 Treaty between the Netherlands and Great Britain on the suppression of the slave trade. As a footnote we may add that slavery itself was abolished in the (former) Dutch colonies during the 1860s only.

Another example can be found in Art. 250ter. It was enacted in 1911 in order to implement the 1910 International Convention for the Suppression of White Slave Traffic, and amended in 1927 after ratification by the Netherlands of the 1921 International Convention for the Suppression of Traffic in Women and Children. Both conventions required the contracting parties to criminalize the conduct proscribed in them.[25]

Article 250ter in its present form contains a general prohibition of traffic in persons for the purpose of prostitution. A thorough revision of the provision in 1994 has codified case law in the matter. It is now an offence to deceive or exert any form of pressure on another person resulting in that person entering into prostitution, or to do the same knowing or having serious reasons to believe that the other person will thereby end up in prostitution. It is also an offence to recruit, escort or abduct another person for the purpose of prostitution in another country. Here, the use of pressure or deception is not a requirement. Thus, the idea is abandoned that inducing another person to enter into prostitution is an offence against that person's individual liberty.[26] Finally, to induce minors to enter prostitution is also an offence regardless of whether any pressure or deception has been exerted. Case law equates the preventing of a person from leaving prostitution with forcing him or her to enter prostitution.[27] The offences carry a maximum penalty of six years' imprisonment. Aggravated cases may be punished by imprisonment of eight or ten years' duration.

---

25 The Netherlands has also ratified the 1933 International Convention for the Suppression of the Traffic in Women of Full Age as well as its 1947 Protocol. It also ratified the 1947 Protocol to the 1921 Convention and the 1949 Protocol to the 1910 Convention. Ratification of the 1950 UN Convention for the Suppression of the Traffic in Persons and of the Exploitation of the Prostitution of Others was, however, refused, the reason being that exploitation of prostitution should not be criminalized if adult persons have freely chosen to prostitute themselves. Cf. *Noyon/Langemeijer/Remmelink*, Het Wetboek van Strafrecht, Aantekening 7 op Art. 250ter.

26 In this respect, the provision may be considered to be a *specialis* of the crime of assisting or trying to assist, for the purposes of gain, an alien to enter or to reside within the country, criminalized by Art. 197a of the Penal Code. This Article was adopted in 1993 in order to implement Art. 27 of the 1990 Convention applying the Schengen Agreement.

27 HR 19 May 1992, NJ 1992, 716.

A third, more recent, example of the protection of human rights is provided by the provisions in the Penal Code on various forms of discrimination. These were introduced in 1971 in order to implement the 1966 International Convention on the Elimination of All Forms of Racial Discrimination. They also covered discrimination based on religion or belief, not dealt with by the convention. In 1992, the provisions were revised and now also extend to discrimination based on sex and sexual preference.[28] Their scope is, therefore, very wide indeed.

Article 90quater of the Code defines discrimination as any distinction, exclusion, restriction or preference which has the purpose or effect of nullifying or impairing the recognition, enjoyment or exercise, on an equal footing, of human rights and fundamental freedoms in the political, economic, social or cultural or any other field of public life.[29] In Art. 137c, the public defamation of groups of persons because of their race, religion or belief, their sex or sexual preferences is prohibited.[30] Whether or not a statement is defamatory has to be determined according to the context in which it has been made; its defamatory character may, however, be obvious without looking into these circumstances.[31] Article 137d prohibits incitement to hatred, discrimination or violence because of any of the grounds mentioned. Articles 137e, 137f and 137g prohibit the dissemination of discriminatory statements, the participating in activities aimed at discrimination, and the intentional discrimination of persons in the exercise of an office, a profession or a business activity. In addition to Art. 137g, Art. 429quater prohibits unintentional forms of discrimination; indirect discrimination is also covered by this provision. With the exception of Art. 429quater all offences are crimes, carrying maximum terms of imprisonment varying from a year to three months.

International sanctions

In the past, organs of the United Nations, in particular the Security Council, have taken decisions or passed resolutions urging member states to apply sanctions against political regimes endangering international peace and security.

---

28 This revision bears no direct relationship with the 1979 Convention on the Elimination of All Forms of Discrimination against Women, ratified by the Netherlands in 1991.
29 Cf. Art. 1 of the 1966 Convention.
30 The word 'race' has to be understood in the broad meaning of Art. 1 of the 1966 Convention. Cf. HR 1 July 1986, NJ 1987, 217; HR 14 March 1989, NJ 1990, 29.
31 HR 11 February 1986, NJ 1986, 689; HR 11 December 1990, NJ 1991, 313.

Article 39 of the Charter of the United Nations empowers the Security Council to take decisions binding on all member states in order to maintain or restore international peace and security. The obligation to comply with measures taken by the Council under Chapter VII derives from Art. 25 of the Charter. A well-known example of the use of Arts. 39 and 41 by the Security Council is provided by its decisions with respect to the unilateral declaration of independence by Southern Rhodesia in the 1960s. Various difficulties in implementing the decisions of the Council showed the inadequacy of Dutch legislation existing at the time.[32] As a result, new legislation was enacted. The vehicle for implementing sanctions now is the Sanctions Act 1977 *(Sanctiewet 1977)*.

The Sanctions Act 1977 enables the quick and efficient implementation of binding decisions as well as non-binding resolutions taken or adopted by international organizations in order to maintain or restore international peace and security or to preserve the international legal order. Non-binding resolutions will, however, be implemented only if they have attracted a high degree of international consensus. While its main importance lies in the implementation of sanctions imposed or recommended by the organs of the United Nations, the Act is by no means limited to them. It also enables the implementation of decisions and resolutions by other international organizations such as the International Atomic Agency, the European Union or NATO. The same is true for decisions or resolutions by groups of states. However, sanctions unilaterally imposed by the Netherlands fall outside its scope. In recent years frequent use has been made of the Act.[33]

The Act enables the Government to issue a Decree which is binding on all persons. The usual practice is to include the original text of a decision or resolution in a Decree rather than a translation in the Dutch language. Thus, disputes over the correctness of a translation are avoided. Usually, a Decree enters into force two months after its promulgation. To infringe the provisions of a Decree constitutes an offence within the meaning of the Economic Offences Act. If intentionally committed it carries a maximum penalty of two years' imprisonment, otherwise that of six months' detention.

---

32 For a case study of the implementation of sanctions against Rhodesia by the Netherlands see *Kuyper*, The Implementation of International Sanctions; The Netherlands and Rhodesia.
33 E.g. with respect to South Africa, Iraq, Libya, Serbia and Montenegro, Haiti.

Narcotic drugs and psychotropic substances

The Netherlands is a party to numerous treaties on narcotic drugs and psychotropic substances. The most important ones include the 1961 Single Convention on Narcotic Drugs and its 1972 Protocol, the 1971 Convention on Psychotropic Substances and the 1988 United Nations Convention against Illicit Traffic in Narcotic Drugs and Psychotropic Substances.[34] Articles 70 to 76 of the 1990 Convention applying the Schengen Agreement are also relevant here.[35] Where necessary these treaties have been implemented in the 1928 Opium Act. We must also mention EC Regulation 3677/90 and EC Directive 92/109, implemented by the 1995 Act on the prevention of misuse of chemical substances *(Wet voorkoming misbruik chemicaliën).*[36]

The 1928 Opium Act *(Opiumwet)* prohibits the importation and exportation, the extraction, preparation, sale, delivery, procuring and transport, the possession and the production of narcotic drugs and psychotropic substances indicated on two schedules which form an integral part of the Act. It distinguishes between intentional offences and non-intentional ones, which carry a lesser maximum penalty. We will limit our discussion to intentional offences.

Of basic importance is the distinction between narcotic drugs and psychotropic substances covered by Art. 2 and indicated on Schedule I on the one hand and narcotic drugs covered by Art. 3 and Schedule II on the other. Drugs and psychotropic substances mentioned in the first Schedule correspond with what are usually called hard drugs. They include heroin, cocain, amphetamine and many other substances such as LSD, MDMA, MDA and MDEA. The

---

34 The provisions of Art. 3, paras. 6 to 8, of the UN Convention have been accepted by the Netherlands 'only in so far as the obligations under these provisions are in accordance with Dutch criminal legislation and Dutch policy on criminal matters'. See Appendix II p. 391.

35 For the sake of completeness we may mention the 1988 bilateral Agreement between the Netherlands and Venezuela on the prevention, control and suppression of the abuse of illicit traffic in and the illicit production of narcotic drugs, psychotropic substances and related chemical substances. The 1995 Council of Europe Agreement on Illicit Traffic by Sea, implementing Art. 17 of the United Nations Convention against Illicit Traffic in Narcotic Drugs and Psychotropic Substances, has not yet been ratified.

36 Regulation 3677/90 of 13 December 1990 laying down measures to discourage the diversion of certain substances to the illicit manufacture of drugs and psychotropic substances, 1990 OJ L 357/1, and Directive 92/109 on the manufacture and placing on the market of certain substances used in the illicit manufacture of narcotic drugs and psychotropic substances, 1992 OJ L 370/76.

second Schedule, which is concerned with so-called soft drugs, mentions cannabis and all products derived from it. Different regimes apply to offences with respect to the two categories.

According to Arts. 2 and 10 of the Act the importation and exportation of narcotic drugs and psychotropic substances carry a maximum penalty of twelve years' imprisonment. In the case of extraction, preparation, sale, delivery, transport, procurement and production the maximum penalty amounts to eight years' imprisonment. A maximum of four years applies to possession. However, possession of a small quantity for one's own use is a misdemeanour carrying a maximum penalty of six months' detention.[37] In the case of offences covered by Arts. 3 and 11 of the Act maximum penalties are considerably lower. They amount to a maximum imprisonment term of four years where the importation and exportation of drugs is concerned, and of two years in the case of extraction, preparation, sale, delivery, procurement, transport, production and possession.[38] However, mere possession of a quantity not exceeding thirty grams for one's own use has been made a misdemeanour carrying a maximum penalty of one months' detention.

The normal rules of the Penal Code with respect to attempt and participation apply to drug offences. However, in addition to them Art. 10a of the Act criminalizes a number of preparatory acts. They include the procuring of opportunity, means, or information in order to commit offences, and the possession of objects, means of transport, substances or financial means, knowing or having serious reason to believe that they will be used for the purpose of committing offences; these offences carry a maximum penalty of six years' imprisonment. One also has to bear in mind that Art. 140 of the Penal Code, discussed earlier, is frequently used both in domestic cases and as a basis for granting extradition or mutual assistance. Taken together the provisions in Dutch law seem to correspond to the rather specific provisions on various forms of involvement in drug offences contained in the 1961 Single Convention and the 1988 United Nations Convention. Article 10a of the Opium Act does not apply to the offences covered by Arts. 3 and 11, nor does it apply to pre-

---

37 The Act does not define what a small quantity amounts to. Guidelines adopted by the Public Prosecutions Department mention a quantity which the average user needs on one single day. In the case of heroin or cocain the estimate is 0.5 grams. For the text of these guidelines see *Krabbe*, De Opiumwet, p. 285.

38 In view of the fact that cannabis is increasingly produced within the Netherlands itself the Government are now considering elevation of the maximum penalty for production to four years.

paratory acts committed in order to procure for oneself the possession of hard drugs covered by Arts. 2 and 10.

From the discussion of the Act's basic outlines two major conclusions emerge. Firstly, a sharp distinction has been made between so-called hard drugs and soft drugs.[39] Secondly, a rather sharp distinction has also been made between offences involving the consumption of drugs and psychotropic substances on the one hand and other offences on the other; in other words between persons who consume drugs and persons who supply them. The first distinction is based on the belief that it is desirable to distinguish between drugs which present an unacceptable risk to health and other drugs. In this view, interests which have to be protected by criminal law are primarily health interests. The second distinction rests on the conviction that the primary aim of any policy with respect to drug addiction should be to limit its adverse social consequences and to ensure the integration of drug users in society. To some extent the two distinctions are interrelated. By creating different legal regimes for hard and soft drugs, resulting in a separation of different 'markets', it is hoped that those who consume soft drugs will less readily turn to hard drugs.

The 1995 Act on prevention of misuse of chemical substances prohibits a number of acts with respect to chemical substances used in order to produce narcotic drugs or psychotropic substances. Infringements of its provisions constitute economic offences within the meaning of the Economic Offences Act. They carry maximum penalties varying from six years' imprisonment to six months' detention.

From a comparative viewpoint, the Dutch Opium Act is rather exceptional in making a systematic distinction between hard and soft drugs and between the demand for and the supply of drugs. However well-considered legislative choices may have been, it cannot be denied that they may easily produce contradictions and paradoxes. This is perhaps even more true for enforcement policies developed on the basis of the Act. One of the major problems is how to reconcile rather liberal rules and policies with respect to the demand for drugs with strict and efficient repression of supply, given the fact that all demand generates supply. It is also unmistakably true that liberal policies with respect to demand produce transnational effects, notably in the form of drug tourism to the Netherlands. At least one other European country has openly and repeatedly made it known that they violate the 1990 Convention applying the Schengen Agreement in this respect. Finally, the question arises whether and

---

39 This distinction also appears in the provision on jurisdiction in the Act. See infra pp. 72-73.

to what extent the policies based on the Act can still be reconciled with a faithful implementation of such treaties as the 1988 United Nations Convention.[40]

Within the confinements of this book it is hardly possible to explain or take sides in the ongoing national, and increasingly European, debate on the merits and defects of domestic legislation and policies. Suffice it to say here that the Dutch Government have published a policy paper on the matter recently.[41] In it the Government evaluate past policies and announce a number of revisions. In some respects enforcement policies will become more strict. The Government admit that denouncing international treaties is not an option open to the Netherlands.[42]

Insider trading

At the beginning of 1989, a new provision was introduced in the Penal Code prohibiting insider trading. In 1992, the provision was amended slightly and transferred to the 1991 Act on the supervision of securities transactions *(Wet toezicht effectenverkeer)* in order to make the offence an economic offence within the meaning of the Economic Offences Act. If intentionally committed the offence carries a maximum penalty of two years' imprisonment. Transfer of the provision also served the purpose of adapting it slightly in order to implement EC Directive 89/592.[43] In 1994, the Netherlands became a party to the 1989 Council of Europe Convention on Insider Trading and its Protocol.

Article 31a of the Act prohibits any person who has obtained prior knowledge to effect or bring about any transaction in the Netherlands in respect of securities listed on a securities exchange authorized under Art. 16 of the Act insofar as any benefit may result from that transaction.[44] The same prohibition

---

40 Cf. e.g. *De Hullu/Tillema*, De verdragsverplichtingen en de wetgevingsgeschiedenis, p. 62. For a discussion of policies see also *Rüter*, Drugs and the Criminal Law in the Netherlands, pp. 147-156; *Silvis*, Enforcing drug laws in the Netherlands, pp. 41-58.

41 It has been translated into the English language under the title Drugs Policy in the Netherlands; Continuity and change. Published in October 1995, it was discussed in parliament in the winter of 1996.

42 In Annex III to the paper the legal aspects of denouncing various treaties are methodically reviewed by an independent expert.

43 Directive 89/592 of 13 November 1989 coordinating regulations on insider dealing, 1989 OJ L 334/30.

44 Benefit means any financial advantage whatever its nature, including the avoidance of disadvantages or losses.

applies to any person acting in the Netherlands to bring about transactions quoted on a securities exchange outside the Netherlands. The definition of prior knowledge is a rather complex one. Prior knowledge means knowledge of any special circumstance concerning the legal entity, company or institution to which the securities concerned relate or concerning the trade in securities

a. of which the person who is aware of such circumstances knows or should reasonably suspect that the same is not in the public domain and could not have been brought outside the circle of persons who have a duty of confidentiality without violating a secret, and

b. of which the disclosure may reasonably be expected to affect the quotation of the securities concerned.

In a recent decision the Supreme Court had an opportunity to elucidate three different aspects of the provision.[45] According to the Court, the requirement that any benefit may result from a transaction refers to a benefit directly resulting from the transaction itself. It does not include later benefits which might be acquired depending on uncertain new developments taking place after the transaction has been brought about. Another important point decided by the Court concerns the definition of prior knowledge. In its view, the requirement that disclosure may reasonably be expected to affect the quotation of securities supposes not only that, according to objective criteria, it could reasonably be expected that disclosure of information would affect quotation but also in which direction the market would react. Finally, the Court said that a duty of confidentiality does not only arise from provisions in the Penal Code. It may also derive from other circumstances, such as a contractual relationship, a decision taken within a company or usual practices.

Comparing the Act with the Council of Europe Convention we may note that the concept of insider trading in the Act seems to be broader in some respects. While, for instance, Art. 1 of the Convention enumerates the persons who may trade information, the Act covers a larger group. Moreover, the concept of securities seems to be somewhat broader in Dutch law. As far as the EC Directive is concerned, domestic law and EC law seem roughly to correspond, although there may be minor discrepancies.[46]

---

45 HR 27 June 1995, NJ 1995, 662.
46 For a closer study see *De Serière*, The Netherlands, pp. 112-116.

Money laundering and confiscation of proceeds

A major revision of the Dutch Penal Code in the matter of money laundering
offences preceded ratification of the 1988 United Nations Convention against
Illicit Traffic in Narcotic Drugs and Psychotropic Substances and the 1990
Council of Europe Convention on Laundering, Search, Seizure and Confiscation
of the Proceeds from Crime by the Netherlands in 1993. When ratifying the
Council of Europe Convention the Dutch Government declared that its Art. 6,
para. 1, will only be applied to predicate offences that qualify as crimes under
domestic law.[47] The purpose of this declaration will become clearer when we
discuss Dutch law in the matter.

Money laundering offences are not a separate category in the Penal Code.
The revision of the Code, effected in 1991, made money laundering a form of
the already existing crime of receiving stolen goods. Articles 416, 417, and
417bis of the Code deal with several different forms of receiving. Article 416
now makes it a crime for a person to acquire, possess or transfer property, or
to establish or transfer a contractual right or an encumbrance on such property,
while at the time of acquisition or possession of the property or at the time of
the creation of the personal right or the encumbrance he knew that such
property had been obtained by means of a crime. Guilty of receipt is also the
person who intentionally, for the purpose of personal gain, possesses or
transfers an item of property deriving from a crime, or who transfers a
contractual right or an encumbrance in respect of such property. Those guilty
of intentional receipt may be punished by a maximum term of four years'
imprisonment. The same punishment applies to those who intentionally derive
benefit from the proceeds of any property deriving from a crime. In addition,
Art. 417 of the Code deals with intentional receipt in an aggravated form. A
person who regularly engages in intentional receipt is liable to a maximum term
of six years' imprisonment. Finally, Art. 417bis covers negligent receipt. The
maximum term of imprisonment here is one year.

Making a few comments on these provisions, we may first note that money
laundering relates to all types of predicate offences which generate wealth,
provided that these offences qualify as crimes under Dutch law. There is no
limitation to drug trafficking or to other types of offences. Secondly, it does
not matter whether or not the predicate offence has been committed in the
Netherlands or elsewhere; jurisdiction over predicate offences is not a requirement. Finally, expanding the traditional concept of receiving in such ways as

---

47 See Appendix II p. 399.

to include money laundering entails a consequence that may appear strange at first sight. Since receiving has always been considered an act facilitating the commission of crimes by other persons, it is legally not possible for a person to receive items which he himself acquired by committing a crime. Consequently, a person who commits a predicate offence may not be convicted of laundering the proceeds of that crime at the same time. This explains why it was thought necessary to make a declaration with respect to Art. 6 of the Council of Europe Convention.

Two other statutes are important where investigating money laundering offences is concerned: the 1993 Act on the identification of clients of financial institutions *(Wet identificatie bij financiële dienstverlening 1993)* and the 1993 Act on the disclosure of unusual transactions *(Wet melding ongebruikelijke transacties)*. Both statutes aim to implement the 1991 EC Directive 91/308 on prevention of the use of the financial system for the purpose of money laundering.[48]

Ratification of the United Nations Convention and the Council of Europe Convention was preceded by yet another major revision of domestic law. Effected in 1992, it related to the system of penalties and measures and was aimed primarily at widening the possibilities of confiscating proceeds from crime.

Confiscation, defined by both treaties as the permanent, or final, deprivation of property, may be effected under Dutch law in three different ways. A criminal court may impose the penalty of forfeiture *(verbeurdverklaring)* on the basis of Arts. 33 to 34 of the Code. Pursuant to Arts. 36b to 36d a court may order the withdrawal of goods from circulation *(onttrekking aan het verkeer)* as a measure. Or it may, on the basis of Art. 36e, impose the measure of confiscation of the proceeds from crime *(ontneming van het wederrechtelijk verkregen voordeel)*.[49] To a considerable extent these sanctions overlap, thereby offering the courts an opportunity to choose one way rather than another.

Simplifying matters slightly one may state that forfeiture essentially is a penalty resulting in the deprivation of proceeds acquired from an offence and of instrumentalities used or intended to be used to commit it. Objects may be

---

48 1991 OJ L 166/77. For a discussion of Dutch law in the English language see *Graaf*, Netherlands, pp. 123-140.

49 Moreover, the obligation to pay compensation to the victim of a crime may also result in the rendering of proceeds.

forfeited, together with rights attached to them. However, objects representing proceeds must, as a rule, belong to the accused. The purpose of withdrawal of goods from circulation is to prevent the free circulation of these goods contrary to the law or to the general interest. Objects which may be withdrawn from circulation are largely the same as those which may be forfeited. However, the measure of withdrawal may be imposed regardless of whether the accused has been found guilty or not and regardless of whether or not the objects belong to the accused. Finally, there is the measure of confiscation, the most far-reaching sanction of all three. While, in Dutch law, the penalty of forfeiture is a form of object confiscation, the measure of confiscation of the proceeds from crime is a form of value confiscation. The measure requires a person to pay a sum of money not exceeding the value of proceeds. It may only be pronounced after the accused has been convicted of an offence.

As far as the relationship between that offence and the proceeds is concerned, Art. 36e distinguishes four different situations. The simplest situation is that in which advantages are being confiscated which derive from the offence of which the accused has been convicted. But the law also permits the confiscation of proceeds from other offences. If a person has been found guilty of an offence by the court, that court may also confiscate proceeds generated by similar offences with which the accused has not been charged. A court may decide to take that step if it has become apparent from the evidence before it that the accused is likely to have committed these offences; the court need not be convinced beyond reasonable doubt. Similarly, the court may confiscate proceeds from other offences not similar to the one or the ones it has convicted the accused of. Article 36e, however, permits confiscation with respect to the most serious crimes only. Meanwhile, the most far-reaching form of confiscation is the fourth. If the court has found the accused guilty of a crime carrying a maximum term of imprisonment of six years or more, it may confiscate proceeds from any other offence if it is likely that the accused has gained economic advantages from it, regardless of whether the offence had been committed by the accused himself or by other persons. The court may only do so if, in accordance with Arts. 126 to 126f of the Code of Criminal Procedure, a special financial investigation, the so-called criminal financial investigation, has been carried out into advantages which the accused may have obtained from crime in the past.

Confiscation must always be pronounced by the court in a separate order. The law requires the court to impose detention on the accused, to be enforced if the accused does not pay the amount of money he is obliged to pay. Its maximum is six years' detention.

The system of confiscation discussed here does not apply to fiscal offences. Confiscation of proceeds from fiscal offences is left to the tax authorities since proceeds from these offences are deemed to be taxes that have not been paid. This approach is not without consequences for international cooperation in confiscating proceeds. When ratifying the Council of Europe Convention the Netherlands made a declaration to the effect that it will not apply Art. 2, para. 1, of the Convention with respect to the confiscation of proceeds from tax offences.[50]

Violations of the Revised Rhine Navigation Act

The Revised Rhine Navigation Act, concluded at Mannheim in 1868, aims at achieving free navigation on the Rhine and its mouths from Basle to the open sea.[51] Part of the system created by the Act is the Central Commission for Navigation on the Rhine, established at Strasbourg and composed of representatives of the Rhine states. The Commission is competent to lay down rules with respect to navigation on the Rhine.

Article 32 of the Act penalizes violations of police ordinances jointly decided upon by the Rhine states. While the rules contained in police ordinances are of international origin, enforcing them is a national as well as an international matter. An offender convicted in the first instance by a national court has a right to appeal to a judicial body especially created for that purpose: the Appeals Chamber of the Central Commission for Navigation on the Rhine. However, he may prefer to appeal to the appellate body established in accordance with domestic law of the Rhine state where the court of first instance has its seat. Articles 36 and 37 of the Act offer the offender a choice here.

Violations of police regulations are liable to fines up to 2500 Special Drawing Rights, converted to the national currency. Detention for non-payment of a fine may not be imposed.[52]

---

50 See infra pp. 241-242.
51 Parties to the Act are Belgium, France, Germany, Italy, the Netherlands, the United Kingdom and Switzerland.
52 CCNR 25 February 1981, NJ 1981, 471; HR 9 June 1981, NJ 1981, 472.

Jurisdiction

Marius Teengs Gerritsen

Basic characteristics

The limits of national jurisdiction, over offences committed on the territory of a state as well as outside its territory, are determined by international law. Article 8 of the Dutch Penal Code explicitly refers to those limits by declaring that Arts. 2 to 7 of the Code are applicable only to the extent reconcilable with international law. However, it is not very clear what these limits imply. Usually, a reference is made here to the decision of the Permanent Court of International Justice in the *Lotus* case.[1] In it, the Court stated that international law leaves states 'a wide measure of discretion which is only limited in certain cases by prohibitive rules' where establishing extraterritorial jurisdiction is concerned.

The most important provisions on jurisdiction in Dutch law are to be found in Arts. 2 to 8 of the Penal Code. Dating from 1881, these provisions were originally characterized by a strong emphasis on national sovereignty. On the one hand, sovereignty implied that Dutch courts had jurisdiction over offences committed on Dutch territory. The territoriality principle, therefore, formed the self-evident backbone of the provisions on jurisdiction. On the other hand, national sovereignty was also considered to be a concept limiting jurisdiction. It was thought not proper to extend the jurisdiction of Dutch courts over offences committed outside the Netherlands unless there were compelling reasons for doing so. To extend jurisdiction over extraterritorial offences would, moreover, create a danger of jurisdictional conflicts with other states. That danger should be reduced as much as possible. The emphasis on the territoriality principle and the desire to avoid conflicts of jurisdiction are also at the basis

---

1   PCIJ 7 September 1927, Series A, no. 10, pp. 18-19.

of Art. 68, para. 2, the provision of the Code which deals with *res judicata* of foreign courts.[2]

The foregoing explains why extraterritorial jurisdiction was basically limited to offences which jeopardize vital national interests and to crimes committed by Dutch nationals abroad; their extradition was not permitted at that time. There was little inclination to establish extraterritorial jurisdiction for the sake of international solidarity. The universality principle applied to the offence of piracy only.

Later, especially in the period after the Second World War, a process of expanding extraterritorial jurisdiction set in. Initially, the primary motive behind the expansion was to afford national interests better protection. Increasingly, however, legislative changes were also introduced as a consequence of ratifying multilateral treaties with respect to international crimes. Not only were the provisions in the Penal Code amended frequently, in many other statutes additional jurisdictional rules were introduced. The situation in 1996 is, therefore, rather different from that in 1886, the year in which the Code entered into force. However, it still remains true that Dutch law on extraterritorial jurisdiction is marked by a measure of self-imposed restraint, and in this respect it still differs from the law of many other continental European states. Respect for the sovereignty of other states and the desire to avoid conflicts of jurisdiction with these states have remained important motives despite the expansion of extraterritorial jurisdiction in recent times. They explain why, as will become apparent from our discussion of the law, the protective principle, the passive personality principle and the universality principle are still looked upon as principles which should be made use of as sparingly as possible.[3]

In this part of the book we will first discuss the provisions of the Penal Code on jurisdiction. Articles 2 to 8 of the Code not only apply to all offences under the Code itself but also to those contained in other statutes unless a statute provides otherwise. We will then turn to specific provisions in other statutes which deviate from the rules of the Code. Since it is not possible to deal with all statutes here, we will have to make a selection and will pay special attention to statutes aimed at implementing international treaties.

---

2   See infra pp. 78-80.

3   For a historical analysis of Dutch law in the matter see *Rüter/Swart*, De toepasselijkheid van de Nederlandse strafwet; van locus delicti naar goede rechtsbedeling, pp. 243-274; *Swart*, Jurisdiction in Criminal Law: Some Reflections on the Finnish Code from a Comparative Perspective, pp. 527-543.

The Penal Code

The territoriality principle

According to Art. 2 of the Penal Code, the criminal statutes of the Netherlands are applicable to anyone who commits any offence within the Netherlands. Here, the determining factor is the place where the offence has been committed.

That Dutch criminal law may be applied to offences committed on Dutch territory is 'not only undisputed, but also indisputable', according to the Government in its explanatory notes to the Draft Penal Code.[4] In the *Lotus* case, the Permanent Court of International Justice also held that 'in all systems of law the territorial character of criminal law is fundamental'.[5] That criminal law first and foremost applies to a state's own territory is so logical that to give a more thoroughgoing justification for this rule is often thought unnecessary.[6] Solid arguments are, however, not difficult to find. If an offence is committed on the territory of a state, its consequences will be felt mainly in that state. Moreover, the authority of a state over what happens on its territory is generally recognized and should, in principle, be respected by other states. One may add that the state on whose territory the offence was committed has sole jurisdiction, to the exclusion of other states, to conduct investigations on its territory. Finally, the most important evidence of the offence usually can be found in its own territory.

Two questions are important in connection with Art. 2. The first relates to what Dutch territory includes, the second is what criteria determine whether an offence has been committed on this territory.

Concerning the first question, the borders between the Netherlands on the one hand and Belgium and Germany on the other have been fixed by various treaties.[7]

On the coast, the boundaries between territorial and international waters have been set by the 1985 Act on the boundaries of the Netherlands territorial sea *(Wet grenzen Nederlandse territoriale zee)* at twelve nautical miles from the

---

4 *Smidt*, Geschiedenis van het Wetboek van Strafrecht, Vol. I, p. 110.
5 Cf. also *Oehler*, Internationales Strafrecht, p. 115.
6 Cf. *Rüter/Swart* (supra note 3), p. 247.
7 For the border between the Netherlands and Belgium see the treaties of 5 November 1842, *Staatsblad* 1843, 3, and 8 August 1843, *Staatsblad* 1844, 12. For that between the Netherlands and the Federal Republic of Germany see the treaties of 8 April 1960, *Tractatenblad* 1960, 68, and 10 September 1984, *Tractatenblad* 1984, 118.

Dutch coast. The primary reasons for extending the territorial waters from three to twelve nautical miles were linked with the desire for better regulation of shipping traffic and better protection of the marine environment.[8] As a coastal state of the North Sea, the Netherlands is entitled to exercise sovereign rights over its part of the North Sea continental shelf for the purpose of exploring it and exploiting its natural resources.[9] Three different statutes have been adopted in order to lay down rules in the matter. The 1964 Act on installations in the North Sea *(Wet installaties Noordzee)* declares Dutch criminal law applicable to anyone who commits any offence on or against an installation on the Dutch part of the North Sea continental shelf. The 1965 Continental Shelf Mining Act *(Mijnwet continentaal plat)* and the 1974 Act on the sea bed materials of the North Sea *(Wet bodemmaterialen Noordzee)* have no separate jurisdictional provisions. Since violations of these Acts constitute economic offences, the special regime of the 1950 Economic Offences Act *(Wet op de economische delicten)* applies to them.[10]

Pursuant to developments within the European Communities, the 1977 Act enabling the establishment of a fishery zone *(Machtigingswet instelling visserijzone)* gives the Government the power to establish an exclusive fishery zone that extends two-hundred nautical miles from the coastline. In a Royal Decree, the boundaries of this zone have been so determined that they coincide with the Dutch part of the North Sea continental shelf.[11] Following this Act, Art. 58 of the 1963 Fisheries Act *(Visserijwet)* declares Dutch criminal law applicable to persons who commit any of several fishery offences outside territorial waters but within this zone. These also constitute economic offences.

Unlike the penal codes of some other European countries, the Dutch Penal Code contains no provision with respect to the place where an offence is committed. During the parliamentary debates on the Draft Penal Code the Government designated the place where the physical action occurs and the place where an instrument used by the offender has its effect as possible locations of the offence. The place where the consequences of an offence are felt was not mentioned. The Government, however, found that the development of precise criteria should be the task of legal scholars.[12] Initially, the courts kept strictly

---

8   The Netherlands is a party to the 1958 Convention on the Continental Shelf and the 1982 United Nations Convention on the Law of the Sea.
9   See for its delimitation the North Sea Continental Shelf Cases, ICJ Reports 1969.
10   See infra p. 72.
11   Royal Decree of 23 November 1977, *Staatsblad* 665.
12   Cf. *Smidt* (supra note 4), Vol. I, p. 112.

to the place where the offender acted as the only criterion for the location of the offence. Later on, however, a broader approach was favoured. Of special importance here is a 1954 decision of the Supreme Court.[13] This was a case of fraud in which the perpetrator, located in Singapore, had convinced the victim, residing in Amsterdam, by letter to deliver goods. The Supreme Court held that Amsterdam could also be considered one of the places where the fraud took place. This decision is generally interpreted as implying that the place of the offence may also be the place where the instrument used by the perpetrator has its effect. The result of the Supreme Court's decision is that the place where an offence is committed may be determined on the basis of two different criteria that complement each other. In other words, under certain circumstances an offence can be committed in more than one place. In the case of offences of pure omission, determination of the place is not a problem; it is where the offender should have acted.[14]

Neither are there rules to be found in the Penal Code relating to the question of how to localize the offence in the case of attempt to commit and participation in an offence. For attempt the answer is simple: the location of the offence is where the attempt was made.[15] With regard to those who can be considered participants in an offence, however, the answer is more complex. Unlike in many countries, the construction that the participant is considered to have acted in the same place as the principal is not generally used in the Netherlands. On the contrary, there is a tendency in case law to give each participant his own place, which does not necessarily have to be the same place as where the principal acted. This approach is probably linked with the view that each participant in an offence bears his own share of criminal liability which must be distinguished from that of the others. Apart from that, this tendency is not equally strong with regard to every type of participation. Therefore, we cannot avoid giving a brief description of all the different types of participation below. The case law will be presented only in outline form.[16]

The first type of participation is that of co-authorship *(medeplegers)*. Concerning this type of participation, the courts assume that the acts of a co-author abroad are also committed in the Netherlands if the other co-author has

13 HR 6 April 1954, NJ 1954, 368.
14 Cf. e.g. HR 8 June 1936, NJ 1936, 954; HR 27 April 1993, NJ 1993, 744.
15 The same would have to apply to carrying out preparatory acts in so far as they are punishable under Dutch law. See supra p. 23.
16 See also *Strijards*, Internationaal strafrecht, strafmachtsrecht, pp. 260-264; *Keijzer*, Participation in Crime – Developments in Dutch Law, pp. 500-501.

acted in the Netherlands.[17] Those who use other persons as instruments for committing offences *(doen plegers)* are usually considered to have committed the offence at the place where the person they used as an instrument committed the physical act.[18] This is different for those who solicit others to commit criminal offences *(uitlokkers)*, who are considered to have their own place. Therefore, if someone in a foreign country incites another person to commit a criminal offence on Dutch territory, he is considered not to have acted in the Netherlands.[19] As a rule, the same applies to those who lend support to the committing of offences by others *(medeplichtigen)*.[20] Furthermore, it must be assumed that, with regard to participants, the place of the criminal offence may also be where they themselves acted, as well as where the instruments they used had their effect. Finally, it is necessary to say something about those within a legal person who ordered an offence or who did not prevent the offence from being committed by the legal person while they were in a position and under a duty to do so. Case law assumes that they have committed the offence where the legal person has done so.[21] The foregoing has made it clear that the localization of participation is a rather complicated matter. This partly explains the fact that different regulations have been included in the 1950 Economic Offences Act and the 1928 Opium Act,which apply the protective principle to participation abroad in an offence committed in the Netherlands. These regulations are discussed further below.[22]

Jurisdiction over vessels and aircraft

In Art. 3 of the Penal Code, the criminal law of the Netherlands is declared applicable to anyone who, being outside the Netherlands, commits an offence on board a Dutch vessel or aircraft. Here the location of the offence is the reference point for jurisdiction, as is the case under Art. 2 of the Code. In the application of Art. 3 the question may also arise as to where an offence was committed. This must be answered on the basis of the criteria discussed above.

Jurisdiction over vessels and aircraft is usually considered to be an extension of the territoriality principle. This is correct to the extent that under interna-

---

17 HR 17 November 1981, NJ 1983, 84; HR 24 January 1995, NJ 1995, 352.
18 HR 11 May 1982, NJ 1983, 3.
19 HR 25 June 1917, NJ 1917, 821.
20 HR 1 November 1897, W 7040; HR 15 March 1943, NJ 1943, 375.
21 HR 16 February 1986, NJ 1987, 321; HR 18 October 1988, NJ 1989, 496.
22 See infra pp. 72-73.

tional law an offence committed on board a vessel on the high seas is considered to have been committed on the territory of the state whose flag the vessel flies. In order to justify Art. 3, the Government maintained at that time that offences committed on Dutch vessels could not remain unpunished. Without the rule of Art. 3, a legal vacuum could occur in two different situations. The first would be when a Dutch vessel is on the high seas. The freedom of the high seas implies, after all, that no state may validly purport to subject any part of them to its sovereignty, while international law also prohibits states from exercising jurisdiction over vessels flying the flag of another state.[23] In the second place, a legal vacuum could occur if the Dutch vessel is located within the territorial waters of a state that honours the principle 'ship is territory'. That would mean that the law of the state does not apply to offences committed in its territory on board the Dutch vessel.

Articles 86 and 86a of the Penal Code define what is meant by Dutch vessels and aircraft. The definition of aircraft in Art. 86a is in line with the 1970 Convention for the Suppression of Unlawful Seizure of Aircraft and the 1971 Convention for the Suppression of Unlawful Acts against the Safety of Civil Aviation.

The protective principle

Article 4 of the Penal Code declares the criminal law of the Netherlands applicable to anyone who commits any of the offences listed in this article outside the Netherlands. They are grouped in nine categories. The protective principle is applicable to some of these and the universality principle to others, while in the case of one category the passive personality principle applies. Here we shall only discuss the offences to which the protective principle applies.

The main reason for applying the protective principle is that the legal order of a state may well be violated from abroad and the vital interests of that state jeopardized. In general, such violations are not criminally sanctioned by the state where the offence was committed because the purpose of its criminal law is not to protect the interests of other countries.[24] Meanwhile, the protective principle should be used with restraint. Application of the protective principle

---

23 Cf. Arts. 2 and 6 of the 1958 Convention of the High Seas and Arts. 87 and 92 of the 1982 Convention on the Law of the Sea.
24 Cf. *Oehler* (supra note 5), p. 384.

normally means that a state declares its criminal law applicable to acts outside its territory which are not usually punishable in the place where they were committed. This is a predicament, especially when the perpetrator of the offence is a citizen of the state where he committed the act. Prosecution of this offender could easily be viewed as interference in the domestic affairs of the state of the *locus delicti*. Secondly, application of the protective principle may result in foreigners being subjected to laws they do not know.

There is no simple answer to the question of when the protective principle may be applied. The view is often held that the protection of vital interests of the state must be involved. The security of the state and its own monetary system are examples of such interests. But with respect to the protection of other interests, such as industrial interests and the state's own tax system, there is less consensus.[25] It is also clear that there are considerable differences in the way states apply the principle.[26]

From a comparative point of view, it seems that the Netherlands is relatively restrained in its use of the protective principle. The list of offences to which the principle has been declared applicable has, however, become longer in the course of time. This broadening is partly the result of the ratification of multilateral treaties.

The two first categories of Art. 4 relate to a number of offences against the state, offences against the royal dignity and other offences in so far as they are directly connected with the two first categories.[27] Among the aforementioned provisions there are also some aimed at protecting both the interests of the Dutch state and those of its allies. These are Arts. 98 to 98c, prohibiting the dissemination of information which must be kept secret in order to protect the interests of the state and of its allies.

In the third, fourth and fifth categories, several offences have been included that comprise falsification of official documents, issued by or on the authority of the state of the Netherlands, and the use of such documents.[28] Further, in the fifth category are two shipping offences and the offence of impeding the Dutch authorities in their investigation of criminal offences outside Dutch territory.[29]

---

25 Cf. *Cameron*, The Protective Principle of International Criminal Jurisdiction, pp. 347-362.
26 Cf. *Oehler* (supra note 5), pp. 368-375.
27 Arts. 92 to 96, 97a, 98 to 98c, 105, 108 to 110, 131 to 134, and 189 of the Code.
28 Arts. 216, 226.
29 Arts. 409 to 410, 446a. See for extraterritorial investigations infra pp. 224-225.

The sixth category concerns just one offence: committing perjury before an international court. Perjury before an international court is criminalized in Art. 207a of the Penal Code, with the limitation that the international court must be established by or pursuant to an international treaty to which the Netherlands is a party. The criminal provision came into existence as a result of the 1964 Benelux model law on perjury before an international court.[30] It is obvious that this provision, like Arts. 98 to 98c, does not only protect purely Dutch interests but also those of other states. These might, for instance, be member states of the European Union, of the Council of Europe or of the United Nations.[31]

— Finally, the seventh and eighth categories of Art. 4 declare the protective principle applicable to criminal provisions that are partly aimed at the implementation of a number of multilateral treaties.[32] These are the 1970 Convention for the Suppression of Unlawful Seizure of Aircraft, the 1971 Convention for the Suppression of Unlawful Acts against the Safety of Civil Aviation and its 1988 Protocol, and the 1988 Convention for the Suppression of Unlawful Acts against the Safety of Maritime Navigation and its Protocol.

In Art. 7 of the Penal Code, the criminal law of the Netherlands is declared applicable to the master and other persons on board a Dutch vessel located outside the Netherlands, also while not on board, who have committed certain maritime or aviation offences.[33] These provisions are of limited importance. As an addition to Art. 3, Art. 7 is only significant insofar as it covers offences committed off the vessel. Moreover, in Art. 4 the protective principle is gradually being declared applicable to more and more maritime and aviation offences.

---

30 Cf. *Noyon/Langemeijer/Remmelink*, Het Wetboek van Strafrecht, aantekening 2 op Art. 207a.
31 Cf. Art. 27 of the 1957 Protocol to the Statute of the Court of Justice of the European Economic Community. Perjury before the *ad hoc* tribunals created by the UN Security Council pursuant to Resolutions 827 (1993) and 955 (1994) to adjudicate crimes committed in the former Yugoslavia and in Rwanda also constitutes a crime within the meaning of Art. 207a. Although both courts were created by resolutions of the Security Council, the Council itself derives its power to do so from the Charter of the United Nations. See also infra p. 94.
32 Arts. 166, 168, 350, 352, 354, 385a, 385b and 385c.
33 Arts. 381 to 415 and 469 to 475. Art. 85 of the Code contains definitions.

The passive personality principle

By virtue of a long-standing tradition, Dutch law tends to reject the passive personality principle. It is applied only in special statutes on the repression of offences committed in time of war. The objections of the Dutch legislature against acceptance of the principle for offences committed in peacetime are in accordance with those which are generally put forward. The passive personality principle would appear to show a lack of trust in and respect for the justice systems of other states. It would also foster the creation of positive conflicts of jurisdiction. Like the protective principle, this principle also entails the danger that foreigners will be subjected to laws they do not know or could not know. For all these reasons, a principle that makes jurisdiction dependent upon the nationality of the victim is not in line with the assumptions underlying Arts. 2 to 8 and 68 of the Penal Code.

Neither have there been any fundamental changes to this disapproving attitude during recent decades. The opposition to the passive personality principle explains why the Netherlands waited until 1988 to become a party to the 1973 Convention on the Prevention and Punishment of Crimes against Internationally Protected Persons. Article 3 of the Convention requires each state party to establish its jurisdiction over crimes set forth in Art. 2, when the crime is committed against an internationally protected person who enjoys his status as such by virtue of functions which he exercises on behalf of that state. The Convention was ratified despite the objections to this provision, in the expectation that in actual practice there would be few cases in which Dutch jurisdiction would be based on the passive personality principle. For implementation of the Convention, the principle has now been included in the ninth category of Art. 4 of the Penal Code. This provision, however, requires that the act in question is also an offence in the state where it was committed. Furthermore, the applicable Dutch criminal provisions require that the offender knows the international status of the victim.[34] On the other hand, the passive personality principle has not been declared applicable to the offence of hostage taking, the International Convention against the Taking of Hostages leaving discretion to the states parties in the matter. The same is true for the Convention for the Suppression of Unlawful Acts against the Safety of Maritime Navigation and its Protocol.

---

34 Arts. 117, 117a, 117b, 285.

The active personality principle

Article 5 of the Penal Code declares the criminal law of the Netherlands applicable to offences committed by Dutch nationals outside the Netherlands. The first paragraph of this provision distinguishes two categories of cases. The first category, indicated in para. 1.1°, lists several penal provisions which, when violated, make a Dutch national liable to punishment wherever in the world he may have committed the offence. The second category, indicated in para. 1.2°, includes all crimes under Dutch law. For these, a Dutch national may only be tried in the Netherlands if his act is also an offence under the law of the state on whose territory the act was committed.

The distinction made by the Penal Code in Art. 5 corresponds to a certain extent with the justifications that can be put forward for the active personality principle.[35] On the one hand, it is important to every state that its citizens also observe its own law outside its own borders. On the other, if this requirement extends to the entire national criminal law, then it undoubtedly goes too far. Then the situation could arise that a state would require 'such acts from its citizens abroad as are forbidden to them by the Municipal Law of the land in which they reside, and (order) (...) them not to commit such acts as they are bound to commit according to the Municipal Law of the land in which they reside.'[36] The requirement, therefore, should be limited to laws, the compliance with which is also considered especially important abroad.[37] The question is then which laws these would be.

A second justification for the principle may be found in international solidarity. In this case, the principle sees to it that nationals do not escape punishment for criminal offences which they commit on the territory of another state, by returning to their own state. Impunity, after all, could be the result of the rule in force in many states that nationals will not be extradited; in the Netherlands this rule was also fully applicable until 1986. One could say that, in such cases, the active personality principle expresses an abstract form of solidarity with other states.[38] Abstract, because the possibility to prosecute a national for criminal offences committed in a foreign country does not depend on the condition that the other state has made a request to that effect. Dutch law does not require such a request.

---

35 Cf. e.g. Extraterritorial criminal jurisdiction, Report of the European Committee on Crime Problems, Council of Europe, Strasbourg 1990.

36 *Oppenheim/Lauterpacht*, International Law, A Treatise, Vol. I, p. 237.

37 Cf. *Oehler* (supra note 5), pp. 456-457.

38 Cf. *Oehler* (supra note 5), p. 143.

Article 5 of the Penal Code raises the question of what is meant by a Dutch national. The answer to this question is determined by the 1984 Nationality Act *(Rijkswet op het Nederlanderschap)*, which is an Act of the Kingdom. Another statute of importance here is the 1976 Act on the legal status of Moluccans *(Wet betreffende de positie van Molukkers)*. Under this statute, Moluccans are to be treated like Dutch citizens in the application of most laws. Moluccans are a community of persons who served in the former Dutch colonial army and were repatriated to the Netherlands after Indonesia gained independence, together with their descendants.

Now that legal persons, too, can commit criminal offences under Dutch law, it is obvious that Art. 5 also applies to Dutch legal persons.[39] The question is then what constitutes a Dutch legal person. Under Dutch private law, the nationality of a legal person is determined on the basis of the formal criterion of whether it has been incorporated under Dutch law. There have been arguments in the literature for taking the existence of an actual link between the legal person and the Netherlands as a criterion for the application of Art. 5. That would particularly be the case if the legal person has its registered office or principal place of business in the Netherlands.[40] There is no case law on these questions.

A related question is that of the status of those natural persons within a legal person who ordered the offence or who did not prevent the offence from being committed by the legal person while they were in a position and under a duty to do so. Case law assumes that they must possess Dutch nationality. It is not necessary, however, that the legal person for which they work also possesses that nationality.[41] Neither is there any requirement that the state where the offence had been committed accepts the criminal responsibility of legal persons.[42]

Regardless of whether or not the act in question has been criminalized in the country of the *locus delicti,* Art. 5, para. 1, first category, prohibits Dutch nationals from committing certain offences abroad. In the first place, this

---

39 HR 11 December 1990, NJ 1991, 466.

40 Cf. e.g. *Mok/Duk*, Toepassing van Nederlands strafrecht op buiten Nederland begane delicten, p. 131; *Van Strien*, De rechtsmacht van Nederland ten aanzien van rechtspersonen, p. 61. Cf. also Art. 4 of the Act on the transfer of enforcement of criminal judgments, discussed infra p. 193.

41 HR 12 February 1991, NJ 1991, 528.

42 HR 18 October 1988, NJ 1989, 496.

concerns crimes against state security and crimes against royal dignity.[43] Inclusion of these crimes under the active personality principle expresses the special bond between the Dutch state and its citizens and is also important for the reason that the acts prohibited usually will not be punishable elsewhere.[44] This part of Art. 5 then mentions Arts. 206 (making oneself unsuitable for military service), 237 (bigamy), 272 to 273 (revealing secret information) and 388 to 389 (privateering).

Article 5, para. 1, second category, applies the active nationality principle to all crimes under Dutch law provided that they constitute offences under the law of the state where they have been committed. This provision, introducing the requirement of double criminality, owed its existence mainly to the fact that Dutch law did not permit the extradition of Dutch nationals until 1986. Even though their extradition is now a possibility in certain cases, the provision is still an important one.

Double criminality is determined *in abstracto*. In determining the punishability of the offence charged according to foreign law, it is sufficient to examine whether the act also falls within the scope of a foreign criminal provision. An assessment of the foreign law on the issue of justifications and excuses is not necessary.[45] Neither is an examination required as to whether there are other reasons under the law of the state of the *locus* which would prevent conviction.

A special problem in the determination of double criminality within the framework of Art. 5 occurs where domestic penal provisions specifically protect Dutch interests. For example, this is the case for most crimes against state security and many crimes against public order, but other criminal provisions may also have such limitations, either implicitly or explicitly. Case law assumes that double criminality is lacking in such situations even though similar conduct is prohibited by the law of the state where the offence was

---

43 Arts. 92 to 114 of the Code.
44 It has already been mentioned above that Arts. 98 to 98c of the Code do not exclusively protect Dutch interests but also those of allies of the Netherlands. Arts. 100 to 107 prohibit certain acts in time of war. According to Art. 107a war also means another armed conflict in which the Netherlands is involved, either for individual or collective self-defence or for restoring international peace and security.
45 Although some authors argue in favour of including justifications in the assessment. See *Noyon/Langemeijer/Remmelink* (supra note 30), comment 8 on Art. 5.

committed.[46] This is different from the manner in which double criminality is determined within the framework of requests for extradition and other requests for legal assistance.[47] A somewhat related problem comes up with respect to criminal provisions that prohibit certain actions without a license. Case law assumes that these provisions do not extend to actions outside the territory of the Netherlands.[48]

— The second paragraph of Art. 5 stipulates that the person who acquires Dutch nationality after having committed a crime may also be prosecuted in the Netherlands for that crime.[49]

Finally, we must mention Art. 6 here. This provision applies to Dutch public servants who commit any of the crimes included under Arts. 355 to 380 of the Penal Code outside the Netherlands. The determining factor here is not the Dutch nationality but the capacity of being a Dutch public servant. It is conceivable that a non-Dutch citizen may be considered a Dutch public servant. An example is the honorary consul working abroad.

— Neither the Penal Code nor any other statute describes what is generally meant by a Dutch public servant. Case law assumes that a public servant is someone who has been appointed by the public authorities to a public position in order to perform part of the task of the state or its organs.[50] Its principal criterion is the actual task to be fulfilled.

The universality principle

The universality principle is pre-eminently the jurisdictional principle that expresses international solidarity. The idea behind this principle is that states have an interest in combating and punishing certain forms of crime in unison. That is why they place themselves under obligations to prosecute the alleged perpetrators of certain offences, which include cases in which the offence committed does not directly or immediately damage their own national interests.

— Although Dutch law does not reject the idea of international solidarity, it has always had strong reservations with regard to the universality principle, in

---

46 For example, refusal to obey the Norwegian authorities does not constitute the offence under Art. 184 of the Penal Code. See HR 17 March 1987, NJ 1987, 887 *(Linquenda)*.

47 See for example infra pp. 99-100, 183-184, 193.

48 Cf. e.g. HR 31 May 1983, NJ 1983, 768 (carrying a gun without licence).

49 See also HR 30 June 1950, NJ 1950, 646.

50 HR 30 January 1911, W 9149; HR 25 October 1915, NJ 1915, 1205.

its traditional form as well as in its more modern variant as the principle of *aut dedere aut punire* (either extradite or punish). These reservations do not apply so much to the idea of international solidarity itself, as to the way it is almost always laid down in treaties. In the first place, that formulation creates the risk of jurisdictional conflicts. Such conflicts may consist of two states parties wanting to prosecute and punish the same alleged offender at the same time. They may also take the form of shifting cases onto another state party. This would occur if a state party which is directly affected by the offence purposely does not prosecute an alleged offender for political reasons, and thus leaves prosecution of the person to less involved states. It is the absence of a hierarchy of jurisdictional principles in virtually all treaties that creates this risk. In the second place, the universality principle may easily result in the alleged offender being exposed to double jeopardy. Both these objections weigh heavily because the avoidance of conflicts of jurisdiction and double jeopardy has always been regarded as one of the most important objectives of jurisdictional rules in the Netherlands.

The hesitations with regard to the universality principle in Dutch law have not been without consequences. Application of the principle is only accepted if an explicit basis can be found for it in international law, either in the form of a rule of customary international law or that of a treaty provision. Where a treaty basis is concerned, there must be an obligation to create universal jurisdiction; it is not sufficient that the treaty allows the establishing of universal jurisdiction.[51] Finally, the Netherlands has made reservations to a number of treaties in order to prevent as much as possible a situation whereby the Netherlands could be obliged to prosecute an alleged offender solely on the grounds that the latter is present in its territory. Behind this lies the view that the person who has committed an international offence can best be prosecuted by the states with the strongest jurisdictional claims. Against the background of Arts. 2 to 8 of the Penal Code, those are the state on whose territory the offence was committed and the state of the alleged offender's nationality.

In the Penal Code, the universality principle has been declared applicable without restrictions to piracy and counterfeiting currency.[52] Here, the basis for universal jurisdiction lies in customary international law, the 1958 Convention

---

51 For example, the universality principle is not accepted for criminal offences covered by the 1910 International Convention for the Suppression of White Slave Traffic. Neither does Dutch law accept the rule of *aut dedere aut punire* where drug offences are concerned. See infra p. 73.

52 Arts. 381 to 385 and 208 to 215 of the Code.

on the High Seas and the 1929 International Convention for the Suppression of Counterfeiting Currency. This was done in categories 3 and 4 of Art. 4.

The universality principle with specific stipulations can be found in categories 7 and 8 of Art. 4. Here, the restriction applies that the alleged offender must be present in the territory of the Netherlands. The penal provisions to which these categories refer serve to implement the 1970 Convention for the Suppression of Unlawful Seizure of Aircraft, the 1971 Convention for the Suppression of Unlawful Acts against the Safety of Civil Aviation and the 1988 Convention for the Suppression of Unlawful Acts against the Safety of Maritime Navigation and its Protocol.[53] As mentioned above, the protective principle applies to these offences as well.

The three aforementioned treaties are not the only ones under which the Netherlands has the duty either to prosecute an alleged offender itself or to extradite the person to another contracting party. Here we may also mention the 1973 Convention on the Prevention and Punishment of Crimes against Internationally Protected Persons, including Diplomatic Agents, the 1979 International Convention against the Taking of Hostages, the 1980 Convention on the Physical Protection of Nuclear Material, the 1988 Protocol for the Suppression of Unlawful Acts of Violence at Airports serving International Civil Aviation to the 1971 Convention for the Suppression of Unlawful Acts against the Safety of Civil Aviation, and the 1977 European Convention on the Suppression of Terrorism.[54] The Netherlands has made reservations to all of these conventions, with the exception of the European Convention, which have as effect that the Netherlands accepts jurisdiction exclusively based on the fact that the alleged offender is present in its territory only under certain circumstances. The reservations mean that the Netherlands is willing to do so only if it has received and rejected a request for extradition of that person from another state party. The same reservation has also been made to the 1988 Protocol for the Suppression of Unlawful Acts against the Safety of Fixed Platforms located on the Continental Shelf to the Convention for the Suppression of Unlawful Acts against the Safety of Maritime Navigation. As far as the European Convention is concerned, its Art. 6 already limits the obligation for contracting parties to prosecute to cases in which the suspected offender is present in their territory and they do not extradite him after receiving a request for extradition.

---

53 Arts. 166, 168, 350, 352, 354, 385a to 385c. For the implementation of the 1984 Torture Convention see infra p. 69.
54 For the implementation of the 1949 Geneva Conventions and Protocol I see infra pp. 68-69.

The purpose of these reservations is clear. They are intended to establish that international offences as a rule are prosecuted by contracting parties with a strong jurisdictional claim. As we noted already, these are first and foremost the state where the offence has been committed and the state whose nationality the offender has. Dutch legislation is in line with these reservations. According to Arts. 2 to 7 of the Penal Code, prosecution of the international offences in question on the own initiative of the Dutch authorities is generally only possible if these offences have been either committed on Dutch territory or on board a Dutch vessel or aircraft, or by a person of Dutch nationality. For a limited number of offences, prosecution is also possible on the basis of the protective principle or the passive personality principle.[55] In all other cases jurisdiction will exist only after a request for extradition by another contracting party is directed to the Netherlands and this request is rejected. Jurisdiction in these cases is provided for in the Arts. 4a of the Penal Code and 552hh of the Code of Criminal Procedure, discussed below.

The 'representation' principle

The so-called 'representation' principle implies that a state derives jurisdiction over an extraterritorial offence solely from the fact that it wishes to act for and in the interest of another state which is more directly involved in that offence.[56] Like the universality principle, it is an expression of international solidarity.

Until recently, the representation principle was foreign to Dutch law. It was introduced in a new Art. 4a of the Penal Code in 1985, on the occasion of the ratification of four conventions. The most important of these conventions are the 1972 European Convention on the Transfer of Proceedings in Criminal Matters and the 1977 European Convention on the Suppression of Terrorism.[57] It goes without saying that the unrestricted acceptance of this principle would not be in line with the views prevailing in the Netherlands on extraterritorial

---

55 See supra pp. 55-58.
56 Cf. Extraterritorial Criminal Jurisdiction p. 14. Other expressions used are the principle of vicarious jurisdiction and the principle of subsidiary jurisdiction. See also *Meyer*, The Vicarious Administration of Justice: An Overlooked Basis of Jurisdiction, pp. 108-116.
57 The other two treaties are the 1974 Benelux Treaty on Transfer of Proceedings in Criminal Matters and the 1979 Agreement between the Member States of the European Communities on the Application of the European Convention on the Suppression of Terrorism. However, neither of these two treaties has entered into force.

jurisdiction. Therefore, Art. 4a contains two important restrictions. First of all, criminal proceedings on the basis of the representation principle are allowed only in cases where a treaty creates the competence for the Netherlands to take proceedings against a person pursuant to this principle. Furthermore, the provision requires that proceedings have been transferred to the Netherlands by another state on the basis of that treaty. This second condition is to prevent the application of the representation principle from resulting in conflicts of jurisdiction and double jeopardy. Supplementary conditions have been included in the provisions of the Code of Criminal Procedure on transfer of proceedings in criminal matters.[58]

Article 4a of the Penal Code is important in the first place in cases where another state wishes to transfer criminal proceedings but the other provisions of Arts. 2 to 7 do not make prosecution by the Netherlands possible. In that case, the request from the other state creates jurisdiction for the Netherlands if there is a treaty basis for doing so. The most important treaty provision creating this basis is Art. 2 of the European Convention on the Transfer of Proceedings in Criminal Matters.[59]

Article 4a has an additional function. It also serves as the domestic legal basis for implementing the obligation either to extradite or prosecute an alleged offender, contained in a number of multilateral treaties. The provision empowers Dutch authorities to prosecute the alleged offender in cases in which the only link between the offence and the Netherlands is that the alleged offender is present in its territory. However, they may do so only after having received a request for proceedings from another contracting party. This requirement must be read in connection with Art. 552hh of the Code of Criminal Procedure. Para. 1 of that Article stipulates that for the application of a number of treaties, an extradition request which has been refused is to be regarded as a request for proceedings which has been granted. Para. 2 of the Article lists six treaties to which this system applies. The first of them is the European Convention on the Suppression of Terrorism. The other five are the treaties to which the Netherlands has made a reservation with respect to the obligation to prosecute an alleged offender who is present in its territory; they have been discussed above.

It must be noted here that Art. 552hh makes use of a legal fiction. It is not certain that the state whose extradition request has been refused will lose

---

58 See infra pp. 186-187.
59 See for other relevant international instruments *Baaijens-van Geloven*, Overdracht en overname van strafvervolging, pp. 89-116.

interest in prosecuting the alleged offender itself. This shows that conflicts of jurisdiction cannot wholly be ruled out by unilateral measures.

Limitations in international law

Jurisdiction over extraterritorial offences is limited by international law. Article 8 of the Penal Code explicitly acknowledges this principle by laying down that the applicability of Arts. 2 to 7 of the Penal Code shall be limited by exceptions recognized in international law.

That international law prevails over national law is a rule that also applies without Art. 8 having stipulated it. Nevertheless, the provision is not superfluous. It enables the courts to suspend the operation of Arts. 2 to 7 if their application would not be reconcilable with rules of customary international law or treaties. In this respect, the provision goes even further than Art. 94 of the Constitution, which does not provide the possibility for the courts to test national legislation against customary international law.

Article 8 of the Code only refers to the provisions on jurisdiction in the Code itself. It does not mention the many provisions on extraterritorial jurisdiction which have been included in other statutes since 1886. It is self-evident that these provisions should not be applied either, if so doing would violate rules of international law. Case law assumes that Art. 8 confers the power on the courts where necessary to refrain from applying these provisions as well.[60]

Article 8 is aimed primarily at the immunity under international law of persons and objects on Dutch territory. In the first place, here, one may think of foreign heads of state, government leaders and ministers. The provision also has other persons in mind, including ambassadors, consuls, the military and representatives of international organizations. Finally, among other things that come to mind are objects such as warships and military aircraft.[61]

A striking example of suspension of the application of Art. 2 of the Penal Code is provided by a recent decision of the Supreme Court on the application of the 1951 NATO Status of Forces Agreement. In it, the Supreme Court held that the Dutch authorities were not entitled to prosecute an American soldier for having murdered his wife in the Netherlands, since, under Art. VII, para. 3,

---

60 Cf. BRvC 17 February 1947, NJ 1947, 87 *(Ahlbrecht)*, discussed supra p. 30.
61 For Dutch law on the matter, see *Rüter/Helder/Swart*, Immunity, Exterritoriality and the Right of Asylum in the Netherlands, pp. 553-563.

of the Agreement, the primary right to exercise jurisdiction rested with the United States.[62]

Other statutes

Crimes against the peace and security of mankind

Jurisdiction over crimes against the peace and security of mankind is a rather complicated matter. This is due to the fact that these crimes are governed by a number of different statutes discussed by other authors.[63]

Jurisdiction over violations of the laws and customs of war is regulated by the 1943 Royal Decree on criminal law in exceptional circumstances *(Besluit Buitengewoon Strafrecht)* and the 1952 Act on criminal law in time of war *(Wet Oorlogsstrafrecht)*. Since the Decree hardly has any practical significance nowadays, we shall discuss the Act only.

Article 3 of the Act applies the universality principle to all violations of the laws and customs of war regardless of whether or not these violations constitute grave breaches of the 1949 Geneva Conventions and Additional Protocol I. As we have seen, however, there is no consensus on the question of whether the Act itself applies to wars other than those in which the Netherlands has become involved.

The Act is also concerned with crimes which, without being international crimes, jeopardize national interests and interests of Dutch nationals in time of war. The principles of active and passive nationality and the protective principle apply to these offences.

As has been discussed elsewhere, crimes against humanity as a separate category have been criminalized by the 1943 Decree only. The 1952 Act deals with them as circumstances aggravating war crimes.

Jurisdiction over genocide is regulated by two different statutes. In addition to the rules of the Penal Code, Art. 5 of the 1964 Act implementing the Genocide Convention *(Uitvoeringswet genocideverdrag)* applies the unrestricted active nationality principle to offences committed outside the territory of the

---

62 HR 11 September 1990, NJ 1991, 250 *(Short)*. Another, more important example is provided by BRvC 17 February 1947, NJ 1947, 87 *(Ahlbrecht)*.

63 See supra pp. 30-33.

Netherlands. Double criminality is not a requirement here. Obviously, Art. VI of the Genocide Convention is not interpreted by the Netherlands as imposing a prohibition on jurisdiction over extraterritorial offences.[64] Moreover, Art. 3 of the Act on criminal law in time of war applies the universality principle to genocide committed during war time.

More extensive jurisdiction over the crime of torture is conferred by the 1988 Act implementing the Torture Convention *(Uitvoeringswet folteringverdrag)*. Under Art. 5 of this Act, the universality principle is applicable to torture. At first sight this may be surprising, since, as we have seen above, it has become the policy of the Dutch Government in recent years to ratify treaties containing the *aut dedere aut punire* principle under the reservation that jurisdiction solely based on the fact that the alleged offender is present in its territory will be exercised only if a request for extradition has been made and rejected.[65] That reservation has not been made to the Torture Convention. On the one hand, the Government held that application of the universality principle to torture was not self-evident. By virtue of its character, this crime would seldom have a cross-border nature and application of the principle would not be required by international solidarity and the common interests of the states most involved. That, nonetheless, no reservation has been made, rests on two different considerations. First of all, the circumstances in a state where torture takes place could change radically, through which the prosecution of torture by the Netherlands might well be interpreted as a token of international solidarity. More weight was carried by the second argument that the inability to prosecute torture in the Netherlands would be unacceptable in situations in which those who committed this crime were to come eye to eye with their victims on Dutch territory.

The 1995 Act implementing the 1993 Chemical Weapons Convention *(Uitvoeringswet verdrag chemische wapens)* applies the unrestricted active nationality principle to extraterritorial offences. Consequently, double criminality is not a requirement, nor does it matter whether the offence qualifies as a crime under Dutch law. A similar provision is absent from the 1981 Act implementing the 1972 Biological Weapons Convention *(Uitvoeringswet verdrag biologische wapens)*.

---

64 For criticism see *Röling*, NJB 37 (1962), pp. 377-384.
65 See supra pp. 62-65.

Infringements of the provisions of both acts constitute economic offences within the meaning of the Economic Offences Acts. As a result, special rules apply with respect to the localization of offences.[66]

International sanctions

Like almost all the special statutes discussed above, the Sanctions Act 1977 *(Sanctiewet 1977)* applies the unrestricted active nationality principle to offences covered by the Act. Since infringement of its provisions constitutes an economic offence within the meaning of the 1950 Economic Offences Act, special rules apply with respect to extraterritorial offences.[67]

Military offences

Article 4 of the 1903 Military Penal Code *(Wetboek van militair strafrecht)* declares Dutch criminal law applicable to members of the military who commit any offence outside the Netherlands. The unrestricted application of the active personality principle means that is irrelevant whether the act constitutes a criminal offence according to the law of the state where the offence has been committed. Neither is it relevant whether the offence constitutes a crime or a misdemeanour under Dutch law. On the other hand, one can easily imagine a situation in which a member of the Dutch military commits an offence according to the law of the state where he is stationed which does not constitute an offence under Dutch law, or only if directed against Dutch interests or on Dutch territory.[68] To remedy this situation, Art. 170 of the Military Penal Code, introduced in 1963, makes it an offence under Dutch law to commit offences under the law of other states which are not punishable under Dutch law. The offence carries a maximum penalty of six months' detention, which in some cases may be far below the maximum punishment under the law of the state where the offence was committed. Finally, we may mention here that Art. 5 of the Code applies the protective principle to offences committed in time of war which are subject to the jurisdiction of the courts martial.

---

66 See infra p. 72.
67 See infra p. 72. For a more detailed discussion of the Act see supra p. 25.
68 See supra pp. 61-62.

With respect to the exercise of jurisdiction over members of the Dutch military abroad, two situations may be distinguished. The first is that in which the 1951 NATO Status of Forces Agreement applies. Article VII of that treaty contains elaborate rules with respect to the exercise of jurisdiction by the sending and the receiving state. It is relevant to note here that the Netherlands is a party to a number of supplementary agreements which may contain rules different from those of the 1951 Agreement.[69] Secondly, the stationing of members of the Dutch military outside NATO territory usually takes place within the framework of peacekeeping operations. Normally, the Netherlands will conclude *ad hoc* agreements with other states to the effect that the sending state has exclusive jurisdiction.[70]

Fiscal offences

Article 73 of the 1959 General Act on Taxes *(Algemene wet inzake rijksbelastingen)* applies the protective principle to fiscal offences which constitute crimes under Dutch law. The question of what constitute fiscal offences is answered mainly by Art. 68 of the General Act, Arts. 44 to 51 of the 1995 Customs Act *(Douanewet)*, Art. 64 of the Recovery of Taxes Act 1990 *(Invorderingswet 1990)*, and Arts. 97 to 102 of the 1991 Act on Excises *(Wet op de accijns)*. According to Art. 72 of the General Act on Taxes, these offences must be considered crimes if they carry the penalty of imprisonment. Article 76b of the Act extends the protective principle to a misdemeanour, a rarity in Dutch law.[71]

With regard to fiscal offences, most cases concern intentional failure to declare or intentionally incorrect declaration, withholding information partly or in full, and not keeping proper records. Since the applicable statutes require declaration and the providing of information and access to the books to the Dutch tax inspector or other Dutch fiscal official, these offences are usually assumed to have taken place in the Netherlands. If they consist of complete failure to fulfil an obligation, the offence is then localized where the person in

---

69 Cf. notably the 1959 Supplementary Agreement with respect to foreign forces stationed in the Federal Republic of Germany.

70 Cf. *Siekmann*, Juridische aspecten van de deelname met nationale contingenten aan VN-vredesmachten (Nederland en Unifil).

71 The misdemeanour under Art. 48, para. 1, section b, sub 3, of the Customs Act. Another example of the application of the principle to misdemeanours is provided by Art. 5, para. 4, of the Penal Code which refers to Art. 446a of the Code.

default should have fulfilled his obligation in time. In most cases this will be the Netherlands.[72] If one does not properly fulfil one's obligations from abroad, then the offence may perhaps be localized in the Netherlands *via* the doctrine of the instrument. Thus, Arts. 73 and 76b of the General Act on Taxes seem to be superfluous and to have become inactive in practice.[73]

Economic offences

Article 3 of the 1950 Economic Offences Act *(Wet op de economische delicten)* contains a special provision on extraterritorial economic offences. Under this Article, participation in an offence committed within the Netherlands is punishable even if the participant has acted outside the Netherlands. From the above discussion of the case law on the localization of the offence in relation to those who have solicited others to commit offences and accessories abroad, it has appeared that it is not, or not always, assumed that they have acted in the same place as the principal.[74] Article 3 of the Economic Offences Act solves that problem by applying the protective principle to acts of participants committed outside the Netherlands. Since the Act serves as a vehicle for implementing so many international instruments, this provision is not without significance.

Narcotic drugs and psychotropic substances

The general rules of jurisdiction under the Penal Code apply to drug offences covered by the 1928 Opium Act *(Opiumwet)*. However, Art. 13, para. 3, of the Act contains two provisions which create broader extraterritorial jurisdiction over offences related to the importation and exportation of so-called hard drugs.[75] They were introduced in the Act in 1985. The first of these provisions concerns attempts to import or export, and participation in the importation and exportation of narcotic drugs and psychotropic substances to and from the Netherlands. The provision establishes jurisdiction over attempt and participation occurring outside the Netherlands. It fulfils a function which is similar to that of Art. 3 of the 1950 Economic Offences Act discussed above. The second

---

72 Cf. HR 8 June 1936, NJ 1936, 954.
73 Cf. *Wattel*, Fiscaal straf- en strafprocesrecht, pp. 166-167.
74 See supra p. 54.
75 For the difference between hard drugs and soft drugs see supra pp. 40-41.

provision establishes jurisdiction over preparatory acts committed with the intent to import or export narcotic drugs or psychotropic substances. Where preparatory acts to import these substances are concerned, the provision may be considered to apply the protective principle. In the case of preparatory acts to export, international solidarity seems to be the primary underlying motive. Jurisdiction over preparatory acts committed outside a state's territory is clearly permitted by the 1961 Single Convention on Narcotic Drugs and its 1972 Protocol as well as the 1988 United Nations Convention against Illicit Traffic in Narcotic Drugs and Psychotropic Substances.[76]

It must be noted that the Opium Act has never made use of the universality principle. Nor does it accept jurisdiction over alleged offenders who cannot be extradited, regardless of where an offence has been committed and of the nationality of the alleged offender. As we have seen earlier, such steps are taken only if a rule of international law imposes the obligation upon the Netherlands to do so.[77] However, neither Art. 36 of the Single Convention and its Protocol nor Art. 4 of the United Nations Convention, although they would allow such steps, makes them mandatory. Consequently, an alleged offender who cannot be extradited to another state may only be prosecuted in the Netherlands if the offence has been committed on Dutch territory or on board a Dutch vessel or aircraft, if the person possesses Dutch nationality or if the offence is covered by Art. 13 of the Opium Act.

---

76 For a critical analysis of the provisions see *Haentjens*, DD 14 (1984), pp. 38-48.
77 See supra pp. 62-65.

Ne Bis in Idem

Peter Baauw

Ne bis in idem in Dutch criminal law

Article 68, para. 1, of the Dutch Penal Code provides that no one shall be tried again for the same offence when the judgment made concerning him is final. The justification of this provision rests on two considerations. The first is that certainty in the legal order is in the public interest.[1] *Res judicata* should be respected and the general interest is served by the court not having to repeat or contradict itself.[2] A second consideration is the importance of protecting the person being tried against constant uncertainty.[3] An individual benefits from the certainty that – once the legal battle being fought against him has ended – he will not be troubled a second time with the same offence *(nemo debet bis vexari)* nor be subject to punishment twice for the same offence *(ne bis in idem)*. As such the *ne bis in idem* provision in Art. 68 of the Penal Code may also be considered a necessary extension of the legality principle laid down in Art. 1 of the Code. The guarantee contained in the requirement of a previously laid down criminal provision would be merely an illusion if a person could be troubled continually with various aspects of the same offence.[4]

An exception to the rule that no one may be prosecuted twice for an offence upon which a Dutch court has made a final judgment can be found in the first paragraph of Art. 68. This exception concerns the special remedy of review, regulated in Art. 457 of the Code of Criminal Procedure. Under this provision there are two cases in which the convicted person may appeal to the Supreme Court from a final decision. The first is when different court decisions are

---

1   *Pompe*, Handboek van het Nederlandse strafrecht, p. 543.
2   *Hazewinkel-Suringa/Remmelink*, Inleiding tot de studie van het Nederlandse strafrecht, p. 590.
3   *Pompe* (supra note 1), p. 543.
4   *Jörg/Kelk*, Strafrecht met mate, p. 108.

incompatible with each other. The second is when evidence subsequently made available makes it plausible that the accused has been convicted unjustly. Review is a remedy for the benefit of the convicted person, which makes it possible to have miscarriages of justice corrected in his favour. Strictly speaking this cannot be considered a new prosecution.[5]

Article 68 applies exclusively to criminal court decisions. According to case law, the provision does not prevent the prosecution of a person upon whom a sanction has previously been imposed by an administrative authority or administrative tribunal.[6] Some statutes do, however, contain provisions that preclude the imposition of administrative sanctions in addition to criminal sanctions or that stipulate that account must be taken of a previously imposed criminal sanction in imposing an administrative sanction. Examples are the 1959 General Act on Taxes *(Algemene wet inzake rijksbelastingen)* and the 1990 Military Disciplinary Sanctions Act *(Wet militair tuchtrecht)*.

Article 68, para. 1, applies only to decisions by the criminal courts in which judgment has been given on the substance of the charges. The provision only concerns judgments involving acquittal, dismissal of the charges or conviction. Other court decisions to dismiss cases because of their provisional nature do not prevent renewed proceedings. These are decisions in which the court holds that the indictment is null and void, that it has no jurisdiction in the matter, that the public prosecutor is barred from prosecuting, or that there are reasons for suspending proceedings. The decision to dismiss the charges *(ontslag van rechtsvervolging)* requires further clarification. According to Dutch law, charges have to be dismissed if the facts are proved but do not constitute an offence. The same decision is made if the facts are proved but the accused has been successful in invoking a justification or a defence. However, if the defence is that the accused was not responsible for his actions because of mental deficiency or mental illness, the court may impose a criminal measure committing him to a psychiatric institution or imposing a hospital order. Since many legal systems and treaties only distinguish between acquittal and conviction, problems of interpretation may easily arise in applying Art. 68 to foreign judgements.[7]

---

5   *Hazewinkel-Suringa/Remmelink* (supra note 2), p. 591.
6   HR 5 February 1991, NJ 1991, 402; HR 21 May 1991, NJ 1991, 728.
7   See infra pp. 79-80.

Many criminal cases do not come to trial because an agreement has been concluded between the public prosecutor and the accused in which the former agrees not to prosecute or to drop prosecution in exchange for certain consider-ations from the latter. This concerns the out-of-court settlement (*transactie*) regulated in Arts. 74 to 74c of the Penal Code, which is somewhat similar to plea bargaining in common law systems. In minor cases the police also have the power to propose such settlements. Case law takes the view that a settle-ment out of court prevents any further prosecution of the offender.[8] Similarly, on the basis of Art. 511c of the Code of Criminal Procedure the public prose-cutor and the accused or convicted person may make an agreement regarding the rendering of the proceeds from crime.

Article 68 of the Penal Code is not the only provision protecting the accused or convicted person against *bis in idem* or *bis vexari*. There is also Art. 255 of the Code of Criminal Procedure. According to this provision, there are four circumstances which prevent the public prosecutor from proceeding with the case, even though there has been no final decision within the meaning of Art. 68 of the Penal Code. The most important circumstance is where the accused has submitted a notice of objection against the indictment and the court has honoured this objection because it considers it highly unlikely that the accused would be convicted after a public hearing of the case. The other three cases also usually involve situations in which it is unlikely that the trial court will convict. Article 255, however, does not provide absolute protection against the resumption of prosecution. The protection is lost when new evidence becomes available shedding a different light on the case.

The most important question arising with regard to Art. 68 of the Penal Code and Art. 255 of the Code of Criminal Procedure is what is meant by 'the same offence'. This is not an easy question to answer. The word *feit* (literally: fact) might be understood to refer to a historical event which may or may not consist of several offences. A final decision in the case of one of these offences would then preclude prosecution of the others. However, it is also possible to give that word the meaning of 'offence'. As a consequence, a decision in the case of one offence would not at all stand in the way of prosecuting the other offences which were part of the same historical event. The courts do not choose either of these meanings but take an approach in between which is not easily summa-rized in a simple formula. Factors playing a role are simultaneous behaviour,

---

8   HR 17 December 1963, NJ 1964, 385.

the purpose of the various criminal provisions and the nature of the reproaches that can be made to a person.[9] In a recent case, the Supreme Court overturned the decision of a lower court which had ruled that the export of a load of hashish from the Netherlands and its import into Belgium constituted two different offences within the meaning of Art. 68 of the Penal Code.[10]

Res judicata of courts in the Netherlands Antilles and Aruba

Article 68, para. 1, of the Penal Code places *res judicata* of courts in the Netherlands Antilles and Aruba on a completely equal footing with those of the courts in the European part of the Netherlands. This is explained by Art. 40 of the 1954 Charter for the Kingdom of the Netherlands *(Statuut voor het Konink-rijk der Nederlanden).*[11] Under this provision, criminal sentences pronounced by the courts in the Netherlands Antilles and in Aruba may be enforced out in the Netherlands. The same applies to enforcement of the sentences of Dutch courts in the Netherlands Antilles and Aruba. That is why Dutch judgments in turn preclude prosecution for the same offence in the Netherlands Antilles and in Aruba.[12]

Foreign res judicata

Article 68, para. 2, of the Penal Code applies to the criminal judgments of foreign courts. A foreign judgment always rules out a second prosecution in the Netherlands when the person concerned has been acquitted, i.e. the foreign court finds that the facts have not been proved. The same applies to a decision by a foreign court which under Dutch law is considered the equivalent of dismissal of the charges *(ontslag van rechtsvervolging)*. A foreign decision which is the equivalent of a conviction under Dutch law prevents any new prosecution in the Netherlands when the court has convicted the person without imposing punishment. When punishment has been imposed, a new prosecution is only ruled out if the punishment has been completely enforced, it has been

---

9   Cf. *Hazewinkel-Suringa/Remmelink* (supra note 2), pp. 592-603; *Corstens*, Het Nederlands strafprocesrecht, pp. 189-191.
10 HR 13 December 1994, NJ 1995, 252.
11 See supra p. 2.
12 Cf. *Hofstee/Schalken*, Strafrecht binnen het Koninkrijk, p. 32.

the subject of a pardon or if it can no longer be enforced because of lapse of time. Punishment includes the imposition of criminal measures.

It is clear that protection against double jeopardy goes less far for foreign than for Dutch judgments. The explanation for this difference is that until recently foreign judgments could not be enforced in the Netherlands. Even now this is only the case where provided for by treaty.[13] Nevertheless, Art. 68 of the Penal Code does offer a considerable degree of protection against double jeopardy as a result of a foreign judgment. It has opted for a system whereby prosecution in the Netherlands is completely ruled out, rather than one which takes the foreign judgment into consideration in meting out punishment. Moreover, the provision does not make any distinction as to the state where the foreign judgment has been pronounced, the place where the offence was committed, the nature of the offence or the jurisdictional basis of the foreign judgment.[14] Not surprisingly, it is sometimes criticized in legal doctrine as being too generous. In this regard, mention has been made of the fact that juries sometimes reach verdicts on emotional grounds which would not have had any influence on a Dutch professional judge.[15] Another objection is that an acquittal abroad must always be respected even when it is clear that in the Netherlands more evidence is available against a person. With regard to acquittals by foreign courts for the reason that the act does not constitute an offence under foreign law, the criticism has been expressed that in some cases there may well be an offence according to Dutch law.[16] Nonetheless, neither this nor other criticism has ever led to a statutory restriction of the provision, which has been in existence since 1886. One could say, however, that case law has removed some of the law's sharp edges.

Special problems arise in deciding whether a foreign judgment in which a custodial measure has been imposed because of the diminished responsibility of the offender should be taken as the equivalent of a dismissal of the charges or a conviction under Dutch law. In the first situation a new trial in the Netherlands is unconditionally ruled out, in the second only if the custodial measure has been completely enforced. If there is any doubt, the courts show

---

13 See infra pp. 194-196.

14 Cf. *Krabbe/Poelman*, Enkele aspecten van het *ne bis in idem*-beginsel in internationaal verband, p. 138; *Orie/Van der Meijs/Smit*, Internationaal strafrecht, p. 66; *Schutte*, Ars Aequi 35 (1986), p. 35.

15 *Hazewinkel-Suringa/Remmelink* (supra note 2), p. 604.

16 *Pompe* (supra note 1), p. 558.

a preference for the second possibility, as in the case of two Dutch boys who were committed to a mental institution by a Swedish court for having murdered a Dutch friend in Stockholm and were released after a short time.[17]

A foreign conviction will only bar renewed prosecution in the Netherlands if the sanction imposed has been completely enforced. Article 68 of the Penal Code does not oblige Dutch courts to take any account of a foreign sentence which has not been completely enforced. Nor do the courts attach any importance to the reason why the foreign sentence was not completely enforced. They make no distinction between the case in which further enforcement is impossible because the convicted person has evaded it and that in which enforcement has been suspended prematurely by the foreign authorities.[18] Conditional sentences are a separate case. According to most legal writers, they preclude a second trial in the Netherlands only when they have become irrevocable under foreign law.[19]

In 1985, a new obstacle to prosecution was added to Art. 68. A new paragraph 3 now lays down that prosecution in the Netherlands is barred when the accused has agreed to a settlement out of court in the foreign country and has completely fulfilled the conditions of this settlement. This ensures that a foreign out-of-court settlement of the case is put on an equal footing with a transaction or a similar settlement under Dutch law as far as protection against double jeopardy is concerned.

While Art. 68 of the Penal Code goes far towards putting a foreign judgment on an equal footing with a Dutch one, Art. 255 of the Code of Criminal Procedure lacks such a provision. As a result, the decisions of foreign authorities that no trial should take place do not rule out prosecution in the Netherlands for the same offence.

Article 68 of the Penal Code and international law

Six treaties are discussed below which contain general provisions on double jeopardy. The question here is what significance they have for the application

---

17 HR 4 February 1969, NJ 1970, 352 *(Drost)*.
18 HR 4 February 1969, NJ 1970, 352 *(Drost)*.
19 *Hazewinkel-Suringa/Remmelink* (supra note 2), p. 603; *Corstens* (supra note 9), p. 192.

of Art. 68 of the Penal Code. The Netherlands is a party to five of these six treaties.

Article 14, para. 7, of the 1966 International Covenant on Civil and Political Rights provides that no one shall be liable to be tried or punished again for an offence for which he has already been finally convicted or acquitted in accordance with the law and penal procedure of each country. According to the Dutch Government, it is not clear whether the provision lays down only the national or also the international application of the *ne bis in idem* principle. For this reason the Netherlands has made a declaration that it does not wish the application of the *ne bis in idem* principle to extend any further than Art. 68 of the Dutch Penal Code as it applied at the moment of ratification of the Covenant by the Netherlands. The Netherlands' fear later proved to be unfounded. According to the Human Rights Committee the provision does not apply to foreign *res judicata*.[20]

In contrast to the International Covenant, the 1950 European Convention on the Protection of Human Rights and Fundamental Freedoms contains no provision on the *ne bis in idem* principle. Complaints about being placed in double jeopardy by a contracting party after having been tried by another contracting party have in the past always been dismissed by the European Commission of Human Rights.[21] The 1984 Seventh Protocol to the European Convention does contain such a provision. Article 4, para. 1, of the Protocol states: 'No one shall be liable to be tried or punished again in criminal proceedings under the jurisdiction of the same State for an offence for which he has already been finally acquitted or convicted in accordance with the law and penal procedure of that State.' As is apparent from its wording, the provision does not apply to decisions of foreign courts.[22] In the Explanatory Report to the Protocol it is stated that several Council of Europe instruments, including the 1970 European Convention on the International Validity of Criminal Judgments and the 1972 European Convention on the Transfer of Proceedings in Criminal Matters

---

20 UN Human Rights Committee 2 November 1987, Report 204/1986, *A.P. v. Italy*, RV 1988, 95. Cf. also *Vermeulen*, Panopticon 15 (1994), p. 217.
21 Cf. i.a. European Commission 13 December 1983, Application 8945/80, *S. v. Germany*, 39 Decisions and Reports 43 (1984).
22 Cf. European Commission 2 December 1992, Application 15521/89, *Manzoni v. Italy*, unreported.

govern the application of the *ne bis in idem* principle at the international level.[23] The Netherlands has not yet become a party to this Protocol.

The Netherlands is a party to the European Convention on the International Validity of Criminal Judgments and to the European Convention on the Transfer of Proceedings in Criminal Matters. It is one of the few states which have ratified these conventions. The provisions in both conventions which apply to *ne bis in idem* on an international level can be found in Arts. 53 to 57 of the former and Arts. 35 to 37 of the latter convention, and have practically the same content. For both, the most important principle is that a person who has been tried by one party to the convention shall not be tried again for the same offence by another party if he has previously been acquitted or convicted by a final court judgment and the sanction imposed has been completely enforced or is being enforced, has been wholly or with respect to the part not enforced the subject of an amnesty or pardon, or can no longer be enforced because of lapse of time. However, both conventions make exceptions to this principle. They relate to the nature of the damaged interests, the public status of the offender and the place of the offence. Where a second trial is not ruled out, the prosecuting state should deduct any period of deprivation of liberty enforced under the first sentence from the sentence to be imposed.

The provisions of both conventions have relatively little significance for Dutch law, since no exceptions are made here with regard to the nature of the interest damaged by the offence, the public status of the offender or the place of the offence. Nevertheless, adjustment has been necessary on two points. The fact that under the conventions a second trial is ruled out if the sanction imposed is being enforced seems to imply that a conditional sentence pronounced elsewhere would bar prosecution in the Netherlands even though the time within which this sentence can be revoked has not yet lapsed. Secondly, both conventions sometimes require deduction from the sentence where Art. 68 of the Penal Code does not.[24]

Since both European conventions have been ratified by very few states, it is not surprising that, in Europe, new instruments were created later which provide for recognition of the *ne bis in idem* principle on the international level. New

23 Explanatory Report on the Seventh Protocol to the European Convention, Strasbourg 1984, par. 27.
24 Cf. *Hazewinkel-Suringa/Remmelink* (supra note 2), p. 605.

provisions can be found in the 1987 Convention between the Member States of the European Communities on Double Jeopardy and in Arts. 54 to 58 of the 1990 Convention applying the Schengen Agreement. Both conventions basically adopt the solutions of the two older European conventions, but lay some restrictions on the exceptions allowed by the other conventions to the *ne bis in idem* principle.[25] For the Netherlands these restrictions imply that in cases where a second trial is still permitted, a Dutch court now also has to take account of sanctions other than custodial sanctions imposed elsewhere, notably fines.

Ne bis in idem and international cooperation

Article 68 of the Penal Code goes relatively far in recognizing international *ne bis in idem*. It is not surprising that this provision has had much influence upon various laws that determine the conditions under which the Netherlands is willing to render mutual assistance to other states and on the Dutch position with respect to conventions which provide for cooperation with other states. The implication is that the Netherlands will more readily refuse assistance to other states on the grounds of double jeopardy. The relevant Dutch legislation is discussed elsewhere.[26] Several general characteristics are, however, pointed out below.

One characteristic of Dutch legislation is that it not only requires the Dutch authorities to refuse international cooperation in cases in which the *res judicata* originates from a Dutch court. In addition, cooperation must always be refused in cases where the *res judicata* comes from a court in a third state. This explains why reservations with respect to double jeopardy have been made to the 1957 European Convention on Extradition, the 1959 European Convention on Mutual Assistance in Criminal Matters and the 1964 European Convention on the Supervision of Conditionally Sentenced or Conditionally Released Offenders.

---

25 Cf. *De Doelder/Van der Hulst*, SEW 11 (1993), p. 722; *Jung*, Zur 'Internationalisierung' des Grundsatzes 'ne bis in idem', p. 499; *Swart*, Police and security in the Schengen Agreement and Schengen Convention, pp. 105-106.
26 See infra pp. 110-112, 140-141, 185, 194.

Another characteristic of Dutch law on international cooperation is the influence of Art. 255 of the Code of Criminal Procedure. Usually, cooperation has to be refused if proceedings for the same offence in the Netherlands or in a third state have ended in a decision that the case should not be brought to trial.[27] This is all the more remarkable since Dutch law does not rule out prosecution in the Netherlands for a case that has been settled elsewhere in a similar manner.

Finally, it may be said that there is a certain discrepancy between out-of-court settlements in the Netherlands and in other states. Under Art. 68, para. 3, of the Penal Code, a settlement between the accused and a foreign authority in principle rules out prosecution for the same offence in the Netherlands. Dutch law, however, does not state in so many words that cooperation with another state must be refused if a settlement has already been reached between the accused and the Dutch authorities. Nevertheless, the relevant statutory provisions are so broadly formulated that they are open to such an interpretation. Moreover, it may be said that case law generally places settlements on the same level as final judgments.[28]

---

27 See infra pp. 110, 140, 185, 194. The exception here is transfer of proceedings to the Netherlands.
28 See supra p. 77.

Extradition

Bert Swart

The concept of extradition[1]

Article 1 of the 1967 Extradition Act *(Uitleveringswet)* defines extradition as 'the removal of a person from the Netherlands with the object of surrendering him to another State for the purpose of a criminal investigation concerning him in that State or of enforcing a penalty or measure imposed on him in that State'. This definition contains three elements: a purpose, a means to achieve that purpose and, more hidden, the existence of a link between the two. A closer look at these key elements will reveal in more detail what is understood by extradition in the Netherlands and what legal consequences attach to it.

Obviously, the general purpose of extradition according to the definition in the Act is to assist another state in enforcing its criminal law. This may be done in two ways. Either a person is surrendered in order to face trial before a criminal court in the requesting state. Or his surrender may enable the requesting state to enforce a sentence imposed on the person by a national court, whether the sentence consists of a penalty or a measure, or of both. The importance of indicating the purpose of extradition in the Act lies especially in making clear what ends extradition cannot serve. Two points are important here.

Firstly, in accordance with state practice, the definition excludes extradition for the purpose of enforcing other parts of the law of the requesting state, such as administrative or disciplinary provisions. From other provisions of the Act it also follows that a sanction must have been imposed by a criminal court in

---

1   For an exhaustive analysis of Dutch extradition law see *Swart*, Nederlands uitleveringsrecht. Introductions are given by *Remmelink*, Uitlevering; *Strijards*, Uitlevering. For an outline of Dutch extradition law in the English language see *Kuyper*, The Netherlands Law of Extradition, pp. 203-245.

the requesting state. Sanctions of a penal nature imposed by other authorities are not relevant in this respect. However, it is debatable whether the Act intends to exclude such sanctions if an appeal lies open from the decision of an administrative authority to a criminal court. As a matter of fact, in two treaties the Netherlands has agreed to extradite persons for the purpose of enforcing these sanctions.[2]

It also follows from the definition that surrender of a person to another state with the purpose of enforcing a sanction imposed by a Dutch court does not constitute extradition within the meaning of the Act. Transfer of persons to that end is governed by the 1986 Act on the transfer of enforcement of criminal judgments *(Wet overdracht tenuitvoerlegging strafvonnissen)*. On the other hand, extradition may be a means of surrendering a person to another state following transfer of criminal proceedings from the Netherlands to that state, since transfer of these proceedings implies that 'a criminal investigation in that State' is taking place. As a matter of fact, transfer of proceedings to other states coupled with or followed by extradition of the suspect is a rather frequent occurrence in Dutch practice. It is relevant to note here that the provisions in the Code of Criminal Procedure on transfer of proceedings to other states do not themselves allow for the surrender of a person.

According to the definition of the Extradition Act, extradition consists of (physical) removal of a person from the Netherlands. Again some implications of this definitional element should be pointed at.

Physical removal and surrender to the authorities of another state normally supposes that one acts without the consent of the person being removed and surrendered. However, removal with the consent of the requested person is also seen as extradition in the Act. Articles 41 to 45 of the Act apply here.

The definition speaks of removal 'from the Netherlands'. This implies that surrendering a person to the competent foreign authorities acting within Dutch territory may, regardless of the purpose of surrender, not be considered to be extradition. Such forms of surrender notably occur where deserting crew members of ships and members of a foreign military force stationed in the Netherlands are concerned. Somewhat superfluously, Art. 61 of the Act declares both forms of surrender to be outside its scope. As far as the surrender of members of the military is concerned, its terms are mainly determined by the

---

2   The 1978 Second Additional Protocol to the European Convention and the 1979 Agreement between the Federal Republic of Germany and the Netherlands to supplement and facilitate the application of the European Convention on Extradition.

1951 NATO Status of Forces Agreement and the 1953 Act implementing the Agreement.

Taken literally, transit of extraditees from one state to another over Dutch territory does not constitute extradition within the meaning of the Act either. The Act recognizes this explicitly by classifying transit as an 'other form of assistance' in Art. 48. The same argument is probably valid where the transfer of arrestees by the Belgium police from the Belgian enclave Baerle-Hertog over Dutch territory to other parts of Belgium is concerned.[3] Finally, within the meaning of the Act extradition of a person to a third state by the state who obtained his extradition by the Netherlands cannot be considered a removal from the Netherlands.

It is often held that extradition may be refused by the requested state if it is obvious that to grant extradition would definitely not serve the purpose it is supposed to promote. For instance, if it has become manifest that the requested person cannot possibly have committed the offence, extradition would serve no legitimate end. Similarly, if it has been established beyond reasonable doubt that legal obstacles prevent the requesting state from successfully trying the person or punishing him, e.g. he has become immune by reason of lapse of time, the requested state would be entitled to refuse extradition since the only possible outcome would be acquittal or dismissal of the charges in the requesting state.

May we consider this limitation to be an implicit element of the definition of the Extradition Act? There is no general agreement on the answer, but both the Act itself and case law have adopted the idea that extradition should serve a useful purpose, albeit with the necessary caution. According to Art. 28 of the Act, courts will have to refuse extradition if it has been established beyond any doubt that the requested person cannot have committed the offence. They have to do this regardless of whether an extradition treaty explicitly entitles the requesting state to refuse extradition.[4] As far as case law is concerned, it steadfastly adheres to the view that courts are not required to investigate into matters of foreign law. The requesting state must be trusted to apply for

---

3   In HR 8 November 1985, NJ 1986, 123, 18 NYIL 400-402 (1987) *(Kamer)*, a Dutchman was arrested in the Belgian enclave and transferred to Belgium where an extradition request of the United States was awaiting him. The Supreme Court held that his transportation did not amount to transit within the meaning of Art. 21 of the 1962 Benelux Treaty on Extradition and Mutual Assistance in Criminal Matters and that, therefore, no prior approval of transfer needed to be given by the Dutch authorities.

4   For a more detailed discussion see infra pp. 117-118.

extradition only if there is a reasonable chance of convicting the requested person.[5] However, case law accepts the, almost purely theoretical, possibility that a court refuses extradition because it has become convinced that, for whatever reason, extradition cannot serve any useful purpose.[6]

One striking feature of the definition remains to be discussed. Most definitions of extradition mention that extradition is granted by a state at the request of another state. They do this in order to stress the fact that extradition is based on an agreement between two states. The Extradition Act, however, makes no mention of a request by another state. It would be wrong to conclude from this that the Act allows for extradition without any extradition request. From the parliamentary history of the Act it appears that the purpose has been quite the contrary. In omitting from the definition the element 'request' the Government wanted to stress the fact that every form of removing a person from the Netherlands with the purpose to put him at the disposal of the criminal justice system of another country amounts to extradition within the meaning of the Extradition Act. The very fact that this purpose is being pursued without respecting the conditions and procedural provisions of the Act makes such removal an act that is forbidden by it. In other words, the definition wants to stress that there is only one proper way to assist other states in enforcing their laws by removing a person, and that is extradition on the basis of the Act.

Article 1 of the Act forbids disguised extradition. But it leaves open the question of when the removal of a person constitutes disguised extradition. According to established case law, expulsion of an alien may be considered to be disguised extradition if the authorities remove him to another state thereby intending or producing the effect of an extradition without there being an imperative need to do so.[7] Whether this will be the case is a matter of the correct application of the law on admission and expulsion of aliens. Case law requires the scrupulous observance of all legal conditions and formalities of that part of the law. More specifically, there must be serious objections to the continued presence of the person on Dutch territory for reasons of Dutch public order and the person has to be given an adequate opportunity to choose his own country of destination. While, in principle, case law does not accept removal of a person to the requesting state pending extradition proceedings, it leaves room for exceptions if speedy removal seems to be in the public interest. Case

---

5   Cf. e.g. HR 5 December 1972, NJ 1973, 285; HR 14 May 1991, NJ 1991, 730.

6   HR 16 October 1990, NJ 1991, 134.

7   See especially HR 13 September 1963, NJ 1963, 509 *(Wallace)*; HR 13 February 1987, NJ 1987, 582; HR 18 November 1994, NJ 1996, 579 *(Reeve)*.

law on abduction and other methods of getting hold of persons is discussed in another contribution to this book.[8]

Sources of the law

Until 1983, Art. 4, para. 2, of the Constitution for the Kingdom of the Netherlands stated that 'the general conditions on which extradition treaties may be concluded with other states shall be laid down by statute'. On the occasion of a total revision of the Constitution in 1983, this Article was abrogated. It has been replaced by a new Art. 2, para. 3, stating that extradition shall take place only pursuant to a treaty. Paragraph 3 further requires that extradition be regulated by statute.

Ratification of extradition treaties needs prior approval of parliament. This follows from Art. 91 of the Constitution and Art. 2 of the 1994 Act on the approval and publication of treaties *(Rijkswet goedkeuring en bekendmaking verdragen)*, which is an Act of the Kingdom.

The present Act governing extradition is the 1967 Extradition Act which replaced its forerunner of 1875. It has been closely modelled after the 1957 European Convention on Extradition. The Act is only concerned with extradition of persons from the Netherlands. Extradition to the Netherlands is governed by a few provisions in the Penal Code and the Code of Criminal Procedure.[9]

The Extradition Act is supplemented by the 1954 Act relating to surrender in respect of war crimes *(Wet overlevering inzake oorlogsmisdrijven)*. This Act allows the extradition of persons on the basis of the four 1949 Geneva Conventions and the 1977 Additional Protocol I to other parties to these treaties. The alleged offence must constitute a grave breach of one of their provisions. Mention should also be made of the 1964 Act implementing the 1948 Genocide Convention *(Uitvoeringswet genocideverdrag)*. Article 5a of the Act declares that genocide may not be considered to be a political offence for the purpose of extradition. Finally, there is the 1994 Act containing provisions relating to the establishment of the International Tribunal for the prosecution of persons responsible for serious violations of international humanitarian law committed in the territory of the former Yugoslavia since 1991. It aims to implement

---

8   See infra pp. 220-223.
9   See infra pp. 121-122.

Arts. 27 and 29 of the Tribunal's Statute. Pursuant to Art. 4 of the Act, surrender may only be refused if it cannot be established that the person brought before the Dutch court is the person whose surrender has been requested or if surrender has been requested on account of offences in respect of which the Tribunal is not competent under its Statute. Draft legislation is pending with respect to the surrender of persons to the Rwanda Tribunal.

The Extradition Act of 1967 achieves a number of different purposes. In conformity with former Art. 4 of the Constitution, the Act lays down the conditions which the Government must include in extradition treaties with other states. In this respect the Act limits the power of Government to freely negotiate the terms of an extradition treaty. However, as is apparent from the Act itself, it does not completely rule out the possibility that Government conclude a treaty that, in some way or another, does not conform to the provisions of the Act. Allowing that this may, on occasion, be necessary or desirable, Art. 3 of the Act obliges the Government to submit a Bill to amend the Act in order to re-establish a close correspondence between the terms of the treaty and the provisions of the Act. A number of provisions in the Act have been introduced to meet the requirement of Art. 3.[10] However, in actual practice bills have not always been introduced to amend the Act where a treaty deviates from it. Apart from that, extradition treaties which were concluded before the Extradition Act of 1967 came into force 'deviate' from it in many respects. It has not been deemed necessary to renegotiate the terms of these treaties on occasion of the replacement of the Act of 1875 by the Act of 1967.

    Secondly, the Extradition Act also provides the authorities dealing with extradition requests with criteria to decide upon those requests. The conditions for concluding extradition treaties are also criteria for deciding upon specific requests for extradition. Since, however, according to constitutional rules, international law takes precedence over national law the importance of the Act is necessarily limited in this respect. Articles 93 and 94 of the Constitution require that provisions of Dutch law be disregarded if they conflict with treaty provisions which are directly applicable. Dutch courts will, therefore, not apply provisions of the Extradition Act which conflict with the contents of an extradition treaty.[11] They will apply the Act only to the extent permitted by due respect for treaty obligations. This may occur especially where treaties

---

10 E.g. Arts. 6, 10 para. 4, and 12 para. 6, take account of specific provisions in the Benelux Treaty on Extradition and Mutual Assistance in Criminal Matters.
11 Cf. e.g. HR 3 June 1969, NJ 1969, 382; HR 22 July 1974, NJ 1974, 501, 6 NYIL 353 (1975).

leave it to the contracting parties to decide whether or not they consider a specific circumstance a sufficient reason for refusing extradition.

—Finally, the Extradition Act indicates the authorities competent to deal with extradition requests and contains detailed rules for handling these requests.

A complete list of treaties which are relevant where extradition by the Netherlands is concerned will be found in the documentary part of this book. Here, we limit ourselves to some general remarks on various types of treaties.

The classical type of extradition treaty is the bilateral treaty. A number of bilateral treaties are in force between the Netherlands and other states, a majority of them dating from before 1967. Older treaties link the Netherlands with fifteen other states. Since 1967, new bilateral treaties have been concluded with Australia, Canada, Hong Kong, Suriname and the United States.

By far the most important treaty in operation is the 1957 European Convention on Extradition. It links the Netherlands with some thirty other, almost all European, states. The Netherlands has also ratified its 1975 Additional and its 1978 Second Additional Protocol. The Netherlands and the Federal Republic of Germany have concluded the 1979 Wittem Agreement to supplement and facilitate the application of the European Convention between them.

A second important multilateral treaty is the 1962 Benelux Treaty on Extradition and Mutual Assistance in Criminal Matters, concluded between Belgium, Luxembourg and the Netherlands. This treaty differs from the European Convention, as well as from the Extradition Act, in that it makes extradition between the three countries easier in a number of respects.

An agreement which supplements both the European Convention and its Benelux counterpart is the 1990 Convention applying the Schengen Agreement of June 14, 1985, between the Benelux countries, the Federal Republic of Germany and France on the Gradual Abolition of Checks at their Common Borders. Austria, Greece, Italy, Portugal and Spain have acceded to the Convention later.

Apart from the bilateral and multilateral extradition treaties there are other types of (multilateral) treaties that have a bearing upon extradition.

The first type is the multilateral treaty that, without being an extradition treaty itself, supplements existing extradition treaties in force between the parties to the treaty. This may be done by declaring that specific offences are deemed to be included in extradition treaties in force between the parties or in some other way, e.g. by declaring that specific offences shall not be considered to be political offences for the purpose of extradition. Examples are provided by the 1929 International Convention for the Suppression of Counterfeiting Currency and the 1948 Genocide Convention.

—— Partly overlapping the first type is the multilateral treaty which requires the contracting parties either to extradite or punish *(aut dedere aut punire)* the offenders of specific crimes. One could think of the four 1949 Geneva Conventions here, or of the 1977 European Convention on the Suppression of Terrorism.

—— Finally, a third type of multilateral treaty, exemplified by the 1970 Hague Convention for the Suppression of Unlawful Seizure of Aircraft, should be mentioned. Treaties of this type all include a provision stating that a contracting party may at its option consider the treaty itself as a legal basis for extradition in relation to other contracting parties with which it has no extradition treaty.[12] Article 51a of the Extradition Act allows extradition of persons to other contracting parties to a list of treaties of this type.[13] To the extent that the Netherlands has not concluded a specific extradition treaty with another contracting party, Art. 51a declares the provisions of the Act and those of the European Convention on Extradition applicable. This is done because multilateral treaties of the third type do not themselves specify conditions for extradition.

Case law assumes that extradition treaties, like the Extradition Act, have retroactive effect in the sense that they also create obligations to extradite for offences that have been committed prior to their entering into force.[14] However, extradition requests which have been submitted before that date will be

---

12 E.g. Art. 8, para. 2, of the Hague Convention.
13 The list includes in the following order:
    – the 1970 Convention for the Suppression of Unlawful Seizure of Aircraft;
    – the 1971 Convention for the Suppression of Unlawful Acts against the Safety of Civil Aviation and its 1988 Protocol;
    – the 1961 Single Convention in Narcotic Drugs, as amended by its 1972 Protocol;
    – the 1973 Convention on the Prevention and Punishment of Crimes against Internationally Protected Persons, including Diplomatic Agents;
    – the 1979 International Convention against the Taking of Hostages;
    – the 1984 Convention against Torture and Other Cruel, Inhuman or Degrading Treatment or Punishment;
    – the 1980 Convention on the Physical Protection of Nuclear Material;
    – the 1988 Convention for the Suppression of Unlawful Acts against the Safety of Maritime Navigation and its 1988 Protocol;
    – the 1988 Convention against Illicit Traffic in Narcotic Drugs and Psychotropic Substances.
14 HR 28 April 1970, NJ 1971, 5; HR 16 January 1973, NJ 1973, 281, 5 NYIL 309-311 (1974) *(Pauksch)*; HR 7 November 1978, NJ 1979, 188.

declined, even if the Dutch authorities have to decide upon the request after that date.[15]

The treaty requirement

Article 2, para. 3, of the Constitution states that extradition may take place only pursuant to a treaty. The same provision can be found in Art. 2 of the Extradition Act. The two provisions are supplemented by Art. 51a of the Extradition Act. As we have seen, it deals with a number of multilateral treaties which, while not being extradition treaties themselves in the usual sense, may be regarded as a legal basis for extradition under the Act.

Article 2, para. 3, of the Constitution forms part of a chapter on fundamental individual rights. It confers upon individual persons a right to be extradited pursuant to the terms of an extradition treaty only. The extradition treaty clearly is thought to be an indispensable legal safeguard. Why should this be so?

The constitutional provision assumes that to extradite a person to another state should be possible only if the criminal justice system of that state warrants enough faith and confidence where its respect for basic individual rights is concerned. However, to decide on that question in each single extradition case would create difficult problems for the courts and other authorities. They would have to inquire into matters in the requesting state. Investigations that are not only time consuming and difficult to carry out but also politically unattractive. A more simple and objective yardstick is to be preferred. Since extradition treaties should only be concluded with states in whose systems of justice one can have confidence, the treaty requirement is seen by the Constitution as capable of providing this yardstick. It is the method *par excellence* of protecting individual persons against unfair treatment elsewhere. This requirement has a corollary effect in Dutch law. Since ratification of an extradition treaty requires the consent of parliament, it is not for the executive branch but solely for the legislature to decide whether another country is worthy of maintaining extradition relations with.

The constitutional provision does not create difficulties where bilateral treaties are concerned. Multilateral treaties, however, create constitutional problems. For in the situation of those treaties it is not for the Netherlands to decide what states may become parties to them. Sometimes, notably with

---

15 HR 2 April 1985, NJ 1985, 890, 17 NYIL 278-280 (1986).

respect to the European Convention on Extradition, indirect guarantees exist
that the other parties to the treaty will have adopted appropriate standards of
criminal justice. For the parties to that treaty are, with the exception of Israel,
all members of the Council of Europe and most of them have, in that capacity,
accepted the right of individual petition under the European Convention of
Human Rights. However, now that the Council has expanded its membership
considerably in recent years the logic has become less compelling.

Similar functional equivalents do not exist in the case of treaties such as the
Hague Convention for the Suppression of Unlawful Seizure of Aircraft to
which all states of the world may become parties. And, indeed, among the
parties to these treaties are states the Netherlands would not wish to conclude
an extradition treaty with. Article 51a of the Extradition Act tries to cope with
that difficulty by declaring that these treaties may, but need not, be considered
to be extradition treaties within the meaning of the Extradition Act, and this
conforms to the rules laid down in those convention themselves. Moreover,
under Art. 51a the Government are free to refuse extradition if they think
respect for human rights would justify refusal. However, it is difficult to
contend that the treaty requirement fulfils its function of providing the
authorities with an objective yardstick here. It is fair to say that, as a matter of
fact, Art. 51a conflicts with the logic behind the Constitution.[16] Similar
objections may be voiced against the Act relating to surrender in respect of war
crimes, allowing extradition to all parties to the Geneva Conventions and
Additional Protocol I. Since Art. 91 of the Constitution allows the approval of
treaties which deviate from its provision by a parliamentary majority of two
thirds, the constitutionality of approving multilateral treaties seems to depend
on whether this qualified majority has been obtained.

The surrender of an accused to the Yugoslavia Tribunal is not based on a
treaty but on Security Council Resolution 827 (1993). However, since the
Security Council derives its powers from the Charter of the United Nations, it
is assumed that the Charter itself constitutes a treaty within the meaning of the
Constitution.

Strongly linked to the treaty requirement is the rule of non inquiry. If faith and
confidence in a state's criminal justice system is a necessary requirement for
concluding an extradition treaty with that state, it is only natural that the

---

16 See for the constitutional debate on this point in the Netherlands *Schutte*, Volkenrechtelijke
    aspecten van het Nederlandse uitleveringsrecht, pp. 35-41; *Swart*, Nederlands uitleveringsrecht,
    pp. 61-67; *Swart*, Toelating, uitzetting en uitlevering in de herziene Grondwet, pp. 83-91.

existence of a treaty becomes proof of the fact that the requesting state will respect basic individual rights.

In case law this linkage is recognized. On many occasions the Supreme Court has held that, since the requesting state must be assumed to pay due respects to human rights, it is not up to a Dutch court to inquire into that matter except for cases in which the extradition treaty expressly enables it to do so. This is sometimes referred to as the 'confidence principle' *(vertrouwensbeginsel)*. A typical example of that approach is provided by a case involving the United States as the requesting state. The Supreme Court held that there was no reason to examine a complaint raised by the requested person since it must be assumed that the Netherlands, in negotiating the 1980 extradition treaty with the United States, had managed to adjust the result of the bilateral negotiations 'to take account of the nature and the extent of the recognition of (...) fundamental principles in the other state'.[17]

Recently, however, the courts have mitigated their application of the rule of non inquiry to some extent. The judgment of the European Court of Human Rights in the *Soering* case has forced them to revise their position.[18] We will discuss the matter in more detail when looking at the impact of human rights conventions on Dutch extradition law.[19]

Due to the treaty requirement courts will deny extradition if the terms of the treaty have not been fulfilled. They will consider it irrelevant in this respect whether treaty provisions intend to protect individual rights and whether the Extradition Act would have allowed the conclusion of an extradition treaty with broader terms.[20]

The fact that individual persons have a constitutional right to be extradited pursuant to a treaty only, does not imply that they may never be expelled to a state to which they could not have been extradited. In that sense the Constitution creates no individual rights.[21] However, methods of removing persons from the territory that aim at circumventing extradition procedures, such as disguised extradition or abduction, may be considered to amount to violations of a constitutional right.[22]

---

17   HR 1 July 1985, NJ 1986, 162, 17 NYIL 280-284 (1986) *(Geller)*.
18   ECHR 7 July 1989, Series A 161.
19   See infra pp. 112-115.
20   HR 3 April 1973, NJ 1974, 407, 6 NYIL 350 (1975); HR 20 May 1975, NJ 1975, 391.
21   See supra p. 88.
22   Cf. Rechtbank Den Haag 29 June 1984, NJ 1985, 815.

Reciprocity

There is no general requirement of reciprocity in the Extradition Act. This is explained by two considerations. On the one hand, extradition treaties, by creating mutual rights and obligations, start from the idea of reciprocity already. On the other, it was felt that one should not, as a matter of course, refuse to extradite a person, however desirable his extradition might be in an individual case, for the sole reason that one could not obtain the extradition of a person from another state in similar circumstances.[23] From the system of the Act it follows that extradition may be refused if the extradition treaty leaves room for doing so, but need not be refused. In actual practice, extradition is frequently granted without assurance of reciprocity. In particular, the fact that the requesting state bases its jurisdiction on a rule not known in Dutch law is usually considered no sufficient reason for refusing extradition.[24]

Double criminality

An indispensable condition for extradition to be granted is that the act for which extradition has been requested constitutes an offence according to the laws of both the requesting and the requested state. It is a condition present in all extradition treaties to which the Netherlands is a party. The Extradition Act lays down the requirement in Art. 5. In its definition of extraditable offences this provision closely follows Art. 2 of the European Convention on Extradition. Case law on both provisions is abundant. Here, we are able to discuss the most important aspects only.

Like the European Convention, the Extradition Act in defining extraditable offences has opted for a system of elimination. Extradition may be granted in respect of an offence punishable under the law of the requesting state and of the Netherlands by a custodial sentence of at least one year. Moreover, where extradition is requested for the purpose of enforcing a sentence the custodial sentence imposed must amount to a period of at least four months. Article 6

---

23 This is not to suggest that the Netherlands is not interested at all in maintaining reciprocity where the content of treaty obligations is concerned. Cf., for instance, the Dutch reservation to Art. 7, para. 2, of the European Convention on Extradition.

24 A typical example is provided by German extradition requests on the basis of the universality principle. While German law applies this principle to drug offences Dutch law does not. Cf. HR 31 August 1981, NJ 1982, 154; HR 18 December 1984, NJ 1985, 650.

allows for lower minima where extradition to other Benelux countries is concerned. Finally, like Art. 25 of the European Convention, Art. 7 of the Act equates measures involving deprivation of liberty that may or have been imposed by a criminal court in addition to or instead of a custodial sentence with custodial sentences for the purpose of the Act.

The European Convention and the Extradition Act raise a number of questions. In looking at the question of what punishment can be imposed in respect of the offence one has, of course, to take into account classifications which may exist in the law of the requesting or the requested state to the extent they are relevant. For example, Arts. 300 to 304 of the Dutch Penal Code distinguish between no less than twelve different forms of assault occasioning bodily harm, each carrying its own maximum sentence. It is less clear whether one should also look at more general rules that may influence the maximum punishment permitted. While, for instance, the fact that there has only been an attempt or that the offender was of minor age implies that, according to Dutch law, the maximum is less severe, the reverse is true where such factors as recidivism are concerned. To this question case law does not provide an unambiguous answer. Differences between the laws of the two states as to the length or nature of custodial sentences are generally held to be irrelevant in case law.[25]

When a person has been convicted for an offence, the length of the custodial sentence which has been imposed determines whether the offence is an extraditable one. From this case law infers that it is irrelevant whether detention on remand or detention for the purpose of extradition has been or will have to be deducted from the sentence.[26] Neither does it matter what part of the sentence remains to be enforced at the moment of the extradition request.[27] Most importantly, although the language of both the European Convention and the Extradition Act seems to suggest differently, it is assumed that the four months' requirement is also met if a foreign court has imposed a sentence of that length, or a longer sentence, with regard to several offences taken together.[28] Finally, it is not relevant whether a Dutch court would have

25 E.g. it does not matter whether the offence carries the same maximum in both states or whether some custodial sentences in other states are coupled with forms of forced labour. Cf. HR 10 April 1979, DD 1979, 256.
26 HR 26 June 1971, NJ 1972, 267; HR 3 February 1981, NJ 1981, 318, 13 NYIL 347-349 (1982).
27 HR 24 October 1978, NJ 1979, 157. See, however, Recommendation No. R (80)7 of the Committee of Ministers of the Council of Europe.
28 HR 12 October 1978, NJ 1979, 141; HR 10 April 1979, NJ 1979, 433.

imposed a sentence of similar length or whether the case would have been brought before a Dutch court in a similar situation.

The requirement of a four months' custodial sentence has been adopted in the Convention and the Act in order to exclude more trivial offences from extradition. In itself it does not logically imply that extradition should be refused for the purpose of enforcing other forms of punishment which may have been imposed together with a custodial sentence. Case law, however, has taken the view that on the basis of both the Convention and the Act extradition is not permissible where such sanctions as fines, confiscation, payment of the costs of criminal proceedings or contributions to a fund for compensation of victims of crime, etcetera are concerned.[29]

Article 2, para. 2, of the European Convention provides for a possibility of allowing extradition for offences which do not meet the requirements of para. 1, on the condition that the extradition request does at least contain one offence which does meet these requirements. A similar provision is absent from the Extradition Act. However, on the basis of Art. 12, which deals with the rule of speciality, permission will usually be granted to the requesting state to prosecute or punish these offences.[30]

The central question in all extradition cases is whether the act constitutes a punishable offence according to the laws of both the requesting and the requested state.

As far as punishability according to the laws of the requesting state is concerned this is simply assumed by the Dutch courts as a matter of course. The requesting state must be presumed to have sufficiently verified that matter already.[31]

In verifying whether the act constitutes an offence under Dutch law courts proceed on the basis of the statement of the facts (exposé des faits) contained in the extradition request. That is given a liberal interpretation often. The question then is whether, assuming these facts to be true, they may come within reach of a provision of Dutch law declaring similar behaviour to be a criminal

---

29 See e.g. HR 18 April 1978, NJ 1978, 697; HR 4 May 1971, NJ 1972, 225; HR 3 February 1981, NJ 1981, 317; HR 17 October 1989, NJ 1990, 220. Consequently, where a custodial sentence has replaced a fine that has not been paid or a financial obligation that has not been fulfilled, extradition also has to be refused.

30 Even wider possibilities of accessory extradition are offered by the 1978 Second Additional Protocol to the European Convention and the 1979 Agreement between Germany and the Netherlands.

31 Cf. HR 5 February 1991, NJ 1991, 404.

offence. In answering that question foreign law is not taken into account. Punishability according to the laws of the requesting state and those of the requested state are considered to be quite different questions which should be sharply differentiated. As a result, it does not matter at all whether or not the laws of both states place the offence within the same category of offences or denominate an offence by the same terminology.[32] Neither, for instance, it is relevant whether the act constitutes a similar form of participation.[33]

As is apparent from case law, double criminality presents no difficulties in a very large majority of cases. Interesting differences between the laws of the Netherlands and that of other states occasionally come to the fore, however.[34] They sometimes reveal more structural differences between legal systems. To common law countries, for example, it may be important to realize that the legal concept of criminal conspiracy is, as such, not known in Dutch law although a functional equivalent of that concept may be found in a provision of the Penal Code on criminal organizations. Case law on the matter provides perfect examples of the irrelevance of different legal qualifications for double criminality to exist.[35] Another general feature that should be noted here is that the Penal Code of the Netherlands goes less far in criminalizing breaches of contract and torts than that of various other countries on the European continent.[36]

A specific rule of interpretation with respect to double criminality is contained in Art. 5, para. 2, of the Act. For double criminality to exist it suffices that the act constitutes an offence of the same nature according to Dutch law. This provision is especially relevant where criminal provisions contain implicit

---

32 Cf. i.a. HR 2 March 1976, NJ 1976, 415, 8 NYIL 275 (1977); HR 15 November 1977, NJ 1978, 190.
33 HR 29 May 1984, NJ 1985, 107.
34 Some examples of acts not punishable according to Dutch law: escape from prison (HR 4 May 1971, NJ 1972, 225); selling lemon tea pretending it to be heroïn (HR 20 September 1982, NJ 1983, 253); not carrying an identity document (HR 28 June 1983, NJ 1984, 79); mailing pornographic material by closed envelope on request of the addressee (HR 30 October 1984, NJ 1985, 293).
35 Art. 140 Penal Code. The concept of criminal organization is in some respects narrower than that of criminal conspiracy. For instance, it does not apply to an agreement between persons to cooperate on one occasion only. See HR 28 February 1989, NJ 1990, 9 (refusal of extradition on a charge of conspiracy to Australia). However, quite regularly having conspired is thought by the courts to amount in the given circumstances to participation in a criminal organization within the meaning of Art. 140. An example is provided by HR 2 May 1989, NJ 1989, 773. See also the explicit provision in Art. 2, para. 4, of the treaty between the United States and the Netherlands. Cf. also supra p. 23.
36 E.g. HR 22 July 1974, NJ 1974, 501, 6 NYIL 353 (1975); HR 3 May 1983, NJ 1983, 588.

or explicit territorial or other limitations. For example, offering resistance to an officer in the exercise of his duty constitutes an offence only if the officer is a Dutch officer. Paragraph 2 of Art. 5 provides the opportunity to extradite for similar offences according to the law of the requesting state. The offence must be thought to be one of the same character.[37]

For double criminality to exist according to the law of the requested state, case law considers the legal situation at the time of the extradition request and the decision on that request to be decisive. The act need not be an offence according to Dutch law at the moment of its commission too. On the other hand, if the act constituted an offence at the time of its commission but not any more at a later date extradition will have to be refused.[38]

Jurisdiction, statutes of limitation, minor age, pardon and amnesty

A difficult problem of extradition law is to know what exactly is meant by double criminality. In a narrower sense the requirement can be understood only to require that the act for which extradition has been requested constitutes a punishable offence according to the laws of the requesting and the requested state. This is sometimes referred to as double criminality *in abstracto*. But the requirement can also be given a wider meaning. It would then justify refusal of extradition if the requested state would, in a similar situation, not be able to prosecute the offender or enforce a judgment against him. This is usually referred to as double criminality *in concreto*. On the basis of this interpretation the requested state could, for instance, refuse extradition if it would, in a similar situation, not be able to prosecute or to punish a person because it would have no jurisdiction in the matter, or because its statutes of limitation would prevent this.

Like the European Convention on Extradition, the Extradition Act requires a narrow interpretation of the concept of double criminality.[39] In relation to that requirement it only matters whether the act constitutes a punishable offence according to the laws of the requesting state and the Netherlands. Other

---

37 For a different approach of the problem where jurisdiction over extraterritorial offences is concerned see supra pp. 61-62.

38 HR 16 January 1973, NJ 1973, 281, 5 NYIL 309-311 (1974) *(Pauksch)*; HR 1 July 1977, NJ 1977, 601, 9 NYIL 292-293 (1978) *(Pauksch)*. A complaint in the first case with the European Commission of Human Rights was rejected. See European Commission 6 July 1976, 6 Decisions and Reports 184-186 (1977).

39 Cf. HR 3 February 1981, NJ 1981, 318, 13 NYIL 347-349 (1982).

obstacles that would, in a similar situation, prevent prosecution or punishment according to Dutch law are relevant only if the Act mentions them explicitly. The Act contains fewer obstacles than the European Convention.

Article 7 of the European Convention allows the requested state to refuse extradition if the offence has been committed on its territory. Moreover, extradition may be refused if the offence has been committed outside the territory of the requesting state and the law of the requested state does not allow prosecution for the same category of offences when committed outside the latter state's territory.

Similar provisions are absent in the Extradition Act. As far as the Act is concerned there is no imperative reason for refusing extradition because the offence has been committed on Dutch territory or because Dutch courts would not have jurisdiction in a similar case. It is a matter of applying treaty provisions only. As we have seen already in discussing reciprocity, in actual practice extradition is never refused for the reason that a Dutch court would not have jurisdiction in a similar situation. However, mandatory treaty provisions may lead to extradition being refused since the Act requires that extradition take place on the basis of a treaty.

In attaching consequences to statutes of limitation, the Extradition Act follows the European Convention on Extradition. According to Art. 9, para. 1, sub-para. *e*, of the Act, extradition must be refused if the requested person has become immune from prosecution or punishment by reason of lapse of time, either according to the laws of the requesting state or those of the Netherlands. Case law assumes that, under this provision as well as under Art. 10 of the European Convention, in the case of extradition for the purpose of enforcing a sentence one should also examine whether the person would have been immune from prosecution by reason of lapse of time according to the law of the requested state.[40]

In examining the situation according to the laws of both states courts proceed in the same manner as has been explained in discussing double criminality. They will assume as a matter of course that no problems exist where the law of the requesting state is concerned. As far as Dutch law is concerned, on the basis of the facts as they appear from the extradition request courts will consider whether, according to Arts. 70 to 77 of the Penal Code, the requested person would have become immune by reason of lapse of time, and whether the

---

40 HR 26 June 1984, NJ 1985, 57.

facts disclose circumstances that would have brought about interruption or suspension of the statutory period of time.[41] As in the case of double criminality the examination of the situation under foreign law and under Dutch law are sharply differentiated.[42]

The Extradition Act is silent on other circumstances that would bar prosecution or punishment according to Dutch law, such as minor age, amnesty or pardon, and the absence of a complaint of the victim if that complaint is a condition for prosecuting the offender. Consequently, they have no relevance where extradition is concerned. An exception must, however, probably be made for minor age. Minors who were below the age of twelve years at the time of their committing an offence cannot be prosecuted. Although Art. 77a of the Penal Code states that the age of the offender is a bar to prosecuting him only, one must assume that this provision considers children below the age of twelve not to be criminally responsible for their acts. In their case, therefore, the requirement of double criminality would not be fulfilled.

Notwithstanding the foregoing, amnesty or pardon may constitute reasons for refusing extradition under the Act if the requested person in committing an offence has not only contravened the law of the requesting state but also that of the Netherlands. We will discuss that matter below when dealing with *non bis in idem* provisions.

Political, military and fiscal offences

Article 11, para. 1, of the Extradition Act exempts offences of a political nature, including offences connected with these offences, from extradition. Paragraph 2 makes an exception to that principle where the taking or attempted taking of the life of a Head of State or a member of his family is concerned.

Both provisions of the Act closely follow the wording of Art. 3 of the European Convention on Extradition. No definition is given of what offences

---

41 E.g. HR 1 July 1981, NJ 1981, 665; HR 29 April 1980, DD 80.237. If the act was not a punishable offence according to Dutch law at the time of its commission but had become one at the time of the extradition request courts will consider whether, supposing that the act did constitute a punishable offence at the time of its commission, the offender would have become immune. See HR 1 July 1977, NJ 1977, 601, 9 NYIL 292-293 (1978) *(Pauksch)*.

42 Cf. for a different provision, requiring that the law of the requesting state be applied in matters of interruption and suspension of time periods, Art. V of the 1979 Agreement between Germany and the Netherlands.

constitute political offences. However, during the parliamentary debates on the Extradition Bill the Government declared that they considered the following offences to be political offences within the meaning of Art. 11:

'1. offences which in accordance with their legal description are always – i.e. regardless of the circumstances – to be considered as such (the purely political offences);

2. offences committed with the intent to change the political order;

3. offences committed for the purpose of making the foregoing offences possible or of escaping prosecution thereof or of escaping discriminatory prosecution and punishment.'

The Government added that, as far as the second category is concerned, what matters is the (objective) purpose of the offence and not the (subjective) motive of the offender. This summing up more or less follows traditional doctrine. The first category comprises purely political offences, including the so-called *complex* offences. The third category consists of *connex* political offences. As far as the second category of offences is concerned they seem to cover what are sometimes called *relative* political offences, i.e. offences that, without having a direct connection with purely political offences, are being committed in the course of a struggle for political power.

Prior to the 1967 Extradition Act no case law had developed on political offences. This explains why the remarks of the Government have been rather influential on the developments after 1967. Moreover, as far as relative political offences are concerned Dutch courts have been influenced by Swiss case law.

In considering whether an offence is a political offence case law distinguishes between offences that have been committed in the course of a political struggle in which the requesting state is directly involved and offences showing no such involvement. In the latter case they will deny the political character of the offence. A clear example of that approach is provided by a case in which Belgium applied for the extradition of a Moroccan national and political opponent to the Moroccan Government for having burglarized the Moroccan embassy in Brussels.[43]

---

43 HR 14 September 1971, NJ 1974, 50, 3 NYIL 280 (1972) *(Joudat)*. See also HR 8 November 1977, NJ 1978, 35 *(Gallagher)*. The approach is the same as that of the House of Lords in *Cheng v. Governor of Pentonville Prison*, [1973] 2 Weekly Law Reports 746-772.

Extradition for purely political offences will always be declared inadmissible.[44] The same is true for complex and connex political offences, regardless of the circumstances in which they have been committed. The leading case here is that of *Folkerts*, a member of the *Rote Armee Fraktion* whose extradition had been requested by the German Government. In that case the Supreme Court, among other things, held that the kidnapping of a prominent German businessman and the killing of four persons escorting him constituted political offences within the meaning of the Extradition Act since they had been committed in order to put pressure on the German Government to release other members of the *Rote Armee Fraktion* from prison, an offence that the Supreme Court considered to be a purely political offence.[45] It is obvious that the Court, in doing so, followed what had been said by the Government during parliamentary discussions on the Extradition Bill.

Quite different is the approach of the Supreme Court where so-called relative political offences are concerned. Here a restrictive view prevails. The leading case again is that of *Folkerts*, together with that of *Wackernagel*, also a member of the *Rote Armee Fraktion*.[46] From these cases it appears that the political character of such offences will only by accepted if a number of conditions have been met. First, the offender must have acted with a political motive. Motive, however, is not enough. Other circumstances will determine whether an offence is of a 'predominantly' political character. The decisive factor here is whether the offender could reasonably have expected that the offence would yield any result directly related to the political goal he was pursuing. This the Supreme Court denied in the cases of *Folkerts* and *Wackernagel*, in which extradition was requested for a number of violent crimes. In adopting the predominance test the Supreme Court was clearly influenced by Swiss case law. Its purpose may be summarized by saying that senseless violence which cannot possibly yield any favourable political results to the offender is excluded from the political offence exception. However, the Supreme Court applies this test also to non-violent offences like desertion.[47]

---

44 Purely political offences, according to the Supreme Court, are the offences summed up in Arts. 92 to 130 of the Penal Code. These provisions are mainly concerned with protecting the security of the state. Cf. HR 8 May 1978, NJ 1978, 314, 10 NYIL 465-471 (1979) *(Folkerts)*; HR 20 December 1988, NJ 1989, 702, 21 NYIL 410-413 (1990).

45 HR 8 May 1978, NJ 1978, 314, 10 NYIL 465-471 (1979) *(Folkerts)*.

46 HR 8 May 1978, NJ 1978, 315 *(Wackernagel)*. See also HR 9 November 1976, NJ 1977, 75, 8 NYIL 267-269 (1977). Cf. for a more detailed discussion of case law *Swart*, ZStW 91 (1979), pp. 779-791.

47 HR 28 February 1984, NJ 1984, 497, 16 NYIL 486-487 (1985).

There is no example in case law in which the Supreme Court considered the predominance test to have been fulfilled.

The case law of the Supreme Court is remarkable in that it applies different tests for connex offences on the one hand and relative offences on the other. It has been criticized for not explaining why it should be necessary to deal with connex offences more leniently than with relative offences. Another criticism is that the political offender is invited by Dutch case law to combine common offences with a purely political one in order to make them connex offences.

It is a curious feature of Dutch case law that it considers Art. 11 of the Act not to be applicable where the interpretation of treaties is concerned which have been concluded before 1967. In the cases of *Kelly* and *McFarlane*, two members of the *Irish Republican Army* whose extradition had been requested by the United Kingdom, the Supreme Court held that the provision on political offences in the 1898 extradition treaty between that country and the Netherlands should be explained against the background of the Extradition Act of 1875. It further assumed that only purely political offences were excluded from extradition under that Act.[48] The obvious objection against this approach is that it makes provisions on political offences in older extradition treaties redundant since purely political offences are already excluded from their lists of extraditable offences.

In interpreting the political offence provision in the European Convention on Extradition case law will base itself on Art. 11 of the present Extradition Act. It is, therefore, irrelevant whether other contracting parties interpret the treaty provision in the same way.[49]

In a number of treaties to which the Netherlands is a party provisions may be found which differ from Art. 11, para. 1, of the Extradition Act. The first treaty is the 1948 Genocide Convention, which declares in the Art. VII that genocide shall not be considered as a political crime for the purpose of extradition. A similar provision can be found in the 1975 Additional Protocol to the European Convention on Extradition. To these provisions Art. 5a of the Act implementing the Genocide Convention gives effect. The Additional Protocol to the European Convention also excludes grave breaches of the four

---

48 HR 1 July 1986, NJ 1987, 255 *(Kelly)*; HR 1 July 1986, NJ 1987, 256 *(McFarlane)*. See also HR 21 October 1986, NJ 1987, 257 *(Kelly)*; HR 21 October 1986, NJ 1987, 258, 19 NYIL 462-470 (1988) *(McFarlane)*.

49 HR 16 April 1985, NJ 1986, 478, 18 NYIL 370-372 (1987) *(McCann)*. While France had previously refused extradition on the basis of the political offence exception the Supreme Court denied the political character of the offences.

1949 Geneva Conventions as well as comparable violations of the laws and customs of war from the political offence exception in the European Convention. As far as grave breaches of the Geneva Conventions and of Additional Protocol I thereto are concerned, the Act relating to surrender in respect of war crimes makes no mention of political offences. On the other hand, the Dutch Government did not want to depoliticize offences committed during non-international armed conflicts. They therefore declared that they did not accept Art. 1 of the Protocol to the European Convention since it did not permit partial reservations.

The Netherlands has also become a party to the 1977 European Convention on the Suppression of Terrorism. However, it has made a declaration under Art. 13 of the Convention, enabling it to evaluate the political character of the relevant offences in the light of the circumstances. A similar declaration has been made to the 1979 Agreement on the Application of the European Convention on the Suppression of Terrorism between the Member States of the European Communities. Article 11, para. 3, of the Extradition Act declares para. 1 not to be applicable where the European Convention is concerned.

Finally, mention should be made of Art. 3 of the Benelux Treaty on Extradition and Mutual Assistance in Criminal Matters, declaring that desertion from military service may not be deemed to be a political offence.

In para. 4 of Art. 11 the Extradition Act deals with military offences. The provision is limited to purely military offences, i.e. offences under military law which are not also indictable offences under the general criminal law of the Netherlands. Extradition for purely military offences is precluded by para. 4 unless provided for otherwise by treaty. From this it is clear that the Act does not object to extradition for military offences as a matter of principle. It only requires an express provision on the matter in a treaty. However, until now the Benelux Treaty is the only treaty creating obligations to extradite for military offences. Paragraph 5 of Art. 11 refers to that treaty.

With respect to fiscal offences Art. 11, para. 4, of the Act follows the same system. Extradition for fiscal offences will be discussed in another contribution to this book.[50]

---

50 See infra pp. 234-235.

Nationality and other personal circumstances

In Art. 4, para. 1, of the Extradition Act extradition of Dutch nationals is excluded. On the other hand, by virtue of Art. 5 of the Penal Code the courts have jurisdiction over crimes committed by Dutch nationals abroad.[51] Traditionally, prosecuting Dutch nationals in the Netherlands is preferred to extradition. Article 1 of the Act equates with them aliens who are treated as Dutch nationals by virtue of a special statute. One statute is relevant in this respect: the 1976 Act on the legal status of Moluccans *(Wet betreffende de positie van Molukkers).*[52] It is assumed that in case of multiple nationality Dutch nationality prevails.[53] Nationality is determined as at the time of the decision concerning extradition.[54]

In 1986, on the occasion of the adoption of the Act on the transfer of enforcement of criminal judgments *(Wet overdracht tenuitvoerlegging strafvonnissen)*, a second paragraph was added to Art. 4. It allows the extradition of Dutch nationals in certain cases and under certain conditions. Henceforth they may be extradited for the purpose of standing trial in another state. However, that state must guarantee that the person will be returned to the Netherlands to serve his sentence there if, following his extradition, a custodial sentence other than a suspended sentence or a measure depriving him of his liberty has been imposed upon him. According to the Act, it is for the Minister of Justice to obtain that guarantee from the requesting state. Return of the person to the Netherlands implies that enforcement of the foreign sentence is transferred. Case law assumes the Minister of Justice to be obliged to obtain the guarantee from the requesting state that transfer of enforcement will be effected in the form of conversion of sentence rather than continued enforcement, unless an extradition treaty does not offer room for making that condition.[55]

In linking extradition of nationals for the purpose of facing trial elsewhere to transfer of enforcement of criminal judgments the Extradition Act aims to eliminate one of the main objections which traditionally existed in the Nether-

---

51 See supra pp. 59-62.
52 See supra p. 60.
53 HR 8 April 1935, NJ 1935, 826.
54 HR 5 June 1874, W 3761.
55 HR 31 March 1995, NJ 1996, 382 *(Van Doesburg)*. The main difference between the two modes of transfer is that conversion of sentence, unlike continued enforcement, offers the courts of the administering state an opportunity to alter the sentence imposed in the sentencing state. See for a more detailed discussion infra p. 204. See also *Paridaens*, De uitlevering van eigen onderdanen door Nederland, pp. 107-117.

lands to extraditing nationals: the belief that sanctions consisting in deprivation of liberty are normally best executed in the state where the offender has his social roots, both from a humanitarian viewpoint and with a view to his social rehabilitation.[56] It is important to note here that, according to the Act, extradition may, but need not, be granted. It is for the Minister of Justice to decide whether extradition or prosecution of the offender in the Netherlands serves the interests of justice best in a particular case.

As far as extradition for the purpose of enforcing a foreign sentence is concerned, this is categorically excluded by the Act, the reason being that transfer of enforcement of that sentence to the Netherlands is the preferred option. Here, as well as with respect to extradition for the purpose of prosecuting the person, it must be noted that the Act on the transfer of enforcement of criminal judgments makes transfer to the Netherlands possible pursuant to a treaty only.[57]

The system of the Act represents an attempt to take an intermediate position between common law systems and civil law systems where extraditing nationals is concerned. Extradition of Dutch nationals has become a regular occurrence, both to common and civil law systems. On the whole it seems to function well. One may, however, wonder whether the system of the Act has found sufficiently clear reflection in recent extradition treaties concluded with other states.[58]

In a declaration to Art. 6 of the European Convention on Extradition the Netherlands has declared that for the purpose of the Convention the word 'nationals' is to be understood as meaning 'persons of Netherlands nationality as well as foreigners integrated into the Netherlands community in so far as they can be prosecuted within the Kingdom of the Netherlands for the act in respect of which extradition is requested, and in so far as such foreigners are not expected to loose their right of residence in the Kingdom as a result of the imposition of a penalty or measure subsequent to their extradition'.[59]

The importance of the declaration is rather limited where persons not possessing Dutch nationality are concerned. This is due to the fact the Penal Code does not, as a general rule, apply the active personality principle to them.

---

56 Cf. *Swart*, Human Rights and the Abolition of Traditional Principles, p. 532. For a more thorough discussion of the Dutch system see also *Paridaens*, RIDP 62 (1991), pp. 515-521.

57 See infra pp. 194-196.

58 That question notably arises with respect to the 1980 treaty between the United States and the Netherlands.

59 A similar declaration has been made to Art. 3 of the 1983 Convention on the Transfer of Sentenced Persons. See infra p. 196.

For acts committed by them outside the territory of the Netherlands the courts have jurisdiction in a limited number of cases only. On the other hand, Arts. 7 and 8 of the European Convention already enable the Netherlands to refuse extradition for offences committed within Dutch territory. However, pursuant to the Act on the legal status of Moluccans the active personality principle does apply to persons envisaged in that Act. Case law has consistently refused to equate other aliens with Dutch nationals within the meaning of Art. 4 of the Extradition Act.[60]

According to Art. 10, para. 1, of the Extradition Act, extradition shall not be granted if there are good grounds for believing that if the request were to be granted 'the person claimed would be prosecuted, punished or otherwise harassed on account of his religious or political opinions, nationality or race or of the population group to which he belongs'. Like the corresponding provision in Art. 3, para. 2, of the European Convention on Extradition, this provision has been inspired by the 1951 Convention relating to the Status of Refugees. However, the Extradition Act and the European Convention seem to differ from the Refugee Convention in one important respect. While the Refugee Convention requires that a person is likely to be 'persecuted' on one of the grounds enumerated in order to be considered a refugee, the Act and the European Convention are less demanding. For a person to be protected by their provisions it already suffices that his position may be 'prejudiced' for any of these reasons.

Finally, the Extradition Act contains a hardship clause. In Art. 10, para. 2, it is said that extradition shall not be granted if its consequences would cause particular hardship to the person claimed, for example, because of his youth, advanced age or state of health. A similar reservation has been made to Art. 1 of the European Convention on Extradition.
   A question arises as to the relationship between the reservation to Art. 1 of the European Convention and the declaration to Art. 6. Does the fact that the person claimed is a Dutch national or is integrated into Dutch society in itself amount to a particular hardship? An affirmative answer would imply that Dutch nationals and integrated aliens could never be extradited. Case law, therefore, assumes that having Dutch nationality or being integrated in Dutch society are

---

60 Cf. HR 28 June 1983, NJ 1984, 756, 16 NYIL 484-486 (1985).

only factors that should be taken into account when it is decided whether a person's extradition would cause particular hardship.[61]

Concurrent jurisdiction and ne bis in idem

Article 9 of the Extradition Act deals with offences with respect to which jurisdiction of the courts in the requesting state and those in the Netherlands concur. It distinguishes between situations in which proceedings for the same offence are pending, have been discontinued and have ended in a final verdict of a court.[62]

As long as proceedings for the same offence are pending in the Netherlands extradition may not be granted. Article 9, para. 1, sub *a*, of the Act gives unconditional priority to criminal investigations in the Netherlands. However, on the basis of para. 2 of the same Article the Minister of Justice may order that proceedings be discontinued. He may do so up to the moment a trial has begun.[63] In actual practice proceedings are frequently discontinued in order to make extradition of the suspect for the offence possible. Notably, it is the official policy of the Dutch authorities with respect to aliens who have only been permitted to stay in the country for a maximum period of three months or remain there without permission and who have committed the offence on Dutch territory, to promote them being brought before the courts of their country of origin as much as is reconcilable with other interests. It is assumed that a proper administration of justice, including the interests of the suspect himself, is normally best served by extraditing him. In such cases extradition may, in fact, become transfer of proceedings to the requesting state.[64]

According to Art. 9, para. 1, sub *b*, extradition may not be granted if proceedings for the same offence have been discontinued and their reopening is excluded by the Code of Criminal Procedure. Article 255 of the Code, to which the Extradition Act refers, deals mainly, but not exclusively, with situations in which, despite investigations having been carried out, there is not enough evidence to warrant a trial. According to the provision of the Code, however, a case may be reopened if fresh evidence becomes available. To this system

---

61 HR 26 July 1987, NJ 1987, 835, 20 NYIL 322-324 (1989).
62 For the concept of 'same offence' see supra pp. 77-78.
63 HR 28 February 1984, NJ 1984, 490.
64 See infra p. 175.

para. 3 of Art. 9 makes two exceptions. First, extradition may be granted if the decision to discontinue proceedings was due to the fact that investigations have made it clear that Dutch courts have no jurisdiction to try the offence. Secondly, extradition is allowed if, prior to the extradition request, the Dutch authorities had already decided to transfer proceedings to the state which requested extradition.

Article 9 does not govern the situation in which the authorities have decided not to start proceedings against a person. The decision whether or not to extradite lies entirely with the Minister of Justice.

Finally, para. 1, subparas. c and d, of Art. 9 deals with the consequences of decisions of the Dutch trial courts. According to subpara. c extradition shall not be granted if the person claimed has been acquitted or the charges against him have been dismissed. Subparagraph d attaches the same consequence to verdicts finding accused guilty and convicting him, but only in one of the three following circumstances. The first is that in which the sentence or measure imposed has been fully served. This situation includes amnesty and pardon as a result of which enforcement of a judgment has ended. Secondly, extradition is excluded if the sentence or measure imposed, or what remains to be enforced of them, is conditional. Finally extradition may not take place if the court held the defendant guilty without imposing punishment.[65]

Subparagraphs c and d attach to final judgments of Dutch courts the same consequences for the purpose of extradition as Art. 68, para. 2, of the Penal Code does where the negative effects of foreign court decisions within the Dutch legal order are concerned. However, while Art. 68, para. 3, of the Code puts out-of-court settlements on an equal footing with final judgments as far as double jeopardy is concerned, the Extradition Act is silent on that point. It is only fair to refuse extradition in such cases and one may well hold the view that refusal is justified under most extradition treaties in force.

It is a remarkable characteristic of subparas. c and d that they also preclude extradition as a consequence of final judgments rendered by courts of third states. As a matter of fact, they make no difference between final judgments of Dutch courts and those of other courts.[66] Again, this can be explained by the

---

65 Subpara. e needs no discussion here since it deals with a purely theoretical situation that may never occur in practice. See *Swart* (supra note 1), pp. 240-241.

66 Cf. also the Dutch reservation to Art. 9 of the European Convention on Extradition and Art. 2 of its Additional Protocol.

fact that Art. 68 of the Penal Code attaches similar consequences to foreign court decisions in the Dutch legal order.[67]

Other impediments to extradition; human rights

In Art. 5, para. 3, of the Extradition Act it is provided that extradition for the purpose of enforcing a judgment rendered *in absentia* shall be granted only if the person claimed has had or will still be given an adequate opportunity to defend himself. This provision has been inspired by Art. 6 of the European Convention on Human Rights, granting every accused the right to defend himself in person or through legal assistance of his own choosing. It has been read as implying the right of the accused to be tried in his presence.[68] A corresponding reservation has been made to Art. 1 of the European Convention on Extradition.[69]

A judgment rendered *in absentia* will not automatically lead to refusal of extradition, as is apparent from the provision in the Act. For instance, case law assumes that the person claimed should, wherever possible, take appropriate steps to be kept informed of the date of the trial.[70]

Article 8 of the Extradition Act deals with capital punishment. Pursuant to that provision, extradition for offences which are punishable by death under the law of the requesting state may only be granted if an adequate assurance has been given that the death penalty, if imposed, will not be carried out. It is for the Minister of Justice to decide what guarantees he considers to be sufficient.[71]

Although the Extradition Act contains several provisions aiming at the protection of basic individual rights of the person claimed, it does not offer an overall protection against infringements of human rights by the requesting state. Moreover, the provisions of the Act can be applied only to the extent permitted by due respect for treaty obligations, since provisions of Dutch law which

---

67 See supra p. 83.
68 Cf. ECHR 12 February 1985, Series A 89 *(Colozza v. Italy)*.
69 Cf. also the Second Additional Protocol to the European Convention and Art. II.3 of the 1979 Agreement between Germany and the Netherlands.
70 HR 25 June 1968, NJ 1969, 23, 1 NYIL 216 (1970). See also HR 5 March 1968, NJ 1968, 238, 1 NYIL 214 (1970); HR 29 November 1983, NJ 1984, 349; HR 3 April 1984, NJ 1984, 724.
71 Cf. Rechtbank Den Haag 23 May 1978, NJ 1978, 360, 10 NYIL 471-472 (1979).

conflict with treaty provisions must be disregarded. Not all extradition treaties to which the Netherlands is a party offer the same protection as the Extradition Act does. It is not surprising, therefore, that the Supreme Court has been confronted frequently with the question of whether the person claimed may invoke provisions of human rights treaties to which the Netherlands is a party in order to prevent his extradition. All in all case law comprises some forty cases, a very large majority of them dealing with extradition requests on the basis of the European Convention on Extradition and the Benelux Treaty on Extradition and Mutual Assistance in Criminal Matters. In discussing these cases we may distinguish between case law before and after the well-known decision of the European Court of Human Rights in the case of *Soering* v. *United Kingdom.*[72]

As far as case law during the pre-*Soering* period is concerned, in all cases but one the appeal was dismissed. It is hard to summarize the Court's approach, the reason being that it shows such variety in motives for not accepting the appeal. From a point of view of principle the most interesting cases are the ones in which the Supreme Court held that no investigation of a complaint should be made because the requesting state, being a party to the European Convention for the Protection of Human Rights and Fundamental Freedoms, must be assumed to live up to its obligations under the Convention.[73] It sometimes added that the requesting state had recognized the right of individual complaint under the Convention.[74] Or that, according to the law of the requesting state, the person sought has the right to invoke the provisions of the Convention in court proceedings.[75] In a case concerning an extradition request from the United States, a state not a party to human rights conventions at that time, the Supreme Court held that there was no reason to examine a complaint since it must be assumed that the Netherlands, being bound by the European Convention of Human Rights, 'has managed to adjust the results of the bilateral negotiations' leading to the 1980 extradition treaty between the United States and the Netherlands 'to take account of the nature and the extent of the recognition of (...) fundamental principles of law in the other state'.[76] The one

---

72 ECHR 7 July 1989, Series A 161.
73 HR 28 May 1985, NJ 1985, 892; HR 21 October 1986, NJ 1987, 258, 19 NYIL 462-470 (1988); HR 17 February 1987, NJ 1987, 873; HR 17 March 1987, NJ 1988, 312.
74 E.g. HR 21 October 1986, NJ 1987, 258, 19 NYIL 462-470 (1988).
75 HR 28 May 1985, NJ 1985, 892.
76 HR 1 July 1985, NJ 1986, 162, 17 NYIL 280-284 (1986) *(Geller)*. A complaint to the European Commission was declared inadmissible on 10 October 1985 (unreported). See also *Trechsel*, EuGRZ 14 (1987), p. 73.

exception in case law is an extradition request from Turkey. It concerns violation by the Turkish authorities of the right to be tried within a reasonable time. The Supreme Court considered that it should examine the claim, since the requesting state had 'failed to show willingness to recognize the competence of the European Commission of Human Rights to receive petitions'. It then declared extradition to be inadmissible.[77]

It is obvious that the Court has struggled with the matter. Its strong reluctance to examine claims derived from human rights conventions has to do with two considerations mainly. The one is that Dutch courts are not really equipped to make inquiries into all sorts of circumstances in the requesting state. The other is that to do so would amount to a breach of obligations arising from extradition treaties. A breach which is all the less desirable since it must be assumed that the Netherlands had concluded extradition treaties with states that pay due respect to human rights only.

The first case to have been decided by the Supreme Court (civil chamber) after the *Soering* case concerned the surrender of *Short* (an American soldier suspected of having murdered his wife in the Netherlands) to the American military authorities in the Netherlands.[78] The case involves the application of the 1951 NATO Status of Forces Agreement. The American authorities refused to give any assurance that the death penalty would not be imposed or carried out, as they were perfectly entitled to refuse under the Agreement. The Court held that the situation amounted to an irreconcilable conflict of international obligations, to surrender *Short* under the Status of Forces Agreement and not to do so under the Sixth Protocol to the European Convention on Human Rights, to which the Netherlands had become a party. It denied that the European Convention and its Protocol took precedence over the Agreement under international law, which would have freed the Netherlands from its contractual obligations towards the United States. But it went on to say that the case should be decided by balancing the various interests at stake against each other. On that basis it decided that *Short's* interest in not being handed over should prevail over the Government's interest in doing so.[79]

The criminal chamber of the Supreme Court has followed suit. More clearly than before, it recognizes that human rights conventions may bar extradition. Repeating the language of the European Court of Human Rights in the *Soering* case, the Court has stated the European Convention may stand in the way of

---

77 HR 27 March 1984, NJ 1984, 611, 16 NYIL 488-489 (1985).
78 HR 30 March 1990, NJ 1991, 249, 22 NYIL 432-438 (1991) *(Short)*.
79 *Short* was later surrender after the US authorities informed the Dutch Government that he would not be charged with a capital offence.

extradition if there is a real risk that the person sought would suffer a flagrant denial of a fair trial in the requesting state.[80] If, however, that state is a party to the European Convention it must be assumed that it will honour its obligations under the Convention unless the person sought is able to show that this is not or will not be the case.[81] With respect to states that are not parties to the European Convention or to other human rights conventions, the court adopts a similar approach. The fact that the Netherlands has recently concluded an extradition treaty with another state implies that this state must be assumed to respect human rights unless the risk of a flagrant violation can be shown.[82]

As yet there is no indication that the Supreme Court considers it to be relevant whether the requesting state has accepted the right of individual complaint under the European Convention or similar rights under other conventions. Nor has the Court made clear whether it is relevant that the provisions of a human rights convention can be invoked in court proceedings in the requesting state. Until now the Supreme Court has not found claims to be well-founded.

The rule of speciality; re-extradition to a third state

It is an established principle of extradition law that the person who has been extradited may not be proceeded against, sentenced or detained for any offence committed prior to his surrender other than that for which he was surrendered, nor be restricted in his personal freedom for any other reason. In Art. 12, para. 1, of the Extradition Act this rule of speciality is laid down as a general condition that the Minister of Justice must pose when granting extradition to the requesting state. In the case of an extradition request being granted for some offences but not for others a difficulty may arise if extradition has been requested for the purpose of enforcing a sentence. From the extradition request it will not always be clear which part of the sentence has been imposed for which offence. Case law assumes that it is for the authorities of the requesting state to determine which part of the sentence should be enforced.[83]

---

80 HR 29 May 1990, NJ 1991, 647; HR 9 April 1991, NJ 1991, 696.
81 HR 5 March 1991, NJ 1991, 547; HR 29 June 1993, NJ 1995, 227.
82 HR 9 April 1991, NJ 1991, 696, concerning extradition to the United States.
83 HR 9 November 1976, NJ 1977, 75, 8 NYIL 267-269 (1977); HR 20 May 1980, NJ 1980, 540.

In paras. 2 and 5 of Art. 12 a number of exceptions to the speciality requirement have been made.

Paragraph 2 allows the Minister of Justice to refrain from requiring compliance with the speciality condition. He may do this in two situations. The first is the one in which the requesting state could have obtained extradition of the person from the Netherlands on the basis of the treaty in force between the two countries if it had requested so. Moreover, the Minister of Justice may consent to the person being prosecuted or punished for other offences if, on the one hand, the requirement of double criminality is met and, on the other, Arts. 8 to 11 of the Extradition Act would not bar extradition.

Article 12 of the Act lays all decisions concerning application of the rule of speciality exclusively in the hands of the Minister of Justice. It does not require that the courts decide on the matter. Moreover, from the wording of the Article it appears that no prior request of the state having obtained extradition is required for the Minister to decide. He may already allow the requesting state to proceed against the person with respect to other offences the moment he grants extradition.

In accordance with state practice in the matter para. 5 of Art. 12 states that any condition regarding speciality lapses when the person, having had an opportunity to leave the territory of the state which has obtained his extradition, has not done so within a certain period. The period envisaged in the Act is thirty days.

Paragraph 3 of Art. 12 deals with re-extradition to a third state. Without consent of the Minister of Justice the state which has obtained extradition may not extradite the person to a third state for offences committed prior to his surrender by the Netherlands. The Minister may consent if the offences could have given rise to extradition of the person by the Netherlands to the third state. Again, no consent is needed if the person has been given an opportunity to leave the territory of the other state of at least thirty days.

Extradition procedure

Extradition procedure in the Netherlands is a process which involves courts as well as administrative authorities. It essentially consists of two stages: a judicial stage in which a court decides on the admissibility of extraditing a person and an administrative stage in which the Minister of Justice decides on the question of whether or not extradition will be granted. A decision of the court declaring extradition inadmissible binds, with one exception, the Minister. On the other hand, the fact that a court allows extradition only amounts to an advice, the Minister of Justice being free to decide otherwise. Another general feature of extradition procedure is that a court decision on admissibility does not cover all legal aspects of the case. The Extradition Act leaves certain issues for the Minister to decide only. Whether the person claimed runs a risk of being persecuted in the requesting state, whether extraditing him would amount to severe hardship, whether, in the case of concurrent jurisdiction, extradition should be preferred to prosecution in the Netherlands, and a number of other questions, are not for the courts to decide. They belong to the exclusive competence of the Minister and the task of the courts is, here, limited to that of giving him advice.

As soon as an extradition request has been received it will be examined by the Minister of Justice, who has to perform a preliminary check. Articles 19 and 20 of the Extradition Act empower him to refuse extradition if it is obvious that there is no chance of the request being granted, or to invite the requesting state to submit more or other information if the request shows shortcomings which can be repaired.

The request will then be sent to the public prosecutor of the court district where the person claimed remains. It is the duty of the prosecutor to submit the extradition request to the district court. That court will hear the public prosecutor and the person claimed during a public hearing. The person claimed has the right to consult all documents and to be assisted by counsel. If it appears at the hearing that he has no counsel, the court will assign one *ex officio*. During the hearing the court will verify the person's identity and nationality and listen to the arguments of the public prosecutor and the person claimed as to the admissibility of extradition as well as to the question of how the Minister of Justice should decide. If the person claimed argues that he is able to show his innocence forthwith the court must investigate that matter. Witnesses and experts may be heard.

After closing of the hearing the court has to decide on a number of questions summed up in Art. 28 of the Act. It has to declare the extradition request inadmissible if the documents supplied by the requesting state do not satisfy the requirements of the relevant treaty. A second reason for declaring the request inadmissible is that it cannot be granted on the basis of the extradition treaty in combination with the Extradition Act. For instance, because double criminality is lacking, the offence is a political one, a statute of limitation applies. Finally the court must pronounce the request inadmissible if it has no doubt that the person claimed cannot possibly have committed the offence.

The last reason for declaring extradition inadmissible requires some explanation. Neither the Extradition Act nor the majority of treaties to which the Netherlands is a party require that the requesting state submit evidence showing that there is a *prima facie* case against the defendant. The Acts adopts the point of view that the authorities of the requesting state must be presumed not to request extradition without good reasons, and in this respect it follows an established practice on the European continent. However, as a safety valve it provides the courts with an opportunity to declare extradition inadmissible in exceptional cases in which the person claimed cannot possibly have committed the offence. In such cases to allow extradition would not only not serve a useful purpose but also be unfair to the person claimed. In actual practice, many persons argue that they are able to show their innocence without delay, but cases in which they succeed in convincing the court are extremely rare indeed. Case law assumes that the system of the Act does not contravene the presumption of innocence enshrined in Art. 6, para. 2, of the European Convention on Human Rights.[84] If, on the other hand, the extradition treaty requires that *prima facie* evidence be submitted courts will investigate whether the requesting state has lived up to that requirement.[85]

If the District Court declares extradition to be admissible it is its duty to give advice to the Minister of Justice as to questions which the Court is not competent to decide itself.

Against the decision of the District Court both the public prosecutor and the person claimed may appeal to the Supreme Court on points of law. Moreover, the Extradition Act also provides for an appeal 'in the interest of the law' by the procurator-general to the Supreme Court.

The judicial phase having ended the Minister of Justice has to decide on the extradition request. If the court has held extradition to be inadmissible his only option is to refuse the request. However, in the case of inadmissibility for the reason that the documents supplied by the requesting state did not satisfy the requirements of the relevant treaty, instead of denying extradition the Minister may invite the authorities of the requesting state to repair the shortcomings, after which the request will be submitted to the court again.[86]

---

84 Cf. HR 2 March 1976, NJ 1976, 415, 8 NYIL 275 (1977).
85 HR 3 April 1973, NJ 1974, 407, 6 NYIL 350 (1975); HR 16 September 1991, NJ 1992, 63.
86 Article 33, para. 3, of the Act. However, it is not unusual for courts to postpone a decision on admissibility if the documents seem to be insufficient. In so doing an opportunity is offered to the requesting state to repair shortcomings at an earlier moment.

The request having been declared admissible the Minister of Justice will have to decide whether extradition should be granted or not. As has become apparent already this decision is a more complex one, the court not having decided all the issues that may arise in a given case. Moreover, in granting extradition the Minister will sometimes have to make additional choices. Article 34 of the Extradition Act deals with plurality of extradition request and provides the Minister with some yardsticks to make a choice between requests from different states. Article 39 has regard to postponed and conditional surrender.

The Extradition Act offers the person claimed no appeal against the Minister of Justice's decision to extradite him, the reason being that a district court has already decided on admissibility and has given advice to the Minister on matters not related to admissibility. Article 8:5 of the 1992 General Act on administrative law *(Algemene wet bestuursrecht)* rules out an appeal to an administrative court. However, on the basis of what is now Art. 6:162 of the New Civil Code the person claimed may approach a district court for an injunction ordering the Government not to surrender him. In actual practice, such procedures are not uncommon and on several occasions an injunction has been granted.[87] Finally we may mention here that complaints may be raised against the Netherlands with the European Commission of Human Rights or the Human Rights Committee on the basis of the European Convention for the Protection of Human Rights and the International Covenant on Civil and Political Rights.[88]

In Arts. 41 to 45 the Extradition Act provides for a special procedure, the so-called expedited procedure, with respect to persons who do not resist extradition. Consent of the person makes the intervention of a district court superfluous. Moreover, it is not the Minister of Justice but the public prosecutor who, in this case, decides on the extradition request.

According to Art. 41 a person may, up to the day before the extradition request would have been dealt with at a court hearing, declare that he consents to being extradited. Unless provided for otherwise by treaty, he will have to

---

87 The most important example is provided by the *Short* case, discussed above. For an example of denial of an injunction see Rechtbank Den Haag 2 December 1986, KG 1987, 547, 19 NYIL 470-474 (1988) *(Kelly and McFarlane)*.

88 E.g. see European Commission 6 July 1976 (7512/76, *Pauksch*), 6 Decisions and Reports 184-186 (1977); 15 December 1977 (8088/77, *Gallagher*), NJ 1978, 381; 14 July 1982 (9058/80, *Leenaert*), RV 1982, 119; 7 October 1986 (9573/81, *Widmaier*), 48 Decisions and Reports 14-20 (1986); 2 December 1986 (12543/86, *Kelly* and *McFarlane*), 51 Decisions and Reports 272-282 (1987).

make his declaration before an examining magistrate. The magistrate is obliged to explain the consequences of his choice to him. Counsel has a right to be present; the person must be informed of his right to be assisted by counsel.

The person having consented it is for the public prosecutor to decide whether extradition should be granted. He may not do so if, on the basis of the extradition treaty, the person could not have been extradited. Moreover, the public prosecutor must check whether the person still has to serve a sentence in the Netherlands and whether criminal proceedings are pending against him. The main consequence of consent is that Art. 12 of the Act no longer applies. The requesting state, therefore, is free to prosecute or punish the person for other offences than the one or the ones for which extradition has been granted.

In enabling the authorities to deprive the person claimed of his liberty during extradition proceedings the Extradition Act distinguishes between deprivation of liberty before and after the receipt of a formal extradition request. Provisional arrest before a formal request is permitted only in so far as provided for by treaty and only at the request of the competent foreign authorities.[89] The total duration of custody before receipt of an extradition request may not exceed twenty-five days unless provided for otherwise by treaty. Custody after receipt of the extradition request may, of course, take much longer. It is decided upon by the district court dealing with the request and re-examined every thirty days. The Act does not make custody compulsory. It is for the competent authorities to decide whether deprivation of liberty is necessary with a view to ensuring surrender. They may conditionally suspend custody. According to Art. 59 of the Act, the person claimed may recover damages suffered as a consequence of custody if the case has ended in a final verdict of a court declaring extradition inadmissible. Some other damages or expenses may also be compensated for on the basis of that Article.

Handing over of property and transit

Articles 46 and 47 of the Extradition Act allow for the seizure of property found in the possession of the person claimed at the request of the foreign authorities. The decision to hand it over to these authorities lies with the district court which has to decide on the extradition request. It may order that certain

---

89 An exception to the latter requirement is made in Art. 13a of the Act, implementing Art. 41, para. 6, of the Convention applying the Schengen Agreement.

objects be delivered only on the condition that they will be returned immediately after they have been used for the purpose the requesting state needed them. Property cannot be handed over to the requesting state if extradition of the person claimed is not granted.[90]

The provisions in the Extradition Act with regard to transit are rather complicated. Articles 48 to 50 of the Act distinguish between four different situations. Generally, transit may only take place pursuant to a consent of the Minister of Justice. That consent, however, need not be given for transit by air during which no landing is made on Dutch territory. Transit by land may only be consented to on the basis of a treaty. Finally, in the case of an unforeseen landing of an airplane consent must be requested as soon as possible after landing. In all cases requiring consent, the Minister must refuse it if Arts. 8 to 11 of the Extradition Act would have made extradition of the person impossible.

Extradition to the Netherlands

The Extradition Act only governs extradition by the Netherlands and contains no rules relating to extradition to the country. A number of provisions of the Penal Code and the Code of Criminal Procedure are relevant here.

The initiative to request extradition will normally be taken by the public prosecutor who is dealing with the criminal case. His proposal is forwarded to the Minister of Justice and, if need be, to the Minister for Foreign Affairs, depending on the extradition treaty in force, and sent to the competent authorities of the requested state. Article 66, para. 2, of the Code of Criminal Procedure empowers the District Court to order detention on remand of the suspect in order to obtain his extradition from another state. However, this provision is rarely used, most extradition treaties no longer requiring that a court of the requesting state has ordered that the suspect be detained. In most cases, therefore, a detention order issued by the public prosecutor on the basis of Arts. 57 and 58 of the Code of Criminal Procedure suffices. Article 216 of the Code contains a provision that is relevant in the case of an extradition treaty requiring the requesting state to submit evidence justifying the person's

---

90 However, case law assumes that the objects seized may be handed over to the requesting state on the basis of a treaty on mutual assistance in criminal matters between that state and the Netherlands. Cf. HR 18 June 1991, DD 91.357.

committal for trial. Article 216 empowers the examining magistrate to take sworn statements from witnesses for the purpose of collecting the evidence.

Extradition having been obtained from the requested state the extraditee may, according to established case law, invoke the speciality provision of the relevant treaty.[91] Article 27 of the Penal Code obliges the courts to deduct any period of detention applied to the extraditee in the requested state as a consequence of an extradition request from the sentence that the court might impose. If a person has already been convicted Art. 27 a of the Code obliges the competent authorities to deduct that period from a sentence that has already been imposed. Moreover, according to Art. 15 of the Penal Code, detention for the purpose of extradition to the Netherlands is relevant to the determination of the date of early release from prison. Finally, Art. 89 of the Code of Criminal Procedure offers the extraditee the possibility of requesting financial compensation for detention on the basis of an extradition request if the case ends with no punishment being imposed on him.

There is hardly any case law on the consequences of disguised extradition to the Netherlands and of other irregular methods of getting hold of persons, the courts having had to face such issues very rarely.[92]

---

91 HR 28 June 1960, NJ 1960, 566; HR 27 September 1983, NJ 1984, 96.
92 For a discussion see *Swart*, RIDP 65 (1994), pp. 397-398.

Mutual Assistance in Criminal Matters

Rijnhard Haentjens

The concept of assistance

The internationalization of criminal justice has made national police and judicial authorities increasingly dependent on international cooperation. A dense network of treaties links the Netherlands with other states. Most of these treaties deal with one form of cooperation only. They provide a basis for extradition, mutual assistance in criminal matters, transfer of criminal proceedings or transfer of the execution of criminal sentences. Others, such as the 1988 Vienna Convention against Illicit Traffic in Narcotic Drugs and Psychotropic Substances, while limiting themselves to specific offences, deal with all forms of cooperation within one single framework.

Mutual assistance, sometimes also called minor assistance, may play a special role in international cooperation since the applicable rules are relatively free of formality, both under international treaties and under national legislative schemes. The protection of individual rights, as well as the assurance of fairness in criminal proceedings, however, must not be compromised by the flexibility of the rules.

It is typical for mutual assistance that the requested state bears no responsibility for the way the requesting state makes use of the results obtained. This is different from transfer of proceedings and transfer of the enforcement of criminal judgments. Here, the requested state becomes responsible for what is being asked: the prosecution of a criminal case or the enforcement of a sentence. On the other hand, mutual assistance is different from extradition in that is does not involve the surrender of individual persons to the authorities of the requesting state. Transfer of suspects or witnesses for the purposes of questioning or confrontation as a form of mutual assistance occurs on a temporary basis only.

Rules of mutual assistance consist of legal norms which apply in cases when one state (the requested state) at the request of another state (the requesting

state) or, more rarely, on its own initiative, offers assistance in the investigation, prosecution and adjudication of a criminal offence by the requesting state.
It may also consist in rendering assistance in other proceedings in criminal
matters.

Following the language of the 1959 European Convention on Mutual
Assistance in Criminal Matters Art. 552h of the 1921 Code of Criminal
Procedure *(Wetboek van Strafvordering)* defines mutual assistance as assistance
'in connection with' criminal proceedings. Obviously, the provision is concerned with acts of assistance which may help another state in investigating,
prosecuting and adjudicating a criminal case. But it has a broader meaning. It
also covers such forms of assistance as are mentioned, for instance, in Art. 3
of the 1978 Additional Protocol to the European Convention and in Art. 49 of
the 1990 Convention applying the Schengen Agreement. As examples we may
mention here proceedings for compensation in respect of unjustified detention
on remand, proceedings involving requests for pardon, the service of documents
concerning the enforcement of a sentence, the recovery of a fine or the payment
of costs of proceedings, measures relating to the suspension of pronouncement
of a sentence or of its enforcement, or to conditional release.[1] One may also
think of assistance in the identification and tracing of instrumentalities,
proceeds and other property liable to confiscation, although most forms of
assistance in this field are not governed by Art. 552h of the Code of Criminal
Procedure but by the 1986 Act on the transfer of enforcement of criminal judgments *(Wet overdracht tenuitvoerlegging strafvonnissen)*.

However wide a definition of mutual assistance in criminal matters may be,
it will normally exclude assistance in civil and administrative matters. We must
mention one exception though. Some international treaties, such as the Convention applying the Schengen Agreement and the 1979 Agreement between
Germany and the Netherlands to supplement and facilitate the application of the
European Convention on Mutual Assistance in Criminal Matters, create an
obligation to render assistance where the imposition of administrative penalties
by administrative authorities is concerned. For the purpose of Art. 552h of the
Code of Criminal Procedure assistance requested on the basis of these treaties
has to be equated with assistance in criminal matters.[2]

---

1   Cf. *Haentjens*, Schets van het Nederlandse kleine rechtshulprecht in strafzaken, pp. 85-86;
    Sjöcrona, De kleine rechtshulp, pp. 83-86.
2   Cf. *Sjöcrona* (supra note 2), pp. 81-82.

The provisions in the Code of Criminal Procedure on mutual assistance in criminal matters are concerned with requests for assistance made by the authorities of a foreign state. This limits their scope in several respects.

In including the request of a foreign state as an element of the definition of mutual assistance Art. 552h of the Code of Criminal Procedure rules out the rendering of assistance without request. However, provisions in other statutes do allow the Dutch authorities to render assistance spontaneously or automatically.

Secondly, Art. 552h of the Code excludes the rendering of assistance to entities other than states. International organizations such as the United Nations or the European Communities cannot be considered states within the meaning of the provision. Cooperation with the institutions of the European Communities in repressing infringements of Community law takes place on the basis of special regulations. Assistance to the International Tribunal for the prosecution of persons responsible for serious violations of international humanitarian law committed in the former Yugoslavia since 1991 is regulated by a special statute.[3] Also outside the scope of Art. 552h is cooperation in criminal matters between the three parts of the Kingdom of the Netherlands.[4]

Finally, the language of Art. 552h makes clear that mutual assistance is conceived as a transaction between authorities. The provision precludes requests from individual persons. Specific rights have been granted to suspects, witnesses and other persons in various provisions of the Code but the right to initiate proceedings for assistance is not among them.

In this part of the book we will first look at the sources of Dutch law relating to mutual assistance in criminal matters. We will then discuss procedures for dealing with foreign requests for assistance and the forms assistance may take. After reviewing grounds for refusal and conditions attached to the granting of assistance we will pay attention to assistance to the Netherlands.

Our discussion of mutual assistance will not cover all aspects and forms of cooperation. Given its growing importance international cooperation between police authorities is discussed in a separate contribution to the book. Assistance with a view to confiscating proceeds from crime in the Netherlands at the request of another state is better discussed within the framework of transfer of enforcement of criminal judgments, since in Dutch law it is governed by the Act on the transfer of enforcement of criminal judgments. Finally, another

---

3   Act of 21 April 1994, *Staatsblad* 308. See also Appendix I pp. 315-318.
4   Cf. HR 12 June 1990, NJ 1991, 236. See also supra pp. 3-4.

author deals with mutual assistance relating to fiscal offences and its links with administrative cooperation in tax matters. We will, therefore, focus mainly on what has been the traditional core of mutual assistance between civil law countries: forms of cooperation between judicial authorities, i.e. between courts and public prosecutors.

Sources of the law

The most important multilateral treaties on mutual assistance in criminal matters to which the Netherlands is a party are:
– the European Convention on Mutual Assistance in Criminal Matters (Strasbourg 1959) and its Additional Protocol (Strasbourg 1978);
– the Additional Protocol to the European Convention on Information on Foreign Law (Strasbourg 1978);
– the Benelux Treaty on Extradition and Mutual Assistance in Criminal Matters (Brussels 1962);
– the Benelux Convention on cooperation between administrative and judicial authorities in matters pertaining to the Benelux Economic Union (The Hague 1969);
– the Convention applying the Schengen Agreement (Schengen 1990);
– the NATO Status of Forces Agreement (London 1951).
Other, more recent treaties containing provisions in the field of mutual assistance include the Convention on Laundering, Search, Seizure and Confiscation of the Proceeds from Crime (Strasbourg 1990) and the United Nations Convention against Illicit Traffic in Narcotic Drugs and Psychotropic Drugs (Vienna 1988).

In addition to these multilateral conventions, the Netherlands is also a party to a number of bilateral treaties which may be of special relevance in practice:
– the Agreement between the Kingdom of the Netherlands and the Republic of Suriname on Extradition and Mutual Assistance in Criminal Matters (The Hague 1976) and its Protocol (The Hague 1993);
– the Agreement between the Kingdom of the Netherlands and the Federal Republic of Germany to Supplement and to Facilitate the Application of the European Treaty on Mutual Assistance in Criminal Matters, known as the Wittem Agreement (Wittem 1979);
– the Treaty between the Kingdom of the Netherlands and the United States on Mutual Assistance in Criminal Matters (The Hague 1981);

- the Treaty between the Kingdom of the Netherlands and Australia on Mutual Assistance in Criminal Matters (Canberra 1988);
- the Treaty between the Kingdom of the Netherlands and Canada on Mutual Assistance in Criminal Matters (The Hague 1991);
- the Agreement between the Government of the Kingdom of the Netherlands and the United States of America regarding mutual cooperation in the tracing, freezing, seizure and forfeiture of proceeds and instrumentalities of crime and the sharing of forfeited assets (Washington 1992);
- the Agreement between the Kingdom of the Netherlands and the United Kingdom to supplement and facilitate the Operation of the Convention of the Council of Europe on Laundering, Search, Seizure and Confiscation of the Proceeds from Crime (London 1993).

Turning our attention to domestic law we note that the most important statute in the matter is the Code of Criminal Procedure. Articles 552h to 552q of the Code contain a number of detailed provisions on the rendering of mutual assistance to other states. They were introduced in the Code in 1967, on the occasion of the ratification by the Netherlands of the European Convention on Mutual Assistance in Criminal Matters and the Benelux Treaty on Extradition and Mutual Assistance in Criminal Matters. Their content is largely inspired by the two conventions. Articles 552h to 552q also provide a basis for rendering assistance pursuant to other treaties. Moreover, they enable the Dutch authorities to render assistance without a treaty basis, although, as will be seen below, possibilities are more limited here.

In addition to the Code of Criminal Procedure we must mention other statutes regulating the rendering of assistance in specific areas. The 1967 Extradition Act *(Uitleveringswet)* contains provisions on the temporary transfer of suspects and witnesses as well as on the seizure of property within the framework of extradition proceedings. The 1955 Judicial Records Act *(Wet op de justitiële documentatie)* allows the communication of data from judicial records to foreign judicial authorities. Of ever growing importance is the 1990 Police Files Act *(Wet politieregisters)*, providing a new legal basis for the exchange of information contained in police data bases to foreign police authorities. Mention must also be made of the 1988 Act on the transfer of enforcement of criminal judgments. Its provisions enable the Dutch authorities to carry out investigations and take provisional measures at the request of another state with a view to confiscating instrumentalities and proceeds from crime. Finally, there is the 1953 Act implementing the NATO Status of Forces Agreement.

Statutes and treaties form a complex system for rendering mutual assistance in criminal matters to other states. We have noted already that Dutch legislation does not require the existence of a treaty as a general precondition for rendering assistance. In this respect the legal situation is different from extradition and transfer of the enforcement of criminal judgments. Both the Extradition Act and the Act on the transfer of enforcement of criminal judgments rule out cooperation without a treaty basis completely. However, this is not to say that the treaty requirement is of no importance at all where mutual assistance in criminal matters is concerned. No less than three provisions in the Code of Criminal Procedure require the existence of a treaty. Their cumulative effect is that assistance outside the framework of a treaty may be rendered only if collecting evidence or information does not require the application of provisional measures or only with the voluntary cooperation of a person involved. Likewise, the Extradition Act allows the temporary transfer of suspects and witnesses pursuant to a treaty only. Finally, the Act on the transfer of enforcement of criminal judgments does not enable the Dutch authorities to carry out investigations and take provisional measures without a treaty basis. On the other hand, neither the Judicial Records Act nor the Police Files Act contains a similar requirement.

Procedures for dealing with foreign requests

The provisions of the Code of Criminal Procedure and those of other statutes hardly contain any rules on the form and content of requests for assistance, on the foreign authorities which are deemed competent to make requests or on the authorities competent to receive their requests. They are primarily concerned with the entirely different question of who is competent to decide on requests. In stating that requests for assistance are to be addressed to a judicial or police authority in the Netherlands, whether indicated by name or not, Art. 552h merely assumes the existence of rules with respect to the communication and content of requests that have to be observed by the foreign authorities.

Therefore, the answer to the question of how requests for assistance should be transmitted and what requirements apply as to their form and content has to be found primarily in treaties to which the Netherlands is a party. While very few treaties still require the diplomatic channels to be followed, a majority of them require that, as a rule, requests are communicated from ministry of justice to ministry of justice. The European Convention on Mutual Assistance in Criminal Matters is the most important example. However, treaties usually have provisions allowing the use of more direct ways of communication in cases of urgency. In more recent treaties direct communication between the competent authorities is the rule rather than the exception. As an example we may mention Art. 53 of the Convention applying the Schengen Agreement. Where direct communication is accepted, frequently use can be made of Interpol's services. All treaties seem to assume that requests are made in writing but they frequently permit more direct and rapid contacts in advance of formal requests.

As a matter of course Dutch authorities will check whether all applicable rules have been observed by the requesting state.[5] Courts, however, show little inclination to give a broad interpretation to treaty requirements with respect to the form and content of requests.[6] They also refrain from passing judgment on the question of whether the request was an urgent one.[7] Where provisions of different treaties to which the requesting state is a party seem to contradict each other they will choose an interpretation which benefits efficiency most.[8]

The Code of Criminal Procedure accords a central role to the public prosecutor in the handling of requests for assistance. As a general rule, Art. 552i, para. 1, of the Code requires all other public authorities who may have received requests to forward them to the public prosecutor in the district in which the request is to be dealt with. Article 552j makes that prosecutor competent to decide on the action to be taken on the request.

The basic choice facing the public prosecutor is whether he will dismiss a request for assistance or decide that it should be complied with. Several provisions in the Code limit his discretion in making choices. The first is Art. 552k. It requires the public prosecutor to make every effort to comply with requests for assistance where a treaty carries the unconditional obligation to do so. In cases in which a treaty leaves discretion to the requested party whether or not it will satisfy a request, as well as in cases in which a request is not based on a treaty, the prosecutor may honour the request if he considers it to be a reasonable one. However, he must refuse it if compliance would contravene Dutch law or would be contrary to instructions from the Minister of Justice. Moreover, in making his decision the public prosecutor must observe the mandatory grounds for refusal listed in Art. 552l of the Code. Article 552m, on the other hand, requires him to obtain prior authorization from the Minister of Justice before granting requests that involve political or fiscal

---

5 Cf. e.g. HR 7 October 1980, DD 81.015.
6 HR 12 June 1984, NJ 1985, 173; HR 26 June 1990, NJ 1991, 359; HR 14 September 1993, DD 94.105.
7 HR 12 June 1984, NJ 1985, 174.
8 HR 11 October 1994, NJ 1996, 409.

offences. In making a decision the public prosecutor may, of course, also take into account grounds for refusal which are not contained in the Code but mentioned in the applicable treaty.

Having decided that a request for assistance should be complied with the public prosecutor is responsible for its execution. Here, Art. 552n of the Code distinguishes between two categories of requests. On the one hand there are requests that cannot be complied with without the cooperation of an examining magistrate. On the other hand, there are those which the public prosecutor may satisfy himself or charge other public officials to satisfy without interference of a court. The distinction is a fundamental one and we will have to look at it in more detail later. Suffice it to say here that it makes the examining magistrate the only authority competent to apply various measures of coercion for the purpose of complying with requests for assistance. Other authorities have not been empowered to do so, not even to use the powers of coercion which the law grants them in domestic criminal cases.

Although the public prosecutor has been made the central authority responsible for handling requests for assistance it would be wrong to assume that all requests have to be submitted to him. Actually, in a large majority of cases there is no need to do so at all. Article 552i of the Code of Criminal Procedure has always allowed other public officials to deal with requests for assistance on their own authority. Recently, on the occasion of the ratification of the Convention applying the Schengen Agreement in 1993, their competence to do so has even been enlarged. Para. 2 of Art. 552i now enables them to satisfy all requests for assistance provided that their sole aim is to obtain information and that no coercive measures are needed to collect that information; in other words, information which is already in their possession or is easily acquired.

The recent change of the Code illustrates the rapidly growing importance of police authorities in the field of mutual assistance and their emancipation from the tutelage of the Public Prosecutions Department. Parallel to that development is a tendency to replace informal modes of police cooperation by a set of written rules which aim at structuring and regulating their activities.

The second paragraph of Art. 552i does not itself indicate the authorities competent to deal with requests for information. The answer to that question has to be found in other parts of legislation as well as in instructions or circular letters. For instance, requests for information on legal matters on the basis of the Protocol to the European Convention on Information on Foreign Law or on the basis of other treaties will normally be handled by the Ministry of Justice, and requests for information concerning judicial records by the Judicial Records Service. Of major importance here are the 1990 Police Files Act and the 1991

Police Files Decree, which govern the exchange of information between the regular Dutch police authorities and those of other countries. We may also mention here the Guideline on the application of Art. 552i of the Code, issued by the heads of the Public Prosecutions Department to the police authorities in 1994.[9]

Paragraph 3 of Art. 552i requires all authorities involved in supplying information on request to keep record of their activities. Records must contain basic information on requests as well as on the response that has been given to them. Paragraph 4 of the same Article obliges them to comply with general and specific instructions for handling requests that have been issued by the public prosecutor. This provision constitutes the legal basis of the Guideline we just mentioned. Its content will be discussed in another contribution to this book.[10] It goes without saying that all authorities handling requests for information have to observe the same conditions and restrictions which apply to the activities of the public prosecutor himself. Articles 552k, 552l and 552m also apply to them.

As we have noted already, some requests for assistance require the public prosecutor to obtain the cooperation of an examining magistrate. Article 552n of the Code of Criminal Procedure makes it necessary for him to do so if:
– a person has to be examined and that person is unwilling to appear or to make a declaration;
– the requesting state has made it known that it wants to obtain a sworn statement or a statement made before a court;
– it is necessary to enter private premises without the consent of the inhabitant or to seize objects in order to comply with a request;
– the interception of telecommunications has been requested.
In other cases the public prosecutor may approach the examining magistrate as he thinks fit. For instance, he may do so if he anticipates that a sworn statement will be of special value to the requesting state.[11] All requests have to satisfy two conditions. They must have been made by judicial authorities of the requesting state. Moreover, they must have a treaty between that state and the Netherlands as their basis. The second condition, of course, considerably restricts the possibilities for granting assistance in certain types of cases.

---

9   *Staatscourant* 1994, 242.
10 See infra p. 152.
11 *Sjöcrona* (supra note 2), p. 232.

Once he has granted a written request of the public prosecutor, it is the examining magistrate who is in charge of performing all that is necessary in order to satisfy the foreign state's request for assistance. Article 552o of the Code of Criminal Procedure requires him to proceed as if he were conducting a preliminary judicial examination in a domestic case. For instance, a suspect must be informed of his right to remain silent during interrogations and may have the assistance of counsel. A witness may invoke testimonial privileges accorded to him by Dutch law. The examining magistrate may apply coercive measures as he deems necessary, although his powers to do so are in a number of respects more limited than in domestic cases. This is especially true where seizure of property is concerned. We will pay more attention to these restrictions when discussing the various forms of assistance in the next section.

After having performed his functions the examining magistrate returns the request for assistance to the public prosecutor, together with the recorded statements of persons who have been examined and a report of his activities. However, matters are more complicated where property seized and information obtained by intercepting telecommunications are concerned. Here, Art. 552p of the Code requires the examining magistrate to obtain prior authorization from the district court before handing over the evidence to the public prosecutor. In the ensuing proceedings before the district court interested parties have a right to be heard and to oppose the forwarding of property seized to the requesting state. The court must satisfy itself that all requirements for rendering assistance have been met. It may attach certain conditions to the use of evidence by that state. They will be discussed at the end of this chapter.

For the public prosecutor and the interested parties, appeal lies open to the Supreme Court. In the event the Supreme Court quashes the decision of the district court, it refers the case to a court of appeal. Pending proceedings, evidence may not be forwarded to the requesting state.[12] Thus, the whole process of rendering assistance may become time-consuming indeed. The system adopted hardly squares with the idea that international assistance should be granted as easily and quickly as possible. On the other hand, it does offer adequate legal protection to the suspect and to third parties.

From the foregoing discussion of Dutch law the conclusion may be drawn that requests for assistance can be settled quickly if the following conditions are met: the applicable treaty provides for direct contact between the competent

---

12 HR 12 June 1984, NJ 1985, 175.

authorities, there is no need to involve an examining magistrate in the matter, and there are no grounds for refusal. To a considerable extent the same is true for requests which are not based on a treaty. Surely the quickest form of cooperation is that between police authorities who know each other well and may act upon their own authority in rendering assistance. In other cases satisfying requests may take considerable time. Foreign authorities are well advised to take this into account when considering making a request.

Forms of assistance

Many treaties on mutual assistance in criminal matters to which the Netherlands is a party contain loose and broad definitions of what assistance may consist of. Thus, for instance, Art. 1 of the European Convention creates the obligation to afford 'the widest measure of mutual assistance'. Article 1 of the bilateral treaty between the Netherlands and the United States sums up different forms of assistance but declares that assistance shall not be limited to them. Usually, treaties contain more elaborate and detailed provisions with respect to the most important specific forms of assistance.

The provisions of the Code of Criminal Procedure on mutual assistance take the same approach. This is not surprising since one of their aims was to implement the European Convention on Mutual Assistance in Criminal Matters and the Benelux Treaty on Extradition and Mutual Assistance in Criminal Matters. Borrowing from the language of the European Convention Art. 552h, para. 2, lists the various forms assistance may take. They include the conducting of investigations for the purpose of gathering evidence as well as the lending of assistance in such investigations on the one hand, and the providing of records, documents and other pieces of evidence as well as the transmission of information on the other; in other words, the execution of letters rogatory. To them the paragraph adds the service and issuance of a variety of documents. Although the enumeration covers a broad range of acts, not all forms of assistance are included. The transfer of persons for evidentiary purposes and the taking of provisional measures for the purpose of confiscating proceeds from crime are governed by the Extradition Act and the Act on the transfer of enforcement of criminal judgments.

As a matter of course letters rogatory will be executed in the manner provided for by Dutch law. However, this does not prevent the authorities from taking the laws of the requesting state into account when performing their duties. There is no provision in the Code or in any other statute forbidding them to do so. One may even argue that this would be perfectly in line with

Art. 552k of the Code, requiring that every effort be made to comply with treaty-based requests.[13] Some bilateral mutual assistance treaties, for example the ones with the United States and Canada, provide for an obligation to follow procedures specified by the requesting state. Of course, applying foreign law is not permitted when it would actually conflict with domestic law.

The first form of assistance mentioned by Art. 552h consists of carrying out investigations for the purpose of gathering evidence. Some forms of investigations are regulated in more detail: taking testimony of persons, search and seizure, intercepting telecommunications.

As we have seen already, the use of coercive measures for the purpose of gathering evidence and information is in the sole hands of the examining magistrate. In itself this does not rule out all investigative activities by other authorities. For example, they may be able to gather evidence or information with the voluntary cooperation of a suspect or a third person. Or they may carry out investigations without any interference with individual rights. Ascertaining the location of a person, examining sites and conducting a technical analysis are but some examples of what can be done.

Article 552h of the Code raises the important question of whether foreign authorities may be present during investigations and take part in them or, for that matter, conduct their own investigations.[14] Neither Art. 552h nor any other provision in the Code of Criminal Procedure rules out the presence of foreign authorities. Whether and to what extent they may actively participate in investigations is less obvious and seems to depend on the circumstances, it being clear, however, that the competent Dutch authorities remain in charge. Since, apart from being the head of investigations in domestic cases, the public prosecutor is the central authority in dealing with requests for assistance, in most cases his consent will be required. A number of mutual assistance treaties explicitly state that authorities of the requesting state have a right to be present during investigations. The matter is discussed in more detail elsewhere.[15]

One of the most important forms of investigation is the taking of testimony or statements of persons. As we have seen in the previous paragraph, the power to examine suspects, witnesses and experts is, in principle, reserved to the

---

13 Cf. *Klip*, Buitenlandse getuigen in strafzaken, p. 205.
14 Cf. *Haentjens* (supra note 2), pp. 98-99; *Sjöcrona* (supra note 2), pp. 93-100.
15 See infra pp. 164-165, 218-219.

examining magistrate. In proceedings he may make use of the powers granted to him in conducting a preliminary judicial inquiry in domestic cases.

Suspects may be compelled to appear before the magistrate. They have a right to remain silent and must be advised of that right. They may be assisted by counsel during interrogations. The examining magistrate may confront them with other persons.

Witnesses and experts must appear before the examining magistrate and must answer questions truthfully. Committing perjury is a crime under Dutch law. The witness may invoke testimonial privileges accorded to him by Dutch law in domestic cases. Counsel for the accused has a right to be present and to forward questions. However, the examining magistrate may limit these rights in order to protect a witness from violence or intimidation. As a rule, all questioning is done by the magistrate himself. However, there no longer seem to be strong objections against having an interrogation in the form of a cross examination. Cross examination is made possible in the recent bilateral assistance treaties with the United States, Australia and Canada. The bilateral agreement between the Netherlands and Germany supplementing the European Convention on Mutual Assistance in Criminal Matters also confers upon the parties to the case the right to be present.

Another way of assisting the requesting state in obtaining testimony or statements of persons is their temporary transfer to the requesting state. Article 51 of the Extradition Act allows the transfer of persons who are being detained in the Netherlands for the purposes of testifying as a witness or of confrontation; some treaties allow their transfer also for other purposes. Transfer may only be effected on the basis of a treaty. Consent of the person is needed unless otherwise provided in the applicable treaty; so far, the Benelux Treaty on Extradition and Mutual Assistance in Criminal Matters is the only treaty allowing transfer without consent. Articles 9 and 10 of the Extradition Act apply. Transfer, therefore, has to be refused if the case has been or is being tried in the Netherlands, if it would expose the person to discriminatory treatment or would present special hardship to him. Article 50a of the Extradition Act allows the transfer of detained persons from a foreign state to the Netherlands. Here, the requirements of treaty and consent do not apply.

The providing of records, documents and other pieces of evidence as well as the exchange of information will normally be effected by the authorities who are in possession of them or in the best position to obtain them. The handing over of items included in files *(dossier)* of a criminal case requires prior authorization by the competent public prosecutor. Special rules apply to the seizure of documents and other objects in the possession of third persons, which will be discussed below.

A number of special statutes govern the providing of information. We have already mentioned the Judicial Records Act and the Police Files Act. We may add here the general 1988 Data Protection Act *(Wet persoonsregistraties)* which applies to the providing of computerized information to the authorities of foreign states by authorities other than the regular police. As an example we may mention the Fiscal Intelligence and Investigation Department.[16] While Art. 552h of the Code of Criminal Procedure assumes that information is provided on request only, these statutes also allow the spontaneous or automatic exchange of data.

A few rules on the service of documents on behalf of the requesting state are to be found in Art. 552q of the Code of Criminal Procedure. Its scope is wide. Documents may include summonses to appear before an authority of the requesting state, judicial verdicts and proposals for settling cases out of court, notices to third parties informing them of their rights or of current developments in proceedings in the requesting state.

As far as summonses to appear are concerned, Dutch law follows the international practice of not attaching legal consequences to a refusal of a witness to appear before an authority of the requesting state. A person who refuses to appear commits no offence under Dutch law and cannot be compelled by the Dutch authorities to comply with a summons. The notable exception here is Art. 34 of the Benelux Treaty on Extradition and Mutual Assistance in Criminal Matters, implemented by Art. 192 of the Penal Code.

Service of judicial decisions does not imply any involvement in enforcing them. It is strictly limited to notifying a person of the decision and handing over a copy of it. The same is true for e.g. official documents relating to settlements out of court or the revocation of conditional sentences. Enforcing foreign judgments is a matter governed by the Act on the transfer of enforcement of criminal judgments.

The service of documents is effected in accordance with Dutch law. However, if the requesting state so wishes, there is no objection against notifying persons in the way preferred by that state. Article 552q specifically requires the Dutch authorities to transmit a document to the addressee in person if the requesting state so desires. It is hardly likely that to comply with requests of the requesting state would ever contravene Dutch law.

---

16 See infra pp. 233, 246.

Article 552q of the Code does not envisage the possibility that a foreign state addresses procedural documents directly by post to persons who are staying in the Netherlands. However, some treaties enable the contracting parties to do so. The most important examples are the Benelux Treaty and the Convention applying the Schengen Agreement.

The use of coercive measures, or rather measures that infringe upon individual rights, for the purpose of satisfying requests for assistance is subject to considerable restrictions. We have mentioned already that they may be applied only if the request is based on a treaty and only by an examining magistrate. To these restrictions we must now add a third. From Art. 552o, para. 3, it follows that only those measures may be applied which are necessary to comply with requests which have to be submitted to the magistrate on the basis of Art. 552n. For instance, while in domestic cases the magistrate may order an examination of the suspect's body or mental faculties or the taking of body material for the purpose of analysis, Art. 552o does not permit him to do so since this would go beyond what may be required in order to take testimony or statements of a person. However, para. 3 of Art. 552o leaves open the possibility that a treaty provides otherwise.

Paragraph 2 of Art. 552o deals with search and seizure. It requires that the offence motivating the request is punishable under Dutch law and that the execution of the request is consistent with it.[17] Moreover, property may be seized for evidentiary purposes only.[18] Seizure for the purpose of confiscation is, however, made possible in the Act on the transfer of enforcement of criminal judgments.

Finally, Art. 552o, para. 2, imposes yet another restriction upon seizing property for evidentiary purposes. According to that provision, the offence motivating the request, apart from being punishable under Dutch law, must also be an extraditable offence. Whether the offence is an extraditable one has to be determined according to the extradition treaty with the requesting state.[19] Consequently, if no extradition treaty is in force between the requesting state and the Netherlands seizure is never possible. And in the case of an extradition treaty, its terms will determine whether or not the offence is an extraditable one and, therefore, property can be seized. Thus, it may occur that seizure is not

---

17 The same requirements would also have applied to intercepting telecommunications had not serious technical mistakes been made during the legislating process. For an explanation see Appendix I p. 259.

18 HR 12 June 1984, NJ 1985, 173. Cf. also *Haentjens*, DD 15 (1985), p. 741.

19 Cf. *Haentjens* (supra note 2), p. 96; *Sjöcrona* (supra note 2), p. 263.

permitted because the offence is a political, military or fiscal offence for which the extradition treaty rules out extradition.[20] Immunity by lapse of time and nationality of the offender, on the other hand, do not matter here.[21] One may conclude that para. 2 of Art. 552o, modelled after Art. 5 of the European Convention on Mutual Assistance in Criminal Matters, makes seizure of property rather difficult. However, more liberal rules may have been adopted in a number of mutual assistance treaties to which the Netherlands is a party, and the third paragraph of Art. 552o refers to that possibility. The most important treaty here is the Convention applying the Schengen Agreement. Another example is provided by the mutual assistance treaty between the Netherlands and the United States.

Grounds for refusal and conditions

In recent years, concern for efficient cooperation in criminal matters has led to a reduction of formalities in applying for and in rendering assistance as well as to an expansion of the forms which assistance may take. The tendency to facilitate cooperation as much as possible reveals itself also in the limitation of grounds for refusal in the Code.

Compared to the Extradition Act the Code of Criminal Procedure shows considerable restraint indeed in introducing grounds for refusal. That the provisions on mutual assistance aim at providing the widest measure of assistance is, for instance, apparent from the fact that double criminality is no general requirement for rendering it. Nor do they, as a rule, distinguish between serious offences and other offences. There is no exception at all for military offences.[22] Assistance in the case of political and fiscal offences is not ruled out completely but subject to certain restrictions only. There are no grounds for refusal related to the nationality of the offender nor to the kind of punishment which can be imposed for the offence. The most important barrier for rendering assistance is the treaty requirement. Although the existence of a treaty is no general requirement for rendering assistance, the distinction between treaty-based requests and other requests is an important one in several respects.

The grounds for refusing assistance in Dutch legislation are more limited in number and scope than those contained in most mutual assistance treaties.

---

20 HR 4 February 1986, NJ 1986, 672, 20 NYIL 344-346 (1989), a case involving fiscal offences.
21 HR 26 June 1990, NJ 1991, 359, and, probably, HR 24 June 1990, NJ 1991, 57.
22 However, mutual assistance in such cases will usually be granted on the basis of the 1953 Act implementing the NATO Status of Forces Agreement.

There is, for instance, no provision similar to Art. 2 of the European Convention on Mutual Assistance in Criminal Matters, allowing the requested state to refuse help if it considers that execution of the request is likely to prejudice the sovereignty, security, *ordre public* or other essential interests of its country.[23] Of course, the Code of Criminal Procedure does not prevent the Dutch authorities from invoking grounds for refusal which are contained in treaties but not in domestic legislation. Absence of double criminality might, for instance, lead to refusal of assistance in specific cases if to render it would run counter to basic values protected by Dutch law. Similarly, the competent authorities might show special caution in rendering assistance in cases involving the possibility of a death penalty.[24] Broad exception clauses like the one in the European Convention on Mutual Assistance may also enable the authorities to verify whether rendering assistance would run counter to the obligations arising out of the European Convention on the Protection of Human Rights and Fundamental Freedoms or other human rights treaties for the Netherlands.[25]

Special rules apply to requests for assistance concerning political and fiscal offences. Article 552m of the Code of Criminal Procedure is applicable here.

According to the first paragraph of Art. 552m, rendering assistance for political offences and offences connected with political offences is allowed only if the request is based on a treaty. Moreover, assistance may not be granted without prior authorization of the Minister of Justice. The Minister of Justice must consult the Minister for Foreign Affairs before granting authorization. The decision whether or not to grant assistance has to be communicated to the requesting state by diplomatic channels. The provision does not define political offences. In determining whether an offence constitutes a political offence or an offence connected therewith one has to consult Art. 11 of the Extradition Act and case law concerning that provision.[26] According to the second paragraph, there is no need for obtaining prior authorization nor for using diplomatic channels in the case of requests based on the European Convention on the Suppression of Terrorism and the Agreement between the Member States

---

23 As a rule, essential interests do not include interests of private companies. Cf. Raad van State 20 December 1976, AB 1979, 70. See, however, also the Explanatory Report on the Additional Protocol to the European Convention on Mutual Assistance in Criminal Matters, Strasbourg 1978 at 7.
24 Cf. the Guideline on the application of Art. 552i.
25 Case law is rather cautious on this point. Cf. HR 4 February 1986, NJ 1986, 672, 20 NYIL (1989), pp. 344-346.
26 See supra pp. 102-105.

of the European Communities on the Application of the European Convention on the Suppression of Terrorism.

Paragraph 3 of Art. 552m creates a similar regime where fiscal offences and offences related thereto are concerned. Assistance without treaty basis is ruled out. Requests based on a treaty may only be granted after authorization by the Minister of Justice. Moreover, the provision requires the Minister of Justice to consult the Minister of Finance before granting authorization. This provision is discussed in more detail elsewhere in this book.[27]

Finally, Art. 552l of the Code of Criminal Procedure lists three different mandatory grounds for refusing assistance.

Paragraph 1 of Art. 552l does not allow the rendering of assistance if there are substantial grounds for believing that a request has been made for the purpose of prosecuting or punishing a person on account of his religious or political opinions, his nationality, race or the group of the population to which he belongs, or that the person's position may be prejudiced for any of these reasons. Paragraph 2 requires the competent authorities to submit a request to the Minister of Justice if they have reasons for believing that this would be the case.

Paragraph 1 also requires the refusal of assistance if compliance with the request would run counter to the principles enshrined in Art. 68 of the Penal Code and Art. 255, para. 1, of the Code of Criminal Procedure. Thus, assistance may not be granted if a final judgment has been passed with respect to the same offence by a Dutch court or a court of a third state since Art. 68 of the Penal Code would bar prosecution of a person in the Netherlands in similar circumstances. On the other hand, the reference to Art. 255 of the Code of Criminal Procedure means that mutual assistance must be refused if, in a similar case, prosecution would be barred because a Dutch court would have held it highly unlikely that the case would end in a conviction and therefore would have dismissed the case before the beginning of a trial. It is arguable that the *ne bis in idem* principle enshrined in Art. 68 of the Penal Code would also be violated by rendering assistance in a case if a settlement out of court with respect to the same offence has been reached in the Netherlands or in a third state. For a more thorough discussion of double jeopardy in Dutch law we may refer to another contribution to this book.[28]

---

27 See infra pp. 235-236.
28 See supra pp. 75-84.

judgment on that matter themselves.[32] On the other hand, there is support in case law for the view that domestic provisions with respect to collecting evidence are not wholly irrelevant. Methods in another state may be so different from those accepted in domestic law that to use evidence thus collected would be contrary to fundamental principles of the domestic legal order. The issue was raised before the Supreme Court in a case involving the taking of a blood sample from a Dutch soldier stationed in Germany by the German authorities on suspicion of drunken driving. The Court held that rules applying in Germany on the taking of blood samples were not so different from those in force in the Netherlands as to prevent the results of the blood test from being used as evidence.[33]

A final question regarding requests for assistance relates to the significance of treaties for making requests. According to established case law, the fact that a treaty exists between the Netherlands and the requested state does not automatically imply that every request should have the treaty as its basis. There is room for cooperation outside the terms of that treaty.[34] Generally, the view that a treaty does not constitute an exclusive basis for cooperation seems to be correct. However, matters are different where a treaty confers rights on individual persons which they do not derive from domestic law of the requesting state, or not to the same extent. That, for instance, is the case with several treaties conferring upon the accused the right to question witnesses who are heard by the requested state on request of the Netherlands.[35] In these situations, to assume that a statement of a witness may be used as evidence despite the accused not having been able to question him because of the fact that the request for hearing the witness was not dealt with on the basis of a treaty, effectively nullifies the rights of the accused.[36] It is relevant to note here that domestic law of the Netherlands is rather generous in permitting the use of hearsay evidence when compared with the law of common law systems or, for that matter, many other civil law systems.[37]

---

32 Cf. European Commission of Human Rights 6 March 1989 (12592/86, *X. v. Austria*), 60 Decisions and Reports 201-204 (1989).

33 HR 4 November 1986, NJ 1987, 812.

34 HR 16 April 1985, NJ 1986, 769, 18 NYIL 376 (1987); HR 14 September 1987, NJ 1988, 301.

35 Cf. Art. V of the 1979 Wittem Agreement between Germany and the Netherlands; Art. 5 of the mutual assistance Treaty Between the Netherlands and the United States and Art. 10, para. 4, Mutual Assistance Treaty with Australia.

36 As was done in HR 14 September 1987, NJ 1988, 301.

37 For a more detailed discussion of the issue see *Klip* (supra note 13), pp. 51-58, 180-181.

Finally, the consequences of violations of rules with respect to the gathering of evidence abroad should be discussed. Here, we may distinguish between three different situations. The rules violated may be those of the Netherlands, those that hold in the requested state, or rules of international law, whether customary law or provisions of treaties.[38]

As far as the first category of violations is concerned, from our discussion of Dutch law it has appeared that it is hard to tell in what respects domestic law governs the requesting of assistance from other states. However, disregard of applicable rules may lead to exclusion of evidence or have other consequences.[39] Moreover, as is discussed elsewhere in this book, in carrying out investigations abroad Dutch authorities are bound to comply with the provisions of the Code of Criminal Procedure.[40]

The second situation is the one in which rules of the requested state have been disregarded. As yet there is no case law on the question of what consequences attach to a violation by foreign authorities of rules of their own legal system. It is, therefore, hard to predict how Dutch courts would react. Moreover, with the exception of Arts. 126 to 130 of the Convention applying the Schengen Agreement, all treaties in force are silent on the matter. We may only note here that there is something approaching an established practice as far as the reversed situation is concerned: the case in which Dutch authorities have granted assistance to foreign authorities without being permitted to do so. The practice entails that the consequences will be made undone as far as possible. Where activities of Dutch authorities abroad are concerned, disregard of the rules of the state on whose territory they are acting will almost always coincide with a violation of international law.

To violations of rules of international law by Dutch authorities the courts will attach consequences that they deem appropriate.[41] Since such situations usually involve these authorities acting on the territory of other states without authorization of the local authorities, case law in the matter is discussed in more detail in another contribution to this book.[42]

---

38 Cf. also *Swart* (supra note 30), pp. 394-396.
39 E.g. the return of property to the authorities of the requested state. See HR 29 September 1987, NJ 1988, 302.
40 See infra pp. 224-225.
41 Cf. HR 22 January 1952, NJ 1952, 146; HR 16 December 1986, NJ 1987, 562; HR 15 December 1987, NJ 1988, 707, where the issue of summonses is concerned. See also HR 26 April 1988, NJ 1989, 186 (unauthorized cross-border pursuit): HR 25 March 1993, NJ 1993, 784 (unauthorized interview of witnesses).
42 See infra pp. 225-226.

Police Cooperation

Julian Schutte

Police cooperation and judicial assistance

Police cooperation may be defined as mutual assistance between national police forces for the purpose of carrying out police tasks. Several reasons make it important to devote special attention to this form of international cooperation. Firstly, the number of contacts between national police forces has increased enormously in recent years and the forms cooperation takes have become more diverse. Moreover, while police cooperation was largely left unregulated in the past, that situation is now rapidly changing. The ever increasing need for cooperation at the police level has led to a growing number of national statutes and international treaties laying down basic rules and principles of cooperation. Another reason for paying special attention to international contacts between police forces is that, in most legal systems, their responsibilities are not limited to investigating crime. Traditionally, the police have wider responsibilities, notably including the prevention of crime and the preservation of public order and security. In the 1990 Convention applying the Schengen Agreement and in Title VI of the 1992 Treaty on European Union these wider responsibilities have found recognition. The provisions of both treaties acknowledge the fact that investigating crime may go hand in hand with preventing crime or preserving public order and security.

In legal systems of justice belonging to the civil law tradition, a distinction is usually made between police cooperation on the one hand and judicial assistance on the other. Judicial assistance is defined as assistance between judicial authorities, i.e. authorities charged with performing judicial tasks. What authorities may be considered to be judicial authorities and what tasks may be considered to be judicial tasks, varies from legal system to legal system. The answers depend on how, in a system of justice, the investigation and prosecution of criminal offences have been structured and on what powers have been conferred upon various authorities.

In continental European systems of justice, among them that of the Netherlands, the power to perform judicial functions is exclusively vested in the members of the judicial branch of government. That branch includes the Public Prosecutions Department (public prosecutors at the courts of first instance, procurators general and advocates general at higher instances) on the one hand and the judiciary on the other. Among the members of the judiciary the examining magistrates deserve special mention since they play a prominent role in the field of international judicial assistance. Examining magistrates are charged with carrying out preliminary judicial examinations in more serious cases, and they possess exclusive competence to apply or to authorize others to apply coercive measures such as detention on remand, the search of houses or other premises, the intercepting of telecommunications, the opening of letters, or compelling witnesses to appear and testify during preliminary examinations.

In the Dutch system of criminal justice, the Public Prosecutions Department plays a central role in the investigation and prosecution of criminal offences. On the one hand, the Department directs all criminal investigations; in investigating criminal offences police officers always act under its authority. On the other hand, the Department is solely responsible for prosecuting offences, i.e. for bringing criminal cases before the courts, adducing evidence and demanding that punishment be imposed. Some categories of senior police officers are authorized by law to fulfil the function of assistant public prosecutor. In that capacity they may, in urgent cases, make use of certain powers of coercion on a provisional basis. However, their actions and decisions need to be confirmed or prolonged by the public prosecutor and, in some cases, by the examining magistrate. The fact that a police officer has the status of assistant public prosecutor does not make him a member of the judicial branch of government.

The importance of making a distinction between police cooperation and judicial assistance lies mainly in the fact that different international regimes apply to the two forms of cooperation. Many international instruments are available with respect to mutual judicial cooperation, and they often regulate the matter in considerable detail. Among them one may mention treaties on mutual assistance in criminal matters, on extradition, on transfer of proceedings in criminal matters and on transfer of enforcement of criminal judgments. The same is not true of police cooperation. International instruments are much rarer here and generally of a more recent date. Moreover, it cannot be said yet that these instruments present a complete inventory of the forms police cooperation may take. The law on police cooperation is still very much in the process of being developed, and existing instruments merely offer a fragmented picture. However, one may expect that codification of the law on police cooperation will make headway in the coming years, especially within the framework of Title VI of the Treaty on European Union with its structure for consultation and decision-making in the fields of justice and home affairs.

Treaties

The Netherlands is a party to a number of treaties which deal with police cooperation in criminal matters. We will briefly discuss the most important instruments here.

The 1962 Benelux Treaty on Extradition and Mutual Assistance in Criminal Matters contains a provision on cross-border hot pursuit. On the basis of that provision, police officers of one Benelux country are permitted to continue the pursuit of persons, caught in the act of committing a criminal offence, in the territory of another country with a view to apprehending the person. Pursuit may be continued over a distance of twenty kilometers. However, arrest is permitted within a strip of ten kilometers alongside the border only. More liberal provisions can be found in the 1969 Benelux Convention on cooperation between administrative and judicial authorities in matters pertaining to the Benelux Economic Union. The provisions of both treaties, which have served as models to the 1990 Convention applying the Schengen Agreement, are discussed in more detail elsewhere in this book.[1]

Article 9 of the 1988 United Nations Convention against Illicit Traffic in Narcotic Drugs and Psychotropic Substances, to which the Netherlands became a party in 1993, also deals with police cooperation. Its provisions invite the contracting parties to conclude bilateral or multilateral agreements on the matter and indicates what forms of cooperation such agreements should envisage.

The most comprehensive instrument on police cooperation is the 1990 Convention applying the 1985 Schengen Agreement on the Gradual Abolition of Checks at their Common Borders, concluded between France, Germany and the three Benelux countries. Austria, Greece, Italy, Portugal and Spain entered into agreements of accession to both conventions at later dates. The 1990 Convention entered into force between the five original signatories as well as Portugal and Spain in December 1993; its provisions became operative as of March

---

1 See infra pp. 213-214, 215-216.

1995. It is the purpose of the 1985 Agreement to abolish border controls at the common land borders of the contracting parties as well as at their airports for internal flights and their sea ports for regular trans-shipment connections exclusively from or to other ports within the territories of the contracting parties. The 1990 Convention, on the other hand, is concerned with developing a complex set of compensatory measures in order to cope with the consequences of abolishing border controls. The measures envisaged *inter alia* deal with control of persons at external borders and with cooperation in the fields of police and security.

The 1990 Convention contains two different sets of provisions which are of special importance to international police cooperation. On the one hand, Arts. 39 to 47, together constituting Chapter 1 (Police Co-operation) of Title III (Police and Security), are devoted to various forms of police cooperation; more will be said about them below.[2] On the other, Title IV, comprising Arts. 92 to 119, envisages the creation of a joint automated database, the so-called Schengen Information System (SIS). The SIS is a database containing information about persons and objects in respect of which, if found, a specific action is required. Thus, for instance, data may be stored with respect to persons for the purpose of refusing their entry into the territory of the parties to the Convention or, if they are found within that territory, their deportation. Similarly, data may be stored relating to persons who are wanted for arrest for extradition purposes or whose whereabouts are to be reported for a variety of reasons. Moreover, data may relate to persons who are to be specifically checked or discretely surveyed. Data relating to objects sought concern missing objects identifiable by number (e.g. motor vehicles, identification documents, firearms, registered bank notes).

The Schengen Information System provides a database which is accessible *via* terminals to the police authorities and authorities charged with border control, and identical in all connected countries (although translated into each country's own language). It enables these authorities to know almost immediately whether or not data relating to persons or objects have been stored and, if that turns out to be the case, for what purpose. The system is designed for

---

2   See infra pp. 163-167. On the basis of Art. 39, para. 5, of the Convention more detailed
    agreements have been concluded between the Netherlands and neighbouring states on police
    cooperation in border regions. An example is provided by the 1995 Hasselt Agreement with
    regard to the exchange of information on drug addiction and drug related criminality, con-
    cluded between the various Belgian and Dutch police forces in border regions. Earlier
    agreements on the same subject-matters were concluded in 1993 and 1994. None of them have
    been published.

national authorities to use in addition to national data files, which may serve broader purposes.

The provisions on data protection and on securing the system against improper or unauthorized use are an important part of its set-up. In this respect, Arts. 102 to 118 of the 1990 Convention offer a detailed codification, at a European level, of a system of individual rights and duties of Governments.

Negotiations are now in progress with the aim of creating an information system comparable to SIS for the use of all member states of the European Union. Although the purpose of these negotiations is to conclude a separate Convention on the establishment of a European Information System (EIS) between the member states of the European Union, in actual practice this boils down to making SIS available to member states which do not want to become parties to the 1990 Schengen Convention (at the present moment Ireland and the United Kingdom). While the drafting of a Convention on the establishment of a European Information System (EIS) to a large extent amounts to copying the relevant provisions of the Schengen Convention, it is by no means certain that it will be adopted. That seems to depend on the adoption of yet another convention, the Convention on the crossing of the external frontiers of the member states of the European Union. Negotiations on that convention have been at a stalemate for some time, partly due to a dispute between the United Kingdom and Spain over the status of Gibraltar.

Finally, the activities aimed at creating a European Police Office (Europol), mentioned in Art. K.1 of the 1992 Treaty on European Union (often called the Treaty of Maastricht), must be briefly discussed. In the language of the Treaty on European Union, Europol consists of a 'Union-wide system for exchanging information'. The member states of the Union are in agreement that the establishment of Europol should be based on a treaty in which the status, seat, tasks and powers of, as well as the responsibility for this institution are laid down. Their negotiations have now resulted in the adoption of the Convention on the establishment of a European Police Office (Europol) of 26 July 1995.[3] Meanwhile, in 1993, in anticipation of the entering into force of the convention, the ministers of the member states of the European Communities responsible for police affairs signed a ministerial agreement setting up the European Drugs Unit on a provisional basis. In 1995, the agreement was replaced by a Joint

---

3   1995 OJ C 316/1.

Action of the Council of the European Union.[4] The Europol Drugs Unit consists of liaison officers of member states, each of whom has direct access to all criminal information and intelligence of his own state with respect to certain categories of offences and related offences (notably the laundering of proceeds from these offences) and is entitled to exchange that information on a mutual basis. However, until the Europol Convention has entered into force the Unit's own database may contain non-personal data only. Moreover, the Unit is not permitted to establish direct contacts with third bodies (e.g. Interpol). Europol Drugs Unit is located in The Hague and became operative as of 1 January 1994. While in 1993 its mandate was limited to cross-border drug offences, this has subsequently been broadened to include cross-border trafficking in radioactive and nuclear substances, crimes involving clandestine immigration networks, traffic in human beings and illicit vehicle trafficking.

Article 3 of the 1995 Convention sets out the principal and additional tasks of Europol. One of its principal tasks is to facilitate the exchange of information between the member states. Another is to obtain, collate and analyse information and intelligence. According to Art. 3, Europol will shall also have to notify the competent national authorities without delay 'of information concerning them and of any connections identified between criminal offences'. Its fourth principal task is to aid investigations in the member states by forwarding all relevant information to them. Finally, the fifth and most important task is to maintain a computerized system of collected information. Among the additional tasks entrusted to Europol one may mention the providing of strategic information, the preparation of general situation reports, the providing of assistance where the training, equipment, organization and work methods of national police forces are concerned.

According to Art. 6 of the Convention, Europol is to maintain a computerized system of collected information consisting of three different components: an information system, work files, and an index system. The information system may be used to store, modify and utilize a restricted number of data relating to persons who are suspected of having committed a criminal offence or with respect to whom there are serious grounds for presuming that they will commit criminal offences for which Europol is competent under Art. 2 of the Convention. Direct access to the system is accorded to national units maintaining official contacts with Europol, liaison officers of the member states seconded to Europol, and Europol officials. The second system consists of work files for the purposes of analysis. Since analysis of groups of persons or sets

---

4   1995 OJ L 62/1.

of events cannot be performed without the necessary data, work files may contain comprehensive information. On the other hand, access to work files is limited to an analysis group designated for each individual file. Finally, the index system enables liaison officers of member states to establish whether or not a work file contains data concerning the seconding state.

Statutes

Dutch legislation with respect to international cooperation between judicial authorities is both comprehensive and detailed. Three different statutes are of special importance here: the 1967 Extradition Act *(Uitleveringswet)*, the 1986 Act on the transfer of enforcement of criminal judgments *(Wet overdracht tenuitvoerlegging strafvonnissen)*, and the 1921 Code of Criminal Procedure *(Wetboek van Strafvordering)*, dealing with mutual assistance and transfer of proceedings in criminal matters. The legal situation with respect to police cooperation is rather different. Statutory provisions are rare here. They are not to be found in the 1993 Police Act *(Politiewet)* but in the Code of Criminal Procedure, notably Arts. 552h, 552i and 552k, and in the 1990 Police Files Act *(Wet politieregisters)*.

Article 552h of the Code of Criminal Procedure contains a general definition of international legal assistance in criminal matters. Here, assistance is defined as 'assistance in connection with a criminal case'. The definition not only covers assistance given by judicial authorities but also that rendered by police officials.[5]

That police officials may grant assistance also follows from Art. 552i of the Code. While the Article has made the public prosecutor the central authority responsible for handling requests for assistance, it does not rule out the possibility that other public officials decide on them. The second paragraph of Art. 552i states that, if a request is for information only and no coercive measures are required to obtain that information, the request need not be forwarded to the public prosecutor. The public official having received the request may, in that case, decide on the request himself. This provision is of special importance to the police. It enables them to offer assistance on their own authority. Until recently, their powers to do so were more restricted. Information could only be provided if it was already in their possession or

---

5   See supra pp. 130-131.

could be obtained without conducting an investigation. In all other cases the request had to be forwarded to the public prosecutor. In 1993, on the occasion of the ratification of the Convention applying the Schengen Agreement, their powers have been widened. The police are now entitled to conduct an investigation in order to obtain the information requested, on the one proviso, however, that no coercive measures are applied. Coercive measures imply the use of compulsion or other forms of interference with individual rights, as is, for instance, the case when a person's home is entered or his property seized without his consent or when telecommunications are intercepted. The change effected in the Code in 1993 has widened the scope of police cooperation considerably, as that concept was traditionally understood.

Nevertheless, the legislature did not wish police cooperation to take place without any supervision. The third paragraph of Art. 552i obliges the police authorities to keep written record of all requests received and of all action taken on them. These records are available to the competent public prosecutor, with whose instructions the police have to comply pursuant to the fourth paragraph of Art. 552i. Moreover, in 1994, the heads of the Public Prosecutions Department issued a 'Guideline on the application of Article 552i by the Public Prosecutions Department and on the providing of information by the police within the framework of mutual legal assistance in criminal matters'.[6] The Guideline explains the relevant provisions of the Code to the police in some detail. It also limits in a number of respects their discretion to act on foreign requests for information on their own authority. Thus, requests may not be decided upon by the police if there is reason for believing that mandatory or optional grounds for refusal apply in the case. In such situations, the request should be forwarded to the competent public prosecutor. The same rule applies if, in order to obtain the information requested, it might be necessary or desirable discreetly observe persons or objects, to lend assistance to controlled deliveries, or to permit undercover agents or informers to act on Dutch territory within the framework of a foreign investigation. Furthermore, the Guideline allows individual public prosecutors to conclude further agreements with the police. Finally, the Guideline states that, in providing information, the police authorities should always comply with Art. 13 of the Police Files Decree, a provision that will be discussed below. It goes on to state that providing information is not forbidden for the sole reason that this might result in the arrest by foreign authorities of persons residing in the Netherlands.

---

6   Guideline of 23 November 1994, *Staatscourant* 1994, 242.

Pursuant to Art. 552k of the Code of Criminal Procedure requests for information need not be based on a treaty.[7]

The second statute of major importance to police cooperation is the 1990 Police Files Act *(Wet politieregisters)*. The Act provides a legal framework for the maintenance and use of automated personal data files for police purposes. The term 'police purposes' not only covers the investigation of criminal offences but also other police tasks such as the prevention of crime and the preservation of public order and security. Article 18 of the Act requires an Order in Council to lay down provisions with regard to the communicating of data from automated personal data files in use with the police, whether through the intermediary of Interpol or otherwise, to the police authorities of other countries, as well as with regard to conditions which may be attached to the use of that information by them.

Article 13 of the 1991 Police Files Decree *(Besluit politieregisters)* serves to implement Art. 18 of the Act. Paragraph 1 allows the police authorities to communicate, either spontaneously or on request, data from automated personal data files to the police authorities of another state with a view to the proper discharge of police tasks either in the Netherlands or in the other state. According to para. 4, in deciding whether or not data will be communicated regard must be had of the safeguards against improper use of data and the level of data protection existing in the other state. Paragraph 5 requires the authorities to communicate data only on the condition that no use will be made of them for purposes other than those for which they have been transmitted. In special cases, however, exceptions may be allowed. Pursuant to para. 7, communication of data must, as a rule, take place through the intermediary of the Central Criminal Intelligence Department *(Centrale Recherche Informatiedienst, CRI)*. Direct communication is, however, permitted on the basis of special agreements with the police authorities of other countries.[8] Paragraph 8 of Art. 13 lists a number of mandatory and optional grounds for refusing to communicate personal data. This provision is largely inspired by Arts. 552m and 552l of the Code of Criminal Procedure.[9]

Both the Act and the Decree purport to implement the provisions in the 1990 Convention applying the Schengen Agreement with regard to the

---

7   See supra pp. 127-128.
8   On the basis of this provision agreements have been concluded between the Dutch and the Belgian police forces in border regions. See supra note 2.
9   For a discussion of these provisions see supra pp. 139-141.

Schengen Information System as well as other provisions on the non-automated communication of data in the Convention. They also codify existing practices with regard to the communication of data to Interpol.

The significance of ICPO-Interpol

The Netherlands was one of the founders of Interpol's predecessor, the *Commission Internationale de Police Criminelle*, and of the organization which was to succeed the *Commission* after the Second World War under the name of International Criminal Police Organization Interpol (ICPO Interpol). The Netherlands continues to play an active part in the organization, as is witnessed by a recent initiative taken together with the United Kingdom for the establishment of a crime analysis project.

The function of the Netherlands National Central Office is now being discharged by a branch of the Central Criminal Intelligence Department *(Centrale Recherche Informatiedienst, CRI)*, called Interpol-The Hague and located in Zoetermeer. One may note here in passing that the police forces of national states, rather than states themselves, are members of the organization. Thus, the police forces of the three component parts of the Kingdom of the Netherlands – the Netherlands, the Netherlands Antilles, and Aruba – are all independent members of Interpol. Each has its own National Central Office with its own connections to the Headquarters in Lyon. The Netherlands Office belongs to Zone 2 of the radio network of the organization, while the Office of the Netherlands Antilles in Willemstad and that of Aruba in Oranjestad belong to Zone 8. In view of the importance of maintaining direct Interpol radio connections within the Caribbean region for enforcing criminal law in the Netherlands Antilles and Aruba, the Government of the Kingdom of the Netherlands deems it a matter of great importance that the independent membership of the police forces of all parts of the Kingdom be preserved. This is the most important reason why there is opposition to proposals to turn Interpol into an intergovernmental organization of which independent states may only be members.

Nowadays, the vast majority of requests for assistance at a police level to and from the Netherlands are channelled through Interpol. At the CRI, many tens of thousands of requests are registered annually. About eighty percent of the requests coming from abroad are forwarded to local police forces. The remaining twenty percent are handled by the CRI itself on the basis of data already at its disposal or which it may obtain easily. These are mostly requests for verification of personal data, the checking of fingerprints, verification of names under which number plates of vehicles are registered, and similar requests. Delays in handling requests occur especially when they have to be dealt with by the local police, since it is not always possible for them to make the execution of foreign requests a priority.

New developments may lead to a relative decrease of the importance of Interpol in the future. In this respect, one may think of the introduction of the Schengen Information System, and its intended expansion into the European Information System, whereby all kinds of data which were transmitted through Interpol may be directly entered into and obtained from a joint automated information system. Moreover, it is not impossible that the establishment of the European Police Office Europol may, in the shorter or longer run, result in that organization taking over, at a European level, some of the functions which Interpol now fulfils. This could lead to rivalry between the two organizations, with negative consequences for the effectiveness of police cooperation at a global level. It is the responsibility of those who have created Europol to ensure that such consequences are minimized.

Participation by the Netherlands in international police consultations

While, within Europe, several fora provide for regular consultations on police matters, the Council of Europe has never been one of them. Within that organization, the view prevailed that it is too large to offer a suitable frame-work for structured consultations on matters of policing. Instead, cooperation in criminal matters within the Council has always concentrated on crimino-logical research, cooperation in the penitentiary and penological field, and on developing instruments for international judicial assistance.

During the 1970s, in response to a wave of terrorism striking several European countries, the ministers of the member states of the European Communities responsible for combating terrorism and violent crimes established a form of collaboration between national authorities in the field of police and security. This platform for cooperation became known as the TREVI group (presumably an acronym for *Terrorisme, Radicalisme, Extrémisme et Violence Internatio-nale*). Initially, TREVI consisted of three working groups. One of these was engaged in exchanging sensitive information and analysing threats in the field of terrorism. The second concerned itself with consultations with regard to methods for combating terrorism, including matters of training and technical equipment. The third concentrated on consultations with respect to other forms of serious cross-border criminality, notably drugs offences. The TREVI groups were concerned with exchanging information and expertise only and did not draft any legal documents. They prepared reports for the benefit of the responsible ministers, who met twice a year in order to be informed of any progress made and to give further guidance.

Later, in 1989, a fourth working group came into being. Its task was to discuss measures to be taken by the member states in the field of policing with a view to the imminent realization of free movement of persons as an integral part of the truly common market envisaged by the 1986 Single European Act. This working group, called TREVI '92, was dissolved as of 1 January 1993 as a consequence of the Treaty on European Union entering into force. It has been replaced by another working group, charged with preparing the establishment of the European Drugs Intelligence Unit (EDIU), the forerunner of the European Drugs Unit and the European Police Office Europol. Meanwhile, within the framework of Title VI of the Treaty on European Union, the former TREVI working groups have been restructured. In the fields of justice and home affairs there now exists a multitude of working groups. Among these are working groups on terrorism, police cooperation, drugs and organized crime, customs cooperation and extradition.

In the past, the Netherlands has played an active part in the various TREVI groups. In some fields, notably measures against money laundering, techniques for intercepting telecommunications and crime analysis techniques, it has acted as a forerunner.

The 1990 Convention applying the Schengen Agreement has also created specific forms of police consultation between the contracting parties.

First, mention should be made of the working party on the practical and technical aspects of combating offences involving narcotic drugs, envisaged by Art. 70 of the Convention. Already before the entering into force of the Convention, practical agreements were agreed upon within the working party between Belgium, France, and the Netherlands with regard to these offences and ensuing disturbances of public order. The Schengen working party partly replaces earlier consultations between police officials from Germany and the Benelux countries within the so-called *Ständige Arbeitsgruppe Rauschgift, STAR* (Standing working group on drugs).

Furthermore, in connection with the establishment of the Schengen Information System, a parallel system for transmitting messages has been developed for use between the authorities responsible for the national sections of the SIS. This system for communicating information, called the SIRENE system (Supplementary Information Requests at the National Entry), aims to ensure that actions taken upon reports entered into the SIS may receive an immediate follow-up. Thus, for instance, the network may be used for transmitting without delay a request for the provisional arrest for extradition purposes of a person who has been apprehended following a SIS-report. The SIRENE system creates a multilateral network for transmitting information between national police authorities that does not depend on Interpol or other channels of communication. It has been agreed that English will be the language of communication.

Finally, we should mention the fact that structured practical cooperation between national police forces occurs on a limited scale in border regions. An example is provided by the working party for regional cooperation between the police authorities of Belgium, the Netherlands and the German *Land* Nordrhein-Westfalen, set up as a private association. In it, regular consultations take place between the heads of local police forces. Moreover, the working party provides a framework for organizing joint investigations into specific cases of cross-border forms of criminality.

Instruments of cooperation for special investigation departments

In the Netherlands, police tasks are not only fulfilled by the regular police. With a view to monitoring compliance with specific statutes, special investigation departments have been established which possess the expertise necessary for securing compliance. One may, for instance, think of legislation in the fields of customs and taxes or of legislation regulating economic activities or protecting public health and the environment.

Due to the extent to which such and other matters are subject to regulation, as well as the financial interests involved, chances are considerable that the applicable legislation will be infringed upon. This explains the need for establishing systems of strict supervision, imposing on the citizen duties to provide information to government officials and not to resist investigative measures taken by them, without which it would not be possible to monitor compliance. To that end, a number of specialized investigation departments have been created. Among them one may mention in particular the customs authorities *(douane)* and the Fiscal Intelligence and Investigation Department *(Fiscale informatie en opsporingsdienst, FIOD)*, both falling under the Ministry of Finance, the Economic Inspection Department *(Economische controledienst, ECD)* of the Ministry of Economic Affairs, and the General Inspection Department *(Algemene inspectiedienst, AID)* of the Ministry of Agriculture, Management of the Environment and Fisheries. With a view to supervising compliance and investigating infringements of the applicable legislation, the competent departments have been granted powers which, in a number of respects, exceed those of the regular police when investigating criminal offences under the Penal Code.[10] However, this does not alter the fact that those charged with investigating offences against special statutes should also exercise their powers in ways such as to ensure that during criminal proceedings resulting from their activities basic principles of fairness, such as the presumption of innocence, the privilege against self incrimination, or the right to defend oneself and to be assisted by counsel, are respected.

At present, many statutes for the enforcement of which specialized investigation departments have been made competent, find their basis in instruments of the European Community. This is certainly true for national legislation with regard to customs, value added tax and fisheries as well as the whole broad spectrum of economic activities which the Community is competent to regulate. Since, pursuant to Community law, the enforcement of Community rules is still the responsibility of member states mainly, which actually means that of their own specialized departments, it comes as no surprise that there is a strong need for these departments to cooperate closely with each other at the international level. The need for cooperation is especially strong where the exchange of information and the gathering of evidence are concerned, and, in order to obtain these, national departments must, therefore, be able to exercise the powers granted to them in purely domestic cases. The fact that the interests of the Community itself are at stake in promoting interstate cooperation – it may sometimes directly or indirectly affect the financial interests of the Community or have an influence on the proper functioning of the Community market system – explains why many of the existing international instruments for interstate cooperation between specialized departments are instruments of Community law. This is certainly true for the Netherlands as a member state of the European Community. Among these instruments one may especially mention EC regulations and directives on mutual administrative assistance between the respective customs authorities[11] and tax authorities[12] of the member states. In addition, there are many other regulations and directives which provide a basis for exchanging

---

10 See infra pp. 170-171.
11 EC Regulation 1468/81 on mutual assistance between the administrative authorities of the member states and cooperation between the latter and the Commission to ensure the correct application of the law on customs or agricultural matters, 1981 OJ L 144/1, as amended by EC Regulation 945/87, 1987 OJ L 90/3.
12 EC Directive 77/799 concerning mutual assistance by the competent authorities of the member states in the field of direct taxation, 1977 OJ L 336/15; EC Regulation 218/92 on administrative cooperation in the field of indirect taxation (VAT), 1992 OJ L 24/1.

information between national authorities in certain areas. An important example is provided by the various directives with regard to the supervision of financial institutions (banks, credit institutions, stock markets, insurance companies and investment institutions).[13]

Among international instruments other than EC regulations and directives, the 1969 Benelux Convention on cooperation between the administrative and judicial authorities in matters pertaining to the Benelux Economic Union deserves special mention here. While its scope is limited – it only covers customs duties, excise and value added tax, which are, moreover, areas now largely governed by Community law – the importance of the Convention lies mainly in the fact that it contains detailed provisions on the methods of administrative cooperation and the relationship between this and mutual assistance in criminal matters. In this respect, it may still serve as a model for future instruments to be adopted at the European level.

There is no legislation in the Netherlands providing a general framework for the rendering of international administrative assistance by specialized investigation departments or other administrative authorities charged with supervising compliance with parts of the law. If such legislation is enacted, it would be advisable to regulate each sector separately, given the divergencies in powers and responsibilities conferred by law upon the various specialized departments.[14] In the not too recent past, specific legislation on international administrative assistance was completely lacking. The solution was found in applying international instruments (treaties, EC regulations and directives) directly. Information was communicated to foreign authorities on the basis of general statutory provisions authorizing the competent Minister to lift the obligation of keeping information obtained by national authorities secret.

The first sector with regard to which special legislation has been enacted is that of direct taxation. The relevant Act is the 1986 Act on the rendering of international assistance in the levying of taxes *(Wet internationale bijstandsverlening bij de heffing van belastingen)*. One of the purposes of the Act was to implement an EC directive on the same subject-matter, which dated from 1977(!) and was previously applied 'directly' in the absence of appropriate legislation.[15] The 1986 Act contains detailed provisions on various forms of

---

13 Cf. Directives 73/239, 77/780, 79/267, 85/611, 88/627, 89/592, 89/646, 92/30, 92/49, 92/96.
    Cf. also *Schutte*, Administrative cooperation, pp. 195-197.

14 However, the exchange of information between specialised investigation departments is now partly governed by the 1988 Data Protection Act *(Wet persoonsregistraties)*. See infra p. 160.

15 EC Directive 77/799, 1977 OJ L 336/15.

international assistance (communication of information on request, automatic and spontaneous communication of information, presence of foreign authorities at the execution of requests for assistance). Other provisions of the Act deal with grounds for refusing requests, the obligation to keep information secret, and restrictions as to the use of information obtained. Interested parties may appeal to an administrative tribunal against the intention of the Minister of Finance to render assistance following a request. Finally, requests for assistance made in connection with criminal offences may be granted only after consultation with the Minister of Justice. This enables the Minister of Justice to establish whether or not administrative assistance is being requested in order to circumvent the rules on rendering assistance in criminal matters.[16]

The example of the 1986 Act has not yet been followed in other areas of tax law. There is, for instance, no domestic legislation implementing EC Directive 79/1070[17] and EC Regulation 218/92[18] with regard to administrative assistance in the field of indirect taxation. Even more striking is the situation where customs cooperation is concerned. In the field of international cooperation between customs authorities in particular, international instruments are numerous and detailed; some of them date from several decades ago. In the absence of implementing legislation they are still being applied directly. However, this implies that there is no system of legal protection comparable to that created by the Act on the rendering of administrative assistance in the levying of taxes. There is a lacuna here which needs to be filled, all the more so since of all forms of international administrative assistance customs cooperation is by far the most important one in terms of numbers of cases. Meanwhile, the need for special implementing legislation has decreased somewhat with the adoption of the Data Protection Act *(Wet persoonsregistraties)* in 1988. The 1988 Data Protection Act has created a legal regime for the use of automated information systems comprizing personal data. The provisions of the Act also apply to the automated databases used by the customs authorities.

The need for comprehensive domestic legislation in the area of customs cooperation becomes more urgent as the forms cooperation may take become more varied. Within the framework of the European Union, for instance, the Convention on the use of information technology for customs purposes was adopted in 1995.[19] According to its Art. 2, the aim of the joint automated

---

16 See also infra pp. 244-245. Cf. also *Schutte*, Administrative and Judicial Co-operation in the Fight against EC Fraud, pp. 133-134.
17 1979 OJ L 331/8.
18 1992 OJ L 24/1.
19 1995 OJ C 316/33.

information system envisaged by the Convention is to assist in preventing, investigating and prosecuting serious contraventions of national laws by increasing the effectiveness of the cooperation and control procedures of the customs administrations of the member states through rapid dissemination of information. The term 'national laws' in the Convention refers to virtually all laws or regulations in the application of which the customs administration of a member state has total or partial competence. In most member states, the competence of customs authorities is not limited to tax laws but also extends to laws concerning the importation, exportation and transit of goods, or even a wider range of laws. One may think, for instance, of laws with regard to trafficking in narcotic drugs, stolen art objects, pornographic material or strategic goods. Here, the tasks of customs authorities are not fundamentally different from those of the regular police. This suggests that international cooperation between customs authorities in these fields should be governed by the same rules and principles as apply to police cooperation in general.

In recent years, interesting developments have occurred in other areas of international administrative assistance. First, we may mention here the 1993 Act on the disclosure of unusual transactions *(Wet melding ongebruikelijke transacties)*, which intends to implement EC Directive 91/308 on prevention of the use of the financial system for the purpose of money laundering.[20] The Netherlands is one of the member states which have chosen to implement Arts. 5 and 6 of the Directive by creating an independent Disclosures Office, which serves as a buffer between credit institutions and financial institutions on the one hand and the authorities charged with investigating and prosecuting money laundering offences on the other. Pursuant to the Act, credit and financial institutions have to report financial transactions to the Office which seem to possess an unusual character. The unusual character of a transaction is determined by a set of so-called indicators. On the basis of the information received and of other information available to it the Office will then determine whether or not the transaction is a suspicious one, in which case it will contact the police and the Public Prosecutions Department.[21] According to Art. 3 of the Act, one of the duties of the Disclosures Office is to maintain contacts with similar bodies in other states. Its contacts with them are governed by Arts. 12 and 13 of the Police Files Decree, already discussed above.[22] It is important to note here that

---

20 1991 OJ L 166/77.
21 Cf. *Westerwee/Hillen*, Measures to Combat Money Laundering in the Netherlands, pp. 11-12.
22 See supra p. 153.

the provisions of the Decree distinguish between offices in other countries having the same character as the Disclosures Office and offices which are also authorized by law to investigate money laundering offences themselves. In the latter case, the Office is permitted to communicate data on suspicious transactions only. In the former case, data on all unusual transactions may be communicated. However, these data may not be used by foreign authorities for the purpose of investigating criminal offences without the consent of the Office. If the foreign state wants to use the data received as evidence in a criminal case, the consent of the competent Dutch public prosecutor is needed.[23] The Disclosures Office is now engaged in concluding agreements on the exchange of information with similar bodies in other countries.[24]

A second development to be mentioned here is the revision in 1994 of four different statutes with regard to the supervision of credit institutions and financial institutions. This revision was made necessary by international developments with respect to the lifting of restrictions on the movement of capital, in particular within the European Community. These developments have created a new need for cooperation between national public authorities charged with supervising credit and financial institutions. With a view to implementing international instruments in the matter, notably a number of EC directives, new provisions on international administrative assistance were introduced in the 1986 Act on the supervision of insurance companies *(Wet toezicht verzekeringsbedrijf)*, the 1990 Act on the supervision of investment institutions *(Wet toezicht beleggingsinstellingen)*, the 1991 Act on the supervision of securities transactions *(Wet toezicht effectenverkeer)*, and the 1992 Act on the supervision of the credit system *(Wet toezicht kredietwezen 1992)*. On the basis of the new provisions, the Minister of Finance and the Bank of the Netherlands may now exchange information with foreign public authorities charged with supervising credit and financial institutions, either spontaneously or on request, with a view to assist them in fulfilling their supervisory tasks. Information may not be used for purposes other than those for which it has been provided. Subsequent requests for permission to use the information in connection with criminal investigations may be granted only after consultation with the Minister of Justice. A second aspect of the new provisions is that they allow the Minister of Finance and the Bank of the Netherlands to require credit and financial institutions to provide information or to conduct an investigation themselves in order to obtain the information requested. However, this is permitted only if the

---

23 Cf. *Smid*, Ervaringen vanuit politie en justitie met het meldpunt MOT, p. 195.
24 Cf. *Smid* (supra note 23), p. 196.

foreign request is based on a treaty or a decision of an international organization (EC regulations and directives in particular). In such cases, permission may be granted to foreign authorities to be present at the execution of a request.

Forms of police cooperation

Police cooperation may take a variety of forms. Some of them are described in international instruments. Some are based on informal agreements or consist of habits developed in practice by the police. Others are in the process of being developed and will probably be elaborated in detail in future international instruments.

Exchanging information is the most important form of police cooperation from a quantitative point of view. In the vast majority of cases information is provided on request, sometimes it is being offered spontaneously. Usually, the information provided is already at the disposal of the requested police force or can be easily collected by it. Several provisions of the 1990 Convention applying the Schengen Agreement are devoted to the exchange of information. Among them are Art. 39, dealing with the providing of information on request, and Art. 46, governing the spontaneous providing of information.[25] Of special importance is Art. 39, para. 2. Pursuant to this provision, written information exchanged between police forces may not be used as evidence of a criminal offence other than with the consent of the competent judicial authorities of the requested state. This provision intends to prevent the channels of police cooperation from being used to circumvent those of judicial assistance and to ensure that information contained in police reports will not be used as evidence against persons other than those in whose case a report has been drawn up.

Another form of police cooperation is the practice of exchanging liaison officers. This practice was originally developed with a view to maintaining closer contacts with countries which are producers of narcotic drugs. Notably concerned were countries in Asia and Latin America, with which Interpol contacts are more difficult to maintain than with countries within the European region. Dutch police officers specialized in combating illicit traffic in narcotic drugs (drugs liaison officers/DLOs) are regularly seconded to the embassy of

---

25 See also supra note 2.

the Kingdom of the Netherlands in the country concerned and are accredited by the receiving country, whereby they obtain the status of members of the diplomatic staff. The information collected by the liaison officer is forwarded to his country of origin and on the basis of such information investigations may be initiated or analyses made. Meanwhile, the practice of seconding liaison officers has become widespread and is no longer limited to countries in specific parts of the world. Moreover, use of them is now also made in other areas of law enforcement, such as customs legislation and organized crime. Within the European region, there is a growing practice of seconding liaison officers directly to the police forces of the receiving state rather than to the embassy of the sending state. On the one hand, this means that they no longer enjoy diplomatic status. On the other, it enables them to develop much closer contacts with the police of the receiving state.

Article 47 of the 1990 Convention applying the Schengen Agreement provides a treaty basis for the secondment of liaison officers. Firstly, the contracting parties are invited to exchange liaison officers between each other by seconding them to the police authorities of the other parties. Secondly, the Convention urges them to coordinate their policies with respect to seconding liaison officers to third states, notably states on other continents. The idea is that a liaison officer from one contracting party should be able to also represent the interests of other Schengen states. This would enable them to achieve a better geographical distribution of liaison officers at a global level. More elaborate provisions on liaison officers can be found in the recent Joint Action providing for a common framework for the initiatives of member states concerning liaison officers, adopted by the Council of the European Union in 1996.[26]

Among other things, exchanging liaison officers presents the advantage that they will often have an opportunity to be present at the execution of a request for assistance made by the sending state to the state where they have been seconded. They may then report their findings to their home country. In many cases, however, the liaison officer will hardly be in a position to replace the police officers in charge of the case in the sending state. In such situations, it is usually more attractive to send these officers to the state which is executing the request for assistance. In some treaties, mention is made of the opportunity for authorities of the requesting state to be present at the execution of letters rogatory by the authorities of the requested state. An example is provided by Art. 4 of the 1959 European Convention on Mutual Assistance in Criminal

---

26   1966 OJ L 268/2.

Matters. In a number of recent treaties, authorities of the requesting state have been granted the right to be present. Examples are the 1979 Agreement between Germany and the Netherlands to supplement and facilitate the application of the 1959 European Convention, and the 1981 Treaty between the Netherlands and the United States on Mutual Assistance in Criminal Matters. Notwithstanding the opportunity or the right to be present the responsibility for executing letters rogatory remains wholly with the authorities of the requested state. Protocols of interrogations drawn up by them constitute the primary results of requests for assistance. Of course, the foreign authority present at the execution of a request may draw up his own report. However, that report cannot be considered to be the 'answer' to a request for assistance.

A form of police cooperation that has been regulated in considerable detail in Art. 40 of the 1990 Convention applying the Schengen Agreement is cross-border observation.[27] On the basis of its provisions, teams of police officers engaged in observing persons are entitled to continue their observation in the territory of another contracting party. Observation occurs discreetly and may relate to all persons in whom the police are interested within the framework of a criminal investigation. Not only suspects may be observed but also, for instance, persons who know him and who may put the police on his track. Since organizing a team of observers equipped with the necessary technical means (special cars, electronic equipment) requires time and planning, it will usually be possible to request in advance authorization from the state or the states to whose territories observation is likely to extend. This provides the authorities of the requested state with an opportunity to examine whether they prefer observation to be carried out by a team of their own police officers, if need be joined by a police officer of the requesting state, or to add a local police officer to the team of that state.

Obviously, time and place are uncertain factors. It is often hard to predict over what period of time and to what area observation will extend. Therefore, Art. 40 of the Convention requires the contracting parties to designate a central authority having jurisdiction to grant authorization for the whole territory of the requested state.

Requests to permit cross-border observation must be submitted in the form of a request for judicial assistance, i.e. they must originate from judicial authorities charged with investigating and prosecuting the offence in connection with which observation of a person is felt necessary. However, since carrying

---

27 Cf. *Bevers/Joubert*, Schengen Investigated, pp. 243-248. See also infra pp. 214-215.

out observations is wholly a matter for the police, one might rather consider it to be a form of police cooperation. Article 40 of the Convention lays down in detail the cases in which cross-border observation may be requested and the powers conferred on police officers of the requesting state. Thus, for instance, police officers engaged in cross-border observation are not entitled to apprehend the person under observation, and all operations are subject to a report to be submitted to the authorities of the state on whose territory observation takes place. Article 43 of the Convention contains rules with respect to the reparation of damage caused by police officers during observation.

Similarly detailed are the provisions of Art. 41 of the Schengen Convention on another form of police cooperation: cross-border hot pursuit.[28] This form of cooperation concerns the pursuit of persons caught in the act of committing a criminal offence and of persons escaping from provisional custody or while serving a custodial sentence. On the basis of the Convention, a pursuit may continue in the territory of a neighbouring contracting party. Since checks at the common borders have been abolished between the contracting parties, fugitives from justice in one country may be able to cross a common border without difficulty. It is the purpose of cross-border pursuit to provide an adequate response. This purpose can be achieved either by granting the pursuing police officers the right to apprehend the fugitive after a border has been crossed or by authorizing them to pursue that person as long as is necessary for him to be apprehended by local police officers. In this respect, the Convention enables the contracting parties to make a choice. The Netherlands, Belgium and Germany have chosen the option of permitting foreign police officers to apprehend the fugitive themselves. In the case of the Netherlands and Belgium the right of pursuit is limited to an area of ten kilometers alongside the border; Germany has chosen not to adopt geographical limitations.

Pursuing officers having apprehended a person are not allowed to take him back to the country from which he fled. Instead, they are to hand him over to the local police authorities. Extradition proceedings may then commence. If extradition is ruled out because of the nationality of the fugitive transfer of criminal proceedings might be an alternative. The direct link between cross-border pursuit and extradition explains why, pursuant to Art. 41, pursuit is permitted in connection with extraditable offences only. Finally, Art. 41 contains precise provisions on the powers of the pursuing officers, in particular their right to apprehend a person. Moreover, it lists the police officers entitled

---

28 See also infra pp. 215-217.

to effect cross-border pursuits and requires them to be able to identify themselves at all times.

The forms of police cooperation discussed above consist of police officers of one state acting on their own initiative on the territory of another state. However, one can also imagine forms of cooperation entailing police bodies of two or more states setting up joint investigation teams for the purpose of investigating a case or a string of cases. Experience has shown that teams composed of police officers from various countries cooperating together in one investigation require both thorough preparation and specific working agreements with respect to the deployment of manpower and supporting equipment, leadership, priority-setting and continuity. Indeed, for each country participating in the endeavour a protocol of agreements should be drawn up, to be relied upon during operations. The more countries participating in joint investigation teams, the more complex their set up and organization becomes.

At present, most experience is being gained with a method of investigation which, by its very nature, requires close coordination of investigative activities of police forces of different countries: the method of controlled delivery. The method consists of systematically observing international transports of illegal goods, usually narcotic drugs, with a view to collecting information on the routes followed, means of transport used, suppliers and buyers. It requires that international transports be left undisturbed, although kept under observation, in order to enable the arrest, at the moment of delivery of the goods, not only of those persons who take care of transports or act as couriers but also of buyers and organizers. In such cases, police forces from various countries are expected to cooperate as if they constituted one single mixed team. Provided it is well-organised, controlled delivery has proven to be an important tool for combating various forms of international crime.

Police cooperation need not be limited to the operational level. Exchange of information may also relate to police methods, to experience with respect to newly developed investigative techniques or techniques for collecting and analysing data. Thus, for instance, introducing the same systems of automated data processing with respect to dactyloscopic evidence in different countries may enhance efficiency, or exchanging experiences in preventing and combating terrorist acts may be useful with a view to setting up specialized anti-terror brigades. In Art. 3 of the 1995 Convention on the establishment of a European Police Office (Europol) the collection and dissemination of such information and expertise has been made one of the tasks of Europol.

A relatively new development is the use of computers in the field of crime analysis. This includes the examination of specific behavioural patterns and *modus operandi* of criminal organizations. Its purpose is to identify ways in which such organizations operate. One may think here of the choice of routes followed for transporting narcotic drugs or other illegal contraband or of the kind of packaging used, but also of methods for laundering proceeds from crime or for penetrating into legitimate business with the help of juristic constructs. In the field of crime analysis both the United Kingdom and the Netherlands have made important headway in recent years. Both countries have sponsored a research project within ICPO Interpol aimed at the wider dissemination of knowledge in this field. Crime analysis has also been made one of the principal tasks of Europol.

Police cooperation may also be understood to include cooperation in the training of police officers. Increasingly, the authorities responsible for training domestic police forces in various European countries, but also those of other countries, have meetings with each other. This results in 'international' elements frequently being included in training curricula. These elements may consist of guest lectures, working visits or exchange programmes, but also of the joint development of educational material on international police cooperation.

In particular, recent developments in Central and Eastern Europe have contributed to a marked increase in international cooperation where the development of training programmes is concerned. In Eastern Europe a special need exists to reorganize the structure of policing while, at the same time, these countries are confronted with an enormous increase of all types of crime, property and economic crime in particular. A variety of more or less spontaneous initiatives have been taken by most Western European countries for the most diverse forms of aid and assistance to the police forces of the countries of Central and Eastern Europe, without there being any systematic coordination or exchange of information between them. This, one may assume, leads to a waste of money and energy. Until now, there is no European organization engaged in coordinating aid programmes in the field of policing at an international level. The Council of Europe has not taken any initiative here and TREVI did not offer a suitable framework for assuming that task. Meanwhile, the 1992 Treaty on European Union seems to open better perspectives. It offers sufficient room for adopting structural programmes, not only with respect to developing police cooperation between the member states but also for organizing cooperation with third states, those on the European continent in particular. Whether or not the member states will be willing to explore these opportunities, only time will tell.

Finally, it is worth mentioning the fact that international police cooperation may also cover issues of a purely technical nature. Here, agreements come to mind with respect to the cross-border use of means of communication (e.g. type of equipment and radio frequencies to be used, exchange of equipment) and to the designing of national parts of common computerized information systems, such as the Schengen Information System.

Concluding reflections on restriction of purpose, confidentiality, and protection of privacy

In many legal systems there is no sharp dividing line between international police cooperation on the one hand and international judicial assistance on the other. Judicial assistance may be defined as cooperation between authorities charged with judicial tasks. What authorities may be considered to be judicial authorities depends on the structure of criminal procedure in a given state. In the Netherlands, they include the courts as well as the examining magistrate, who is responsible for conducting preliminary judicial examinations and for applying a range of coercive measures or for authorizing others to apply them. Moreover, the members of the Public Prosecutions Service, responsible for instituting criminal proceedings and for bringing criminal cases before the courts, are also considered to be judicial authorities.

Many criminal investigations taking place under the direction or responsibility of the judicial authorities are actually carried out by the police. While acting under the direction or responsibility of the public prosecutor or examining magistrate, police authorities may, among other things, also maintain contacts with colleagues in other countries. In such cases, all steps taken by them are subject to the authorization of the said judicial authorities.

In actual practice, during the earliest stages of criminal investigations the police will, as a rule, not be acting under the direct supervision of the Public Prosecutions Department. It is true that, in Dutch law, the Public Prosecutions Department bears a responsibility for all police investigations into criminal offences, even if these investigations are still in an early stage and no reports on the findings have been forwarded to the Department yet. However, at this stage the Department is not in a position to give much direction to the police, and this is also true where their contacts with police authorities of other countries are concerned. In other legal systems it may be the case that the responsibility of public prosecutors for the activities of the police is less far-reaching than in the Netherlands and that, therefore, the police enjoy more autonomy *de jure* in deciding whether and how criminal investigations are carried out.

To complicate matters further, in the Netherlands, as well as in other countries, differences exist between the regular police on the one hand and specialized investigation departments on the other, where their relations with the Public Prosecutions Department are concerned. In tax and customs cases, unlike in other cases, the Department is not *dominus litis*, i.e. not solely competent to decide whether or not a case will be prosecuted. Reports of investigations in tax and customs cases are first sent to higher tax authorities, and it is they who decide whether a financial settlement will be offered to the person concerned by the investigation or whether the case will be sent to the Public Prosecutions Department with a view to prosecuting the case. This implies that international administrative assistance with regard to tax and customs offences occurs without the Department being able to exercise control. As a matter of fact, the same situation prevails where the international exchange of data between other specialized departments, such as the Economic Inspection Department *(ECD)* and the General Inspection Department *(AID)*, is concerned. Usually, exchange of data occurs here on the basis of EC regulations and directives with regard to monitoring compliance with Community law. If, as a consequence of exchanging data – or perhaps even at an earlier stage – it is suspected that irregularities have been committed, the exchanging of data will be intensified in order to obtain more certainty. In these situations, it may occur that powers granted for the purpose of monitoring compliance – among them the power to require the person concerned to give information about himself or other persons, or about his business – are used for the purpose of investigating criminal offences.

There is a definite danger here that powers granted under national law for the sole purpose of monitoring compliance with a given set of rules, will, within the framework of international cooperation, be used to further investigations into criminal offences conducted elsewhere. With a view to preventing such and other abuses many international instruments contain provisions limiting the use of data transmitted through the channels of international administrative assistance. Usually, this limitation takes the form of a so-called restriction of purpose: the data receiving state is not permitted to use the data for any purpose other than that for which their transmission has been requested or granted. That purpose is, in principle, administrative; it is to enable the competent administrative authorities of the requesting state to verify whether parts of national legislation are being complied with and to correct irregularities by administrative means. It excludes their use in public court proceedings, except with the express and prior authorization of the competent authorities of the supplying state. The requirement of prior authorization enables the competent authorities of that state to determine whether the same data would have been supplied had their transmission been requested through the channels of judicial assistance. If doubts arise in this regard, they may then indicate that the channels for judicial assistance in criminal matters should be resorted to.

In principle, restricting the use of data to the purpose for which their transmission has been requested, also rules out their use for administrative purposes other than those for which they have been supplied, except with prior authorization. It is, however, doubtful whether such a condition can be very effective. It should not be overlooked that in a number of countries few or no restrictions at all are accepted where the exchange of information between government authorities is concerned. In some other countries there is a general obligation for all authorities to report suspected offences, together with the information on which suspicions are based, to the judicial authorities.

It may, perhaps, be possible to ensure compliance with provisions on restriction of purpose and secrecy where the international exchange of data in tax matters is concerned, since it is characteristic for the mechanisms of enforcing tax laws that far-reaching powers of supervision are accorded to the competent authorities and that they are also empowered to impose administrative penalties for infringements of those laws. But the situation appears to be different in other sectors of administrative law, where the imposition of penalties for irregularities is entirely or almost entirely left to the criminal justice system. Here, imposing sanctions on infringements rapidly becomes the responsibility of the criminal justice authorities, and this often implies that public court proceedings will be instituted. One may wonder to what extent account will be taken in such proceedings of the manner in which data introduced as evidence of a criminal offence have been obtained from abroad. At any rate, it is obvious that the answer to that question may differ from one legal system to another.

Differences between legal systems in the powers granted to their regular police forces and specialized investigation departments, as well as in the duty or the willingness of national courts to inquire into the manner in which foreign authorities have collected evidence, coupled with the increasing tendency to attach more weight than in the past to considerations of efficiency in striking a balance between legality and efficiency, all lead to police cooperation and judicial assistance, administrative assistance and assistance in criminal matters, becoming intermingled to an ever growing extent. The first international instruments have already been adopted in which it is explicitly provided that data obtained through the channels of cooperation in customs matters and relating to illicit trafficking in narcotic drugs, may, without prior authorization of the competent authorities of the supplying state, be communicated to other authorities directly involved in the combating of illicit drug traffic.[29] There seems to be an increasing tendency to eliminate the requirement of prior authorization in other areas too. On the other hand, there is also an increasing tendency to use the instruments designed for international judicial assistance for the purpose of furthering cooperation with regard to investigating and sanctioning so-called administrative offences.[30]

As a result of the various developments discussed here, there is a real need to consider – at some stage – the existing international instruments for police cooperation, administrative assistance and judicial assistance all together, and to develop an integrated approach to them. Only then will it become apparent to what extent checks and balances built into domestic law in order to ensure an equilibrium between collective and individual interests, between efficiency and legality, between publicity and secrecy, can also be introduced and maintained at an international level.

---

29 Cf. Protocol 6, Art. 11, of the 1993 Europe Agreement establishing an association between the European Communities and their member states, of the one part, and the Republic of Hungary, of the other part, 1993 OJ L 347/1. The example of the Agreement has been followed in later Europe Agreements with other states.

30 Cf. Art. 49 of the Convention applying the Schengen Agreement. See also infra p. 124.

Transfer of Criminal Proceedings

Désirée Paridaens

Introduction

Transfer of criminal proceedings concerns a type of international legal assistance in criminal matters in which the judicial authorities of one state are requested by the authorities of another state to institute criminal proceedings. The criminal file is transferred to the other state for this purpose. The requesting state aims in its request either to induce the requested state to initiate proceedings, or, if the same offence is already being prosecuted there, to concentrate proceedings in that state.

For a long time now, the Netherlands has engaged in the practice of transferring criminal proceedings.[1] Transfer of proceedings need not be based on a treaty. This form of mutual legal assistance is a relatively important instrument for the Netherlands, as is reflected in figures published by the Ministry of Justice in an appendix to its 1995 annual budget. Transfer of proceedings takes place considerably more often than extradition occurs.[2] Rather striking in the figures is the sharp decrease since 1990 of the number of cases in which proceedings have been transferred from the Netherlands to other states in cases of violation of driving hours regulations.[3]

---

1   For an exhaustive analysis of Dutch law see *Baaijens-van Geloven*, Overdracht en overname van strafvervolging. Cf. also *Schutte*, The European System, pp. 319-335.
2   It appears that between 1 January 1988 and 31 December 1993 some 15,908 cases were transferred to other states and that 3,390 cases were transferred to the Netherlands. In the same period, the Netherlands sought extradition in 304 cases and received 1,047 requests for extradition.
3   The marked decline in the transfer of proceedings from the Netherlands to foreign countries is due to the fact that, in recent years, foreign drivers caught in the act of violating driving hours regulations are given the opportunity to settle the matter immediately. If a driver is unable or unwilling to pay the fine involved on the spot, he will then be summonsed to appear before a criminal court. Transfer of proceedings no longer occurs.

Traditionally, transfer of criminal proceedings occurred only in cases involving offences which could be prosecuted both in the Netherlands and in the other state involved. It has now become possible to transfer proceedings in cases in which concurrent jurisdiction does not exist. In some cases, only the requested state will possess jurisdiction to prosecute the offence on the basis of its own legislation. In other cases, only the requesting state will. Examples of the first situation are provided by Art. 21 of the 1959 European Convention on Mutual Assistance in Criminal Matters and Art. 42 of the 1962 Benelux Treaty on Extradition and Mutual Assistance in Criminal Matters. Both provisions recognize the fact that a state which does not have jurisdiction over a particular offence, may have relevant evidentiary material which would enable another state to institute criminal proceedings; therefore, both treaties contain provisions facilitating the transmission of the evidence by the first state with a view to proceedings being instituted by the other state. The 1972 European Convention on the Transfer of Proceedings in Criminal Matters provides an example of the reverse situation.[4] Article 2 of the Convention enables a contracting party which has no jurisdiction over an offence under its own law, to institute proceedings on the basis of a request from another contracting party which has jurisdiction over the offence. In other words, a legal basis has been created for instituting criminal proceedings based on what is sometimes called subsidiary jurisdiction.

In addition to treaties which provide a general basis for transferring criminal proceedings to another state, there are also treaties which specifically provide for transfer of proceedings with a view to confiscating the proceeds of crime. This is significant for the Netherlands with respect to the 1988 United Nations Convention against Illicit Traffic in Narcotic Drugs and Psychotropic Substances, the 1990 Council of Europe Convention on Laundering, Search, Seizure and Confiscation of the Proceeds from Crime, and the 1992 Agreement between the Netherlands and the United States regarding mutual cooperation in the tracing, freezing, seizure and forfeiture of proceeds and instrumentalities of crime and the sharing of forfeited assets.[5]

---

4   Ratified by the Netherlands in 1985. The Netherlands also ratified the 1974 Benelux Treaty on the Transfer of Proceedings in Criminal Matters (and Appendix), but this convention has not yet entered into force. Whether it will, depends on ratification by Belgium or Luxembourg. Neither state has ratified the European Convention on the Transfer of Proceedings in Criminal Matters to date.

5   Cf. also the 1993 Agreement between the Netherlands and the United Kingdom to supplement and facilitate the Operation of the 1990 Convention of the Council of Europe on Laundering, Search, Seizure and Confiscation of the Proceeds from Crime.

Statutory provisions concerning transfer of proceedings from and to the Netherlands, particularly provisions of a procedural nature, are since 1985 to be found in Arts. 552t to 552hh of the 1921 Code of Criminal Procedure *(Wetboek van Strafvordering)*. Articles 552t to 552w concern transfer of proceedings from the Netherlands to other states, while Arts. 552x to 552hh deal with transfer of proceedings from other states to the Netherlands. On the one hand, these provisions implement treaties providing for transfer of proceedings. On the other, they contain conditions which must be observed when requests for proceedings are made by or addressed to the Netherlands without a treaty being applicable. Also of relevance are Arts. 4a and 77 of the 1881 Penal Code *(Wetboek van Strafrecht)*. Article 4a provides that Dutch jurisdiction may derive directly from a treaty. Article 77 regulates the lapse of the right to institute proceedings and to enforce criminal judgments in the Netherlands as a consequence of transfer of proceedings to another state, as well as reversion of these rights at a later moment.[6]

Articles 552t to 552hh of the Code of Criminal Procedure are not applicable to the transfer of a criminal file to foreign military authorities on the basis of the 1951 NATO Status of Forces Agreement.[7] Nor are they applicable to transfer of proceedings between the three component parts of the Kingdom of the Netherlands. In these cases, the legal basis must be sought in Art. 36 of the 1954 Charter for the Kingdom of the Netherlands *(Statuut voor het Koninkrijk der Nederlanden)*, which provides that the three countries shall offer help and assistance to one another.[8] Finally, from case law it appears that Arts. 552t to 552w are not applicable when a Dutch public prosecutor intends to transfer proceedings with regard to an offence for which the Netherlands has already received a request for extradition of the person against whom proceedings are directed.[9]

---

6 They revert to the Netherlands if the state which had accepted transfer of proceedings withdraws acceptance of the request, or informs the Netherlands that it will not institute proceedings or will discontinue them. Cf. also Art. 21, para. 2, of the European Convention on the Transfer of Proceedings in Criminal Matters.

7 Cf. Art. VII of the NATO Status of Forces Agreement. See also Art. 4 of the 1953 Act implementing the Agreement, and the circular letter from the Minister of Justice of 15 February 1981, concerning the exercise of jurisdiction with respect to criminal offences committed by foreign military officials.

8 For additional detail in this regard, see *Hofstee/Schalken*, Strafrecht binnen het Koninkrijk, pp. 99-102. Cf. also supra pp. 2-3.

9 Gerechtshof Den Haag 26 May 1988, NJ 1990, 549. See also infra pp. 180-181.

Transfer of proceedings from the Netherlands

Procedure

Transfer of proceedings by the Netherlands usually occurs on the basis of a decision by the Minister of Justice, following a proposal by the public prosecutor. Only requests for transfer of proceedings in cases of violation of driving hours legislation, which are based on Art. 21 of the European Convention on Mutual Assistance in Criminal Matters or on Art. 42 of the Benelux Treaty on Extradition and Mutual Assistance in Criminal Matters, can be made directly – thus without intervention by the Minister of Justice – by the public prosecutor to the judicial authorities of the requested state.[10]

A proper administration of justice

Article 552t, para. 1, of the Code of Criminal Procedure provides that the public prosecutor may direct a reasoned proposal for initiating criminal proceedings in another state to the Minister of Justice, if he considers that proceedings against the suspect in that state would be in the interests of a proper administration of justice. No guidance is set out as to the meaning of the words 'proper administration of justice'.

Interpretation of the term 'proper administration of justice' is aided by the Guideline regarding the transfer of proceedings, issued by the heads of the Public Prosecutions Department on 30 December 1982, when ratification of the 1972 European Convention on the Transfer of Proceedings in Criminal Matters and the adoption of implementing legislation were imminent.[11] In addition, a manual for transfer of proceedings was issued in 1989. Reference is made in the manual to the European Convention on the Transfer of Proceedings in Criminal Matters, in which criteria are included which may be considered to be an elucidation of the expression. On the basis of the criteria contained in the Convention and in the 1982 Guideline, it is possible to assess when a proper administration of justice is supposedly served by transfer of proceedings. Of note is that the criteria of Art. 8 of the European Convention also serve as instructions in making a decision to transfer proceedings in cases in which the

---

10 See Art. 53, para. 5, of the 1990 Convention applying the Schengen Agreement.
11 Published in *Staatscourant* 3 January 1983, 1.

Convention is not applicable, for example because the requested state is not a party to it.

The basic principle of the manual is that proceedings should always be transferred if they relate to a criminal offence presumably committed by a non-resident alien in the Netherlands. If prosecution in another state is a good alternative to instituting criminal proceedings in the Netherlands, then in principle transfer of proceedings is preferred. The manual lists other circumstances in which transfer is deemed to be desirable. This includes a situation where the suspect is being prosecuted in another state for the same or for other offences. Lastly, the circumstances are described in which transfer of proceedings might not be desirable, so that prosecution in the Netherlands should be preferred. Here, mention is made of the following considerations:

- the offence is a serious one and the corresponding shock to the Dutch legal order severe;
- the suspect is in possession of a valid permit for residence in the Netherlands and such permit is unlikely to be withdrawn as a consequence of conviction;
- other persons involved in the same offence can only be prosecuted in the Netherlands (the importance of equality before the law);
- transfer would conflict with the search for truth, particularly where the most important evidentiary material is in the Netherlands and cannot be transferred;
- an offender would not be prosecuted in the Netherlands in a similar case.

Neither the 1982 Guideline nor the 1989 manual take account of recent conventions concerning international cooperation with respect to confiscation of proceeds of crime or of changes in related Dutch legislation.[12] In 1993, a sixth paragraph was added to Art. 552t of the Code of Criminal Procedure. The new paragraph sets out that a proposal of the public prosecutor to transfer proceedings may be limited to proceedings in the foreign state with a view to imposing and enforcing a sanction whose purpose is to deprive the offender of the proceeds from crime. This provision builds forth on Arts. 511b to 511i of the Code, introduced in 1992. While in most criminal cases a measure of confiscation will be imposed by a court decision convicting the accused, Arts. 511b to 511i of the Code make it possible to separate proceedings aimed at confiscation from the main proceedings and to decide upon them at a date

---

12 On confiscation of proceeds in Dutch law see supra pp. 45-47.

later than conviction. Paragraph 6 of Art. 552t now enables the Dutch authorities to transfer confiscation proceedings after a court has convicted the accused. This may promote the interests of a proper administration of justice in cases in which offences have generated proceeds which are to be found entirely or almost entirely in another country. The Dutch legislature considered that there may be good reasons to prosecute the criminal offence itself in the Netherlands, but to leave determination of the magnitude of the proceeds to be confiscated to the authorities of the country where they are found. A condition for successful transfer is of course that the law of the requested state, like the law of the Netherlands, permits separate confiscation proceedings.

Double criminality

Under Art. 552t, para. 1, of the Code the public prosecutor may propose transfer of proceedings only in cases concerning offences under Dutch law. The law does not require that the offence also be punishable under the law of the requested state. Article 7 of the European Convention on the Transfer of Proceedings in Criminal Matters does require double criminality *(in concreto)*. However, in Art. 1 of the Convention, acts dealt with by administrative authorities are equated with criminal offences, subject to the condition that the person may appeal to a court of law. Appendix III to the Convention contains a list of administrative offences which are assimilated to offences under criminal law. By means of a declaration made in 1990, the Government of the Netherlands brought the legal provisions of the 1989 Act on the administrative enforcement of traffic regulations *(Wet administratiefrechtelijke handhaving verkeersvoorschriften)* under Appendix III of the European Convention. Pursuant to the Act, minor traffic violations are prosecuted in administrative rather than in criminal proceedings. The offences brought under the Act are no longer considered criminal offences.

Article 49 of the Convention applying the Schengen Agreement is applicable to the transfer of proceedings to another Schengen state which treats the violation concerned administratively rather than criminally. This provision supplements Art. 21 of the European Convention on Mutual Assistance in Criminal Matters and Art. 42 of the Benelux Treaty on Extradition and Mutual Assistance in Criminal Matters where transfer is concerned. Paragraph (a) provides that mutual legal assistance on the basis of these treaties shall also be afforded: 'in proceedings brought by the administrative authorities in respect of offences which are punishable in one of the two Contracting Parties or in both Contracting Parties by virtue of being infringements of the rules of law, where the decision may give rise to proceedings before a criminal court'.

The interests of the victim

If the victim has expressed an interest in the criminal proceedings with the intention of seeking damages or compensation, the public prosecutor may, pursuant to Art. 552t, para. 3, of the Code, propose transfer of proceedings only if the victim has agreed to transfer in writing. If such consent is not forthcoming, authorization by the competent criminal court is required. Before the public prosecutor may obtain such authorization, however, the victim must be summonsed for a hearing on the matter.[13]

Notice to the suspect

The suspect must be notified of the proposal of the public prosecutor to transfer proceedings and of the decision of the Minister of Justice to request transfer in a limited number of cases only. As will be seen below,[14] this has important consequences for the possibility of opposing transfer.

— Under Art. 552t, para. 2, of the Code, the suspect must be given notice of the proposal of the public prosecutor in cases in which a preliminary judicial examination has been conducted or remand in custody has been ordered with respect to the offence involved. In these cases, it does not matter whether the suspect remains in the Netherlands or abroad. Pursuant to Art. 243 of the Code, the public prosecutor would normally have to notify the suspect of his decision to discontinue proceedings. Certain legal effects are attached to such notice. However, Art. 552t, para. 3, of the Code provides that a notice of discontinuation need not be given in cases in which the public prosecutor declines further prosecution in the Netherlands because he prefers transfer of proceedings to another country. The suspect will instead receive notice of a proposal to transfer proceedings, to which the legal consequences of a normal notice of discontinuation do not attach.

In addition to the foregoing, if the suspect has not agreed to transfer of proceedings and is in the Netherlands, Art 552u, para. 2, of the Code requires

---

13 This follows from Art. 23 of the Code.
14 See infra p. 180.

the Minister of Justice to give written notice to the suspect of his intention to request transfer of proceedings, prior to making the decision to do so. In actual practice, the suspect is often no longer in the Netherlands. This means that the notice requirement no longer applies.

Legal remedies

Pursuant to Art. 552t, para. 5, of the Code, the suspect may lodge an objection to a proposal to transfer proceedings with the competent court of appeal within fourteen days of the day on which notice of the public prosecutor's proposal was served on him. This legal remedy is only available to suspects who have received such a notice as required by the second paragraph of Art. 552t. In principle, a timely filed objection will effect suspension of the procedure to transfer proceedings. Until now, use of this remedy has never resulted in a court of appeal forbidding transfer of proceedings.[15]

In addition, notice of the Minister's intention to request transfer of proceedings enables a suspect who is in the Netherlands and who has not agreed to transfer, to approach a district court for an injunction ordering the Minister not to request transfer. If done within fourteen days after service of the notice, this will have the effect of delaying the Minister's decision (Art. 552u, para. 2).

The law provides no particular legal remedy for cases in which the suspect prefers transfer of criminal proceedings, but where a proposal for transfer is not forthcoming. This situation seldom arises in actual practice. If the public prosecutor is not to be persuaded that transfer of proceeding is desirable, the only remedy available to the suspect is to approach a district court for an injunction ordering the Minister to request transfer.

Transfer of the suspect to the requested state

Transfer of proceedings cannot be used to transfer the suspect. Meanwhile, physical transfer of the suspect is usually not necessary since, more often than not, he is already present in the requested state. However, if the suspect still remains in the state which wants to transfer proceedings, his removal may be effected in a number of ways. As far as the Netherlands is concerned, three

---

15 Cf. Gerechtshof Leeuwarden 16 June 1987, NJ 1987, 896; Gerechtshof Arnhem 7 July 1987, NJ 1988, 86. See also *Baaijens-van Geloven* (supra note 1), pp. 263-264.

different possibilities for removing the suspect offer themselves: extradition, deportation, and transfer of sentenced persons. The first avenue requires the state which intends to accept transfer of proceedings to make a request for extradition to the Netherlands. Such a request may be elicited by the Dutch authorities if necessary. The second possibility exists, of course, only if the suspect is an alien who qualifies for deportation to the requested state. However, the view prevails that transfer of proceedings may be effected only after deportation has taken place, and not concurrently, since disguised extradition should be avoided.[16] The third possibility requires the suspect to have received a final conviction and to serve a custodial sentence of some duration in the Netherlands with regard to a different offence. If transfer of enforcement of that sentence is requested, the competent authorities might decide to request transfer of proceedings with regard to other offences at the same time.[17]

Transfer of proceedings to the Netherlands

Procedure

Generally, a foreign request to transfer proceedings to the Netherlands is received by the Minister of Justice.[18] The request should be refused summarily if it can be established that it satisfies one of the grounds for refusal set out in Art. 552y of the Code of Criminal Procedure.[19] If the request is based on a treaty, such refusal is only possible if the treaty so permits.

If such a summary refusal is not indicated, the request is then sent to the competent public prosecutor for an opinion.[20] In actual practice, the public prosecutor gives his opinion only if there are grounds for believing that an

---

16   Cf. *Baaijens-van Geloven* (supra note 1), pp. 82-84; *Schutte* (supra note 1), pp. 320-322.

17   See infra pp. 206-208 for a discussion of the conditions for transfer of sentenced persons.

18   Cf. Art. 13 of the European Convention on the Transfer of Proceedings in Criminal Matters. For an exception see Art. 53, para. 5, of the 1990 Convention applying the Schengen Agreement.

19   See infra pp. 183-185.

20   In general, this will be the public prosecutor at the district court in the district in which the person involved in the request for proceedings has his fixed abode or place of residence (Art. 552z, para. 1). However, if confiscation of proceeds from crime has been requested and the request relates to an alien whose fixed abode or permanent residence is outside the Netherlands, the Minister must forward it to the public prosecutor in the district in which property is located against which a sanction aimed at confiscation of the proceeds from crime can be enforced (Art. 552z, para. 2).

impediment to instituting proceedings exists. In order to speed up the procedure, if the public prosecutor concludes that no impediment to the transfer exists, he is authorized to institute proceedings immediately after having received the request from the Minister.

— If the public prosecutor gives a negative opinion, the Minister of Justice must then decide whether to grant or refuse a request for transfer.[21] The Minister may, before making a decision, invite the competent authorities of the requesting state to provide additional information within a prescribed time period if such information is needed in order to take a decision on the request.[22] The Minister must notify the public prosecutor and the authorities of the requesting state of his decision. He must also notify these authorities of the outcome of proceedings which have been instituted as a result of the request.

— The granting of a foreign request for transfer of proceedings is not irrevocable.[23] Article 552dd of the Code provides that, as long as the trial has not yet begun, the Minister of Justice may revoke his decision to grant a request for proceedings if, from the preliminary investigation or for some other reason, circumstances emerge which would have led to a refusal of the request had they been known at the time of his decision. The Minister may also withdraw his decision if a sentence which has been imposed on the suspect in the requesting state cannot be enforced in the Netherlands.[24]

Provisional arrest of the suspect

A suspect to whom the criminal law of the Netherlands already applies, may be taken into custody pursuant to Arts. 52 to 93 of the Code of Criminal Procedure. If, on the other hand, jurisdiction of the Dutch courts is exclusively based on a treaty conferring subsidiary jurisdiction upon the Netherlands, a suspect may nonetheless be held in custody before a decision on a foreign

---

21 See infra p. 185.
22 Art. 552cc. Cf. also Art. 14 of the European Convention on the Transfer of Proceedings in Criminal Matters.
23 Art. 552dd. Cf. also Art. 12 of the European Convention.
24 This provision relates to Arts. 8, para. 2, and 11 of the European Convention. Pursuant to Art. 8, a contracting party may request proceedings to be instituted against a person who has been finally sentenced in that state, if it cannot itself enforce the sentence, even by having recourse to extradition, and if the other contracting party does not accept enforcement of a foreign judgment as a matter of principle or refuses to enforce such sentence.

request has been taken. However, Art. 552ff of the Code permits his arrest on the basis of treaty provisions only.[25] The most important treaty provision here is Art. 27 of the European Convention on the Transfer of Proceedings in Criminal Matters, providing for the provisional arrest of a person at the request of another contracting party in anticipation of a formal request for proceedings. However, Art. 29 of the Convention requires the release of the suspect if the requested state does not receive a request for proceedings within eighteen days of the date of the arrest.

Grounds for refusal

Article 552y of the Code contains seven different grounds for summary refusal by the Minister of Justice of a foreign request for proceedings. If the Minister does not summarily reject the request, it is then forwarded to the competent public prosecutor. Article 552bb, para. 2, requires the Minister to reject the request if, taking the negative opinion of the public prosecutor into consideration, the Minister concludes that one of the grounds for refusal mentioned in Art. 552y applies.

The first ground for refusal relates to requests concerning an alien whose fixed abode or place of residence is outside the Netherlands.[26] However, two exceptions apply here. The first exception concerns requests for proceedings aimed at the confiscation of proceeds from crime.[27] Here, the presence in the Netherlands of property which may be confiscated constitutes a sufficient basis for instituting proceedings. A second exception is set out in Art. 552hh, para. 3, of the Code. This exception applies in certain cases in which a foreign state has requested extradition of a person and the Netherlands has refused to grant the request.[28]

The second ground for refusal concerns the absence of punishability under Dutch law. Here, the Code requires punishability in concreto. This implies that the conduct should not only fall under a definition of a criminal offence, but also that no justification or excuse exists which would prevent the suspect from being criminally responsible under Dutch law. Naturally, the offence must have been punishable at the time of its commission and not only at the time of the

---

25 In that case, Arts. 52 to 93 of the Code are applicable by analogy. See Art. 552ff.
26 The Code contains no such requirement with regard to Dutch nationals.
27 See Art. 552y, para. 2, of the Code.
28 See infra pp. 186-187.

request; otherwise the principle of legality would be violated. In contrast to Art. 7 of the European Convention on the Transfer of Criminal Proceedings, the Code does not require that the offence also be punishable under the law of the requesting state. This enables the Netherlands to grant requests for proceedings originating from a state which has no jurisdiction to prosecute the offence itself. Article 21 of the European Convention on Mutual Assistance in Criminal Matters or Art. 42 of the Benelux Treaty on Extradition and Mutual Assistance in Criminal Matters are especially relevant here.[29]

— The third and fourth grounds for refusal are related to the nature of the offence lying at the basis of the foreign request for proceedings. The request must be refused if the offence is of a political nature or is connected with an offence of a political nature. Refusal is also mandatory if the offence constitutes a military offence.[30] However, Art. 552hh, para. 4, of the Code makes an exception to the political offence exception with respect to requests which are based on the 1977 European Convention on the Suppression of Terrorism or on the 1979 Agreement on the application of that Convention between the Member States of the European Communities (not yet in force).

— The fifth ground for refusal concerns statutes of limitation under Dutch law as well as under the law of the requesting state. With respect to requests based on the European Convention on the Transfer of Proceedings in Criminal Matters, Dutch legislation with regard to lapse of time is applicable if the criminal law of the Netherlands already applies to the offence. If proceedings take place on the basis of subsidiary jurisdiction only, the statutory time-limit for proceedings is prolonged by six months, pursuant to Art. 26 of the Convention. Pursuant to the same Art. 26, any act which interrupts time-limitation and which has been validly performed in the requesting state shall have the same effect in the requested state, and vice versa.

— A sixth ground for refusing a request for criminal proceedings is that the request is intended to harass the person whom it concerns on account of his religious or political opinions, his nationality, race or the population group to which he belongs. Article 11 of the European Convention on the Transfer of Proceedings in Criminal Matters contains an optional ground for refusal in such cases.[31]

---

29 See also supra p. 174.
30 For a discussion of these exceptions see supra pp. 102-106.
31 This accords with Art. 3, para. 2, of the European Convention on Extradition. See also supra p. 109.

— The seventh ground for refusal set out in Art. 552y applies if to proceed against the person in the Netherlands would amount to double jeopardy within the meaning of Art. 68 of the Penal Code.[32]

As stated above, if one of the grounds specified in Art. 552y appears to apply, the Minister of Justice will either summarily refuse the request for proceedings, or do so after having received a negative opinion from the competent public prosecutor. In addition, the Minister is required by Art. 552bb, para. 3, of the Code to refuse request which are not based on a treaty if the Public Prosecutions Department is of the opinion that proceedings cannot be instituted against the suspect concerned for the offence with which he is charged. If a request is based on a treaty, the Minister must take account of the grounds refusal contained in the treaty. This is set out in Art. 552bb, para 4. Consequently, a request for proceedings must be refused if the treaty so requires, and may be refused if the treaty so permits.

Legal remedies

No particular legal remedy is available for the purpose of opposing a decision of the Minister to accept transfer of proceedings. Neither is there a general duty to inform a suspect of the fact that a foreign request for proceedings has been received. Article 552aa of the Code limits the requirement of informing him with a view to enabling him to present his views on the matter, to cases in which the jurisdiction of the Netherlands is exclusively based on a treaty.[33]

It is not the policy of the Dutch Government to develop initiatives for transferring proceedings to the Netherlands against Dutch citizens being prosecuted in another state for drug offences. They will rather await a request from other states. In principle, courts will respect this policy and consider that the Government should enjoy a large freedom of action in the area of foreign relations.[34]

---

32 For further discussion of double jeopardy see supra pp. 75-84.
33 Cf. Art. 17 of the European Convention.
34 Cf. Gerechtshof Den Haag 16 March 1989, NJ 1990, 203; Rechtbank Den Haag 19 January 1984, KG 1984, 57.

Transfer of proceedings after a refusal to extradite

In a number of extradition treaties, provisions can be found requiring the contracting parties either to consider whether proceedings should be instituted against an alleged offender or to extradite him to another contracting party. Instituting criminal proceedings may serve as an alternative to extradition here *(aut dedere aut judicare)*. Under some treaties, the obligation to submit the case to the competent domestic authorities arises only in connection with the nationality of the person involved, while other treaties contain a general obligation to make a choice between the alternatives, regardless of the person's nationality.

As examples of the first category of treaties we may mention the 1957 European Convention on Extradition, the 1980 extradition treaty between the Netherlands and the United States and the 1985 extradition treaty between the Netherlands and Australia. Pursuant to the provisions of all three treaties, the obligation for the requested state to submit the case to the competent authorities only arises if the other state so requests. Without request there is no duty to prosecute. In other words, the request and the response to it effect a transfer of proceedings from the requesting state to the requested state. The requested state exercises jurisdiction on the basis of the active personality principle. Articles 552x to 552gg of the Code of Criminal Procedure apply to these requests.

Rather different is the situation with respect to the second category of treaties. Here, the obligation to prosecute is general and, moreover, does not depend on an extradition request having been received and refused, the only exception being the 1977 European Convention on the Suppression of Terrorism. As has been discussed elsewhere in this book, the Netherlands has become a party to a number of multilateral conventions which carry the obligation for the contracting parties either to extradite the alleged offender or to institute proceedings against the person themselves.[35] It has also been shown that the Netherlands is rather reluctant to accept extraterritorial jurisdiction over offences based solely on the fact that the alleged offender is present in its territory. A reluctance which, in the case of five of these treaties, has led to the entering of reservations to the effect that the Netherlands will exercise jurisdiction based solely on the presence of the alleged offender in its territory only after it has received and refused a request for extradition from another contract-

---

35   See supra pp. 63-65.

ing party.[36] Finally, it has been explained that Arts. 4a of the Penal Code and 552hh of the Code of Criminal Procedure serve as the domestic legal basis for implementing obligations to prosecute arising out of the European Convention on the Suppression of Terrorism and these five treaties for the Netherlands.[37]

Article 552hh, para. 1, of the Code sets out the conditions under which a request for extradition will be regarded as a request for proceedings which has been granted. The following conditions apply: a) the person must be present in the Netherlands;[38] b) he is suspected or convicted of a criminal offence within the meaning of the provisions of the six treaties listed in para. 2; c) the extradition request originates from a state which is a party to the treaty in question, and extradition has been either declared inadmissible by a court or refused by the Minister of Justice. If the request for extradition is regarded as a request for proceedings which has been granted, the rules of procedure laid down in Arts. 552y to 552cc of the Code will be considered to have been followed. The foregoing does not imply that proceedings will automatically be instituted in the Netherlands in the case at hand. They will, for example, not take place if the alleged offender is able to show that he did not commit the offence, or if he is being extradited to a third state.

Transfer of proceedings after a request for enforcement of a foreign judgment rendered in absentia

In addition to requests for extradition, request for enforcement of a foreign judgment rendered *in absentia* may, under certain circumstances, also be regarded as requests for proceedings which have been granted. Here, the explanation is provided by the provisions on judgments *in absentia* in the 1968 Benelux Treaty on the Enforcement of Criminal Judgments[39] and the 1970 European Convention on the International Validity of Criminal Judgments.

---

36 The 1973 Convention on the Prevention and Punishment of Crimes against Internationally Protected Persons, including Diplomatic Agents; the 1979 International Convention against the Taking of Hostages; the 1980 Convention on the Physical Protection of Nuclear Material; the Protocol to the 1988 Convention for the Suppression of Unlawful Acts against the Safety of Maritime Navigation; the 1988 Protocol to the 1971 Convention on the Suppression of Unlawful Acts against the Safety of Civil Aviation.

37 See supra pp. 65-67.

38 Fixed abode or place of residence Netherlands is not required. Cf. Art. 552hh, para. 3.

39 Not yet entered into force.

Requests for enforcement of a foreign judgment rendered *in absentia*, made pursuant to the European Convention or the Benelux Treaty,[40] may be served on the sentenced person if there are no impediments to enforcement.[41] The sentenced person may lodge an opposition to the judgment within a specified period of time, which leads to a fresh determination of the charges against him. The opposition will be heard either by a Dutch court or by a court in the sentencing state, the sentenced person having the right to choose between the alternatives. If the person concerned opts for a fresh determination of the charges against him by a Dutch court, one might consider transfer of enforcement to amount to transfer of proceedings. This is also the point of view adopted in Art. 46, para. 2, of the 1986 Act on the transfer of enforcement of criminal judgments *(Wet overdracht tenuitvoerlegging strafvonnissen)*. Pursuant to the Act, a valid opposition with a view to having the case heard in the Netherlands, entails that the request for enforcement of the foreign judgment rendered *in absentia* must be regarded as a request for proceedings which has been granted. The foreign judgment rendered *in absentia* must then be considered null and void.

---

40 Cf. Art. 17 of the Benelux Treaty and Art. 21 of the European Convention.

41 Pursuant to Art. 45 of the 1986 Act on the transfer of enforcement of criminal judgments, a foreign judgment rendered *in absentia* may not be served on the sentenced person if proceedings for the offence on which judgment was passed would have been precluded by lapse of time under Dutch law, or if Arts. 2 to 7 of the Act preclude enforcement of a sentence in the Netherlands; cf. infra pp. 199-200. Moreover, the Netherlands may refrain from serving a judgment if the applicable treaty enables it to invoke a ground for refusing enforcement. Cf. the Explanatory Report on the European Convention on the International Validity of Criminal Judgments, p. 52.

Transfer of Enforcement of Criminal Judgments

Désirée Paridaens

Introduction

Transfer of enforcement of criminal judgments is a form of international co-operation in criminal matters in which the sentencing state transfers the enforcement of a judgment pronounced in that state to another state. The sentenced person may also be transferred at the same time. Whether or not such transfer is necessary is partly determined by the nature of the sanction imposed and the habitual residence of the convicted person. Surrender of the person will only occur if the person involved is still present in the sentencing state and has been sentenced there to deprivation of liberty.

Until 1988, transfer of enforcement of criminal judgments was only possible in the Netherlands to a very limited extent. Article 40 of the 1868 Revised Rhine Navigation Act *(Herziene Rijnvaartakte)* already offered a limited basis for this. It provides for the transfer of enforcement of the judgments of Rhine Navigation Courts in which a fine has been imposed. In addition, Art. VII, para. 7, of the 1951 NATO Status of Forces Agreement provides a basis for assistance from the receiving state in the enforcement of a sentence of imprisonment pronounced by the authorities of sending state. To the extent of my knowledge, neither of these two possibilities has ever been used in practice by the Netherlands.

Since 1 January 1988, the possibilities for transfer of enforcement of criminal judgments have been considerably widened. On that date the Netherlands became a party to the following three Council of Europe Conventions:
- the 1964 European Convention on the Supervision of Conditionally Sentenced or Conditionally Released Offenders;
- the 1970 European Convention on the International Validity of Criminal Judgments;
- the 1983 Convention on the Transfer of Sentenced Persons.

On 1 January 1988, the Act on the transfer of enforcement of criminal judgments *(Wet overdracht tenuitvoerlegging strafvonnissen)* also entered into force.[1] The Act contains substantive conditions and procedural rules for the enforcement of foreign judgments by the Netherlands and for the transfer of enforcement of Dutch judgments to other countries. According to its Art. 1, the Act applies to judgments rendered by a court in respect of criminal offences. However, the definition of the word 'judgment' also includes decisions of administrative authorities in respect of offences and imposing a punishment or measure other than deprivation of liberty , provided that such decisions can be appealed in court. Criminal offences within the meaning of the Act include: offences so designated in national legislation as well as so-called administrative offences. Under Dutch law this also includes acts falling within the scope of the 1989 Act on the administrative enforcement of traffic regulations *(Wet administratieve handhaving verkeersvoorschriften)*.[2]

Since 1988 the number of treaties that can be applied by the Netherlands in this area has been expanded. The following treaties now also offer a basis for transfer:
- the 1988 Treaty between the Netherlands and Australia on Mutual Assistance in Criminal Matters;[3]
- the 1988 United Nations Convention against Illicit Traffic in Narcotic Drugs and Psychotropic Substances;
- the 1989 Treaty between the Netherlands and Canada on Extradition;[4]
- the 1990 Convention applying the Schengen Agreement;[5]

---

1   As is the case for the Extradition Act, the Act is only applicable in the Netherlands and not in the Netherlands Antilles or Aruba. Cf. also supra pp. 3-4.
2   Cf. *Paridaens*, De overdracht van de tenuitvoerlegging van strafvonnissen, p. 182.
3   This treaty provides, among other things, for measures to locate, restrain and forfeit the proceeds of crime at the request of the other state.
4   Art. 3, para. 3, of this treaty provides the possibility for taking over the enforcement of a judgment pronounced against a citizen of the requested state after extradition of the convicted person has been refused.
5   This agreement, which took force in March 1995, supplements the Convention on the Transfer of Sentenced Persons. Art. 68 provides for transfer of enforcement of a judgment in which a sanction involving deprivation of liberty has been imposed, if the person in question has been able to avoid enforcement of that sentence by escaping to his own country. In that case, transfer is not accompanied by transfer of the convicted person and does not depend upon his consent.

- the 1990 Council of Europe Convention on Laundering, Search, Seizure and Confiscation of the Proceeds from Crime;[6]
- the 1991 Treaty between the Netherlands and Canada on Mutual Assistance in Criminal Matters;[7]
- the 1991 Convention between the Member States of the European Communities on the Enforcement of Foreign Criminal Sentences;[8]
- the 1992 Agreement between the Netherlands and the United States of America regarding mutual cooperation in the tracing, freezing, seizure and forfeiture of proceeds and instrumentalities of crime and the sharing of forfeited assets.[9]

The 1988 United Nations Convention and the 1990 Council of Europe Convention in particular required considerable amendments and supplements to the Act on the transfer of enforcement of criminal judgments. These amendments entered into force in 1993. Afterwards the Act was amended, among other reasons, for the purpose of implementing the Agreement with the United States.

Although the existing instruments now provide a wide range of possibilities for transfer of enforcement of criminal judgments to and from the Netherlands, so far the Netherlands has made relatively little use of them in practice. International cooperation has been restricted mainly to transfer of enforcement of

---

6   Also of importance for the application of Arts. 1, 8 to 12, 15, 24, 27, 31, 38 and 42 of this Convention with respect to the United Kingdom is the 1993 Agreement between the Netherlands and the United Kingdom to supplement and facilitate the Operation of the Convention of the Council of Europe on Laundering, Search, Seizure and Confiscation of the Proceeds from Crime.

7   It provides, among other things, for locating, restraining and forfeiting the proceeds of crime and other property, and for enforcement of fines.

8   This convention has not yet taken effect but, pending its coming into force, the Netherlands has declared it applicable in its relations with other member states which have made a similar declaration in accordance with Art. 21, para. 3. It provides for transfer of enforcement of criminal sentences in so far as they involve custodial penalties or pecuniary penalties or sanctions, or a combination of the two. It does not provide for transfer of the sentenced person. The coming into force of a treaty among the member states of the European Communities which was signed earlier, the 1987 Agreement on the application among the Member States of the European Communities of the Council of Europe Convention on the Transfer of Sentenced Persons, cannot be expected at present. This is due to a difference of opinion between Spain and the United Kingdom on the territorial applicability of the agreement to Gibraltar. Therefore, the Netherlands Government has decided that, under such circumstances, becoming a party to the 1987 Agreement would not be desirable.

9   The Netherlands is also a party to the 1968 Benelux Treaty on the Enforcement of Criminal Judgments which has not yet entered into force. In 1996, the Netherlands and Venezuela agreed upon a bilateral treaty with regard to the transfer of sentenced persons.

judgments in which custodial sentences have been imposed. As a rule, this has been based on the Convention on the Transfer of Sentenced Persons. This convention only provides for transfer of enforcement of judgments involving deprivation of liberty, and requires the consent of the countries involved as well that of the sentenced person. Transfer on the basis of this convention always involves the physical transfer of the person to the administering state.

A recently completed evaluation[10] has shown that in the period between 1991-1994, on the basis of the Convention on the Transfer of Sentenced Persons, the Netherlands received 550 requests for transfer of enforcement from foreign authorities. Of these requests, 312 have resulted in the transfer of a sentenced person to the Netherlands and 43 were still pending. The remaining 203 requests will not result in any transfer.[11] In the same period, on the basis of the same convention, the Netherlands made 98 requests for transfer of enforcement of judgments to other countries. So far, 22 of these requests have resulted in transfer and 7 requests are still pending.

The Netherlands has had little or no experience with the application of other treaties. An explanation for this can be found partly in the short time which has passed since the coming into force of a number of these treaties. Since 1988, the Netherlands has received only one request to take over supervision on the basis of the 1964 European Convention on the Supervision of Conditionally Sentenced or Conditionally Released Offenders. In addition, the 1970 European Convention on the International Validity of Criminal Judgments has been applied only incidentally to transfer enforcement of criminal judgments involving the deprivation of liberty against the will of the convicted person. Finally, on the basis of the 1990 Convention applying the Schengen Agreement, which has been in effect since March 1995, transfer of enforcement of a custodial sentence to the Netherlands has been achieved once.

---

10 *Gijzen*, Evaluatie van de Wet overdracht tenuitvoerlegging strafvonnissen, onderzoeksperiode 1991-1994. An evaluation of previous experiences took place in 1991. See *Knaapen/Van der Kallen*, Evaluatie van drie jaren Wet overdracht tenuitvoerlegging strafvonnissen. For a comparison between British and Dutch practice see *Paridaens/Harding*, The Transfer of Prisoners with Special Reference to The Netherlands and the UK.

11 There are various reasons for this. In 60 cases, the sentenced person had already been released by the sentencing state. In 30 cases, the person had withdrawn his consent to being transferred before action had been taken on the request for transfer. The reason for withdrawal of consent is often the expectation that the sentenced person will be released at an earlier date if no transfer takes place. In 113 cases, transfer was refused either by the sentencing state or by the Netherlands.

The Act on transfer of enforcement of criminal judgments only governs the enforcement of judgments rendered by courts of other states. In 1994, the Act containing provisions relating to the establishment of the International Tribunal for the prosecution of persons responsible for serious violations of international humanitarian law committed in the territory of the former Yugoslavia since 1991 was adopted. Articles 11 to 14 of the Act deal with enforcing judgments of the International Tribunal. A number of provisions of the Act on the transfer of enforcement of criminal judgments have been declared applicable.

Transfer of enforcement to the Netherlands

Statutory conditions for transfer

The general conditions for transfer of enforcement of judgments from foreign countries are laid down in Arts. 2 to 7 of the Act on the transfer of the enforcement of criminal judgments. First of all, Art. 2 requires a treaty basis. Article 3 then lays down that the foreign judgment must be enforceable in the sentencing state, and that the sanction imposed may not consist of the payment of the costs of proceedings or an order to pay damages to an injured party. Furthermore, Art. 3 requires that the foreign judgment has been pronounced in respect of an offence which is also punishable under Dutch law, and that, in the event of a conviction, the offender would also be liable to punishment under Dutch law. The Act hereby assumes double criminality *in concreto*. Under Art. 4, a foreign sanction may not be enforced in the Netherlands if it relates to an alien of no fixed abode or place of residence in the Netherlands.[12] However, this condition does not apply insofar as the foreign sanction involves the payment of a fine, forfeiture, or other sanction whose purpose is to deprive the offender of the proceeds from crime. Article 5 contains a non-discrimination clause. It stipulates that a foreign sentence may not be enforced in the Netherlands if the Minister of Justice finds that there is good reason to believe that the decision to prosecute or the imposition of the sanction was motivated by considerations relating to the race, religion, nationality or political opinions of the person involved or was unfavourably influenced thereby. Article 6 concerns immunity by lapse of time under Dutch law and the age of the sentenced

---

12 If the sanction has been imposed on a legal person, it may not be enforced in the Netherlands if the management board of the legal person has no seat or office in the Netherlands, or if its managing director has no fixed abode in the Netherlands.

person. A foreign sentence may not be enforced in the Netherlands if the right to enforce the sentence would be barred by lapse of time under Dutch law or if the sentenced person was under twelve years of age when the offence was committed. Finally, Art. 7 requires refusal of transfer of enforcement if the sentenced person is being prosecuted in the Netherlands for the same offence or if enforcement of the sentence in the Netherlands would not be compatible with the *ne bis in idem* principle underlying Art. 68 of the Penal Code and Art. 255 of the Code of Criminal Procedure.

If one or more of these conditions are not met, the law then requires refusal of transfer of enforcement. Meanwhile, whether or not such refusal is possible also depends upon the applicable treaty; it would have to provide room for refusal. In the remaining instances in which no grounds for refusal apply, the Act leaves discretion as to whether or not the request be refused. However, such discretion may be converted by the applicable treaty into an obligation to refuse transfer if it contains a mandatory ground for refusal which applies in the case.

In addition to the general conditions for transfer of enforcement of foreign judgments to the Netherlands, the Act also contains yet another special ground for refusal which is laid down in Art. 30, para. 1, under d. Pursuant to this provision, the district court charged with granting or refusing *exequatur* must declare enforcement inadmissible if, after due consideration of all the interests involved, it would not be reasonable to decide to enforce the judgment in the Netherlands. The *exequatur* court is hereby able to declare enforcement in the Netherlands inadmissible if, in its opinion, such enforcement would be in conflict with the fundamental principles of the Dutch legal order.

Most of the conditions laid down in Arts. 2 to 7 of the Act are familiar from extradition law. They will not be discussed further here.[13] Articles 2 and 4, however, deserve a more detailed explanation.

The treaty requirement

Article 2 of the Act on the transfer of enforcement of criminal judgments requires a treaty basis for enforcement of foreign judgments in the Netherlands. In this respect, it has been of decisive importance that the Netherlands is not

---

13 See supra pp. 93-112. For an extensive discussion see *Paridaens* (supra note 2).

prepared to enforce criminal judgments which are in conflict with the fundamental principles pertaining to the rule of law. This is even the case when the
sentenced person himself has consented to transfer of enforcement.[14] Enforcement of these judgments is held to conflict with the *ordre public* of the
Netherlands. Moreover, the legislature has taken into consideration that the
Netherlands could be held internationally responsible for enforcement, and thus
the recognition, of these judgments.[15] It has also assumed that treaties are only
concluded with states with regard to whom the Netherlands enjoys sufficient
confidence in the quality of criminal justice, and that a treaty may serve as the
indication of such confidence.

The Dutch legislature has shown a preference for a prior general assessment
of the quality of the criminal justice system in the other state rather than an
assessment *ex post* in each individual case. There are several objections to a
review in the case at hand. Refusal to accept transfer of enforcement might be
more politically sensitive than when the absence of a treaty precludes transfer
from taking place. Furthermore, according to this view, it is preferable that a
court should not be put in the position of having to express an opinion on the
administration of criminal justice in the other state.

During the parliamentary debates on the Bill, the treaty requirement was the
subject of many discussions. The objection was put forward that multilateral
and regional treaty relations do not necessarily justify automatic confidence in
the quality of criminal justice in all of the other contracting parties. Moreover,
it was argued that, on the other hand, the absence of a treaty does not necessarily imply lack of confidence in the quality of criminal justice in a certain state.
Although the Government did indeed recognize the validity of these arguments,
they held that they must be set aside because the alternative, i.e. an assessment
in the case at hand, was considered even less attractive. Finally, humanitarian
objections to the treaty requirement were also brought up. The condition could,
after all, result in the sentenced person being forced to serve his sentence in a
foreign state. This would be especially problematic if it is likely that human
rights of the sentenced person would be violated during enforcement of the
sentence. The Government, however, stuck to the view that the arguments

---

14 The Act itself does not require such consent. Whether or not consent of the sentenced person
    is needed depends upon the applicable treaty.
15 The question whether, and to what extent, the administering state should examine a foreign
    criminal judgment, is discussed in ECHR 26 June 1992, Series A 240, *Drozd and Janousek
    v. France and Spain*. The European Court held, among other things, 'that Contracting States
    are obliged to refuse their co-operation if it emerges that the conviction is the result of a
    flagrant denial of justice'.

pertaining to the rule of law in favour of the treaty requirement should outweigh any opposing humanitarian interests.[16]

Nationality and domicile

Article 4 of the Act requires a legal or factual connection between the sentenced person and the Netherlands, unless transfer of a property sanction is involved. In respect of custodial sanctions, the underlying idea is that they should preferably be served within the society to which the sentenced person will return after his release. This would give him the best chances for resocialization.

Unless enforcement of a property sanction is involved, the requirement is set for aliens that they must have fixed abode or place of reside in the Netherlands. In assessing whether this condition has been fulfilled, not only the person's permanent address in the Netherlands is taken into consideration, but also whether or not he will retain his right of residence despite the foreign sentence.[17]

In respect of Dutch nationals, the law does not require any permanent residence in the Netherlands. However, it is not the policy of the Government to encourage that Dutch nationals who have no connection with the European part of the Kingdom other than their nationality serve their sentences there.

Provisional measures

A sentenced person who − whether or not after being transferred − is present in the Netherlands may on the grounds of Art. 8 of the Act be provisionally arrested in so far as:
− the applicable treaty provides for this,[18] and
− a sentence involving deprivation of liberty has been imposed on him in the foreign state, and

---

16 For a lengthy explanation of the Government's argument see 17 NYIL 156-161 (1986).

17 Cf. also the declaration made by the Netherlands to Art. 3, para. 4, of the Convention on the Transfer of Sentenced Persons.

18 See in this regard Art. 32, para. 1, of the 1970 European Convention; Art. 11, para. 2, of the 1983 Convention; Art. 68 para. 2 of the 1990 Convention applying the Schengen Agreement; Art. 10 of the 1991 Convention between the Member States of the European Community on the Enforcement of Foreign Criminal Sentences.

- at least three months of the sentence still have to be served, and
- there is good reason to expect that the sentence will shortly be enforced in the Netherlands.

A sentenced person who has been arrested pursuant to Art. 8 may continue to be deprived of his liberty either until the foreign sentence has been converted into a Dutch sentence[19] or the Minister of Justice has given instructions for immediate enforcement.[20] Now, too, the condition applies that the applicable treaty must provide the possibility for continued detention.[21]

Arts. 13 to 13f of the Act contain a complex set of rules for seizure of property as a provisional measure with a view to forfeiture or to confiscation, either by the requesting state or the Netherlands.[22] Their complexity is partly explained by the fact that account had to be taken of considerable differences between national legal systems where confiscating the proceeds from crime is concerned. The Act distinguishes three forms of seizure upon request from a foreign state.

— First of all, Art. 13 provides for seizure of property within the framework of a criminal financial investigation. Pursuant to Art. 13, as a result of a request based on a treaty, such an investigation may be instituted in the Netherlands. The main purpose of the investigation is to locate the presence of any proceeds from crime within the Netherlands. These proceeds must belong to or have been obtained within the Netherlands by a person against whom a criminal investigation has been instituted abroad. During the investigation, property may be seized if there are good reasons to expect that subsequently the state requesting the investigation will request enforcement of an order of forfeiture of the property concerned or for enforcement of a sanction whose purpose is to deprive the offender of the proceeds from crime.

— Article 13a of the Act deals with seizure of property outside the framework of a criminal financial investigation. Like Art. 13, it is concerned with seizure in anticipation of requests for enforcement of an order of forfeiture or for enforcement of a sanction whose purpose is to deprive the offender of the proceeds from crime, to be issued by the authorities of the requesting state. Insofar as provided for by treaty, property may be seized at the request of a

---

19 See Arts. 9 to 12 of the Act.
20 See Art. 43, para. 4, in conjunction with Arts. 9 to 12 of the Act.
21 This may present a problem where custody pending the decision on a request for continued enforcement pursuant to the 1983 Convention is concerned. Art. 11, para. 2, of that convention only applies to custody pending the decision with regard to conversion of sentence. See also Art. 43, para. 4, of the Act.
22 For the differences between forfeiture and confiscation in Dutch law see pp. 45-47.

foreign state for three different purposes. According to Art. 13a, property may be seized: a) with respect to which, according to the law of the requesting state, a sanction may be imposed declaring the property forfeit, b) with a view to preserving the right of recovery in respect of a requirement to pay a sum of money which may be imposed for the purpose of confiscation of proceeds from crime according to the law of that state, and c) which may serve as evidence of proceeds from crime. Seizure in the first two situations is permitted only if it is to be expected that the other state will later request enforcement of an order of forfeiture or of a sanction whose purpose is to deprive the offender of the proceeds from crime.

— Seizure of property with respect to which a foreign court has already issued an order which is similar to an order of forfeiture or of confiscation of proceeds from crime is governed by Art. 13b. The request for seizure must – once again – be based on a treaty. Moreover, the Act requires again that a request for enforcement of an order of forfeiture or confiscation will shortly be made.

— While Arts. 13 to 13b assume that enforcement of orders takes place in the Netherlands, Art. 13c provides for the possibility for transfer of the property seized to the requesting state. This Article mainly serves to implement the 1992 Agreement with the United States. It lays down that property which is seized in the Netherlands at the request of another state, is to be handed over to that state with a view to imposing and enforcing an order of forfeiture or a sanction whose purpose is to deprive the offender of the proceeds from crime. Transfer requires permission from the competent district court. Permission may only be given under the condition that, upon delivery of the property to the foreign authorities, the latter agree that they will eventually send it back to the Netherlands or that the requesting state will pay the Dutch state a sum of money to be determined by the Minister of Justice which is equal to (part of) the value of the property.[23]

Transfer procedures

Foreign requests for transfer of enforcement of a criminal judgment to the Netherlands arrive – whether or not *via* diplomatic channels – at the Ministry

---

[23] The Minister of Justice may decide to waive payment of the agreed sum of money if the requesting state is able to prove that the property surrendered has been returned to third-party rightful owners.

of Justice. They are handled on behalf of the Minister by the Office of International Legal Assistance in Criminal Matters *(Bureau Internationale Rechtshulp in Strafzaken)* of the Ministry.

Under Art. 15 of the Act on the transfer of enforcement of criminal judgments, the Minister may reject immediately any request which has come in if he finds that it should be rejected.[24] If there is no reason to do so, then the request, with the accompanying documents, is handed over to a public prosecutor.[25]

The Act distinguishes various procedures for transfer of enforcement of a judgment from a foreign state. The procedure which is followed in a specific case depends, among other things, on the nature of the sanction imposed and the applicable treaty.

First of all, the Act provides for court proceedings, usually called *exequatur* proceedings (Arts. 18 to 33). In these proceedings, the district court decides on the admissibility of enforcing the foreign judgment in the Netherlands. If that appears to be the case the court may, taking into account what is prescribed in the applicable treaty, impose a sanction carried by a similar offence under Dutch law.[26] *Exequatur* proceedings have to be followed unless the Act prescribes one of the other procedures mentioned hereafter.

The Act opens the possibility of enforcing foreign sentences without the consent of a court in three different situations. The first relates to enforcement of judgments imposing a fine only (Arts. 34 to 37). The second involves transfer of supervision of compliance with conditions imposed upon a sentenced person by a foreign court (Arts. 38 to 42). The third concerns immediate enforcement of sanctions involving deprivation of liberty (Art. 43). Moreover, Arts. 44 to 47 contain provisions on transfer to the Netherlands of enforcement of judgments pronounced *in absentia*,[27] and Arts. 48 to 50 on transfer of

---

24 If this does not happen, the Minister of Justice may still reject the request at a later stage. This may result in withdrawal of the public prosecutor's application for permission for enforcement by the *exequatur* court. Under Art. 30, para. 2 of the Act, the public prosecutor may withdraw his application as long as its examination at the hearing of the court has not been completed.

25 This is usually the public prosecutor at the court of the district in which the sentenced person has his fixed abode or place of residence. If the person concerned has no fixed abode or place of residence in the Netherlands and the request is for enforcement of a pecuniary sanction, the documents are sent to the public prosecutor at the court of the district where property is present against which the sanction can be enforced. See Art. 17 of the Act.

26 The practical implications of this are discussed infra pp. 201-202.

27 These provisions serve to implement the 1970 European Convention on the International Validity of Criminal Judgments and the 1968 Benelux Treaty on the Enforcement of Criminal Judgments (ratified by the Netherlands but not yet entered into force).

enforcement of so-called 'partial decisions' based on the 1968 Benelux Treaty on the Enforcement of Criminal Judgments.[28] In these cases, the request for enforcement must be submitted to a district court. Arts. 48 to 50 of the Act are not yet operative because the Benelux Treaty has not yet entered into force.[29]

In actual practice, the *exequatur* procedure and the procedure of immediate enforcement have proved to be the most important. This is linked with the fact that – as was mentioned earlier – international cooperation has been mainly limited to transfer of enforcement of sentences involving deprivation of liberty on the basis of the 1983 Convention on the Transfer of Sentenced Persons. Other than the 1970 European Convention on the International Validity of Criminal Judgments, the 1983 Convention provides for both procedures. While the *exequatur* procedure in the Act corresponds to conversion of sentence under Art. 11 of the Convention, immediate enforcement in the Act is equivalent to continued enforcement under Art. 10.

The exequatur procedure

The *exequatur* procedure is divided into two stages: an inquiry into the admissibility of enforcement of the foreign judgment in the Netherlands, resulting in the granting of permission for enforcement, followed by conversion of the foreign sanction into a sanction under Dutch law.

The procedure starts with the public prosecutor's application for the granting of permission for enforcement of the foreign judgment in the Netherlands. A hearing then follows in which the *exequatur* court examines, in the following order, the sentenced person's identity, the admissibility of the application lodged by the public prosecutor, as well as the possibility of enforcement of the foreign decision in the Netherlands and the facts and circumstances important to the decision of the court. The sentenced person is given the opportunity to be present at the hearing. Where necessary, he has already been transferred from the foreign state to the Netherlands.

According to Art. 28, para. 3, of the Act the *exequatur* court is bound by the findings as to the facts of the case insofar as manifestly established by the foreign court as the basis for its decision. It may not re-investigate these facts;

---

28 These are decisions in which a court in the sentencing state has limited itself to deciding that the defendant has committed the offence with which he is charged and that a punishment or measure should be imposed. The sentencing state then requests the administering state to impose a sanction and to enforce the sentence.

29 The coming into force of the treaty is awaiting ratification by Luxembourg.

the idea is not that the investigation conducted by the court in the sentencing state should be repeated in the Netherlands. However, the Dutch view is that the *exequatur* court is not bound by the foreign court's determination that the person involved is personally responsible for the offence; it may come to the conclusion that the sentenced person is not responsible, or only to a diminished extent.[30] The fact that the *exequatur* court is not bound by the foreign court's assessment of responsibility is especially important in sentencing. This enables it to order committal to a psychiatric institution in cases where the foreign court found that the person concerned was indeed responsible.[31]

Under Art. 30, para. 1, of the Act, the court has to refuse *exequatur* if it finds:

a. that the documents submitted do not fulfil the requirements of the applicable treaty;

b. that the sentenced person was able to rely successfully upon a ground which rules out the punishability of the offence or of the offender under Dutch law but not under the law of the sentencing state, and that he does not need compulsory psychiatric treatment;

c. that enforcement in the Netherlands on the grounds of what is laid down in Arts. 2 to 4 and 6 to 7 may not take place;[32] or,

d. in a case in which according to the applicable treaty enforcement may be refused, that, after due consideration of all the interests involved, it would not be reasonable to decide to enforce the judgment in the Netherlands.

If the court finds that enforcement may be allowed, it then grants permission for enforcement of the foreign decision and, taking into account the relevant provisions of the applicable treaty, imposes a punishment or measure prescribed for the corresponding offence under Dutch law.[33] If a prison sentence is imposed, the court must then order deduction of the time the sentenced person has already been deprived of his liberty in the foreign state due to the sanction

---

30 The justification is to be found in the circumstance that the question whether an offender, in view of his mental capacity, may be held responsible for an offence, cannot really be answered by the establishment of factual circumstances. It is the result of a personal assessment by the court of the inner personality structure or emotional state of the offender. The Dutch *exequatur* court does not have to consider itself bound by this assessment.

31 Committal to a psychiatric institution may be ordered only if the accused cannot be held responsible for his acts.

32 A decision on the question of whether or not Art. 5 precludes enforcement in the Netherlands is reserved for the Minister of Justice. The Act assumes that the Minister is in a better position to pass judgment on the question of whether a person has been the victim of discriminatory treatment.

33 See Art. 31, para. 1.

imposed upon him there, as well as the time involved in transferring him to the Netherlands and the period of provisional arrest in the Netherlands pursuant to Arts. 8 to 12 of the Act. Pursuant to Art. 31a, permission to enforce a sanction whose purpose is to confiscate the proceeds from crime may be limited to enforcement of the requirement to pay a sum of money to the state which only represents part of the proceeds. Article 31a of the Act also makes it possible to order forfeiture of property representing proceeds upon the explicit request from a foreign state. This enables the Netherlands to satisfy requests for enforcement of orders of forfeiture coming from countries having a system of property confiscation. Dutch law is mainly based on value confiscation; in this system, an offender is usually deprived of the proceeds from crime by requiring him to pay a sum of money corresponding to the value of proceeds.[34] Pursuant to Art. 33a of the Penal Code, property which is wholly or primarily obtained by means of the offence may be declared forfeit only if it belongs to the sentenced person or if it can be used wholly or in part for his advantage. This is why Art. 31a of the Act declares that the *exequatur* court is not bound by the restrictions in the Penal Code with respect to the penalty of forfeiture.

Appeal in cassation with the Supreme Court against the decision of the *exequatur* court may be instituted by the public prosecutor as well as by the sentenced person.[35] If the decision is totally or partially overturned, the Supreme Court will settle the case itself where possible.[36]

With respect to transfer of enforcement of judgments involving deprivation of liberty, the Netherlands has always expressed a strong preference for the *exequatur* procedure. The alternative, the procedure of immediate enforcement, was considered less attractive by the Government during the parliamentary debates on the Bill on the transfer of enforcement of criminal judgments because it meant being bound by the duration of the sanction imposed by the foreign court. The *exequatur* procedure, on the other hand, would offer the possibility to replace the foreign sanction by a sanction which, according to Dutch standards, is considered a proper response to the seriousness of the offence, the circumstances under which it was committed and the personality of the offender. Since the sentenced person will normally return to Dutch society after his detention, the Netherlands, as administering state, has a strong

---

34 Cf. supra pp. 45-46.
35 See Art. 32, para. 1, of the Act.
36 If the Supreme Court cannot settle the case itself, it may either refer it back to the district court whose decision was overturned, or refer it to another district court.

interest in his resocialization. That is also why it might be important to be able to adjust the sanction in order to enhance chances for resocialization of the person. At the same time, the legislature realized that the willingness of foreign authorities to consent to enforcement of judgments rendered by their courts in the Netherlands might be influenced by the extent to which changes are made to the sanctions imposed by those judgments. It is therefore emphasized that the *exequatur* court must keep an open mind towards both national and international aspects of conversion.

In recent years, it has become clear that the Supreme Court allows the *exequatur* court considerable discretion in the conversion of foreign sanctions. As a result, practices are varying; whether and to what extent the sentence is reduced appears to depend on the nature of the offence, the sentencing state and the district court taking the decision on requests for transfer of enforcement.[37] The Supreme Court has, however, set some limits on the discretion of district courts to convert sentences. On the one hand, it finds the view that a Dutch *exequatur* court should mitigate the foreign sentence only in exceptional cases, to be unacceptable. On the other, neither does it consider that a foreign sentence should always be adjusted to Dutch standards.[38]

One of the problems confronting the *exequatur* court in practice is related to the condition laid down in Art. 11, para. 1, under d, of the 1983 Convention on the Transfer of Sentenced Persons: when converting the sentence, the competent authority of the administering state may not aggravate the penal position of the sentenced person. According to the Dutch view, if the foreign system of conditional or early release is more favourable than the Dutch system, in determining the length of the sentence under Dutch law account should be taken of the date on which the sentenced person would have been released in the foreign state if enforcement had been continued in that state. In most cases, the foreign system will indeed be more favourable since, under Dutch law, early release is possible only after the convicted person has served two thirds of his sentence. In those cases, the date must be known on which the sentenced person would have been released under foreign law.[39] However, other than in the Netherlands, in some countries remission of sentence may be earned by good behaviour or by doing work in prison. In these cases, in order to determine the sanction under Dutch law, the *exequatur* court will have to

---

37 *Gijzen* (supra note 10), p. 19.
38 For case law on the conversion of sentences see HR 26 June 1990, NJ 1991, 188, HR 26 June 1990, NJ 1991, 200, and HR 21 December 1993, NJ 1995, 199.
39 Cf. HR 26 June 1990, NJ 1991, 189.

have at its disposal an up-to-date summary of the rights to remission of sentence that have been accumulated up to transfer. In regard to requests from Spain in particular such a survey is not often available. In the most extreme cases, this may be a reason for the *exequatur* court to declare enforcement of a foreign judgment inadmissible, since it is not sufficiently clear what part of a sentence would remain to be served in the Netherlands.

Immediate enforcement

Although the legislature has expressed a strong preference for the *exequatur* procedure, the Act also provides for the procedure of immediate enforcement. Moreover, the Netherlands has made no use of the possibility offered by Art. 3, para. 3, of the 1983 Convention on the Transfer of Sentenced Persons to rule out the application of the procedure of continued enforcement, in its relations with other contracting parties. Thus, the option remains open to accept requests for transfer of enforcement made by states which reject conversion of sentences imposed by their courts. In principle, both procedures may be used by the Netherlands. If, however, the request for enforcement of the foreign judgment has been preceded by extradition of the sentenced person to the other state by the Netherlands under a guarantee of return, matters are different.[40] From a recent decision of the Supreme Court it follows that, in such cases, the *exequatur* procedure must always be used;[41] immediate enforcement is thus ruled out. According to the Supreme Court, the parliamentary history of the Act makes clear that extradition of Dutch nationals is acceptable only if an assurance has been given that, after having been extradited to a foreign country and having been sentenced there to deprivation of liberty, they will be returned to the Netherlands with application of the *exequatur* procedure. In its view, the possibility opened by Art. 43 of the Act for immediate enforcement of custodial sentences imposed abroad, has, as far as Dutch nationals are concerned, only been created for persons who – without having been extradited – are already detained in a state that is not willing to cooperate in transfer to the Netherlands with application of the *exequatur* procedure.

---

40 For more details on the guarantee of return of a Netherlands national or a resident alien see supra pp. 107-108.
41 HR 31 March 1995, NJ 1996, 382 *(Van Doesburg)*.

Pursuant to Art. 43, para. 1, of the Act, enforcement or further enforcement of a sentence imposed abroad and involving the deprivation of liberty, may take place in the Netherlands without application of the *exequatur* procedure if a treaty expressly provides for the possibility of immediate enforcement.[42] An instruction to that effect must be given by the Minister of Justice.[43] Before the Minister of Justice may give an instruction:

- it must be evident from a statement signed by the sentenced person that he has consented to being transferred to the Netherlands for the purposes of enforcement or further enforcement of the sanction imposed on him by the foreign state (Art. 43, para. 2);
- advice should be obtained from the execution of sentences chamber of the court of appeal at Arnhem (Art. 43, para. 3).

From the wording of both provisions it is already evident that the legislature has assumed that the decision on following the procedure of immediate enforcement may be taken only after the sentenced person has been transferred to the Netherlands. The underlying idea here was that it was deemed unacceptable to give the undertaking that the procedure of immediate enforcement would be followed before the sentenced person had been transferred to the Netherlands. Nevertheless, a different picture emerges from practice; the person concerned is only transferred from a foreign state to the Netherlands after the Netherlands has agreed to resort to immediate enforcement. In those cases, the consent of the sentencing state to transfer obviously depended on such an undertaking; the alternative would then have been that no transfer of enforcement takes place.

The conditions for application of the procedure of immediate enforcement are that assurance must be given that the sentenced person has consented to being transferred to the Netherlands and that there is no doubt as to his personal responsibility for the offence he committed, nor with respect to the freedom with which he was able to express his consent to transfer. Furthermore, the Minister of Justice must not find that the duration of a sanction involving deprivation of liberty, which according to expectation and experience would actually be served in the foreign state, is totally excessive in proportion to what is considered to be fitting for the offence by Dutch standards. Before taking a decision on whether or not to allow immediate enforcement the Minister of

---

42 Thus far, Art. 43 only serves to implement the 1983 Convention on the Transfer of Sentenced Persons.

43 Actual enforcement of the sanction takes place on the order of the public prosecutor (Art. 43, para. 5).

Justice must seek advice from the execution of sentences chamber of the court of appeal at Arnhem. In preparation of their advice, members of the chamber and a member of the Public Prosecutions Department often visit the sentenced person in the foreign state.[44] In actual practice, the Minister rejects immediate enforcement if the chamber has given negative advice.[45]

From an evaluation report completed in 1996 it has become evident that the execution of sentences chamber is often placed in a dilemma.[46] On the one hand, immediate enforcement would mean that the possibly less favourable Dutch system of early release (permitted only if two thirds of the sentence have been served) is applied to enforcement of the very often stiffer foreign penalties. On the other, from a social point of view, the sentenced person is often better off serving a custodial sentence in the Netherlands. Members of the chamber always inform the prisoner clearly of the consequences of his transfer for the length of his stay in prison. Sometimes it is decided to await the decision of a court or committee in the sentencing state on the date for release in that state. Lately, the chamber has tended to give negative advice in cases in which there is a chance that the sentenced person will be released earlier if he remains in the sentencing state. In these cases, the prisoner will, in its view, probably have considerable difficulties in accepting a longer stay in a Dutch prison. Given the shortage of prison cells in the Netherlands, the chamber does not consider it logical for custodial sentences to be enforced in the Netherlands which would not have been served in the sentencing state if the prisoner had remained there.

Transfer of enforcement from the Netherlands

Statutory conditions for transfer

For transfer of enforcement of Dutch judgments to other states, as opposed to transfer of enforcement of foreign judgments to the Netherlands, there is no treaty requirement. Other statutory guarantees must see to it that confidence in

---

44 *Gijzen* (supra note 10), p. 35.
45 *Gijzen* (supra note 10), p. 22.
46 *Gijzen* (supra note 10), p. 36.

the manner of enforcement in the administering state can be assessed.[47] This is thought preferable to a general, prior assessment *via* the treaty requirement. The absence of a treaty requirement does not, however, change the fact that when a request for enforcement is based on a treaty, the Minister of Justice must take account of the provisions of that treaty in taking his decision on transfer.[48]

The Act on the transfer of enforcement of criminal judgments distinguishes between requests made by the Dutch authorities and requests originating from the authorities of the administering state. If the request comes from the Netherlands, transfer of enforcement of judgments must be in the interest of a proper administration of justice.[49] If the request comes from a foreign state, a proper administration of justice must not stand in the way of transfer.[50] In order to assess this condition, the individual interests of the sentenced person are weighed against the general interests which are served by effectively combating crime. The decision to transfer is, therefore, a policy decision, for which no clear statutory criteria have been laid down and for which the courts – as will be shown – only conduct some marginal review in certain cases.

Furthermore, only persons residing in the Netherlands who have been sentenced to a sanction involving deprivation of liberty and who have not declared their consent to transfer, are given written notice of the intention of the Minister of Justice to transfer enforcement of the sentence. The person concerned may file a notice of objection to the Minister's proposed action with the court which imposed the sanction in the last fact-finding instance.[51] The possibility to file a notice of objection is thus only available to those sentenced persons who have been notified of the Minister's intention to transfer enforcement. The competent court must examine whether the Minister of Justice, after giving due consideration to all the interests involved, could in all fairness take the proposed decision.

---

47 In this respect, it is important that the European Court of Human Rights has decided that a state can be held responsible for transfer of a person to another state if it may be expected that the other state will act in contravention of Art. 3 of the European Convention on Human Rights. See ECHR 7 July 1989, Series A 161, *Soering v. United Kingdom*.

48 See Art. 52, para. 1, of the Act.

49 See Art. 51, para. 1, of the Act.

50 See Art. 56 of the Act.

51 See Art. 52, para. 2, of the Act. Pursuant to Art. 57, para. 1, Art. 52 is equally applicable to a request coming from another state.

Besides the condition that transfer must serve the interests of a proper administration of justice, the Act contains two provisos concerning the consequences of transfer. First, transfer of enforcement may take place only under the general condition that the sanction imposed by the Dutch court will not be altered to the detriment of the sentenced person and that account will be taken of the part of the sentence which has already been served in the Netherlands.[52] Secondly, in the case of the transfer of a sentenced person who has not declared that he consents to transfer, the condition of speciality must be made.[53]

Transfer procedure

Article 51 of the Act places the initiative for Dutch requests for transfer with the Public Prosecutions Department. If the Department finds that a proper administration of justice can best be served by the Dutch sentence being (further) enforced abroad, it directs a reasoned recommendation for transfer to the Minister of Justice. In actual practice, the Public Prosecutions Department hardly makes any use of its right of initiative. The initiative usually comes from the sentenced person who wishes to be eligible for transfer to his native state.

In the Netherlands, prisoners who in principle are eligible for transfer are informed of this by the penal institution in which they are being incarcerated. The prisoner may then by means of a form, through the intervention of the governor of the penal institution, notify the Minister of Justice of his desire to be transferred. A copy of the form is sent to the competent public prosecutor charged with enforcing the sentence. The Minister of Justice then requests a recommendation from him.[54]

If there are good reasons to expect that the sentenced person is eligible for transfer, upon demand by the Public Prosecutions Department he must make a statement before an examining magistrate which shows whether or not he consents to his transfer. The Royal Decree of 18 December 1986 to implement

---

52 See Art. 59, para. 1.
53 See Art. 59, para. 3, of the Act.
54 If the request comes from another state, the Minister not only consults the public prosecutions department, but also the court which had imposed the sanction in the last fact-finding instance on the question of whether or not transfer would conflict with a proper administration of justice. See Art. 56 of the Act.

Art. 58 of the Act[55] contains procedural rules in this respect. Although Art. 58 of the Act serves to implement the 1983 Convention on the Transfer of Sentenced Persons only, the procedure laid down in the Decree is followed also when this convention is not applicable. This is done with a view to the consequences the Act attaches to consent. For example, no possibility is open to the sentenced person who consents to his transfer to file a notice of objection against transfer. Nor is the condition of speciality relevant here.

Pursuant to the Decree, the sentenced person may be assisted by legal counsel when he makes his statement. A consular representative of the state to which the sentenced person is likely to be transferred, is given the opportunity by the examining magistrate to be present when the sentenced person makes his statement. The examining magistrate may also allow other representatives of that state to be present.

Before making his statement, the sentenced person will be informed by the examining magistrate of the consequences of his consent. Once the sentenced person has made a statement to the effect that he consents to being transferred abroad, in principle he may no longer withdraw it. There is one exception to this rule, namely in case transfer of the sentenced person does not take place within four months of the statement having been made. In that case, if the person so desires, he is given the opportunity to make a new statement to the examining magistrate as to whether or not he still consents to transfer.

If the person concerned has consented to being transferred, the Public Prosecutions Department then takes care of the actual transfer. If he has not consented, before transfer can be effected a notice of objection may be lodged pursuant to Art. 52, para. 2, of the Act.[56]

---

55 *Staatsblad* 1986, 703.
56 See supra p. 207.

Extraterritorial Investigations

André Klip

Free movement of persons and goods

Today, the world is more interrelated and interdependent than ever before. Travel and transport between different countries have become day-to-day practice for millions of people and enormous amounts of goods. This is not only a result of technical improvement of means of transport, but also of a gradual abolition or reduction of legal barriers to international travel and transport. For the Netherlands, an important moment in this development is the abolition of passport control between the Benelux countries in the 1960s. With regard to the liberalization of movements of goods, Benelux agreements have also played a major role since 1944, when the Benelux Economic Union was founded. The Benelux Economic Union served as a forerunner for developments within the European Community and the Schengen group of countries. It goes without saying that the freedom of people and goods to move transnationally has had similar consequences in the field of crime, as well. On the other hand, national police officers felt more and more handicapped because their powers still ended at the national border. For a long time, states have concentrated on facilitating economic traffic, thereby neglecting the fact that flows of persons and goods always go together with flows of illegal activities. Therefore, extraterritorial investigations are one of the responses to an increasingly obvious practical need.

Sovereignty

The exercise of authority outside of one's own territory raises questions related to state sovereignty. The Permanent Court of Justice addressed this issue in the

Lotus Case.[1] The Court held that, as a rule, international law prohibits the exercise of state power in another country, stating that: 'The first and foremost restriction imposed by international law upon a State is that – failing the existence of a permissive rule to the contrary – it may not exercise its power in any form in the territory of another State. In this sense jurisdiction is certainly territorial; it cannot be exercised by a State outside its territory except by virtue of a permissive rule derived from international custom or from a convention.' This rule remains in undiminished force today, seventy years later. It is also stated in Art. 2 of the 1988 United Nations Convention against Illicit Traffic in Narcotic Drugs and Psychotropic Substances: 'A Party shall not undertake in the territory of another Party the exercise of jurisdiction and performance of functions which are exclusively reserved for the authorities of that other Party by its domestic law.' The European Commission of Human Rights has also declared that 'foreign authorities may not take evidence in another state unless prior consent is granted.'[2]

Furthermore, it is also assumed by all mutual legal assistance treaties that enforcement jurisdiction is limited to a state's territory. With the territoriality principle as the basic assumption of international mutual legal assistance, a state may, in principle, operate on foreign territory on the basis of a treaty only. Another exception is that a foreign state may grant permission for operations on its territory.[3] The Dutch Government is of the view that 'penal enforcement power' may be exercised outside its territory only if such exercise does not conflict with a prescriptive norm of international law. When investigations on foreign territory are necessary, permission must be obtained from the state concerned. In some countries, the exercise of enforcement jurisdiction by foreign states without permission is punishable as a criminal offence.[4] On the other hand, the United States have taken the view that limited, unintrusive forms of self-help are permitted. According to the United States, the limits of these allowances are constituted by the fundamental rights of citizens.[5]

---

1   PCIJ 7 September 1927, PCIJ Reports Series A, nr. 10, p. 18.
2   European Commission of Human Rights 13 July 1987 (*X v. Germany*, 11853/85), 10 European Human Rights Reports (1988), p. 521.
3   *Siegrist*, Hoheitsakte auf fremdem Staatsgebiet, p. 145. See also Art. 4 of the 1959 European Convention on Mutual Assistance in Criminal Matters.
4   See, e.g., Art. 271 of the Swiss Penal Code and Art. 349 of the Portuguese Penal Code.
5   See *Heymann*, Two Models of National Attitudes Toward International Cooperation in Law Enforcement, pp. 99-107.

Various treaties concluded by the Netherlands provide a basis for police officers operating outside their own country's territory. The wording of these treaties indicates that operations on foreign territory are still considered exceptions to a general prohibition. The practice is one of restraint. Extraterritorial investigations permitted by treaty may be conducted only under the terms of the treaty. In cases in which the treaty terms are not fulfilled, or in the absence of a treaty, the authorities of the foreign state must be requested permission in advance. Whether such permission can be given depends on the national legislation of the state involved. The treaties to which the Netherlands is a party *NL* only allow certain activities. These include activities that arise out of necessity (pursuit), or activities that result in a relatively minor infringement of the involved state's sovereignty and the civil rights of its citizens (evidence collection in cooperation with local authorities). That also explains why, for example, a search of premises or the forced return of persons who have been arrested following cross-border hot pursuit are not permitted under these treaties.[6] In the final analysis, the treaties assume that activities which can be carried out by local authorities should not be performed by foreign authorities.

Foreign investigations and observations within the Netherlands   *treaties*

The Netherlands has concluded several treaties under which foreign officials may be granted authorization to take part in investigations in the Netherlands.[7] The most important treaties are the 1962 Benelux Treaty on Extradition and Mutual Assistance in Criminal Matters, the 1969 Benelux Agreement on cooperation between administrative and judicial authorities in matters pertaining to the Benelux Economic Union, and the 1990 Convention applying the Schengen Agreement. The 1969 Benelux Agreement in particular has adopted a number of measures in the criminal field compensating for the realization of a free movement of persons, goods, capital and services within the Benelux. It is remarkable that the 1990 Convention applying the Schengen Agreement only refers to supplementing the 1962 Benelux Treaty but not the 1969 Benelux Agreement, since the latter deals with extraterritorial investigations more extensively.[8] Police officers from one of the Benelux countries may, with

---

6   See also Resolution II.8 adopted by the 15th International Congress of the AIDP Concerning the Abduction of Persons from Another Country, 65 RIDP (1994), p. 605.

7   This cross border observation must be distinguished from an observation by local authorities on foreign request.

8   See Art. 41, para. 8, as well as declarations of the Benelux countries as to Art. 41, para. 9.

permission of the competent public prosecutor of another state, 'assist in the investigation of criminal offences' (Art. 26, para. 1, Benelux Treaty).[9] They must be in possession of an instruction issued by their superiors. They may provide all information and advice they consider necessary (Art. 26, para. 2, Benelux Treaty).[10] Article 17, para. 3, of the Benelux Agreement supplements Art. 26 of the 1962 Benelux Treaty. Pursuant to its provisions, police officers may, together with the officials of the requested state, relate their findings and activities in a police report. It is also stipulated that a police report drawn up by a police officer of another Benelux country will have the same evidential weight as reports relating to similar acts taken by national authorities.

The 1990 Convention applying the Schengen Agreement provides for the possibility of cross-border observations. On the basis of Art. 40, Belgian and German police officers are authorized to engage in passive observations in which physical force may not be used. Such an observation may only take place in relation to extraditable offences. However, the criminal offence need not yet have been committed at the time of observation. Pro-active operations are therefore possible. In the Netherlands, the National Public Prosecutor for Cross-Border Observation will check the request on the basis of certain criteria, in particular against the principles of proportionality and subsidiarity. In addition, cross-border observation must be likely to advance the investigation, and remand in custody must be permitted for the offence.

In principle, foreign police officers may only engage in observation in another country if local police officers are unable to do it for them. The general rule in Art. 40 of the Convention is that prior authorization must be requested and that conditions may be stipulated. In situations in which observations are being carried out without prior authorization, Art. 40 requires that a competent authority be notified immediately that the border has been crossed. In such cases, a request for assistance outlining the grounds for crossing the border without prior authorization is to be submitted without delay. Cross-border observation is not limited in distance; it may take place on the entire territory of another state. In urgent cases, in which prior authorization could not be obtained, observation must be terminated when the local authorities so request or within five hours of the border crossing (Art. 40, para. 2). In addition, the

---

9   Art. 26 also applies between two non-adjoining Benelux countries, as is the case for the Netherlands and Luxembourg.

10 Advisory role is the basic principle; see the Joint Commentary of the three Governments to the 1962 Benelux Treaty, *Tractatenblad* 1964, 108, p. 11.

officers must comply with local law and they are obligated to follow the instructions of the local authorities. A report of every operation must be submitted to those authorities. Observing officers may be required to appear in person before them. They must also assist the enquiry subsequent to the operation in which they took part, including legal proceedings if such assistance has been requested (Art. 40, para. 3, subparas. a, g and h).

In addition to the treaty-based investigations described hereabove, the Netherlands also authorizes investigations in the absence of a treaty. No clear legal basis exists for granting foreign officials permission to conduct independent investigations. The 1921 Code of Criminal Procedure *(Wetboek van Strafvordering)* does not refer to the matter at all. Only Dutch officials are apparently authorized to investigate criminal offences and use coercive measures under the Code. This is understandable since, in principle, the Code deals with offences under Dutch law only. With the exception of the provisions of the Code which deal with judicial assistance, there is no reference in the Code to foreign criminal proceedings. However, these provisions only deal with actions of Dutch officials with a view to render assistance in foreign criminal proceedings. There is no explicit legal basis for foreign police officers to perform their duties in the Netherlands. Meanwhile, it is often assumed that they may conduct investigations in the Netherlands in cooperation with Dutch authorities, provided that prior authorization has been obtained from the public prosecutor. Under Art. 148 of the Code, the public prosecutor is the head of all criminal investigations, and under Art. 552i of the Code, he is also the person competent to grant requests for assistance. In addition, both the 1962 Benelux Treaty and the 1990 Convention applying the Schengen Agreement point at the public prosecutor as the authority competent to decide on such requests. In practice, without stating any authority, the Government assumes that the public prosecutor is the authority competent to grant permission. Whatever the legal situation might be, it cannot be expected that foreign officers immerse themselves in the question of whether this official abused his powers under Dutch law. Meanwhile, investigations in the Netherlands unauthorized by Dutch authorities are, of course, a violation of Dutch sovereignty.

Cross-border pursuit

Article 27, para. 1, of the 1962 Benelux Treaty permits cross-border pursuit of a person suspected of having committed an extraditable offence into the territory of another state without prior authorization.[11] Belgian police officers are authorized to apprehend the suspect pursued within a ten-kilometer-zone parallel to the border. They must then take the suspect to the Dutch authorities who will perform the arrest (Art. 27, para. 2). It is unclear whether pursuit without apprehension is also permitted outside the ten-kilometer-zone. Paragraph 3 of Art. 27 gives the pursuing police officers the right to prepare a report, in which they give account of their mission. A pursuit (interrupted or terminated) may then serve as the basis of further investigations. The inclusion of rules for pursuit in the 1990 Convention applying the Schengen Agreement does not change the Netherlands' relationship with Belgium.[12]

Under the Dutch declaration, attached to Art. 41 of the Convention applying the Schengen Agreement, German police officers are authorized to continue a pursuit into the Netherlands within a distance of ten kilometers parallel to the common border. They are authorized to apprehend a person pursued on a public road or property provided they have witnessed the suspect committing an extraditable offence on German territory. In urgent cases, a pursuit may take place without prior authorization. The pursuing officers are allowed to hold the subject pursued until local police officers arrive. This applies only to emergency situations in which it is impossible for competent local police officers to take over the pursuit timely.

In the course of the implementation of the 1990 Convention applying the Schengen Agreement, a new paragraph was added to Art. 54 of the Code of Criminal Procedure. This provision authorizes 'a person in public service of a foreign state who is entitled under international law to effect a cross-border pursuit into the Netherlands' to apprehend the suspect.[13] As an additional consequence of the 1990 Convention applying the Schengen Agreement, a general provision has been enacted in the Penal Code. Pursuant to Art. 185a of the Code, it is now a criminal offence to resist a foreign official or an official of an international organization who is performing his duties in the Netherlands in conformity with international law. The Article is meant to implement provisions in international instruments, such as Art. 42 of the 1990 Convention, creating the obligation for the Netherlands to regard officials of other states or

---

11 Article 17, para. 1, of the 1969 Benelux Agreement makes this possible even if the criminal offence involved could not lead to extradition.

12 See Appendix II for the declaration of the Netherlands referred to in Art. 41, para. 9.

13 Article 13a of the Extradition Act *(Uitleveringswet)* further provides a legal basis to hold aliens for questioning if there is good reason to expect that a request for provisional arrest wil shortly be made.

of international organizations as local officials with regard to offences committed against them.[14] Its logical counterpart, a provision making unauthorized activities of foreign officials in the Netherlands a criminal offence, is lacking in the Code.

Liaison officers

On the basis of bilateral agreements as meant in Art. 47 of the 1990 Convention applying the Schengen Agreement, liaison officers may be seconded to the police authorities of another Party for a specified or unspecified period of time. The purpose of secondment is to promote and expedite cooperation (Art. 47, para. 2), in particular by providing assistance in the form of exchange of information for the purpose of fighting crime by preventive and repressive means (subpara. a). Another aim is to promote cooperation by providing assistance where compliance with requests for police and judicial assistance in criminal matters is concerned (subpara. b), as well as to facilitate the transmission of information between the various police forces (Art. 44, para. 2, subpara. a).

Liaison officers have advisory and assistance tasks. They are not authorized to take independent police action. They are to provide information and perform their duties in accordance with instructions given them by the contracting party of origin and by the contracting party to which they have been seconded (Art. 47, para. 3). They are to report regularly to the head of the police department to which they have been seconded (Art. 47, para. 3).

Some liaison officers are officially attached to the embassy of their state, and, consequently, have diplomatic immunity. Their presence is regulated by an exchange of notes between the two Governments. The 1990 Convention applying the Schengen Agreement now provides a basis for secondment to the Dutch police authorities or to the Central Criminal Intelligence Department *(Centrale Recherche Informatiedienst, CRI)*. The Government may extend diplomatic status to the seconded officer, but not for investigative purposes.

Under the 1990 Convention applying the Schengen Agreement, it is provided that a foreign liaison officer seconded to the police or to the CRI will

---

14 Envisaged are, for example, officials of the European Communities. The 1962 Benelux Treaty and 1969 Benelux Agreement already contained provisions carrying the obligation to equate foreign officials with local officials for the purpose of offering them protection in the exercise of their duties (Arts. 28 and 25).

have no operational authority. The officer will primarily follow instructions of the Dutch authorities. These are set out in the 'Guidelines with regard to stationing liaison officers in the Netherlands', which also apply to other liaison officers than those of Schengen states.[15] According to the Guidelines, the task of liaison officers consists of exchanging information for the sake of preventing and combating crime as well as preventing and suppressing disturbances of public order. In addition, they may provide assistance in the execution of requests for mutual judicial assistance. Point 2 of the Guidelines specifies that the actual investigation of criminal offences in the Netherlands will be carried out by Dutch police officers under the authority of the Public Prosecutor Department. The liaison officer must refrain from independent enquiries and investigative activities. If information is not exchanged by liaison officers on the basis of a mutual legal assistance treaty, the state which has provided the information may set conditions for the use of such information.

The Europol Drugs Unit has been operational in the Hague since 1994. Liaison officers seconded to it have no executive powers. They are charged with exchange of information only. Initially, the basis for the activities of the Europol Drugs Unit was a ministerial agreement of the Council of Ministers of the European Union of 2 June 1993. This has since been replaced by a Joint Action of March 10, 1995,[16] based on Art. K.3, para. 2, subpara. b, of the Treaty on European Union. As the host state of the Europol Drugs Unit, the Netherlands has concluded a number of bilateral agreements with the member states of the European Union regarding the secondment of liaison officers to the Europol Drugs Unit. The officers are granted diplomatic status in these agreements.[17] The Europol Convention, concluded on 26 July 1995, which will establish the Europol Police Office in The Hague, has not entered into force yet.[18]

Presence at the execution of requests for mutual assistance

Mutual legal assistance treaties usually contain provisions on the presence of officials of the requesting state at the execution of a request for assistance. In

---

15 Adopted in 1994. See infra pp. 227-229 for the full text.
16 Joint Action of March 10, 1995, 1995 OJ L 62.
17 See Appendix II for information on the exchange of notes between the Netherlands and the other member states of the European Union.
18 See also supra pp. 149-151.

most cases, this involves a discretionary authority of the requested state (Art. 4, 1959 European Convention on Mutual Assistance in Criminal Matters). In mutual legal assistance treaties with the United States (Art. 5, para. 3) and Australia (Art. 10, para. 4), the requested state is required to permit the presence of authorities of the requesting state. In actual practice, the Netherlands usually permits the presence of foreign officials. Requests for permission are generally regarded as requests to carry out or assist in investigations within the meaning of Art. 552h of the Code of Criminal Procedure.[19]

Investigations in military cases

Article VII, para. 1, subpara. a, of the 1951 Agreement between the Parties to the North Atlantic Treaty regarding the status of their forces grants the military authorities of the sending state the right to exercise all criminal and disciplinary jurisdiction conferred on them by the law of the sending state over all persons subject to the military law of that state. Outside the military premises, the employment of military police is subject to arrangements with the authorities of the receiving state, and only insofar as such employment is necessary to maintain discipline and order among the members of the force.[20]

The 1953 Act implementing the Agreement between the Parties to the North Atlantic Treaty regarding the status of their forces *(Wet houdende goedkeuring en uitvoering van het Verdrag van Londen van 19 juni 1951 tussen de staten die partij zijn bij het Noord-Atlantisch Verdrag nopens de rechtspositie van hun krijgsmachten)* does not give foreign military authorities unconditional authorization to carry out investigations in the Netherlands. Article 2 obliges the Dutch authorities to cooperate with the authorities of the sending state charged with the criminal investigations related to their own personnel. A Circular issued by the Minister of Justice[21] limits the meaning of the term 'exercise of jurisdiction', as meant in Art. VII of the Status of Forces Agreement, to prosecution of criminal offences, and does not include investigations. The responsibility for investigations therefore rests with the Dutch authorities. With

---

19 *Sjöcrona,* De kleine rechtshulp, p. 99.
20 This allows military police officers to conduct investigations. See HR 26 November 1991, NJ 1992, 307. See also Appendix II for information on the relevant agreements with the United States of 13 August 1954 and with Germany of 3 August 1959.
21 Circular of 19 February 1981 concerning the exercise of jurisdiction with regard to criminal offences committed by foreign military officials. No official source known. Published in *Buirma,* Militair straf-, strafproces- en tuchtrecht, pp. 226-243.

a view to the use of evidence in foreign criminal proceedings, it is advised that enquiries and investigations be conducted in conjunction with the foreign authorities. Both the Act (Art. 3) and the Circular permit foreign military authorities to hold a military suspect in detention.

Foreign police officers in the Netherlands in practice

There is considerable variety in the manner in which foreign police officers conduct investigations in the Netherlands. Some officers act entirely on their own initiative.[22] Others first take independent action, and then in the course of time begin to work together with the Dutch authorities. In some cases, an operation is set up in cooperation with the Dutch authorities, but includes additional activities which are not covered by the terms of cooperation. There are also operations which, from the beginning, are wholly conducted in cooperation with the Dutch authorities.

In 1978, in an answer to questions raised in Parliament, the Minister of Justice reported that German police officers occasionally come to the Netherlands on the request of Dutch police officers in order to give technical advice in handling certain cases which are also of concern to the German police. Their role is not always limited to giving advice, however. According to the Minister of Justice, in the fall of 1977, German police officers were present in the Netherlands in order to assist in the arrest of Red Army Fraction *(Rote Armee Fraktion)* members.

In reported cases on the involvement of foreign police officers, a variety of complaints were raised about their activities. Quite often, the allegation is that the foreign officers induced suspects to commit criminal offences.[23] One author suggests that this foreign interest in entrapment is related to the dissatisfaction abroad with Dutch drug policies.[24] This would also explain why there are no known cases of the reverse situation. Another explanation would be that difference in national rules on police methods play a role here.[25] This points at certain investigation methods like entrapment, undercover operations

---

22 Gerechtshof 's-Gravenhage, 22 November 1984, NJ 1985, 862, 17 NYIL 299 (1986).

23 Gerechtshof 's-Gravenhage, 22 November 1984, NJ 1985, 862, 17 NYIL 299 (1986).

24 *Swart,* The Protection of Human Rights in International Cooperation in Criminal Proceedings, p. 397.

25 See, e.g., the United States Supreme Court in *Alvarez Machain* (112 S. Ct. 2188 (1992)), and also *Heymann/Heath Gershengorn,* Pursuing Justice, Respecting the Law, pp. 120-147.

and bugging, which may be legal in one country, yet illegal in another. Third, it is possible that diplomatic immunity offers the officer involved such personal protection that he is inclined to pay insufficient respect to Dutch law. The complaint of entrapment has been successful in a few cases only. In those few cases, foreign police officers were engaged in the contested activity without the foreknowledge of the Public Prosecutions Department.[26] Generally speaking, if criminal proceedings are pending abroad, a Dutch court is not readily inclined to investigate whether foreign police officers engaged in unacceptable activities in the Netherlands.[27]

Another complaint which is raised quite often is that a suspect has been lured into crossing the border and leaving Dutch territory. With or without the cooperation of the Dutch authorities, the foreign police officer would have tried to get the suspect to cross the border so that he may be arrested and tried outside the Netherlands. In one of these cases, the District Court of The Hague[28] spoke of a flagrant violation of due process, and it ordered the State of the Netherlands to translate the judgment and send it to the German authorities. Later court decisions protect affected parties to a lesser extent. For instance, those who are prosecuted in the Netherlands may not complain about unsuccessful attempts of foreign police officers to bring them outside the country.[29] Through such a judgment, the Supreme Court has not erected a strong bar against enticement. A case in point is a decision of the Supreme Court in which it held that no violation of rights had occurred because the complainant had intended to leave the Netherlands all along and was not induced to any new action when an American undercover agent brought him to leave a few weeks earlier than he had planned.[30] A few German decisions

26 Rechtbank Amsterdam, 28 May 1980, NJ 1981, 217; Rechtbank Rotterdam, 12 September 1986, NJ 1987, 476.
27 Gerechtshof 's-Gravenhage, 22 November 1984, NJ 1985, 862, 17 NYIL 299 (1986). This case concerned a Dutch suspect who was tried in Germany and who, because he allegedly was induced by German undercover agents in the Netherlands to commit a criminal offence, wanted the Netherlands to request transfer of proceedings from Germany.
28 Rechtbank 's-Gravenhage, 29 June 1984, NJ 1985, 815.
29 HR 9 October 1990, NJ 1991, 98. See also HR 7 June 1988, NJ 1988, 1041. Another (failed) attempt of the DEA to lure a suspect out of the Netherlands is described in Gerechtshof Amsterdam 25 March 1991, NJ 1991, 365. For a crafty inducement to Germany, see Bundesgerichtshof 19 December 1986, StV 1987, 138.
30 HR 9 September 1994, NJ 1995, 44 (Roefen).

were reported with regard to cases in which persons had been removed by force from the Netherlands by German police officers.[31]

There are strong objections to be made against craftily enticing or abducting persons from the Netherlands. The most serious objection is that the person concerned is denied the legal protection of extradition law. According to Art. 2, para. 3, of the Constitution for the Kingdom of the Netherlands *(Grondwet voor het Koninkrijk der Nederlanden)*, extradition may only take place pursuant to a treaty. This is especially important to Dutch nationals as they can only be extradited under the condition that, if convicted, they will be permitted to serve their term of imprisonment in the Netherlands; cf. Art. 4, para. 2, of the Extradition Act *(Uitleveringswet)*. In addition, every person whose extradition is requested has the right of having the request examined by a court of law, which will determine whether his objections to being extradited are valid. Entrapment or abduction may nullify such protection accorded by the law. Furthermore, such a practice may deprive a suspect of the right to being tried by the court to which he is rightfully entitled by law *(jus de non evocando)*. *Heymann* and *Heath Gershengorn* provide an illustration of this with the case of *Van Sichem*.[32] *Van Sichem* was a Dutch national suspected by U.S. authorities of dealing in drugs. After the American authorities had provided the Netherlands with evidence of a number of criminal offences, the Netherlands announced that it was willing to prosecute *Van Sichem* in the Netherlands rather than to extradite him. However, with the help of a Belgian informer, U.S. officers were able to lure *Van Sichem* into Belgium. Belgium then extradited him to the United States.

— A third problem connected with the activities of foreign police officers (both lawful and unlawful) is that they may have negative consequences for the conduct of a criminal trial in the Netherlands. It turns out that foreign officers usually are not prepared to appear in the Netherlands as a witness at a public hearing once their collaboration in the investigation of a criminal case is over. Sometimes, a foreign officer will appear before the examining magistrate during a preliminary investigation and testify as a witness, often remaining anonymous. However, that officer usually does not reappear at the public hearing.[33] In light of the foregoing, a refusal to testify raises the question of

---

31 Oberlandesgericht Düsseldorf, 31 May 1983, NJW 1984, 2050; Bundesgerichtshof, 30 May 1985, EuGRZ 1987, 94; for the same case, see Bundesverfassungsgericht, 6 March 1986, EuGRZ 1987, 92 and StV 1987, 137.

32 *Heymann/Heath Gershengorn* (supra note 25) p. 146.

33 HR 3 July 1989, NJ 1990, 142.

whether the foreign police officer is in fear of being held accountable for his conduct on Dutch territory.

The Government has assured Parliament that in cases of a foreign police officer operating in the Netherlands without prior knowledge of or permission from the Public Prosecutions Department, formal steps will be taken by the Minister of Foreign Affairs and informal steps by the Ministry of Justice. Such a formal step could involve deportation of the police officer concerned. This is the only possibility of dealing with officers to whom diplomatic immunity has been extended.

If the unlawful activities of foreign officers have resulted in the arrest of Dutch nationals in a foreign country, this may lead to a formal request for their return.[34] According to the Government, clear evidence that unlawful activity has taken place is required. Dutch consular officials may advise a Dutch national standing trial abroad to use the defence of unlawfully obtained evidence.[35] In some cases, the Minister of Justice and the Minister of Foreign Affairs have asked the foreign country to discontinue criminal proceedings. In actual practice, however, the strength of the Dutch Government's arguments is often undermined when it turns out that Dutch police officers were also involved in the foreign investigations.[36]

Dutch police officers abroad; treaty provisions

Concerning treaty bases for investigations by Dutch police officers abroad, the reader is referred to the foregoing pages where the basis for investigations by foreign police officers in The Netherlands was discussed. However, a few additional comments may be made here. In contrast to what German police officers are permitted with respect to cross-border pursuit in the Netherlands, Germany has unilaterally granted Dutch police officers a broader authority. In a declaration attached to Art. 41 of the 1990 Convention applying the Schengen Agreement, Germany has provided that the activities of Dutch police officers

---

34 See, e.g., Bundesgerichtshof, 19 December 1986, StV 1987, 138.
35 See also Netherlands Report on Co-operation in Criminal Matters, submitted to the 15th Conference of European Ministers of Justice in Oslo 1986, published in 19 Netherlands Yearbook of International Law 1988, pp. 298-308.
36 The Government has declared that in operations by Dutch liaisons abroad, the basic principle remains 'that Dutch police refrain from attempts to bring Dutch subjects under the jurisdiction of a foreign power unless a specific legal basis exists for doing so'. But see also supra p. 152.

in Germany are unlimited both with regard to where and for how long they are conducted.

On pursuit by Dutch police officers in Belgium, which is possible for extraditable offences, some decisions of Belgian courts are available. In cases where the offence is not an extraditable offence, no basis for pursuit exists according to the 1962 Benelux Treaty. In such cases, resisting a Dutch police officer will not be treated as resisting a police officer in the lawful exercise of his duties.[37] Consequently, Dutch police officers will not be protected on equal footing with their Belgian counterparts on the basis of Art. 28 of the Treaty.

A unilateral provision can be found in the 1992 Treaty providing a framework for friendship and closer cooperation between the Netherlands and Suriname. On the basis of Art. 4, judicial and police experts may be seconded to the Dutch embassy in Paramaribo in order to reinforce the constitutional order and governing apparatus in Suriname, and to support the process of legislation, as well as various aspects of the maintenance of law and order and the departments of general government administration.

Domestic law

In Arts. 539a to 539w of the Code of Criminal Procedure provisions can be found with regard to investigations conducted by Dutch officials abroad. The purpose of these provisions is to provide a basis for investigations in three different situations: investigations on foreign territory; investigations outside of territorial waters[38] and in the air; and investigations in the Netherlands Antilles and Aruba, the two other parts of the Kingdom of the Netherlands. It may be inferred from the wording of Arts. 539c to 539w of the Code that these provisions are intended exclusively for application in investigations at sea and in the air. Unlike investigations at sea and in the air, investigations on foreign territory require the exercise of utmost restraint. This is especially important on land where a competent (foreign) authority as well as applicable local law always exists, contrary to at sea and in the air where there might be a void as to the competent authority and applicable law. This also explains why no

---

37 See Hof van Beroep Antwerpen 8 March 1984, 47 Rechtskundig Weekblad 1983-1984, pp. 2965-2966. See also Cour d'Appel Liège 16 October 1991, 74 Revue de Droit Pénal et de Criminologie 1994, p. 111. See also supra note 14.

38 Notably the North Sea continental shelf.

provision for the use of coercive measures exists for investigations on foreign territory.

The first paragraph of Art. 539a of the Code permits the use of certain powers outside the territorial jurisdiction of a district court. The powers that can be exercised are those in connection with pretrial investigation into criminal offences.[39] Dutch police officers carrying out investigations abroad are bound by the Code, as well as by provisions of criminal procedure contained in special statutes. The use of coercion (such as arrest) is not permitted.

The third paragraph of Art. 539a of the Code provides that the investigations abroad may be conducted only *'in conformity with international and interregional law'*.[40] The most important limitation recognized under international law is the prohibition of violation of the sovereignty of another state. It is important to underline that Art. 539a of the Code creates authorization under Dutch law only. Dutch police officers thus also have to obtain prior authorization from the competent foreign authority before crossing the border into foreign territories.

Military police officers have been given the same powers abroad as their civil colleagues. In drafting Art. 62 of the 1990 Military Criminal Justice Act *(Wet Militaire Strafrechtspraak)*, the Government presumed that an agreement between the Kingdom of the Netherlands and the respective country would be reached to regulate investigations into criminal offences in that country.

In short, Art. 539a Code of Criminal Procedure contains two important instructions for the Dutch police officer conducting investigations abroad: an obligation to respect the law of the other country, and an obligation to comply with Dutch law as well. The latter is important, for example, in cases in which a Dutch police officer questions a suspect. The legal requirement that a suspect be advised that he may refuse to answer questions is also applicable abroad (Art. 29 of the Code).

Case law

Investigations of Dutch police officers abroad come up in Dutch case law with regard to the admissibility of evidence obtained abroad. The first conclusion to

---

39 The authority exists with respect to all offences over which the Netherlands has jurisdiction, regardless of whether the crime has been committed in the Netherlands or not.

40 By interregional law is meant the law that governs the relationship between the three countries of the Kingdom of the Netherlands. See supra p. 2.

draw from a reading of Supreme Court cases regarding Art. 539a of the Code of Criminal Procedure is that a potential violation of international law by Dutch police officers will not bar the use of the evidence obtained abroad if the defence does not raise the matter unless the violation is manifest.[41]

In a 1988 decision, the Supreme Court refused to admit evidence obtained by Dutch police officers while conducting an investigation abroad.[42] The case concerned a charge resulting from a pursuit of a suspect into Belgium. The Supreme Court examined the 1962 Benelux Treaty and concluded that the pursuit had been illegal since, in that case, it did not concern an extraditable offence, as is required by Art. 27 of the Treaty. In 1984, the Supreme Court decided that international law does not allow to board vessels of another state outside the territorial waters of the Netherlands. The competence to do so only lies with the flag state.[43]

Authorization to conduct an investigation in foreign territory will normally be granted by a foreign state before the investigation starts. However, authorization may also be granted later. Permission may be granted by the competent authorities either explicitly or tacitly. Tacit permission was presumed in a case in which the foreign official present at the investigation made no objection to the activities of his Dutch colleague.[44] The importance of an authorization given afterwards is illustrated by a case in which Dutch police officers removed a bullet from a tree on German territory without having obtained prior permission from the German authorities.[45] After the bullet was sent to Germany, it was immediately returned to the Netherlands by the German authorities.

While abroad, police officers are permitted under Dutch law to prepare reports which may be used as evidence in a subsequent criminal trial.[46] With permission from the competent foreign authorities, police officers may conduct investigations and interrogations.[47] It is important that the foreign authority giving permission to the Dutch police officers to question witnesses is aware of the consequences of the evidence gathering for a criminal trial in the

---

41 HR 18 May 1982, NJ 1983, 49; HR 10 April 1984, NJ 1984, 768; HR 16 April 1985, NJ 1986, 769, 18 NYIL 376 (1987).
42 HR 26 April 1988, NJ 1989, 186.
43 HR 24 January 1984, NJ 1984, 538 *(Magda Maria)*.
44 HR 16 April 1985, NJ 1986, 769, 18 NYIL 376 (1987).
45 HR 7 June 1988, NJ 1988, 987.
46 HR 18 May 1982, NJ 1983, 49.
47 HR 16 April 1985, NJ 1986, 769, 18 NYIL 376 (1987). See also, HR 7 June 1988, NJ 1988, 987.

Netherlands. A police report made by a Dutch police officer might constitute the sole basis for a conviction. Therefore, an accused might be convicted on the basis of written evidentiary material containing declarations by witnesses abroad who will not appear at the hearing in the Netherlands at a later date. This may deprive the accused of the opportunity to confront and examine such witnesses. Awareness of this aspect of criminal procedure in the Netherlands is of particular importance for the authorities of a legal system in which a sharp separation exists between pretrial investigations and the trial itself and in which hearsay evidence is admitted in exceptional circumstances only. They should realize that a request for the questioning of a witness by a Dutch police officer will often not be followed by another request, originating from a Dutch court, to have the witness appear at the trial. From a comparative perspective, Dutch case law accepts convictions on the basis of declarations from witnesses who do not appear at the trial rather easily.[48] It is sometimes assumed that the right of the accused to question witnesses, guaranteed by Art. 6 of the European Convention on Human Rights, has been sufficiently respected if he has been given an opportunity to question a witness in writing.

Annex

Guidelines with regard to stationing liaison officers in the Netherlands

21 March 1994 (official translation)

The increasing internationalization of organized crime in particular makes intensification of the international cooperation in combatting this sort of crime necessary.

The liaison officers network gives an important contribution to the improvement of the international cooperation.

Stationing of liaison officers in the Netherlands is aimed at furthering and speeding up the mutual cooperation between the Netherlands and the sending state concerned within the framework of international treaties, especially by providing assistance in:

---

48 See *Klip*, Buitenlandse getuigen in strafzaken, pp. 11-27. Cf. also supra p. 143.

a. the exchange of information for the sake of preventing and combatting crime in general and more especially in the exchange of information with Dutch special criminal investigative services as far as it concerns common activities in the field of the prevention and suppression of crime;

b. the execution of requests for legal assistance in criminal cases;

c. the exchange of information for the sake of preventing and suppressing public order disturbances.

In view of i.a. the TREVI recommendation established in Luxembourg in June 1991 with regard to the exchange of liaison officers it is desirable that liaison officers take the following guidelines in consideration when executing their duty:

1. a. the liaison officers will provide information end execute orders in the framework of instructions given to him by the sending state;

   b. in the execution of his work, the liaison officer can for mediation and assistance appeal to the National Criminal Intelligence Division (CRI) of the National Police Agency (KLPD);

   c. at meetings to be organized by KLPD's CRI, the liaison officer will give an account of his work to KLPD's CRI;

   d. the liaison officer will comply, to the extent possible, with requests made to him by Dutch enforcement officers through KLPD's CRI or otherwise;

   e. the liaison officer will timely make available to KLPD's CRI information from his sending state that is destined for the Dutch police.

2. a. In the Netherlands the actual detection of punishable offences will be conducted by Dutch enforcement officers that fall under the Dutch Public Prosecution Service.

   b. The liaison officer will refrain from carrying out executive law enforcement activities;

   c. The liaison officer shall liaise with the competent Dutch authorities with regard to bilateral investigations.

3. a. When, outside the framework of the relevant treaties on extradition and on legal assistance, information is exchanged between the Netherlands and the sending state through the mediation of the liaison officer, the State in which the information originated will set the terms on which the information may be made use of. The receiving State will commit itself to comply with the terms. Further agreements may be made between the

Netherlands and the sending state about the supply of data from police registers and the use that may be made of the data;

b.   The data mentioned under 3.a. may only be used as evidence in criminal cases if to that end a request for legal assistance, based on the applicable treaty on legal assistance, has been complied with by the State in which the data originated.

4.   Contacts between the liaison officer and informants working for the police in the Netherlands shall be maintained only through the mediation of and with permission of the local, regional or national criminal intelligence service(s).

5.   If the liaison officer is approached by the media with regard to his activities in a particular case, he will beforehand consult the competent Dutch authorities in order to see to it that possible comment does not inflict harm to possible Dutch interests.

6.   These guidelines will not cover the cooperation between the liaison officers and the Customs service on the basis of the existing international customs regulations in the field of the relevant mutual assistance and the Community interests.

Cooperation in Tax Matters

Coen Mulder

Introduction

Traditionally, mutual assistance in criminal matters was refused as a matter of course where fiscal offences were concerned. However, in recent years the exception of the fiscal offence is on the decline. This is certainly true at a European level and in Dutch law. Moreover, an ever denser system of administrative cooperation in fiscal matters has been developed between states. It consists of exchanging information and lending other forms of administrative assistance for the purpose of collecting and recovering taxes. To a considerable extent these forms of administrative assistance seem to fill the gaps created by the traditional reluctance of states to cooperate in the repression of fiscal offences. It is, therefore, indispensable to discuss the relationship between administrative assistance and assistance in criminal matters in Dutch law and in international conventions to which the Netherlands is a party.

That relationship is a complex one. It is made more complicated still by the growing influence of the European Convention on Human Rights on tax law in the Netherlands. For, on the one hand, the European Court of Human Rights has made it clear that the requirements of a fair trial apply to so-called administrative penalties imposed by administrative authorities whenever these penalties have a punitive and deterrent purpose.[1] In Dutch tax law administrative penalties play an important role. On the other hand, the Court's case law on the right of the suspect or the accused not to be compelled to testify against himself may have a certain bearing on the power of tax authorities to investigate the evasion of tax laws.[2] The consequences of these developments for the

---

1   ECHR 21 February 1984, Series A 73, *Öztürk v. Germany*; ECHR 24 February 1994, Series A 284, *Bendenoun v. France*.
2   ECHR 25 February 1993, Series A 256-A, *Funke v. France*; ECHR 17 December 1996, *Saunders v. United Kingdom*, Reports of Judgments and Decisions 1996.

rendering of administrative assistance in tax matters by the Dutch authorities remain, as yet, largely unstudied.

The complexity of the subject-matter discussed here requires a brief look at the basic features of Dutch tax law.

Fiscal offences and their repression in Dutch law

Fiscal offences in Dutch law may be defined as acts made punishable by a statute that regulates the collection of taxes, whatever their name or nature. Taxes consist of all forms of compulsory payments to general government. They may comprise compulsory payments to central government, collected by the tax department of the Ministry of Finance. They may also include compulsory contributions to other agencies of central government, to local authorities or other (semi-) public bodies, including social security agencies. In a number of cases these contributions are collected by the tax department of the Ministry of Finance to the benefit of these authorities or agencies. For simplicity's sake we will limit our discussion of Dutch tax law to taxes collected by the tax department of the Ministry of Finance for the benefit of central government.

Four different statutes govern the repression of offences that violate tax laws. The two most important ones are the 1959 General Act on Taxes *(Algemene Wet inzake rijksbelastingen)* and the 1995 Customs Act *(Douanewet)*. The other statutes are the Recovery of Taxes Act 1990 *(Invorderingswet 1990)* and the 1991 Act on Excises *(Wet op de accijns)*. It is an important feature of these statutes that the repression of tax offences is subject to a regime that, in many ways, differs from ordinary substantive criminal law and criminal procedure. Equally important is the fact that an act constituting a fiscal offence may amount to a common crime at the same time. This is notably true for Arts. 225 and 326 of the Penal Code which deal with the crimes of forgery of documents and swindling. Thus, the difficult and controversial question arises of whether punishment for a fiscal offence as well as for a common offence constitutes a form of double jeopardy.[3] The answer given in case law is usually negative.

In sanctioning infringements of tax laws a two track system is followed. One track is administrative in nature and consists of tax authorities imposing an administrative fine, the fiscal fine, on the offender; against their decisions

---

3   Cf. *Wattel*, Fiscaal straf- en strafprocesrecht, pp. 196-223; *Wortel*, Vervolgen in belastingzaken, pp. 113-131.

an appeal lies to the tax chambers of the various courts of appeal. The Supreme Court assumes that the fiscal fine has a punitive and deterrent purpose. Tax chambers, therefore, have to observe the requirements of a fair trial of Art. 6 of the European Convention on Human Rights in dealing with fiscal fine cases.[4] The other track consists of bringing charges against the perpetrator of a fiscal offence before a criminal court. A number of provisions in tax legislation, so-called anti-cumulation provisions, require the lapse of a fiscal fine if the person concerned is later acquitted or convicted by a criminal court. In actual practice there is a tendency to apply the same approach to the concurrence of fiscal fines with prosecutions for common offences.[5]

Securing compliance with tax laws is a matter for the tax department of the Ministry of Finance. To this end tax officials within the department have been given statutory powers of supervision and coercion. The taxpayer has a duty to cooperate with the authorities when carrying out their inquiries. At the same time some tax officials have been empowered to investigate fiscal offences, and a number of common offences as well. This is especially the case where customs authorities are concerned. Their powers to carry out criminal investigations extend to offences against laws and regulations which prohibit or restrict the importation, exportation and transit of goods.

Within the tax department, a special body has been created that is specialized in investigating fiscal offences and other offences to which the competence of the department extends: the Fiscal Intelligence and Investigation Department *(Fiscale Inlichtingen- en Opsporingsdienst; FIOD)*. All investigating activities in the field of fiscal offences are in fact concentrated with the FIOD. Its officers have unlimited access to all information within the tax administration. According to established case law tax officials, including officers of the FIOD, may continue to make exercise their administrative powers of supervision and coercion after a reasonable suspicion of an offence has arisen. The person who is suspected of the offence equally remains obliged to cooperate in their inquiries. An exception is, however, made with respect to his right to remain silent.[6] The case law of the European Court on the right not to be compelled to testify against oneself has led Dutch courts to assume now that the privilege against self-incrimination also applies to the examination of documents by tax authorities.[7]

---

4   Cf. HR 19 June 1985, NJ 1986, 116.
5   Cf. *Maathuis/Valkenburg*, Bestuurlijke boeten in het fiscale recht, pp. 164-171.
6   HR 26 April 1988, NJ 1989, 390.
7   HR 23 November 1994, NJ 1995, 239. See also ECHR 17 December 1996, *Saunders v. United Kingdom*, Reports of Judgments and Decisions 1996.

Cooperation in criminal matters

Extradition

Article 11, para. 4, of the Extradition Act precludes extradition for fiscal offences unless specifically provided otherwise by treaty. No definition has been given of what constitutes a fiscal offence. It is, however, safe to assume that the term has the same meaning as in Art. 5 of the 1957 European Convention on Extradition, after which the Act has been closely modelled.[8] Envisaged are 'offences in connection with taxes, duties, customs and exchange', in other words acts made punishable by tax laws.[9] Not surprisingly, case law refuses to equate common offences committed for the purpose of evading an obligation to pay taxes with fiscal offences within the meaning of Art. 5 of the European Convention and Art. 11 of the Extradition Act.[10] Unlike Art. 3 of the Convention, Art. 5 does not mention offences 'connected with' fiscal offences. In examining whether an offence constitutes a fiscal offence Dutch courts will look at the nature of the obligation imposed by a penal provision, not at the name of the Act incorporating the provision.[11]

Although Art. 11 of the Extradition Act precludes extradition for fiscal offences, it nevertheless allows the Government to conclude treaties which deviate from the provision.[12] This clearly shows that there is no strong attachment to the exception in Dutch law. Actually, most of the treaties and conventions to which the Netherlands has become a party in the recent past make extradition for fiscal offences a duty or a possibility.

While Art. 5 of the European Convention on Extradition rules out extradition for fiscal offences, the Netherlands has become a party to its 1978 Second Additional Protocol eliminating the exception. Now that the Federal Republic of Germany has also become a party to the Protocol, Art. III of the 1979 Agreement between Germany and the Netherlands to supplement and facilitate the application of the European Convention, which provided for extradition at the discretion of the requested party, has ceased to be applicable in their mutual relations. Nevertheless, the Agreement is still of some relevance to the matter

---

8   See supra p. 89.
9   Cf. *Swart*, Nederlands uitleveringsrecht, p. 282.
10 HR 25 June 1985, NJ 1986, 111.
11 For drugs offences included in foreign customs legislation see HR 9 March 1993, NJ 1993, 574; HR 24 January 1995, NJ 1995, 276; HR 30 August 1996, NJ 1997, 9.
12 On the relationship between the Act and extradition treaties see supra pp. 90-91.

in that its Art. II allows for the (accessory) extradition for offences and other acts liable to administrative penalties to be imposed by administrative authorities.

Like the European Convention, the 1962 Benelux Treaty on Extradition and Mutual Assistance in Criminal Matters rules out extradition for fiscal offences unless specifically provided for on the basis of special arrangements. As yet no such arrangements have been agreed upon by the three countries.

The four recent bilateral treaties between the Netherlands on the one hand and Australia, Canada, Hong Kong and the United States on the other, all provide for extradition for fiscal offences.

Mutual assistance in criminal matters

Article 552m, para. 3, of the Code of Criminal Procedure enables the Dutch authorities to render mutual assistance for fiscal offences. However, important restrictions apply here, while the procedure for rendering assistance in fiscal matters is different from that in ordinary cases. Finally, Art. 552o, para. 2, of the Code imposes further restrictions.

In contrast with Art. 11 of the Extradition Act, Art. 552m, para. 3, of the Code gives an indication of what constitutes a fiscal offence. Following the language of the 1957 European Convention on Extradition the provision speaks of offences connected with duties, taxes, customs and exchange. However, it deviates from the European Convention, as well as from Art. 11 of the Extradition Act, in that it also covers offences 'connected with' fiscal offences. This implies that offences under general criminal law committed with the purpose of evading tax obligations or of escaping prosecution thereof are included.[13] One may, for instance, think of Arts. 225 and 326 of the Penal Code. Moreover, the special regime of Art. 552m also applies to requests for information possessed by the Netherlands tax department or acquired by officials of that department in the exercise of their duties, regardless of whether a request for assistance relates to a fiscal or a common offence. As a consequence, common offences such as drugs offences which customs officials are empowered to investigate are also among the ones covered by the provision. Before acting upon requests for assistance in fiscal and related matters, the competent authorities must obtain prior authorization by the Minister of Justice. Moreover,

---

13 Cf. *Sjöcrona*, De kleine rechtshulp, pp. 177-178.

Art. 552m requires the Minister of Justice to consult the Minister of Finance before granting authorization. Obviously, the purpose of these requirements is to protect the interests of the Dutch treasury, or, in the language of the provision, those of 'the Netherlands tax department'.[14] It also enables the Minister of Finance to check whether a request has been made in order to obtain information that could not have been obtained on the basis of international instruments relating to administrative assistance in tax matters, or on more stringent conditions only. In actual practice the Minister of Finance has delegated his responsibilities to the Fiscal Intelligence and Investigation Department. In carrying out requests for assistance in fiscal and related matters the Department plays a predominant role.

As has been explained elsewhere, the provisions of the Code of Criminal Procedure make the examining magistrate the only authority competent to apply various measures of coercion in executing requests for assistance.[15] The consequences for rendering assistance in fiscal and related matters are considerable. Tax authorities competent to handle these requests are forbidden to exercise their own powers of investigation where fiscal offences and related offences are concerned. Nor may they exercise the administrative powers of supervision and coercion which tax legislation grants them in domestic cases. On the other hand, they are not barred from providing information that they have acquired earlier during the legitimate exercise of their duties. Neither must requests for assistance be refused for the sole reason that, at an earlier stage, administrative assistance has been granted to the fiscal authorities of the requesting state.[16] Obviously, there is a danger here that administrative assistance in fiscal matters is requested and granted in order to circumvent the limitations to rendering assistance in criminal cases. We will discuss that problem in more detail later.

An important restriction on rendering assistance in fiscal and related matters is that it may be granted pursuant to a treaty only. In this respect Art. 552m of the Code of Criminal Procedure again deviates from the general rules applicable to requests for assistance in criminal matters.[17] Meanwhile, most treaties to which the Netherlands has become a party in the recent past have eliminated the fiscal offence exception or have made assistance for fiscal offences an option. They also largely rule out the possibility of refusing requests on the

14 In practice this includes lack of reciprocity.
15 See supra pp. 137-138.
16 HR 30 November 1993, DD 94.161.
17 See supra p. 140.

grounds that granting them might jeopardize the interests of the treasury. Finally, they may contain provisions enabling the competent authorities to grant assistance without prior authorization of higher authorities.

The 1959 European Convention on Mutual Assistance in Criminal Matters opens the possibility of rendering assistance for fiscal offences without creating an obligation to do so. The obligation to do so follows from its Additional Protocol to which the Netherlands has become a party. As the Federal Republic of Germany has also become a party to the Protocol, Art. III of the 1979 Agreement between Germany and the Netherlands to supplement and facilitate the application of this convention has ceased to be applicable in their mutual relations. However, the Agreement is still relevant to the extent that its Art. II equates the imposition of administrative fines with criminal prosecutions.

In Art. 50 of the 1990 Convention applying the Schengen Agreement, the contracting parties have agreed to afford each other assistance as regards infringements of their rules of law with respect to excise duty, value added tax and customs duties. Customs provisions are defined by reference to the 1967 Naples Convention on mutual assistance between customs administrations and EC Regulation 1468/81. Moreover, the Convention applying the Schengen Agreement also equates administrative penalties with criminal penalties.

The 1962 Benelux Treaty on Extradition and Mutual Assistance in Criminal Matters does not permit refusal of assistance for the sole reason that the offence is a fiscal offence. Neither do the recent bilateral conventions on mutual assistance concluded between the Netherlands and Australia, Canada and the United States. It is, moreover, assumed that the 1898 Treaty on extradition between the Netherlands and the United Kingdom, which links the Netherlands with the Bahamas, India, Kenya, Malawi, New Zealand, Uganda, Pakistan and Tanzania, provides a basis for rendering assistance in fiscal matters. The same is true for bilateral extradition treaties between the Netherlands and Argentina, Liberia, Mexico, Monaco, Romania, San Marino, Serbia and Suriname.

Article 552m of the Code raises the question of whether treaties and conventions on mutual administrative assistance in tax matters can be considered treaties within the meaning of the provision. Since the provisions of the Code are strictly limited to assistance in criminal matters the answer must be that instruments of administrative assistance may be considered treaties within the meaning of Art. 552m only in so far as they are explicitly designed to create a framework for cooperation in criminal matters.[18] This is obviously the case for Arts. 16 to 24 of the 1969 Benelux Convention on cooperation

---

18 Cf. *Sjöcrona* (supra note 13), p. 185.

between administrative and judicial authorities in matters pertaining to the Benelux Economic Union. Whether the same can be said of Art. 13 of the Naples Convention is not entirely clear. There is no case law on the question. However, Art. 50 of the Convention applying the Schengen Agreement has made it moot in the relationships with most parties to the Naples Convention.

According to Art. 552o, para. 2, of the Code of Criminal Procedure requests for seizure of property may be granted only if the offence with respect to which a request for assistance has been made is an extraditable offence. The consequences of this provision for assistance in fiscal matters are twofold. Since Art. 2 of the Extradition Act permits extradition pursuant to a treaty only, an extradition treaty must be in force between the Netherlands and the state requesting seizure of property. Moreover, that treaty must contain an obligation to grant extradition for fiscal offences.[19] Thus, the possibilities for effecting seizure of property in fiscal cases are limited indeed. From the combination of Arts. 552m and 552o of the Code it results that two treaties are needed to effect seizure of property in fiscal matters: one carrying the obligation to render assistance for fiscal offences, the other making fiscal offences extraditable offenses.

The double treaty requirement is not often met, there being few states with which the Netherlands is linked by treaties providing for extradition for fiscal offences as well as for mutual assistance for them. The requirement is, for instance, met in relation to states which have ratified both the Second Additional Protocol to the European Convention on Extradition and the European Convention on Mutual Assistance in Criminal Matters. It is also met in relation to Australia, Canada and the United States. On the other hand, seizure of property on the basis of the Benelux Treaty on Extradition and Mutual Assistance in Criminal Matters is ruled out since the former Convention does not make fiscal offences extraditable ones.

However, treaties may contain provisions superseding Art. 552o, para. 2. Thus, Art. 17 of the 1969 Benelux Convention on cooperation between administrative and judicial authorities in matters pertaining to the Benelux Economic Union carries the obligation to seize property under the same conditions as are applicable in domestic cases. Article 51 of the Convention applying the Schengen Agreement states that the admissibility of requests for search and seizure may only be made dependent on two conditions, neither of them requiring that a fiscal offence is liable to extradition. As these provisions

19 HR 4 February 1986, NJ 1986, 672, 20 NYIL 344-346 (1989).

must be considered to be self-executing under Dutch constitutional law, there is no room for applying Art. 552o here. Moreover, since 1993 that Article explicitly mentions the possibility that treaties may contain rules which deviate from its provisions.

Another Act that deals with mutual assistance in criminal matters is the 1990 Police Files Act *(Wet politieregisters)*. Article 13 of the 1991 Police Files Decree *(Besluit politieregisters)* authorizes police officers to provide information, both spontaneously and on request, to the authorities of other states. According to the Article information relating to the offences mentioned in Art. 552m of the Code of Criminal Procedure may be provided after prior authorization of the Minister of Justice only.

Transfer of proceedings

As yet, transfer of proceedings in criminal matters seems to be a rather academic subject where fiscal offences are concerned. However, it could become important, especially in cases in which fiscal offences go together with common offences.

Articles 552t to 552hh of the Code of Criminal Procedure which govern the matter do not contain special provisions on fiscal offences. There is, therefore, no statutory bar to accept transfer of proceedings from other states. Nor do the provisions rule out transfer of proceedings by the Netherlands to other states.

The 1972 European Convention on the Transfer of Proceedings in Criminal Matters, to which the Netherlands is a party, allows refusal of transfer on account of the fiscal nature of the offence without, however, making refusal mandatory.[20] It also allows for transfer of proceedings for the purpose of imposing administrative penalties. A more important basis for transferring proceedings for fiscal offences is the 1969 Benelux Convention on cooperation between administrative and judicial authorities in matters pertaining to the Benelux Economic Union.

---

20 The same is true for the Benelux Treaty on the Transfer of Proceedings in Criminal Matters. Although ratified by the Netherlands it has not yet entered into force.

Transfer of enforcement of criminal judgments

The 1986 Act on the transfer of enforcement of criminal judgments *(Wet over-dracht tenuitvoerlegging strafvonnissen)* does not contain provisions barring transfer of enforcement of sentences imposed for fiscal offences to or from the Netherlands. The Act not only deals with custodial penalties and measures but also with all other penalties and measures which may have been imposed by a court for an offence. Consequently, the Act offers suitable opportunities for transferring the enforcement of sentences imposed for fiscal offences, where financial sanctions occupy a major place. What makes transfer of their enforcement to the Netherlands even easier is that the requirement that the convicted person is domiciled in the Netherlands or that the convicted corporation has its seat in the country does not apply to sanctions of a financial nature.

The Netherlands is a party to the 1970 European Convention on the International Validity of Criminal Judgments, the 1983 Convention on the Transfer of Sentenced Persons and the 1991 Convention between the Member States of the European Union on the Enforcement of Foreign Criminal Sentences. None of these conventions erects a bar against transferring the enforcement of sentences imposed for fiscal offences. Special problems, however, have arisen in the case of the Convention on the Transfer of Sentenced Persons. Since this convention is limited to custodial sanctions, transfer of a person is rarely requested by states which frequently impose customs fines for drugs offences in addition to custodial sanctions and require these fines to have been paid before transfer is considered. This, for instance, explains why transfer of prisoners from France to the Netherlands hardly ever occurs. Among the other conventions in this field to which the Netherlands is a party the 1969 Benelux Convention on cooperation between administrative and judicial authorities in matters pertaining to the Benelux Economic Union deserves special mention since it makes the acceptance of transfer of enforcement of sentences imposed for fiscal offences an unconditional obligation.[21]

Confiscation of the proceeds from crime

According to Dutch law, confiscation of the proceeds from crime is a measure which may be ordered by a criminal court only. Consequently, confiscation can

---

21 For other treaties and conventions in the matter see *Paridaens*, De overdracht van de tenuitvoerlegging van strafvonnissen, pp. 120-149.

only be pronounced at the end of a criminal trial. The sole exceptions to this approach are to be found in the General Act on Taxes and in the Customs Act. Confiscating proceeds from fiscal offences is not a matter for the criminal courts but for the tax department. The explanation for the exception is simple: proceeds from fiscal offences consist of taxes that have not been paid. The recovery of tax debts is better left to the tax authorities.

Although confiscating proceeds from common crimes is a matter that has to be dealt with within the criminal justice system, tax authorities are, of course, deeply involved in investigations which may lead to confiscation measures. Since, in Dutch law, profits from crime are not exempt from taxes most investigations with a view to confiscating proceeds have a fiscal aspect. They almost always concur with investigations concerning tax evasion. Moreover, the tax authorities, in particular the Fiscal Intelligence and Investigation Department, have the financial expertise needed in order to complete investigations into money laundering offences successfully.

Cooperation in criminal matters for the purpose of confiscating proceeds is mainly regulated by the Code of Criminal Procedure and the Act on the transfer of enforcement of criminal judgments. The Netherlands is a party to a number of multilateral and bilateral treaties aiming at international cooperation in searching, seizing and confiscating proceeds from crime.[22] The most important ones are the 1988 Vienna Convention against Illicit Traffic in Narcotic Drugs and Psychotropic Substances and the 1990 Strasbourg Convention on Laundering, Search, Seizure and Confiscation of the Proceeds from Crime. Article 18 of the Strasbourg Convention allows the contracting parties to refuse cooperation if the offence to which a request for assistance relates is a fiscal offence without, however, requiring them to do so. The approach of the Netherlands with regard to fiscal offences is more rigorous. When ratifying the convention the Netherlands has made a reservation to the effect that it will not lend assistance with regard to confiscation of the proceeds from offences punishable under legislation on taxation or on customs and excise. The Government's view is that recovery of fiscal debts is a matter which should be achieved on the basis of international instruments and national legislation concerning administrative cooperation in fiscal matters. This approach can be explained by reference to the system of confiscating proceeds from fiscal offences in domestic law. In itself it certainly does not rule out cooperation in criminal matters for the purpose of imposing custodial sanctions or property sanctions

---

22 See *Paridaens* (supra note 21), pp. 61-149.

which, unlike the measure of confiscation in Dutch law, primarily aim at punishing and deterring perpetrators of fiscal offences. Cooperation for that purpose is, however, not envisaged by the Strasbourg Convention.

Administrative cooperation in fiscal matters

Administrative cooperation and cooperation in criminal matters

At the beginning of our discussion we noted that a system of administrative cooperation in fiscal matters has been developed between states for the purposes of collecting and recovering taxes as well as of recovering administrative fines imposed for infringements of tax laws. As we noted also, cooperation between tax authorities may be of great significance to the investigation of fiscal offences. Information exchanged for the purpose of collecting or recovering taxes may well be of probative value to the requesting state as evidence in criminal cases involving fiscal offences. The same may also be the case where evidence of common offences is concerned since it is not unusual for tax authorities to acquire information regarding such offences in the exercise of their duties. This is, of course, especially true for customs authorities. In most countries they are not only charged with supervising compliance with tax laws but with laws and regulations which prohibit or restrict the importation, exportation and transit of goods as well.

As administrative cooperation in fiscal matters is of great potential significance to criminal prosecutions for fiscal offences and other offences, the question must be asked how this form of international cooperation relates to cooperation in criminal matters. The question is all the more important now that rendering mutual assistance in criminal is matters usually subject to important restrictions where fiscal offences are concerned. Moreover, administrative cooperation and cooperation in criminal matters serve different purposes while conditions and procedures for granting assistance may differ too.[23] Thus, the possibility exists that a state requests administrative assistance from another state with a view to obtaining evidence in a criminal case or, conversely, requests assistance in criminal matters with a view to assessing or recovering taxes. There is also the question of whether and under what conditions information which has been provided for one purpose may legitimately be used for other purposes later. In this respect it is important to note that in gathering

---

23 Cf. *Figge*, Intertax 1980, pp. 86-96.

information which may be used as evidence in a criminal trial the rights of the accused must be respected, notably his right not to be compelled to testify against himself. Similar safeguards usually do not exist where the collecting of information for tax purposes is concerned. In a legal system such as that of the Netherlands these questions acquire a special cogency since tax authorities, notably the Fiscal Intelligence and Investigation Department, are also competent to carry out criminal investigations. Finally, the relationship between administrative cooperation in criminal matters has acquired a new dimension now that the case law of the European Court of Human Rights has equated the imposition of some types of administrative fines with criminal penalties.

The Dutch position on these matters, as can be deduced from legislation, official statements and circular letters, is roughly the following. Since administrative cooperation and cooperation in criminal matters serve different purposes and are subject to different rules and safeguards, they should be kept separate. Requests for administrative assistance should be refused if their main purpose is to obtain evidence in a criminal case. Nor are requests for mutual assistance in criminal matters admissible if their main purpose is to assess or to recover taxes. As a rule, it will be presumed that a request for administrative assistance has been made for the purpose of obtaining evidence in a criminal case if the request has been made after the beginning of criminal proceedings against a person. It is, however, not entirely clear according to what criteria it will be assumed that criminal proceedings have started. Information provided for one purpose may be used for other purposes but after consent of the competent Dutch authorities only. In deciding on whether or not consent will be granted, the authorities will take into account whether assistance could have been granted for these purposes. Cooperation for the purpose of recovering administrative fines is covered by national and international rules on administrative assistance in tax matters unless explicitly provided for otherwise. Administrative cooperation for that purpose should, however, respect the rights of the accused guaranteed by the European Convention on Human Rights. The Dutch position, as summarized here, seems to correspond with the approach taken in most international instruments on administrative cooperation in tax matters. This is, however, not always the case.

Taxes other than customs duties

Administrative assistance in the assessment of taxes other than customs duties is governed by the 1986 Act on the rendering of international assistance in the levying of taxes *(Wet op de internationale bijstandsverlening bij de heffing van belastingen)*. Its scope is limited to taxes to which the General Act on Taxes applies. A number of direct taxes are covered, as well as some indirect taxes such as sales taxes and certain types of excise taxes. A further restriction is that the Act does not deal with mutual assistance in the recovery of tax debts.

It is the purpose of the Act to implement provisions in EC legislation as well as international treaties to which the Netherlands is a party which create binding obligations to provide assistance.[24] Article 13 of the Act excludes the rendering of assistance in other cases categorically.

Articles 5 to 7 of the Act distinguish between three forms of assistance: the providing of information on request, the automatic and the spontaneous providing of information. A key provision in the Act is Art. 8. It enables the Dutch authorities to use their powers of supervision and coercion under the General Act on Taxes in order to acquire information which may benefit other authorities; an exception is, however, made where the spontaneous providing of information is concerned. Article 9 of the Act allows the authorities of other states to be present at their investigations. The Minister of Finance is charged with executing the provisions of the Act. In actual practice he has delegated his responsibilities to the Fiscal Intelligence and Investigation Department.

Two provisions of the Act deal with the relationship between administrative assistance in tax matters and mutual assistance in criminal matters. The first is Art. 5, para. 5. According to this provision, requests for assistance made in connection with an investigation into fiscal offences and offences connected therewith may be granted only after consultation with the Minister of Justice. The purpose of this provision is obvious. It is to distinguish between procedures for rendering administrative assistance and those for rendering mutual assistance in criminal matters. National and international rules on rendering assistance in criminal matters should not be circumvented by requests for administrative assistance in tax matters. It may, therefore, be that, as a result of consultations, the requesting state is advised to make a request for mutual assistance in criminal matters. The provision forms the pendant of Art. 552m, para. 3, of the Code of Criminal Procedure discussed above.[25] The second relevant provision is Art. 15, para. 3, of the Act. It allows the Minister of Finance to consent to the use of information for other purposes than that of assessing taxes. The use of information as evidence in a criminal trial is such a purpose. This provision

---

24 The Act also applies to administrative assistance between the tax authorities of the different parts of the Kingdom of the Netherlands.

25 See supra pp. 235-236. For a more detailed discussion see *Wisselink*, Fiscale informatie-uitwisseling tussen Europese en andere landen, pp. 276-283.

clearly presupposes that the use of information for other purposes than that of assessing taxes is not permitted without the consent of the Minister of Finance.

The Act on the rendering of international assistance also applies to the granting of assistance to the Dutch authorities. Thus, Art. 15, para. 1, for instance, states that information provided by foreign authorities may be used for purposes other than that of assessing taxes only after authorization by these authorities.

While the provisions of the Act make a rather sharp distinction between administrative cooperation and cooperation in criminal matters, it is a distinction without organizational consequences. In actual practice, the Fiscal Intelligence and Investigation Department deals with requests for administrative assistance as well as those for mutual assistance in criminal matters where fiscal offences and related offences are concerned.

Perhaps the most important instrument that the Act on the rendering of international assistance aims to implement is EC Directive 77/779 concerning mutual assistance in the field of direct taxation.[26] We may also mention EC Directive 92/108 and EC Regulation 218/92 in this context.

A second category of relevant international instruments consists of bilateral treaties with respect to taxes on income and on capital. Over forty treaties have been concluded by the Netherlands with other states. In negotiations with other states on concluding treaties use is made of a model treaty which closely resembles the 1977 OECD Model Convention. Article 27 of the Dutch model, dealing with the exchange of information, is identical to Art. 26 of the OECD Model.

Recently, the Netherlands has become a party to the 1988 OECD/Council of Europe Convention on Mutual Administrative Assistance in Tax Matters. A number of reservations have been made. The most important one concerns the right not to provide assistance in relation to certain types of taxes.

Custom duties and customs cooperation

A statute comparable to the Act on the rendering of international assistance in the levying of taxes is lacking where mutual cooperation in customs matters is concerned. This is all the more surprising since administrative assistance in

---

26 1977 OJ L 336/15.

customs matters has acquired a far higher level of intensity than that in other matters.[27]

The Customs Act does not contain provisions on administrative cooperation with the authorities of other states or officials of the European Community. The providing of information to these authorities is governed by the General Act on Taxes and the 1988 Data Protection Act *(Wet persoonsregistraties)*. Article 67 of the General Act imposes on customs authorities the obligation of keeping information confidential. However, the Minister of Finance may grant exemptions. A general exemption with respect to providing information to foreign authorities has been made in para. 2.3 of the 1993 Instruction on the providing of information *(Voorschrift informatieverstrekking)*.[28] Another important instruction dealing with international cooperation in customs matters is the 1990 Instruction on mutual customs cooperation *(Voorschriften wederzijdse bijstand douane)*. It appears from both instructions that cooperation in customs matters, unlike that in other tax matters, need not be based on EC legislation or international treaties. Various tax authorities are charged with rendering assistance. Again, the Fiscal Intelligence and Investigation Department plays an important, although not exclusive, role here.

A major consequence of the lack of specific legislation where customs cooperation is concerned is that the Dutch tax authorities may not exercise their powers of supervision and coercion for the sole purpose of obtaining information to be provided to foreign authorities. Whether EC legislation and international treaties on customs cooperation have altered that situation is a matter that cannot be discussed here.

Paragraph 3.3.1 of the Instruction on mutual customs cooperation deals with the relationship between administrative assistance and assistance in criminal matters. The paragraph clearly demonstrates how difficult, or even artificial, it often is to make a distinction between the two where customs matters are concerned. For in the Netherlands, as well as in a number of other countries, customs authorities are not only involved in assessing and collecting customs duties but also responsible for preventing and investigating offences against laws and regulations concerning the importation, exportation and transit of goods, or even a wider range of common offences. The mere fact that a request for assistance emanates from a customs authority does not, therefore, exclude the possibility that is has been made with a view to further criminal investigations.

---

27 Cf. also supra pp. 160-161.
28 Published in *Staatscourant* 1992, 251.

Recognizing this fact, the Instruction more or less combines administrative assistance and assistance in criminal matters. Requests for assistance based on European and international instruments for customs cooperation are presumed to be requests for administrative assistance. Requests for information within the framework of criminal investigations may be granted by the Dutch customs authorities on the condition that they pay due respect to the various safeguards of criminal procedure. For instance, a suspect must be informed of his right to remain silent. If the application of provisional measures is necessary in order to obtain information, the request must be sent to the competent public prosecutor in order to enable him to decide whether it can be dealt with in accordance with the provisions of the Code of Criminal Procedure or whether it should be sent back to the authorities of the requesting state. Where Dutch requests for administrative assistance to other states are concerned, the Instruction takes the point of view that they should, as a rule, not be made once a Dutch public prosecutor has become involved in the case at hand. As a rule, information provided for one purpose may not be used for other purposes without consent of the competent authorities.

Of major importance in the field of customs cooperation is the 1967 Naples Convention on mutual assistance between customs administrations. Although the Dutch Government has held a different opinion in the past, it is difficult to deny that this convention not only deals with administrative assistance but with assistance in criminal matters as well.[29] Trying to distinguish between the two is particularly inappropriate in the case of the convention since it aims at creating a framework for cooperation between customs administrations regardless of whether they are involved in assessing and collecting customs duties or are dealing with other matters. It may well be that, in actual practice, the Naples Convention has superseded the European Convention on Mutual Assistance in Criminal Matters for the parties to both conventions as the main vehicle for providing assistance in matters which customs authorities are competent to investigate. This is especially so where the direct exchange of information is concerned.

Other conventions on customs cooperation to which the Netherlands is a party include the Benelux Convention on cooperation between administrative and judicial authorities in matters pertaining to the Benelux Economic Union and the bilateral treaties between the Netherlands on the one hand and Estonia, Finland, Israel, Norway, Sweden and the United States on the other. The

---

29 Cf. *Sjöcrona* (supra note 13), pp. 206-207.

bilateral conventions are closely modelled after the Naples Convention. Of importance are also the association agreements concluded by the European Communities and their member states with a number of Eastern European states. Finally, we should mention EC Regulation 1468/81 on mutual assistance in customs and agricultural matters.

Appendix I
Translation of Selected Statutes

1 Penal Code

Act of 3 March 1881, *Staatsblad* 35, as last amended by the Act of 24 May 1996, *Staatsblad* 276.

FIRST BOOK

General provisions

TITLE I

Scope of operation of the criminal law

(...)

Article 2
The criminal law of the Netherlands is applicable to anyone who commits any offence within the Netherlands.

Article 3
The criminal law of the Netherlands is applicable to anyone who commits outside the Netherlands an offence on board a Netherlands vessel or aircraft.

Article 4
The criminal law of the Netherlands is applicable to anyone who commits any of the following offences outside the Netherlands:
1°. the crimes defined in articles 92 to 96, 97a, 98 to 98c, 105 and 108 to 110;
2°. the crimes defined in articles 131 to 134bis and 189, if the offence or crime mentioned in these articles is a crime referred to under 1°;
3°. any crime with respect to coinage or banknotes, or to stamps, seals and marks issued by the Government;
4°. forgery of debt instruments or debt certificates issued by the Netherlands State or a Netherlands province, municipality or public institution, including the counterfoils, dividend coupons and interest certificates pertaining to these documents and the

certificates issued to replace these documents, or the intentional use of such forgery or forged document as if it were genuine and not forged;

5°. the crimes defined in articles 216, second paragraph, 381 to 385, 409 and 410 or the misdemeanour defined in article 446a;

6°. the crime defined in article 207a;

7°. a. the crime defined in article 168, committed against an aircraft in service, if it is a Netherlands aircraft or if the alleged offender is present in the Netherlands;

b. the crime defined in article 385a, committed against an aircraft in flight, if the place of take-off or that of actual landing is situated outside the territory of the state of registration of that aircraft and the alleged offender is present in the Netherlands;

c. the crime defined in article 385b, if the aircraft referred to in that article is a Netherlands aircraft or if the alleged offender is present in the Netherlands;

d. the crime defined in article 385c, if committed either against a Netherlands aircraft or on board an aircraft which subsequently lands in the Netherlands with the alleged offender on board;

8°. the crimes defined in articles 166, 168, 350, 352, 354, 385a, fourth paragraph, 385b, second paragraph, and 385c, if the crime has been either committed against a Netherlands sea-going vessel or on board any other sea-going vessel and the alleged offender is present in the Netherlands;

9°. any of the crimes defined in articles 117, 117a, 117b and 285, insofar as such crimes have been committed against an internationally protected person who is employed by the Netherlands government or belongs to such a person's household, or against his or her protected property, provided that the act constitutes an offence according to the law of the state in whose territory it has been committed.

Article 4a

The criminal law of the Netherlands is applicable to anyone against whom proceedings have been transferred to the Netherlands from a foreign state pursuant to a treaty conferring jurisdiction to prosecute on the Netherlands.

Article 5

1. The criminal law of the Netherlands is applicable to a national of the Netherlands who commits outside the Netherlands:

1°. any of the crimes defined in Titles I and II of the Second Book, and in articles 197a, 197b, 197c, 206, 237, 272, 273, 388 and 389;

2°. an act which constitutes a crime under Dutch law and which has been made an offence according to the law of the state in whose territory it has been committed.

2. Criminal proceedings may also be brought if the alleged offender acquires Netherlands nationality only after the commission of the offence.

Article 6
The criminal law of the Netherlands is applicable to the Netherlands public servant who commits outside the Netherlands any of the crimes referred to in Title XXVIII of the Second Book.

Article 7
The criminal law of the Netherlands is applicable to the master, passengers and crew of a Netherlands vessel who commit outside the Netherlands, even when off the ship, any of the offences defined in Titles XXIX of the Second Book and Title IX of the Third Book.

Article 8
The applicability of articles 2 to 7 shall be subject to the exceptions recognized in international law.

TITLE VIII

Extinction of the right to prosecute and of punishment

Article 68
1. Except in cases in which judgments are susceptible to review, no person may be prosecuted again for an offence in respect of which a court in the Netherlands, the Netherlands Antilles or Aruba has rendered final judgment on the substance of the charges against him.
2. If the final judgment has been rendered by another court, new proceedings against the person for the same offence may not take place in the case of:
   1°. acquittal or dismissal of the charges;
   2°. conviction, if punishment has been imposed, followed by complete enforcement, pardon or lapse of time.
3. No person may be prosecuted for an offence which has been irrevocably disposed of, in relation to him, by the fulfilment of a condition set by the competent authorities of a foreign state to prevent prosecution.

2 Code of Criminal Procedure

Act of 15 January 1921, *Staatsblad* 14, as last amended by the Act of 18 January 1996, *Staatsblad* 39.

FOURTH BOOK

Special procedures

TITLE VIA

Investigations outside the territorial jurisdiction of a district court

First part

General

Article 539a
1. The powers granted by any statutory provision in connection with the investigation of criminal offences or with the examination concerning them other than at the hearing, may, insofar as is not provided otherwise in this Title, be exercised outside the territorial jurisdiction of a district court.
2. The provisions of the first and second part of this Title are applicable only to investigations and examinations outside the territorial jurisdiction of a district court. Insofar as they relate to a person arrested or to property seized, they continue to be applicable also within the territorial jurisdiction of a district court until the person arrested or the property seized have been surrendered to the public prosecutor or to one of his assistant public prosecutors.
3. The powers granted in the provisions of this Title may be exercised only in conformity with international and interregional law.

(...)

TITLE X

International legal assistance

FIRST PART

General provisions

Article 552h

1. The following articles in this title shall apply to requests for legal assistance made by the authorities of a foreign state in connection with a criminal case and addressed to a judicial or police body in the Netherlands, whether or not designated by name, insofar as the processing of such a request is not regulated by the provisions of or pursuant to other legislation.
2. The following shall be deemed to be requests for legal assistance: requests to carry out or assist in investigations, to supply documents, files or evidence or to provide information, to serve documents on or issue documents to or issue notices or notifications to third parties.

Article 552i

1. Requests not addressed to the public prosecutor shall be forwarded immediately by the addressee to the public prosecutor in the district in which the request is to be dealt with or in which the request is received.
2. If a request is for information only and no coercive measures are required to obtain that information the request need not be forwarded to the public prosecutor.
3. Every decision to grant a request in accordance with the second paragraph shall be recorded in a register, the model of which shall be determined by Our Minister. The nature of the request, the capacity of the authority making the request, and the action taken on the request shall be recorded in all cases.
4. In dealing with a request the competent authority referred to in the second paragraph shall comply with the general and specific instructions given by the public prosecutor.

Article 552j

The public prosecutor receiving the request shall decide immediately on the action to be taken. In the interests of speed and efficiency he may transfer the request to the public prosecutor in another district.

Article 552k

1. Every effort shall be made to comply with a request based on a treaty.
2. If a request is reasonable though not based on a treaty, or if the applicable treaty does not make compliance compulsory, the request shall be met, unless such

compliance would be unlawful or contrary to instructions from the Minister of Justice.

Article 552l

1. A request shall not be complied with:
   a. if there are grounds for believing that it has been made in connection with an investigation instituted with a view to prosecuting, punishing or harassing the suspect on account of his religious or political opinions, his nationality or race or the population group to which he belongs;
   b. insofar as compliance would involve assisting in proceedings which are incompatible with the principle underlying article 68 of the Penal Code and article 255, first paragraph, of this Code;
   c. insofar it has been made in connection with an investigation into offences for which the suspect is being prosecuted in the Netherlands.
2. If there are grounds for believing that the request has been made in the circumstances referred to in the preceding paragraph under a, the request shall be submitted to the Minister of Justice.

Article 552m

1. Requests for the purpose of an investigation into offences of a political nature or offences connected therewith shall be complied with only with the authorization of the Minister of Justice. Such authorization may be granted only for requests based on a treaty and after consultation with the Minister for Foreign Affairs. The decision on the request shall be conveyed to the authorities of the requesting state through diplomatic channels.
2. The first paragraph shall not apply to a request made by the authorities of a state which is a party to the European Convention on the Suppression of Terrorism (*Trb.* 1977, 63) or the Agreement on the application of the said Convention between the Member States of the European Communities (*Trb.* 1980, 14) in connection with one of the offences referred to in article 1 or article 2 of the said European Convention.
3. Requests made in connection with an investigation into offences relating to duties, taxes, customs or exchange or offences connected therewith, compliance with which could have consequences for the Netherlands tax department, and requests for information in the possession of the Netherlands tax department or acquired by officials of the said department in the exercise of their duties, shall be complied with only with the authorization of the Minister of Justice. Such authorization may be granted only for requests based on a treaty and after consultation with the Minister of Finance.

Article 552n

1. If a request from the judicial authorities of a foreign state is based on a treaty and is admissible, the public prosecutor shall refer it to the examining magistrate:

     a. if it concerns the examination of persons who are not prepared to appear voluntarily and make the requested statement;

     b. if it expressly requires a sworn statement or a statement made before a judge;

     c. if it is necessary with a view to meeting the request to enter property other than public property against the will of the rightful owner or to seize evidence.

     d. if it concerns the monitoring, tapping or recording of data conveyed through the telecommunications infrastructure or through telecommunications systems used to provide services to the public.

2. In cases other than those provided for in the preceding paragraph, the public prosecutor may refer a request for assistance from a foreign judicial authority to the examining magistrate.

3. A requests shall be submitted to the examining magistrate in the form of a written application setting out the response required of the examining magistrate.

4. An application as referred to in the preceding paragraph may be withdrawn at any time.

Article 552o

1. If an application as referred to in article 552n, third paragraph, is made in order to comply with a request from the judicial authorities of a foreign state and if it is based on a treaty and is admissible, it shall have the same consequences in law as an application for the opening of a preliminary judicial examination insofar as it concerns:

     a. the powers of the examining magistrate in relation to suspects, witnesses and experts to be examined by him and those in relation to ordering the delivery or transfer of evidence, entering and searching premises, seizure of evidence, and tapping or recording of data not destined for the public, conveyed through the telecommunications infrastructure or through telecommunications systems used to provide services to the public;

     b. the powers of the public prosecutor;

     c. the rights and obligations of the persons to be examined by the examining magistrate;

     d. the assistance of counsel;

     e. the duties of the registrar.

2. Evidence may be seized in accordance with the first paragraph of this article if it would be liable to be seized had the offence in question been committed in the Netherlands, and if the offence constitutes grounds for extradition to the requesting state.

3. Unless provided otherwise by treaty, coercive measures may not be used to secure compliance with a request for legal assistance other than in accordance with the preceding paragraphs of this article.

4. Coercive measures may not be used to secure compliance with a request for legal assistance other than in accordance with the preceding paragraphs of this article.[1]

Article 552p
1. The examining magistrate shall return the request to the public prosecutor as soon as possible, enclosing the official reports of the examinations he has conducted and of any other action he has taken in the case.
2. If the district court, taking into consideration the applicable treaty, grants permission, evidence seized by the examining magistrate and information carriers containing data which have been collected through the exercise of any power of investigation in criminal matters shall be put at the disposal of the public prosecutor.
3. Unless it can be assumed that the persons lawfully entitled to the evidence which has been seized do not reside in the Netherlands, the permission referred to in the preceding paragraph may be granted only if it is agreed when the evidence is handed over to the foreign authorities that it shall be returned as soon as it is no longer needed for the purposes of criminal proceedings.
4. The provisions of and pursuant to articles 116 to 119, 552a and 552c to 552e shall apply by analogy. The district court competent to grant permission as referred to in the second paragraph of this article shall take the place of the competent court referred to in the said articles.
5. When information carriers containing data which have been collected by the exercise of any power of investigation in criminal matters are handed over to the foreign authorities, such conditions with respect to their use shall be made as may have been stipulated by the examining magistrate.

Article 552q
1. The statutory provisions governing the service and issue of Dutch documents of a similar purport shall apply by analogy to the service of documents on and the issuing of documents to third parties in compliance with a request for legal assistance.

---

1 Note of the editors: Paras. 3 and 4 of Art. 552o are virtually identical, the only difference being that para. 3 is more liberal in that it allows the use of specific coercive measures on the basis of a treaty. This situation is due to the fact that in 1993 Art. 552o was amended twice by different statutes, neither statute taking the other into account. As a result, the amendments made by the first statute were partly undone by the second. If either statute had taken the other into account paras. 3 and 4 would have read as follows:
3. Data may be tapped or recorded in accordance with para. 1 of this article if they would be liable to be tapped or recorded had the offence in question been committed in the Netherlands.
4. Unless provided for otherwise by treaty, coercive measures other than in accordance with the preceding paragraphs of this article may not be used to secure compliance with a request for legal assistance.

2. If an admissible request expressly indicates that the documents should preferably be served on or issued to the addressee in person, every effort shall be made to do so.

SECOND PART

Offences committed on board aircraft

Article 552r

1. Whenever an inquiry which has to be made into events on board a foreign aircraft, after landing in the Netherlands pursuant to article 13, fourth paragraph, of the Convention on offences and certain other acts committed on board aircraft (*Trb.* 1964, 115), concerns an offence with respect to which the Netherlands does not have jurisdiction, it shall be performed in accordance with the provisions governing the investigation of offences for which remand in custody is not permitted. For the purposes of the application of article 146 the offence shall be deemed to have been committed in the place where the aircraft has landed.
2. In addition to the evidence referred to in article 94, the competent authorities carrying out the inquiry may seize any other evidence which the commander of the foreign aircraft, after landing, furnishes in accordance with the provisions of article 9, third paragraph, of the Convention.
3. The provisions of and pursuant to articles 116 to 118, 119, 552a and 552c to 552e shall apply by analogy. The court within whose jurisdiction the aircraft has landed shall take the place of the competent court referred to in article 117, third paragraph.

Article 552s

1. No inquiry shall be made if there are grounds for believing that the acts of a person on board an aircraft, in connection with which he has been delivered to the authorities pursuant to the provisions of article 9, first paragraph, of the Convention after landing of the aircraft in the Netherlands, constitute an infringement of a provision of criminal law which is based on religious or racial discrimination.
2. If there are grounds for believing that the acts referred to in the preceding paragraph constitute a criminal offence which is of a political nature, an inquiry shall be made only with the authorization of the Minister of Justice. Such authorization may be granted only after consultation with the Minister for Foreign Affairs.

THIRD PART

Transfer of proceedings in criminal matters

Division 1. Transfer of proceedings from the Netherlands

Article 552t
1. If the public prosecutor deems it to be in the interests of a proper administration of justice that a foreign state should institute proceedings against a suspect with respect to an offence which he is responsible for investigating, he shall submit a proposal, stating his reasons and enclosing the criminal file where possible, to the Minister of Justice that a request be made for proceedings to be instituted in the said state.
2. If a preliminary judicial examination has been conducted or if the suspect has been remanded in custody, the public prosecutor submitting a proposal as referred to in the preceding paragraph shall give notice to the suspect that he has recommended that proceedings in connection with the offence to which the preliminary judicial examination related or in connection with which he has been remanded in custody be transferred to a foreign state. The notice shall be served on the suspect.
3. If the notification referred to in the preceding paragraph is given, no notification of discontinuation of proceedings shall be required.
4. If the injured party has expressed the wish to join the proceedings, a proposal as referred to in the first paragraph may be submitted only with his written consent or, if such consent cannot be obtained, with the authorization of the competent court. Such authorization shall be granted upon application by the public prosecutor.
5. The suspect may lodge a written objection to a notification as referred to in the second paragraph with the court of appeal within fourteen days. Articles 12b, 12c, 12e, second paragraph, 12f and 12h to 12l shall apply by analogy, with the proviso that, for the purposes of the application of this paragraph, references in those articles to the complainant or the person whose prosecution is requested shall be taken as referring to the suspect.
6. A proposal as referred to in the first paragraph may be limited to proceedings in the foreign state with a view to imposing and enforcing a sanction whose purpose is to deprive the offender of the proceeds from crime.

Article 552u
1. The Minister of Justice shall decide as soon as possible on the response to be made to a proposal as referred to in the preceding article. He shall take into account the provisions of any treaty on which a request for proceedings to be made to the authorities of a foreign state may be based.
2. If the proposal concerns a suspect who is present in the Netherlands and who has not indicated his consent to transfer of proceedings, the Minister of Justice shall notify the suspect in writing that he intends to agree to the proposal before taking a decision. The suspect shall also be informed that the decision on the proposal of

the public prosecutor will be taken no sooner than fourteen days after the date of the notification.

3. A request for proceedings shall be made to the authorities of a foreign state through the Minister for Foreign Affairs, unless the applicable treaty provides otherwise.
4. A request for proceedings made to a foreign state may be withdrawn at any time until notification has been received concerning the decision taken in that state on the request. The request shall be withdrawn if the court of appeal, in accordance with article 552t, fifth paragraph, orders that proceedings be continued in the Netherlands.

Article 552v
1. After the public prosecutor has submitted a proposal as referred to in article 552t he may not bring the case to trial, nor may he enforce a judgment rendered in the case against the accused, except where:
    a. the proposal is rejected,
    b. the request for proceedings made to the authorities of a foreign state is withdrawn, or
    c. the said authorities issue a notification to the effect that the request has been rejected or that the proceedings instituted in response thereto have been discontinued.
2. In such cases, the public prosecutor shall withdraw a notification as referred to in article 552t, second paragraph. He shall inform the suspect or accused of the withdrawal.

Article 552w
The Minister of Justice shall issue written notification to the public prosector who has submitted a proposal as referred to in article 552t of his decision on the matter and of any communications he receives concerning the decisions of the authorities of the foreign state regarding the request for proceedings made on the public prosecutor's proposal.

Division 2. Transfer of proceedings to the Netherlands

Article 552x
If a request for proceedings to be instituted is addressed by foreign authorities directly to a public prosecutor, that public prosecutor shall forward the request and any supporting documents to the Minister of Justice, together with his opinion.

Article 552y
1. The Minister of Justice shall immediately reject a request for proceedings made by foreign authorities if it can be established without delay that:
    a. the request concerns an alien whose fixed abode or place of residence is outside the Netherlands;

   b. the request concerns an offence:
     1°. which is not punishable under Dutch law;
     2°. which is of a political nature or which is connected with an offence of a political nature;
     3°. which constitutes a military offence;
   c. the request concerns an offence in connection with which proceedings are precluded by lapse of time under Dutch law or under the law of the state making the request;
   d. the request is intended to harass the person whom it concerns on account of his religious or political opinions, his nationality or race or the population group to which he belongs;
   e. proceedings in the Netherlands would contravene the provisions of article 68 of the Penal Code.
2. The condition referred to in the first paragraph, opening words and *a*, shall not apply if the request is for proceedings to be instituted with a view to confiscating the proceeds from crime as referred to in Title III*b* of Book IV.

Article 552z
1. In cases other than those referred to in the preceding article the Minister of Justice shall forward the request for proceedings and supporting documents to the public prosecutor at the district court in the district in which the person whom it concerns has his fixed abode or place of residence. The request and supporting documents shall not be forwarded if the public prosecutor has already given his opinion to the Minister of Justice in accordance with the provisions of article 552x.
2. In the case of a request as referred to in article 552y, second paragraph, and relating to an alien whose fixed abode or permanent residence is outside the Netherlands, the Minister shall forward the request, together with the supporting documents, to the public prosecutor in the district in which property is located against which the measure of confiscation of the proceeds from crime can be enforced.

Article 552aa
1. The public prosecutor to whom a request for proceedings has been forwarded in accordance with the provisions of the preceding article shall give his opinion on it to the Minister of Justice.
2. If the request is based on a treaty and the jurisdiction of the Netherlands to institute proceedings is exclusively based on that treaty, the person whom it concerns shall be heard by the public prosecutor concerning the request, or shall in any event be properly summonsed to be heard.

Article 552bb
1. The Minister of Justice shall decide whether the request for proceedings shall be granted or rejected as soon as possible after receiving the public prosecutor's opinion.

2. The Minister shall in any event reject a request if any of the grounds referred to in article 552y are found to exist.
3. The Minister shall also reject a request not based on a treaty if the public prosecutions department is of the opinion that proceedings may not be instituted in the Netherlands against the person whom the request concerns for the offence with which he is charged.
4. If the request is based on a treaty, the Minister of Justice shall take account of the grounds for rejecting requests for proceedings contained therein.

Article 552cc
Before reaching a decision on a request for proceedings the Minister of Justice may ask the authorities of the state making the request to provide further information within a time limit to be determined by him, if such information is needed in order to take a decision on the request.

Article 552dd
1. Until the investigation at the trial has started the Minister of Justice may withdraw his decision to grant a request for proceedings if circumstances emerge in the course of a preliminary investigation or in any other way which, if they had been known at the time the decision on the request was taken, would have resulted in its being rejected.
2. A decision to grant a request for proceedings may also be withdrawn if the penalty imposed on the accused cannot be enforced.

Article 552ee
1. The Minister of Justice shall notify the public prosecutor and the authorities of the state making the request of his decision on the request.
2. He shall also notify the said authorities of the outcome of proceedings instituted in compliance with the request.

Article 552ff
A person with regard to whom the Netherlands has no jurisdiction to institute proceedings may nevertheless be arrested if such action is in accordance with a treaty. Articles 52 to 93 shall apply by analogy.

Article 552gg
1. The documents concerning official acts, performed with a view to investigating and prosecuting a criminal offence, which the authorities of the state making the request for proceedings submit with their request, shall have the same evidential weight as documents relating to similar acts taken by Dutch authorities, with the proviso that they shall not have greater evidential weight than they would have in the foreign state in question.

2. In the event of a request as referred to in the second paragraph of article 552y being granted, a criminal financial investigation may be opened in accordance with the ninth part of Title IV of Book I.

Article 552hh
1. A request for extradition of a person who is present in the Netherlands and who is suspected or has been convicted of an offence as referred to in one of the treaty articles listed in the second paragraph, shall be regarded as a request for proceedings which has been granted, if it originated from a state which is bound by the provisions of the treaty in question and if extradition of the person concerned has been declared inadmissible by a court or if the request has been rejected by ministerial order.
2. The first paragraph relates to offences referred to in:
   – article 1 of the European Convention on the suppression of terrorism (*Trb.* 1977, 63);
   – article 2, first paragraph, of the Convention on the prevention and punishment of crimes against internationally protected persons, including diplomatic agents (*Trb.* 1981, 69);
   – article 1 of the International Convention against the taking of hostages (*Trb.* 1981, 93);
   – article 7, first paragraph, of the Convention on the physical protection of nuclear material (*Trb.* 1981, 7);
   – article 2 of the Protocol for the suppression of unlawful acts against the safety of fixed platforms located on the continental shelf (*Trb.* 1989, 18);
   – article II of the Protocol for the suppression of unlawful acts of violence at airports serving international civil aviation (*Trb.* 1988, 88).
3. The provisions of article 522y, first paragraph, opening words and *a*, shall not apply to a request for proceedings as referred to in the last clause of the first paragraph.
4. Furthermore, the provisions of article 552y, first paragraph, opening words and *b*, 2°, shall not apply to requests based on the European Convention on the suppression of terrorism or on the Agreement on the application of the said Convention between the Member States of the European Communities (*Trb.* 1980, 14).

3 Extradition Act

Act of 9 March 1967, *Staatsblad* 139, containing new regulations relating to extradition and other forms of international assistance in criminal matters, as last amended by the Act of 12 April 1995, *Staatsblad* 254.

CHAPTER I

Definitions

Article 1
In this Act the following definitions shall apply:
Our Minister: Our Minister of Justice;
extradition: the removal of a person from the Netherlands with the object of surrendering him to the authorities of another State for the purpose of a criminal investigation concerning him in that State or of enforcing a penalty or measure imposed on him in that State;
alien: any person who does not have Netherlands' nationality and who is not treated as a national of the Netherlands by reason of any statutory provision;
person claimed: a person whose extradition has been requested by a foreign Power;
requesting state: the Power requesting extradition.

CHAPTER II

Conditions governing extradition

Article 2
Extradition shall take place only pursuant to a treaty.

Article 3
If a treaty deviating from this Act is presented to the States-General for approval, We shall at the same time submit a Bill to amend the present Act.

Article 4
1. Nationals of the Netherlands shall not be extradited.
2. The first paragraph shall not apply if extradition of a Dutch national is requested for the purpose of prosecuting him and in Our Minister's opinion there is an adequate guarantee that, if he is sentenced to a custodial sentence other than a suspended sentence in the requesting state for offences for which his extradition may be permitted, he will be allowed to serve this sentence in the Netherlands.

Article 5
1. Extradition may be granted only for the purpose of:
    a. a criminal investigation instituted by the authorities of the requesting state on a suspicion that the person claimed is guilty of an offence for which a custodial sentence of one year or more may be imposed under the law of both the requesting state and the Netherlands;
    b. enforcing a custodial sentence of four months or more to be served by the person claimed in the territory of the requesting state for an offence as referred to under *a.*
2. For the purposes of the preceding paragraph, an offence punishable under the law of the Netherlands shall be taken to include an offence violating the legal order of the requesting state if the same violation of the Dutch legal order is punishable under the law of the Netherlands.
3. If, in the case of the first paragraph, under *b*, the judgment imposing the custodial sentence was given in absentia, extradition shall be allowed only if the person claimed has had or will still be given an adequate opportunity to defend himself.

Article 6
The minimum periods of one year and of four months laid down in article 5 shall not apply to extradition to Belgium or Luxembourg.

Article 7
For the purpose of this Act the following shall be equated with:
a. *custodial sentences:* namely measures involving deprivation of liberty imposed by a criminal court in addition to or instead of a penalty;
b. *custodial sentences of more than one year:* namely custodial sentences – including measures as referred to under *a* – for life or for an indefinite period.[1]

Article 8
If the offence in respect of which extradition is requested is punishable by death under the law of the requesting state, the person claimed shall not be extradited unless in Our

---

1   Note of the editors: for the differences between penalties and measures in Dutch law see supra pp. 24-25.

Minister's opinion there is an adequate guarantee that this penalty, if imposed, will not be carried out.

Article 9

1. Extradition of the person claimed shall not be granted for an offence in respect of which:
   a. criminal proceedings are pending against him in the Netherlands at the time a decision on the request for extradition is being made;
   b. he has been prosecuted in the Netherlands, if renewed proceedings are precluded pursuant to article 255, first and second paragraphs, of the Code of Criminal Procedure;
   c. he has been acquitted or the charges against him have been dismissed by final judgment of a Dutch court or a similar irrevocable decision has been made in his respect by another court;
   d. he has been convicted by final judgment of a court in cases in which:
      1. the penalty or measure imposed has already been served, or
      2. such penalty or measure is not susceptible of immediate enforcement or further enforcement, or
      3. the conviction entails a finding of guilt without a penalty or measure having been imposed, or
      4. the final judgment originates from a Dutch court and the power of extradition is not reserved by treaty in such a case;
   e. prosecution or, if extradition has been requested for the purpose of enforcing a penalty or measure, punishment is precluded by lapse of time under Dutch law.
2. An exception shall be made to the opening words and *a* of the preceding paragraph in cases in which Our Minister in deciding to grant the request for extradition at the same time orders that proceedings be discontinued.
3. An exception shall be made to the opening words and *b* of the first paragraph in cases in which proceedings in the Netherlands have been discontinued either because the criminal law of the Netherlands has proved to be inapplicable by reason of articles 2 to 8 of the Penal Code or because preference has been given to proceedings abroad.

Article 10

1. Extradition shall not be granted in cases in which in Our Minister's opinion there are good grounds for believing that if the request were to be granted the person claimed would be prosecuted, punished or otherwise harassed on account of his religious or political opinions, nationality or race or the population group to which he belongs.
2. Extradition shall not be granted in cases in which in Our Minister's opinion its consequences would cause particular hardship to the person claimed on account of his youth, old age or state of health.

Article 11
1. Extradition shall not be granted for offences of a political nature, including offences connected therewith.
2. The taking or attempted taking of the life or liberty of a Head of State or a member of the reigning House shall not be regarded as an offence of a political nature within the meaning of the provisions of the preceding paragraph.
3. The first paragraph shall not apply to extradition for one of the offences defined in article 1 of the European Convention on the Suppression of Terrorism (*Trb.* 1977, 63) to a state which is obliged in a corresponding case not to refuse extradition to the Netherlands on account of the political nature of the offence.
4. Military offences which are not also crimes under the general criminal law of the Netherlands, and fiscal offences shall not constitute grounds for extradition unless specifically provided by treaty.
5. The provisions of the preceding paragraph relating to military offences shall not apply to extradition to Belgium or Luxembourg.

Article 12
1. Extradition shall not be granted except on the general condition that the person claimed will not be prosecuted, punished or restricted in his personal freedom in any other way in respect of offences committed before the time of his extradition and for which he has not been extradited, except with the explicit consent of Our Minister.
2. Our Minister may give the consent referred to in the preceding paragraph with respect to:
    a. offences for which the person claimed could have been extradited to the state requesting consent by virtue of the applicable treaty;
    b. other offences, insofar as these are punishable both under the law of the state requesting consent and under that of the Netherlands and the possibility of extradition in respect thereof is not precluded by articles 8 to 11 of this Act.
3. Furthermore, extradition shall not be granted except on the general condition that the person claimed will not, without the explicit consent of Our Minister, be surrendered to the authorities of a third state in respect of offences committed before the time of his extradition. Such consent may be given as regards offences for which the person claimed could have been extradited by the Netherlands to the third state.
4. The decision of Our Minister regarding a request for consent as referred to in the first and third paragraphs shall be communicated through diplomatic channels to the state making such request, unless some other way has been provided for by treaty.
5. Insofar as provided for by treaty, the consent referred to in the first and third paragraphs shall not be required if the person claimed has had the opportunity for a period of at least thirty days after the time of his extradition to leave the territory of the state making the request for consent.
6. As regards Belgium and Luxembourg, exceptions in cases other than those referred to in the preceding paragraph may be provided for by treaty.

CHAPTER III

Extradition procedure

PART A

Provisional arrest

Article 13

1. In so far as provided for by treaty, the provisional arrest of a person sought in the Netherlands may be ordered – in the cases referred to in the following paragraph – at the request of the competent authority of another state if there is good reason to expect that a request for his extradition susceptible of being granted will shortly be made by that state.
2. Provisional arrest may be ordered when requested:
   a. in connection with a criminal investigation instituted because the person sought is suspected of being guilty of an offence in respect of which a person may be remanded in custody under the law of the Netherlands;
   b. with a view to enforcing a custodial penalty or a measure as referred to in article 7 under *a*;
   c. in cases other than provided for in *a* and *b* if the person sought has no fixed abode or place of residence in the Netherlands.
3. If there is good reason to expect that a request for provisional arrest susceptible of being granted will shortly be made in respect of a person sought who has been delivered by the commander of an aircraft after landing in the Netherlands, pursuant to article 9, first paragraph, of the Convention on Offences and Certain Other Acts Committed on Board Aircraft (*Trb.* 1964, 115), or who is suspected of having committed an act as referred to in article 11, first paragraph, of that Convention on board an aircraft in which he has arrived in the Netherlands, by a state referred to in article 13, fifth paragraph, of the Convention, the provisional arrest of the person sought may be ordered as if it had already been requested.

Article 13a

An alien who has been arrested pursuant to article 54, fourth paragraph, of the Code of Criminal Procedure may, on the order of a public prosecutor or assistant public prosecutor, be held for questioning if there is good reason to expect that a request for provisional arrest as mentioned in article 13 will shortly be made in respect of him. Article 61, second paragraph, of the Code of Criminal Procedure shall apply by analogy.

Article 14

1. Any public prosecutor or assistant public prosecutor may order the provisional arrest of a person sought in accordance with article 13.

2. Within twenty-four hours of being provisionally arrested the person sought shall be brought before the public prosecutor or assistant public prosecutor who issued the warrant for his provisional arrest.
3. After hearing the person sought, the public prosecutor or assistant public prosecutor may order that he be detained in police custody for forty-eight hours from the time of the provisional arrest. The assistant public prosecutor shall inform the public prosecutor in writing of his order as soon as possible.
4. The period of detention in police custody may be extended once for forty-eight hours by the public prosecutor.
5. The person sought may be released at any time by the public prosecutor. If detention in police custody has not yet been extended, the assistant public prosecutor who issued the warrant for provisional arrest shall also have this power.

Article 15
1. The examining magistrate, in charge of dealing with criminal matters, at the court of the district in which a person sought is being detained in police custody in accordance with article 14 may order the person's remand in custody at the request of the public prosecutor at such district court.
2. Before making an order under the preceding paragraph, the examining magistrate shall hear the person sought if possible.

Article 16
1. A person sought whose remand in custody has been ordered by the examining magistrate in accordance with article 15 shall be released, subject to the possibility of further deprivation of his liberty on other grounds:
    a. as soon as this is ordered by the district court, the examining magistrate or the public prosecutor ex officio or at the request of the person or his counsel;
    b. as soon as the period has elapsed within which, according to the applicable treaty, his provisional arrest must be followed by a request for extradition, if no such request has yet been made;
    c. as soon as the remand in custody has lasted for twenty days.
2. In cases in which article 13, third paragraph, applies, the periods referred to in the preceding paragraph under *b* and *c*, after the expiry of which the person sought must be released, shall be extended for four days.

Article 17
Our Minister shall be notified forthwith of every decision made pursuant to any of the provisions of articles 13 to 16.

PART B

Procedure for dealing with a request for extradition

Article 18
1. A request for extradition may be considered only if it satisfies the requirements specified in the following paragraphs of this article.
2. The request shall be made in writing, either through diplomatic channels or – as far as the applicable treaty makes provision therefor – directly to Our Minister.
3. The request must be accompanied by:
   a. the original or an authenticated copy either of an enforceable conviction in respect of the person claimed, or of a warrant for his arrest issued by the competent authorities of the requesting state, or of a document having the same force of law, drawn up in the form prescribed by the law of such state and relating to the offences in respect of which extradition is requested;
   b. a statement of the offences for which extradition is requested, specifying as precisely as possible the time and place at which they have been committed;
   c. the text of the relevant enactments or, in the case of unwritten law, a statement of the purport of such law sufficient to enable the request to be assessed;
   d. the information needed for establishing the identity of the person claimed and – where there is any doubt as to this – his nationality.

Article 19
If in the opinion of Our Minister the documents submitted do not satisfy the requirements of article 18 or further requirements laid down in the applicable treaty, he shall allow the authorities of the requesting state the opportunity to supplement or correct the information supplied within such reasonable period as he may specify.

Article 20
1. Unless Our Minister is from the outset of the opinion that the request for extradition must be refused, he shall pass the request together with the accompanying documents – where necessary after having allowed an opportunity to supplement or correct them in accordance with article 19 – to the public prosecutor at the court of the district in which the person claimed is present.
2. When there has first been a request for provisional arrest, the documents shall be sent to the public prosecutor who has already been concerned with the case in connection with such request.
3. If criminal proceedings against the person claimed are pending in the Netherlands and he has for this reason been provisionally deprived of his liberty, the documents may, notwithstanding the above provisions, be sent to the public prosecutor responsible for such proceedings.
4. If it is not known for the time being in what district the person claimed is present, Our Minister shall send the documents to the public prosecutor in Amsterdam.

Article 21
1. The public prosecutor who has received the request for extradition may order the arrest of the person claimed.
2. The claimed person whose arrest has been ordered in accordance with the preceding paragraph shall be brought before the public prosecutor or, in his absence, before an assistant public prosecutor within twenty-four hours of his arrest. After examination by an assistant public prosecutor, the arrested person shall be brought as soon as possible before the public prosecutor.
3. After the person claimed has been heard, the public prosecutor may order that he continue to be detained in police custody until such time as the district court decides whether to remand him in custody.
4. The order for detention in police custody may be terminated at any time either by the district court or by the public prosecutor ex officio or at the request of the person claimed or his counsel.

Article 22
1. If on the day on which the public prosecutor receives the request for extradition the person claimed has already been detained in police custody or remanded in custody pursuant to articles 14 or 15 as the case may be, he may – contrary to the provisions of article 14, third and fourth paragraphs, or the opening words of article 16 and *c* thereof, as the case may be – continue to be deprived of his liberty by order of the public prosecutor until such time as the district court decides whether he is to be remanded in custody.
2. The public prosecutor shall give immediate notice of an order as referred to in the preceding paragraph to the examining magistrate who has ordered the remand in custody under article 15.

Article 23
1. Not later than the third day following that on which he has received the request for extradition, the public prosecutor shall apply in writing for the district court to deal with the request. In doing so he shall submit the documents to the court.
2. A copy of the application required pursuant to the preceding paragraph shall be served upon the person claimed. He shall at the same time be informed of the offences for which his extradition has been requested, of the times and places at which they have been committed, as specified in the request for extradition, and of the state which has made the request. The above shall also apply in cases in which the public prosecutor has supplemented or altered his application in connection with a request received subsequently. The person claimed shall be informed of the receipt of supplementary documents which are added to the file.
3. After the documents have been submitted to the district court, the person claimed and his counsel may not be denied the right to inspect them. The provisions laid down by and pursuant to article 34 of the Code of Criminal Procedure shall apply by analogy.

Article 24
1. Immediately after receipt of the application referred to in article 23 the president of the competent chamber of the district court shall set the time, allotting the case priority if possible, at which the person claimed will be heard by the court. He may at the same time order that he be brought before the court.
2. The registrar of the district court shall immediately notify the public prosecutor and the person claimed of the time fixed for the hearing. This notification – and, if an order for him to be brought before the court has been made, a copy of such order – shall be served upon the person claimed.
3. If it does not appear that the person claimed already has the services of counsel, the president of the competent chamber of the district court shall instruct the office for legal assistance to assign him counsel.

Article 25
1. The person claimed shall be heard in public unless he asks for the matter to be dealt with in camera or unless the district court orders that the case be heard in camera for reasons of an important nature, to be mentioned in the official record of the proceedings.
2. The public prosecutor shall be present at the hearing.
3. The person claimed may have his counsel assist him at the hearing.
4. If the person claimed does not appear, the district court shall order that he be summoned to appear at a time set by the court, if necessary adding an order that he be brought before the court.

Article 26
1. The district court shall examine the identity of the person claimed, the admissibility of the request for extradition and the possibility of granting it.
2. At the hearing of the court the public prosecutor shall give his views on the admissibility of the request for extradition and shall submit a written summary thereof to the court. The person claimed and his counsel shall also be given an opportunity to make relevant observations regarding the request for extradition and the decisions to be taken in connection therewith.
3. Should the person claimed submit that he is able to show forthwith that he is not guilty of the offences in respect of which his extradition has been requested, the court shall examine this submission.
4. If the court deems this necessary with a view to its examination pursuant to the first or third paragraph of this article, it shall order that witnesses or experts be summoned or given written notice to attend at a time set by the court, if necessary adding an order that they be brought before the court.

Article 27
1. Upon application by the public prosecutor the district court may at the hearing order that the person claimed who has not been deprived of his liberty be remanded in custody.

2. Before the examination at the hearing is closed, the court shall decide ex officio whether the person claimed is to continue to be held in custody, if he has already been either remanded in custody by order of the examining magistrate or detained in police custody.

Article 28
1. As soon as possible after the examination at the hearing is completed, the district court shall render its judgment with regard to the request for extradition. The judgment shall state the grounds on which it is based.
2. If the court finds either that the documents supplied by the requesting state do not satisfy the requirements laid down in article 18 or further requirements laid down in the applicable treaty, or that the request for extradition cannot be granted, or that there is no indication whatever that the person claimed is guilty of the offences for which his extradition has been requested, it shall declare in its judgment that extradition is inadmissible.
3. In cases other than provided for in the preceding paragraph, the court shall declare in its judgment that extradition is admissible, stating the applicable provisions of the relevant statute and treaty, and also the offence or offences for which extradition may be allowed.
4. If extradition is declared admissible notwithstanding a submission by the person claimed in accordance with article 26, third paragraph, then the judgment shall state the findings of the court with regard to such submission.

Article 29
1. Articles 37 to 39, 45 to 49, 50, first paragraph, 268, 269, 274, 275, 277, 283, first and fourth paragraphs, 284 to 308, 318 to 322, 324 to 331, 345, first and third paragraphs, 346, 357 and 362 to 365 of the Code of Criminal Procedure shall apply by analogy. Insofar as the provisions relate to a suspect, they shall apply by analogy to the person claimed.
2. The articles mentioned in the first paragraph shall not apply in so far as they relate to a witness whose identity has not been disclosed or has been disclosed only partially.

Article 30
1. The judgment of the district court shall be served upon a person claimed who was not present when it was read out. He shall at the same time be informed of his right to appeal against such judgment and of the time within which such right of appeal may be exercised.
2. The court shall send Our Minister without delay a certified copy of its judgment. If extradition has been declared admissible, the copy shall be accompanied by the court's opinion on the reply to be given to the request for extradition. The registrar of the court shall give a copy of the opinion to the person claimed and his counsel or send it to them.

Article 31
1. Both the public prosecutor and the person claimed may appeal in cassation against the judgment of the district court.
2. Articles 431 to 433, 436 to 440, 441, first paragraph, 443, 444, 449, first paragraph, and 450 to 456 of the Code of Criminal Procedure shall apply by analogy.
3. The registrar of the district court shall inform Our Minister without delay of any statements waiving the right to appeal in cassation or withdrawing such an appeal.
4. If the district court's decision is quashed in whole or in part, the Supreme Court shall do what the district court should have done.
5. The Supreme Court shall send Our Minister a certified copy of its judgment without delay.

Article 32
Immediately after a court's judgment on the request for extradition has become final, the registrar of the court which last dealt with the matter shall return such request to Our Minister together with the documents pertaining to it.

PART C

Decision on the request for extradition

Article 33
1. After Our Minister has received the documents in accordance with article 32, he shall decide as soon as possible on the request for extradition.
2. If extradition has been declared inadmissible by final judgment of a court, the request shall be refused.
3. If extradition has been declared inadmissible solely on account of the inadequacy of the documents submitted, Our Minister may defer a decision. The same shall apply if extradition has been declared admissible, but Our Minister deems further documents necessary to enable him to take a proper decision.
4. In the event that Our Minister defers his decision, he shall give the authorities of the requesting state the opportunity to submit additional documents within such reasonable time as he may specify.
5. If the additional documents requested are not produced within the time set, Our Minister shall refuse the request for extradition.
6. Our Minister's decision regarding a request for extradition shall be communicated to the requesting state through diplomatic channels unless some other way has been provided for by treaty.

Article 34
1. If Our Minister receives the additional documents within the time set, he may return the file on the matter to the public prosecutor at the district court which dealt with the request for extradition. In that event, articles 23 to 26, 28 to 32 and 33, first and second paragraphs, shall once again apply. If extradition was declared inadmissible

by the Supreme Court on the ground that the documents are inadequate, Our Minister may forward the file with the additional documents direct to the Prosecutor General at the Supreme Court.

2. Insofar as the additional documents provide grounds for this, extradition shall then be declared admissible by the court.

Article 35

If two or more states have requested extradition of the same person, Our Minister shall, in deciding on their requests – insofar as they are admissible and susceptible of being granted – take into account the interests of a proper administration of justice and particularly:

a. the degree of seriousness of the various offences for which extradition has been requested;

b. the place or places where the offences were committed;

c. the times at which the requests for extradition were made;

d. the nationality of the person claimed;

e. the possibility of the person claimed, after his removal to the territory of any of the requesting states, subsequently being surrendered by that state's authorities to the authorities of another requesting state.

Article 36

Our Minister shall immediately notify the public prosecutor at the district court which has dealt with the request of his decision on the request for extradition and also of a deferment thereof in accordance with article 33, third paragraph.

PART D

Continued deprivation of liberty and removal from the Netherlands

Article 37

1. Deprivation of liberty ordered in pursuance of article 27 shall be terminated – subject to the possibility of further deprivation of liberty on other grounds – as soon as:

   a. this is ordered by the district court or by the public prosecutor, either ex officio or at the request of the person in custody or his counsel, or by the Supreme Court in its decision on an appeal in cassation;

   b. the custody has lasted for thirty days unless the district court has meanwhile extended this period upon the application of the public prosecutor.

2. The public prosecutor shall in any event order that deprivation of liberty be terminated as soon as he has been notified of a decision by Our Minister refusing the request for extradition.

Article 38
1. The period referred to in article 37 under *b* may be extended for not more than thirty days at a time.
2. The district court shall not give a decision on an application for an extension until after the person in custody has been heard in respect thereof.
3. Extension may take place only in cases in which:
    a. a court's judgment regarding the request for extradition has not yet become final or has become final less than thirty days prior to the request for extradition;
    b. Our Minister has deferred a decision in accordance with article 33, third paragraph;
    c. extradition has also been requested by a third state and Our Minister has not yet made a decision relating to the request of that state;
    d. extradition has meanwhile been granted but has not yet been able to take place.

Article 39
1. After all or part of the request for extradition has been granted, the person claimed shall be surrendered to the authorities of the requesting state as soon as possible, at a time and place to be decided by Our Minister after consulting the said authorities.
2. The decision regarding the time and place of extradition may be deferred if and for as long as criminal proceedings are pending in the Netherlands against the person claimed or if he has been sentenced by a Dutch court and such sentence can still be enforced in whole or in part.
3. In the cases provided for in the preceding paragraph, Our Minister may, if he considers that there are suitable grounds, order that the person claimed be provisionally and immediately surrendered to the authorities of the requesting state for the purpose of standing trial in that state's territory.
4. If the preceding paragraph is applied to a claimed person who is serving a custodial penalty, the period of his surrender to the authorities of the requesting state shall be deducted from the length of his sentence.

Article 40
1. If this is necessary for the purposes of article 39, first or third paragraph, the person claimed shall be arrested under a warrant issued by a public prosecutor on the instruction of Our Minister.
2. If the competent foreign authorities do not take possession of the person claimed at the time and place fixed by Our Minister, such person may, after the time and place of his extradition have again been fixed, be re-arrested if necessary, in accordance with the preceding paragraph.
3. Deprivation of liberty based solely on a warrant for arrest under the first or second paragraph of this article shall not under any circumstances last longer than forty-eight hours.

PART E

Expedited procedure

Article 41
1. A person sought whose provisional arrest or extradition has been requested by another state may − not later than the day prior to that set for the hearing by the district court in accordance with article 24 − declare that he consents to immediate extradition.
2. Insofar as not otherwise provided for by treaty, a declaration in accordance with the preceding paragraph may be made only before an examining magistrate, in charge of dealing with criminal matters.
3. In making such a declaration, the person sought may be assisted by counsel. Should he appear without counsel his attention shall be drawn to this right by the authority empowered to receive the declaration.
4. Before he makes the declaration, the person sought shall be informed of the possible consequences thereof. An official record shall be made of the declaration.
5. The authority before whom the declaration is made shall send the official record thereof to the public prosecutor who has been concerned under this Act with the request for provisional arrest or the request for extradition.

Article 42
1. After a declaration has been made in accordance with article 41, the public prosecutor may decide that the person sought be surrendered to the authorities of the state making the request for provisional arrest or the request for extradition.
2. The preceding paragraph shall not apply:
   a. if, under any of the provisions of articles 2 and 9, extradition may not be granted for the offence or offences in connection with which provisional arrest or extradition has been requested,
   b. if it appears that criminal proceedings are pending in the Netherlands against the person sought or if he has been sentenced by a Dutch court and all or part of such sentence can still be enforced.
3. The public prosecutor shall inform Our Minister forthwith of every decision taken pursuant to the first paragraph of this article.

Article 43
1. If the public prosecutor has decided in accordance with article 42 that the person sought shall be surrendered to the authorities of the other state, article 23 shall not apply.
2. If the application referred to in article 23 has already been lodged with the court, this shall then be withdrawn forthwith. The registrar of the district court shall then return the request for extradition, together with the documents pertaining to it, to the public prosecutor.

3. The public prosecutor shall inform the person claimed of the withdrawal of such application.

Article 44
1. After the day on which he has made the declaration referred to in article 41, the person sought may be kept in custody on remand or in police custody for not more than twenty days.
2. The preceding paragraph shall not apply if the public prosecutor has decided that no effect will be given to the declaration, and the request for extradition, together with the documents pertaining to it, has been submitted to the district court in accordance with article 23, first paragraph.
3. The period referred to in the first paragraph of this article may, upon the application of the public prosecutor, be extended by the district court. Article 38, first and second paragraphs, shall apply by analogy.
4. Custody may be extended only if extradition cannot be effected within the period of twenty days owing to circumstances of an exceptional nature.

Article 45
1. If article 42, first paragraph, applies, the public prosecutor shall, after consulting the competent foreign authorities, without delay fix the time and place at which extradition will take place.
2. With a view to extradition in pursuance of the provisions of this part, the public prosecutor may if necessary order that the person sought be arrested. Article 40, second and third paragraphs, shall apply by analogy.
3. In the event of extradition by virtue of the provisions of this part, article 12 shall not apply.

CHAPTER IV

Other forms of legal assistance

Article 46
1. Property found in the possession of a person whose extradition or provisional arrest has been requested in pursuance of a treaty may be seized at the request of the competent foreign authorities. Such seizure shall be made by or by order of the public prosecutor or assistant public prosecutor empowered to issue a warrant for arrest or for provisional arrest.
2. Together with the application referred to in article 23, the public prosecutor shall submit to the district court a list of the property seized.

Article 47
1. In its judgment on the request for extradition, the district court shall also decide whether to surrender or return the property seized. Surrender of such property to the

authorities of the requesting state may be ordered only if the request for extradition is granted.

2. In view of possible third party rights, the district court may decide that certain property may be delivered to the authorities of the requesting state only on condition that such property will be returned immediately after it has been used as required for the criminal proceedings.

3. The provisions of articles 116 to 119, 552a and 552c to 552e of the Code of Criminal Procedure and provisions made pursuant thereto shall apply by analogy. Instead of the court competent under such provisions, the court which will act shall be the district court to which the application referred to in article 23, first paragraph, of this Act has been made or – should no such application have been made – the court of the district in which the objects were seized.

4. In the event of extradition in accordance with the provisions of part E of chapter III, the public prosecutor shall decide as to the surrender or return of the property seized, subject to the powers of the district court under the preceding paragraph.

Article 48

1. Aliens who, for the purpose of a criminal investigation or the enforcement of a sentence, are surrendered by the authorities of a foreign state to those of another state may, with Our Minister's consent, be transported across the territory of the Netherlands.

2. Consent for overland transit shall not be given except in pursuance of a treaty.

3. Our Minister's consent shall not be required for transit by air during which no landing is made in the territory of the Netherlands.

4. In the case of an unscheduled landing the alien may, at the request of the authorities accompanying him, be provisionally arrested on the order of the locally competent public prosecutor or assistant public prosecutor. Article 14 shall apply by analogy.

5. Transportation of an alien under provisional arrest may be continued as soon as Our Minister gives his consent. If such consent has not been given after expiry of the remand period or has been refused within such period, the alien shall be released forthwith subject to the possibility of further deprivation of his liberty on other grounds.

Article 49

The consent required under article 48 shall not be given in cases in which, if it was a request for extradition that was involved, such request would have to be refused pursuant to the provisions of articles 8 to 10.

Article 50

1. Where not otherwise provided for by treaty the guarding of the alien shall be entrusted to Dutch officials during overland transit in accordance with article 48.

2. If, owing to circumstances of an exceptional nature, it is not possible for transit through the Netherlands to take place without interruption, the alien may if necessary, pending a suitable opportunity to depart elsewhere, be committed to a

remand prison upon production of a document showing Our Minister's consent to the transit.

Article 50a

1. In cases where a person who has been lawfully deprived of his liberty abroad is temporarily transferred to the Dutch judicial authorities in order to testify as a witness or for purposes of confrontation, he shall be detained in police custody during his stay in the Netherlands, on the order of the competent member of the public prosecutions department. Articles 54 and 56, first paragraph, shall apply by analogy wherever necessary.
2. Police custody shall be terminated as soon as the competent member of the public prosecutions department receives notice that the grounds for deprivation of liberty abroad no longer exist.

Article 51

1. In cases where this is provided for by treaty, Our Minister may allow persons lawfully deprived of their liberty in the Netherlands to be temporarily transferred to the authorities of another state in order to testify as witnesses or for purposes of confrontation.
2. Insofar as the treaty does not provide otherwise, the consent of the person to be temporarily transferred shall be required.
3. Our Minister shall not permit temporary transfer if it is requested for the purpose of a criminal investigation which is instituted in the territory of another state and relates to offences in respect of which no extradition is allowed under article 9 or 10.
4. If the person concerned is serving a custodial sentence in the Netherlands, the time during which he is transferred to the authorities of the other state shall be deducted from the length of the sentence.

CHAPTER V

Final provisions

Article 51a

1. As regards the offences referred to in the second paragraph, which are punishable pursuant to the treaties referred to in that paragraph, extradition may be granted to states party to the relevant treaty.
2. The first paragraph relates to:
    . the crime referred to in article 385a of the Penal Code, insofar as it comes within the definitions of the Convention for the suppression of unlawful seizure of aircraft, concluded at The Hague on 16 December 1970 (*Trb.* 1971, 50);
    . the crimes referred to in articles 162, 162a, 166, 168, 385b, 385c and 385d of the Penal Code, insofar as the offence comes within the definitions of the Convention

for the suppression of unlawful acts against the safety of civil aviation, concluded at Montreal on 23 September 1971 (*Trb.* 1971, 218), or of the Protocol for the suppression of unlawful acts of violence at airports serving international civil aviation, concluded at Montreal on 24 February 1988 (*Trb.* 1988,88);

. the crimes referred to in article 10, second, third, fourth and fifth paragraphs, article 10a, first paragraph, and article 11, second and third paragraphs, of the Opium Act, insofar as the offence comes within the definitions of the first paragraph of article 36 of the Single Convention on narcotic drugs, 1961, as amended pursuant to article 14 of the Protocol amending the Single Convention on narcotic drugs, concluded at Geneva on 25 March 1972 (*Trb.* 1980, 184);

. the crimes referred to in articles 92, 108 to 110, 115 to 117b and 285 of the Penal Code, insofar as the offence has been committed against an internationally protected person or his protected property and comes within the definitions of the Convention on the prevention and punishment of crimes against internationally protected persons, including diplomatic agents, concluded at New York on 14 December 1973 (*Trb.* 1981, 69);

. the crime referred to in article 282a of the Penal Code, insofar as the offence comes within the definition of the International Convention against the taking of hostages, concluded at New York on 17 December 1979 (*Trb.* 1981, 53);

. the crimes referred to in articles 1 and 2 of the Act implementing the torture convention, insofar as the offence comes within the definition of the Convention against torture and other cruel, inhuman or degrading treatment or punishment, concluded at New York on 10 December 1984 (*Trb.* 1985, 69);

. the crimes referred to in articles 157, 161 *quater*, 284a, 285, 310 to 312, 317, 318, 321, 322 and 326 of the Penal Code and the crimes consisting of acts prohibited by or pursuant to articles 15, 19, 21, 26 and 38 of the Nuclear Energy Act, insofar as the offence comes within the definitions of the Convention on the physical protection of nuclear material, concluded at Vienna/New York on 3 March 1980 (*Trb.* 1981, 7);

. the crimes referred to in articles 166, 168, 350, 352, 354, 385a, fourth paragraph, 385b, second paragraph, and 385c, insofar as the offence comes within the definitions of the Convention for the suppression of unlawful acts against the safety of maritime navigation and the Protocol for the suppression of unlawful acts against the safety of fixed platforms located on the continental shelf, concluded at Rome on 10 March 1988 (*Trb.* 1989, 17 and 18);

. the crimes referred to in articles 10, second, third, fourth and fifth paragraph, 10a, first paragraph, and 11, second and third paragraphs, of the Opium Act together with the crimes referred to in articles 131, 140, 189, first paragraph, opening words and 3°, 416 and 417 of the Penal Code, insofar as the offence comes within the definitions of the first paragraph of article 3 of the United Nations Convention against illicit traffic in narcotic drugs and psychotropic substances, concluded at Vienna on 20 December 1988 (*Trb.* 1989, 97).

3. Extradition pursuant to the first paragraph shall be effected subject to the provisions of this Act and, if no other extradition treaty applies, to the provisions of the European Convention on extradition of 13 December 1957 (*Trb.* 1965, 9).

Article 52
Orders for detention in police custody or remand in custody or for extending a period in custody issued pursuant to this Act shall be dated and signed. The grounds for issuing the order shall be stated therein. A copy of the order shall be issued forthwith to the person to whom it relates.

Article 53
1. Warrants or orders for deprivation of liberty issued by virtue of this Act shall be enforceable forthwith.
2. The officials referred to in article 141 of the Code of Criminal Procedure shall be empowered to execute warrants for arrest or provisional arrest or orders for remand in custody.
3. Articles 564 to 568 of the Code of Criminal Procedure shall apply to the execution of warrants or orders for deprivation of liberty and instructions to that effect.

Article 54
Persons held in police custody or remanded in custody by order of the court in pursuance of this Act shall be treated as suspects subjected to a similar measure under the Code of Criminal Procedure.

Article 55
1. The provisions of article 40 of the Code of Criminal Procedure and provisions made pursuant to it shall apply by analogy to a person sought held in police custody pursuant to this Act.
2. If a person is deprived of his liberty in conformity with this Act – other than under a warrant for arrest or provisional arrest or an order for police custody or an extension thereof – the president of the court of the district in which he is present shall instruct the office for legal assistance to assign him counsel. The public prosecutor shall inform the president in writing forthwith that counsel must be provided.

Article 56
1. In cases in which a decision on depriving a person of his liberty may or must be taken under this Act, it may be ordered that such deprivation be conditionally postponed or suspended. The conditions imposed must serve only to prevent abscondence.
2. Articles 80 – with the exception of the second paragraph thereof – and 81 to 88 of the Code of Criminal Procedure shall apply by analogy to warrants or orders issued by virtue of the preceding paragraph by a district court or examining magistrate.

Article 57
Articles 73, 79, 569 and 570 of the Code of Criminal Procedure shall apply by analogy to orders terminating deprivation of liberty made by virtue of this Act and to the execution of such orders.

Article 58
The periods referred to in articles 16 under *c*, 37, first paragraph under *b*, 40, third paragraph, and 44, first paragraph, shall not run during the time the person has evaded the further execution of the orders mentioned in such articles.

Article 59
1. In cases where extradition has been declared inadmissible by final judgment of a court, the district court which heard the case may, at the request of the person claimed, award him a sum to be paid by the state for damage suffered as a result of any deprivation of liberty ordered pursuant to this Act. Damage includes loss other than pecuniary loss. Article 89, third, fourth and sixth paragraphs, and articles 90, 91 and 93 of the Code of Criminal Procedure shall apply by analogy.
2. In cases as referred to in the preceding paragraph, articles 591 and 591a of the Code of Criminal Procedure shall apply by analogy to the payment of costs and damages for the person claimed or his heirs. For this purpose the district court which heard the request for extradition shall take the place of the court referred to in the said articles.

Article 60
Articles 585 to 590 of the Code of Criminal Procedure shall apply by analogy to service, notifications and summonses under this Act.

Article 61
1. The provisions of the preceding chapters hereof shall not apply to:
    a. legal assistance provided for in the Act relating to surrender in respect of war crimes;
    b. the surrender of deserting crew members of ships to authorities of the state to which they belong;
    c. the surrender of members of a foreign military force and of persons equated with them to the competent military authorities insofar as such surrender takes place by virtue of an agreement with one or more states with which the Netherlands maintains an alliance.
2. (...)

Article 63
This Act may be cited as: Extradition Act.

4 Act relating to surrender in respect of war crimes

Act of 19 May 1954 relating to surrender in respect of war crimes, *Staatsblad* 215, as last amended by the Act of 24 June 1992, *Staatsblad* 358.

Article 1
1. Without prejudice to the provisions of extradition treaties concluded with other Powers, persons may be surrendered to another Power for the purpose of prosecuting them with respect to any of the crimes referred to in articles 8 and 9 of the Act on criminal law in time of war, articles 1 and 2 of the Act implementing the Genocide Convention or articles 1 and 2 of the Act implementing the Torture Convention, provided that the crime constitutes a grave breach of one of the following Geneva Conventions of 12 August 1949:
    a. the Convention for the amelioration of the condition of the wounded and the sick in armed forces in the field;
    b. the Convention for the amelioration of the condition of wounded, sick and shipwrecked members of armed forces at sea;
    c. the Convention relative to the treatment of prisoners of war;
    d. the Convention relative to the protection of civilian persons in time of war; or of the Protocol Additional to the Geneva Conventions for the protection of victims of international armed conflicts (Protocol I) of 12 December 1977.

Article 2
Surrender to another Power may take place only if that Power is a party to the Convention breached.

Article 3
1. Unless We have provided otherwise, surrender shall be requested through diplomatic channels.
2. Surrender shall be granted only if the other Power submits an indictment supported by evidence that justifies a committal for trial.

Article 4
1. Persons whose surrender has been requested by another Power in accordance with article 1 may, if they have not yet been deprived of their liberty, be arrested.

2. The warrant of arrest must be served on them within forty-eight hours.
3. Property found in their possession may be seized.
4. The Public Prosecutions Department of the district court which is competent to take cognizance of the crime with respect to which surrender has been requested shall be informed of the arrest within twenty-four hours.

Article 5
1. Before a decision is made on the request for surrender the opinion of the court which is competent to take cognizance of the crime with respect to which surrender has been requested shall be sought.
2. When giving its opinion the court shall decide which property seized shall be either returned to the person claimed or handed over as evidence in the case of surrender.
3. Surrender may not take place if the court has advised against surrender.

Article 6
The Government may permit an alien whose surrender with respect to a grave breach of any of the Conventions referred to in article 1 has been granted by another Power to a third Power to be transported across the territory of the Netherlands in the company of Dutch officials, provided that the Power to which surrender takes place is a party to the Convention breached.

Article 7
Articles 9, 10, 12, 20 to 40, 46, 47 and 51 to 60 of the Extradition Act shall apply by analogy, it being understood that provisional arrest may also be ordered in cases in which a treaty does not provide for that possibility.

Article 8
The surrender of persons suspected of having committed war crimes to other Powers for the purpose of prosecuting them shall, with respect to the Netherlands Antilles and Aruba, be regulated by an Order in Council for the Kingdom, whenever possible in accordance with the Act.

Article 9
1. This Act may be cited as 'Act relating to surrender in respect of war crimes'.
2. (...)

5 Act on the transfer of enforcement of criminal judgments

Act of 10 September 1986, *Staatsblad* 464, containing provisions relating to the taking over of enforcement of foreign criminal judgments and the transfer of enforcement of Dutch criminal judgments to other states, as last amended by the Act of 12 April 1995, *Staatsblad* 254.

CHAPTER I

PART A

Definitions

Article 1

1. In this Act the following definitions shall apply:
    Our Minister: Our Minister of Justice;
    Judgment: a judgment rendered by a court of first instance or a court of appeal in respect of a criminal offence;
    Sanction: any penalty imposed by judgment of a court, including any measure imposed in addition to or instead of a penalty;
    Sentenced person: a person on whom a sanction has been imposed.
2. The term judgment is also deemed to include a decision taken by an administrative authority in respect of an offence and imposing a penalty or measure not involving the deprivation of liberty, in respect of which appeal to a court lies.

PART B

Conditions governing the taking over of enforcement of foreign judgments

Article 2

Enforcement in the Netherlands of foreign judgments shall take place only pursuant to a treaty.

Article 3

1. A sanction imposed in a foreign State may be enforced in the Netherlands only if:
   a. the judgment is susceptible of enforcement in that State;
   b. the sanction does not consist of the payment of the costs of proceedings or an order to pay damages to an injured party;
   c. the judgment was given in respect of an offence which is also punishable under Dutch law;
   d. in the event of conviction, the offender would also have been punishable under Dutch law.
2. For the purposes of the preceding paragraph, an offence shall be deemed punishable under Dutch law if the violation of the legal order which is the subject of the foreign judgment would also be punishable under the law of the Netherlands as a violation of the legal order of the Netherlands.

Article 4

A sanction imposed in a foreign State may not be enforced in the Netherlands if it concerns an alien who has no fixed abode or place of residence in the Netherlands or a legal person whose board of management has no seat or office in the Netherlands or whose managing director has no fixed abode in the Netherlands. This condition shall not apply in so far as the sanction imposed in the foreign State consists of a fine or forfeiture or other sanction whose purpose is to deprive the offender of the proceeds from crime.

Article 5

A sanction imposed in a foreign State may not be enforced in the Netherlands if in Our Minister's opinion there are good grounds for believing that the decision to prosecute or the imposition of the sanction was motivated by considerations of race, religion, nationality or political opinions of the sentenced person or that such considerations have influenced the judgment to his disadvantage.

Article 6

1. A sanction imposed in a foreign State may not be enforced in the Netherlands if the right to enforce the sentence would be barred by lapse of time under Dutch law.
2. A sanction imposed in a foreign State may not be enforced in the Netherlands if at the time of the offence in respect of which the sanction was imposed the sentenced person had not yet attained the age of twelve years.

Article 7

1. A sanction imposed in a foreign State may not be enforced in the Netherlands if the sentenced person is being prosecuted for the same offence in the Netherlands.
2. A sanction imposed in a foreign State may likewise not be enforced in the Netherlands if proceedings in the Netherlands would not be compatible with the principle

underlying article 68 of the Penal Code and article 255, first paragraph, of the Code of Criminal Procedure.

CHAPTER II

Provisional measures

PART A

Provisional arrest

Article 8
Insofar as provided for by treaty, a sentenced person who is present in the Netherlands and on whom a sanction involving deprivation of liberty has been imposed, may, if the part of the sanction which still has to be enforced under the judgment made in the foreign State is at least three months, be provisionally arrested if there is good reason to expect that the sanction in question will shortly be enforced in the Netherlands.

Article 9
1. Any public prosecutor or assistant public prosecutor may order the provisional arrest in conformity with article 8.
2. Within twenty-four hours of his provisional arrest the sentenced person shall be brought before the public prosecutor or assistant public prosecutor who issued the warrant for his provisional arrest.
3. After hearing the sentenced person, the public prosecutor or assistant public prosecutor may order that he be detained in police custody for a period of forty-eight hours from the time of the provisional arrest. The assistant public prosecutor shall inform the public prosecutor in writing of his order as soon as possible.
4. The period of detention in police custody may be extended once for forty-eight hours by the public prosecutor.
5. The sentenced person may be released at any time by the public prosecutor. If detention in police custody has not yet been extended, the assistant public prosecutor who issued the warrant for provisional arrest shall also have this power.

Article 10
1. The examining magistrate, in charge of dealing with criminal matters, at the court of the district in which a sentenced person has been detained in police custody in accordance with article 9 may order the remand in custody of the sentenced person at the request of the public prosecutor at such district court.
2. Before making an order under the preceding paragraph the examining magistrate shall hear the sentenced person if possible.

Article 11
1. Remand in custody may be ordered by the examining magistrate for a period not exceeding fourteen days. It may be extended on the application of the public prosecutor for consecutive periods not exceeding thirty days until remand in custody by order of the district court is pronounced pursuant to article 29, second paragraph.
2. A sentenced person whose remand in custody has been ordered by the examining magistrate shall be released, subject to the possibility of further deprivation of his liberty on other grounds:
    a. as soon as this is ordered by the district court, the examining magistrate or the public prosecutor ex officio or at the request of the sentenced person or his counsel;
    b. as soon as remand in custody by order of the examining magistrate has lasted fourteen days, if the public prosecutor has not yet received the documents referred to in articles 15 or 17;
    c. if the period of detention in police custody and remand in custody exceeds the length of the part of the sanction imposed in the foreign State, which is susceptible of enforcement.

Article 12
Our Minister shall be notified forthwith of every decision made in respect of a request by an authority of a foreign State pursuant to any of the provisions laid down in articles 8 to 11 inclusive.

PART B

Seizure

Article 13
1. In response to a request from a foreign State which is based on a treaty, a criminal financial investigation may be instituted in accordance with the provisions of part nine of Title IV of Book I of the Code of Criminal Procedure with a view to identifying proceeds from crime which are either located in or were obtained within the Netherlands by a person who is the subject of a criminal investigation in the requesting State.
2. The criminal financial investigation may be instituted only if this would also have been possible if the offence or offences which the person is suspected of having committed in the requesting State had been committed in the Netherlands.
3. During the criminal financial investigation, property may be seized in accordance with article 94, second paragraph, and article 94a, second paragraph, of the Code of Criminal Procedure only if there is good reason to expect that a request will be submitted on behalf of the requesting foreign State for enforcement of an order of forfeiture of the property concerned or for enforcement of a sanction whose purpose is to deprive the offender of the proceeds from crime.

4. The public prosecutor shall immediately forward to the Minister a copy of his order for the closing of a criminal financial investigation. In doing so, he shall also inform the Minister of all information which could be of use to the requesting foreign State.

Article 13a
1. Insofar as provided by treaty, at the request of a foreign State property may be seized:
    a. in respect of which, under the law of the foreign State, a sanction declaring the property forfeit may be imposed,
    b. in order to preserve the right of recovery in respect of a requirement to pay a sum of money tantamount to the proceeds from crime, which requirement may be imposed under the law of the foreign State, or
    c. which may serve as evidence of proceeds from crime.
2. Seizure, as referred to in the first paragraph under *a* and *b*, may take place only if the information supplied by the foreign State in conjunction with its request indicates that the competent authorities in that State have issued a seizure order or that they would have done so if the property concerned had been within its territory, and seizure is permitted under Dutch law.
3. For the purposes of the application of the second paragraph, seizure is permitted under Dutch law if it would also have been possible if the offence or offences in respect of which the foreign State has requested seizure of the property had been committed in the Netherlands.
4. Furthermore, seizure of property as referred to in the first paragraph under *a* and *b*, may take place only if there is good reason to expect that a request will be submitted on behalf of the requesting State for enforcement of an order of forfeiture of the property concerned or for enforcement of a sanction whose purpose is to deprive the offender of the proceeds from crime.

Article 13b
1. Insofar as provided by treaty, property in respect of which a court in a foreign State has issued an order whose purpose is similar to that of an order of forfeiture or confiscation of the proceeds from crime may be seized at the request of the foreign State.
2. Seizure as referred to in the first paragraph may take place only in cases in which there is good reason to expect that the order referred to in that paragraph will shortly be enforced in the Netherlands.

Article 13c
1. The provisions of articles 13, third paragraph, and 13a, fourth paragraph, shall not prevent any property seized from being surrendered on request to the requesting foreign State with a view to imposing and enforcing an order of forfeiture or a sanction whose purpose is to deprive the offender of the proceeds from crime. For that purpose any property seized shall be forwarded to the public prosecutor,

provided that the district court, taking account of the applicable treaty, grants permission to do so.

2. The permission required pursuant to the first paragraph may be granted only if it is agreed when the property is handed over to the foreign authorities that it shall be returned, even if its forfeiture or confiscation has been ordered, in which case it shall be returned to the ownership of the Dutch State or the requesting State shall transfer to the Dutch State a sum of money to be determined by Our Minister and corresponding to the whole or partial value of the property. Our Minister may decide to waive the payment of the sum of money agreed if the requesting State shows that the property surrendered has been handed over to interested parties entitled to it.

3. The hearing of a request or application for permission by the district court sitting in chambers shall take place in public. The provisions of part six of Title I of Book I of the Code of Criminal Procedure shall apply by analogy.

4. Appeal in cassation may be lodged by the public prosecutions department within fourteen days after the date of the ruling and by the other participants in the proceedings within fourteen days after the date of forwarding of the letter containing the ruling.

Article 13d

1. The examining magistrate and, insofar as that power is not reserved for the examining magistrate, all public prosecutors and assistant public prosecutors shall be competent to order seizure as referred to in articles 13a and 13b. On the application of the public prosecutor, the examining magistrate may exercise the powers which would be vested in him if he were conducting a preliminary judicial investigation.

2. The provisions of articles 94b, 94c, 94d, 97 to 102, 103, 104 to 114, 116 to 117a, 118, 118b, 119, 552a, 552c to 552e, and 556 of the Code of Criminal Procedure shall apply by analogy.

Article 13e

1. Where article 552a or 552c of the Code of Criminal Procedure applies by analogy, the court shall not re-examine the rights of the interested parties if the foreign court has already rendered judgment on the matter. However, the court may re-examine the matter if:

   a. the judgment relates to rights pertaining to immovable property located in the Netherlands or, in the case of goods whose registration is required, goods registered in the Netherlands;

   b. the judgment relates to the validity, invalidity or dissolution of legal persons established in the Netherlands or decisions by their organs;

   c. the judgment was rendered in absentia without the interested party having been officially informed of the proceedings as long in advance as was reasonably necessary to enable him to prepare his defence;

    d. the judgment is incompatible with a judgment previously rendered in the Netherlands;

    e. recognition of the judgment would be incompatible with the requirements of public policy in the Netherlands.

2. If and so long as proceedings concerning the rights of an interested party are pending before the court of the requesting foreign State, any petition or application lodged by the party concerned shall be inadmissible.

Article 13f

1. Requests as referred to in this part may be considered by the public prosecutor in the district where the action requested is to be performed. If the action requested is to be performed in more than one district, the public prosecutor in any of the districts concerned may consider the request in its entirety. The public prosecutor who is considering the request in its entirety shall, if necessary, ask the public prosecutions departments in other districts to act as intermediaries in carrying out the request. In the interests of dealing with the request efficiently, he may also transfer consideration of the request to the public prosecutor in another district.

2. If requests as referred to in this part are not addressed to a public prosecutor, the addressee shall forward them without delay to the public prosecutor in the district where the action requested is to be performed or where the request has been received.

3. Petitions as referred to in article 552a of the Code of Criminal Procedure and proceedings as referred to in article 552c of that Code shall be lodged or brought at the district court in the district in which the public prosecutor holds office who is considering the request in its entirety.

CHAPTER III

Procedure

PART A

Procedure for dealing with foreign requests for enforcement

Article 14

If in the opinion of Our Minister the documents submitted by the foreign State are inadequate to enable him to take a decision on a request for enforcement, he shall give the authorities of the requesting State the opportunity to submit additional documents or information within a reasonable period of time to be determined by him.

Article 15

1. Unless Our Minister is from the outset of the opinion that the request for enforcement must be refused, he shall pass the request, together with the accompanying

documents, to the public prosecutor at the court of the district in which the sentenced person has his place of residence or is present.

2. When there has first been a request for the person to be provisionally arrested, the documents shall be forwarded to the public prosecutor who has already been concerned with the case in connection with such request.

3. If proceedings have been taken against the sentenced person in the Netherlands, the documents may, notwithstanding the foregoing, be forwarded to the public prosecutor charged with conducting such proceedings.

4. If the sentenced person is a person within the meaning of article 2 of the Military Justice Act, Our Minister shall forward the documents in the case to the public prosecutor at the district court which has jurisdiction over such person by law.

5. If the request concerns the enforcement of a property sanction and the sentenced person is a natural person without fixed abode or place of residence in the Netherlands or a legal person whose board of management has no seat or office in the Netherlands or whose managing director has no fixed abode in the Netherlands, the documents in the case shall be forwarded to the public prosecutor of the district in which property is located in respect of which the sanction can be enforced. When there has first been a request for seizure, the documents shall be sent to the public prosecutor who has dealt with that request.

6. If, for the time being, a public prosecutor cannot be designated in accordance with the foregoing paragraphs, Our Minister shall forward the documents to the public prosecutor in Amsterdam.

Article 16

If the public prosecutor who receives a request for enforcement is of the opinion that the request cannot be granted or that there is reason to make use of one of the grounds for refusing a request defined in the applicable treaty, he shall immediately inform Our Minister accordingly, at the same time submitting his recommendation, and Our Minister shall take a decision on the matter. The public prosecutor shall also immediately inform the sentenced person who is deprived of his liberty pursuant to this Act on which day he submitted his recommendation to Our Minister.

PART B

Procedure for dealing with enforcement in the Netherlands – at the request of the Netherlands – of sanctions imposed by a foreign State

Article 17

1. If a foreign State has consented to the enforcement in the Netherlands of a sanction imposed by it, Our Minister shall forward the documents submitted by such State to the public prosecutor at the court of the district in which the sentenced person has his fixed abode or place of residence or, in the absence thereof, to the public prosecutor in Amsterdam.

2. If the sentenced person is a person within the meaning of article 2 of the Military Justice Act our Minister shall forward the documents in the case to the public prosecutor at the district court which has jurisdiction over such person by law.

PART C

Judicial procedure

Article 18
1. Within two weeks of the day on which he received the documents referred to in article 15 or article 17, the public prosecutor shall apply to the district court in writing for consent to enforcement. With his application he shall send to the district court the documents in the case. A copy of the application shall be served on the sentenced person. The public prosecutor shall also include with his application a list of property seized pursuant to part B of Chapter II.
2. The period referred to in the preceding paragraph shall be suspended from the time when the public prosecutor makes a recommendation to Our Minister pursuant to article 16 until the public prosecutor receives a message from Our Minister that enforcement should be requested.
3. If the sentenced person is deprived of his liberty pursuant to this Act, the suspension shall in any case cease after fourteen days.
4. The provisions of the preceding paragraphs shall not apply if the sanction to be enforced consists solely of a fine.

Article 19
1. The public prosecutor may, under rules to be laid down in an Order in Council, request the assistance of persons and bodies working in probation and after-care or related fields and assign them any necessary tasks.
2. If the sentenced person has not yet attained the age of eighteen years, the public prosecutor shall obtain information from the child care and protection board regarding his character and personal situation.

Article 20
1. The application as referred to in article 18 shall be made to the district court judge responsible for trying minor offences, unless in the initial opinion of the public prosecutor:
   a. the case is not a straightforward one, specifically with regard to whether the offence or the sentenced person is punishable under Dutch law, or
   b. the district court is bound to impose a custodial penalty of which the part still to be enforced in the Netherlands exceeds six months.
2. The district court judge responsible for trying minor offences shall have the power pursuant to this Act to impose a custodial sentence of more than six months, provided the part of this sentence still to be enforced in the Netherlands does not exceed six months.

3. If the district court judge responsible for trying minor offences decides that the case should be dealt with by a full-bench chamber of the court, he shall refer the case to such chamber. The case shall then be dealt with by the full-bench chamber pursuant to the original application.

Article 21
1. If the sentenced person has not yet attained the age of eighteen years, the application referred to in article 18 shall be made to a children's judge, unless in the initial opinion of the public prosecutor and the children's judge:
    a. the case is not a straightforward one, specifically with regard to whether the offence or the sentenced person is punishable under Dutch law, or
    b. the district court is bound to impose a custodial sentence of which the part still to be enforced in the Netherlands exceeds six months.
    If the public prosecutor lodges his application with the full-bench chamber, the children's judge shall participate in the examination conducted at the hearing.
2. The children's judge shall have the power pursuant to this Act to impose a custodial sentence of more than six months, provided the part of this sentence still to be enforced in the Netherlands does not exceed six months.
3. If the children's judge decides that the case should be dealt with by a full-bench chamber of the court, he shall refer the case to such chamber. The case shall then be heard by the full-bench chamber pursuant to the original application. The children's judge shall participate in the examination conducted at the hearing.

Article 22
If the application referred to in article 18 concerns a person referred to in article 2 of the Military Justice Act, the application shall be dealt with, in accordance with article 20, by the military district court judge responsible for trying minor offences or by the military chamber of the district court which has jurisdiction over the person concerned by law.

Article 23
The district court judge responsible for trying minor offences, the children's judge and the military district court judge responsible for trying minor offences shall each have the powers held by the president of a full-bench chamber of the district court.

Article 24
1. As soon as possible after the receipt of the application referred to in article 18, the president of the chamber shall determine when the court will begin the process of considering the application. There must be a period of at least ten days between the date on which notice to appear in court is served on the sentenced person and the date of the hearing.
2. The length of this period may be reduced with the consent of the sentenced person, provided such consent is evidenced in a written statement.

Article 25
The registrar of the district court shall notify the public prosecutor and the sentenced person forthwith of the date set for the hearing of the application. The notification shall also inform a sentenced person who does not have the services of a counsel of his right to select one or more counsel or have counsel assigned to him and of his right to inspect the documents in the case.

Article 26
1. The public prosecutor and the sentenced person shall be empowered to summon witnesses and experts for the purpose of the examination to be conducted by the district court pursuant to this Act and of the decisions it is required to make.
2. The public prosecutor may, by means of reasoned decisions, refuse to summon witnesses or experts if there are reasonable grounds for believing that the sentenced person wishes to summon them for the purpose of making statements at the hearing refuting facts as referred to in article 28, third paragraph. Such a decision shall be notified promptly to the sentenced person in writing. He shall at the same time be informed of the provisions of article 28, sixth paragraph.

Article 27
1. The hearing of the application shall take place in the presence of the public prosecutor. The sentenced person shall be given the opportunity to attend and may be assisted by his counsel.
2. The hearing of the application shall take place in public, unless the district court orders, at the request of the sentenced person or for reasons of an important nature to be mentioned in the official record of the hearing, that the application should be dealt with in camera.

Article 28
1. The district court shall examine the identity of the sentenced person, the admissibility of the application lodged by the public prosecutor, and the possibility of enforcement in the Netherlands of the judgment pronounced abroad and the facts and circumstances which are of importance to its decision.
2. The public prosecutor and the sentenced person and his counsel shall be given the opportunity to be heard by the court.
3. The district court shall be bound by the findings as to the facts of the case in so far as manifestly established by the foreign court as the basis for its decision. The district court shall not re-investigate these facts.
4. Articles 268, 269, 271, 272, 274, 275, 277, 288, 296, 297, with the exception of the third paragraph, 298, first paragraph, 299 to 301, 303, 304, 306, 310, 311, second, third and fourth paragraphs, 315 to 317, 319, 320, 322, first paragraph, 323, first paragraph, 324, 325, first paragraph, and 326 to 331 of the Code of Criminal Procedure shall apply by analogy.
5. If witnesses are called in order to obtain information regarding the character of the sentenced person or if the court deems it necessary to examine facts in order to

establish whether there are grounds under Dutch law, but not under the law of the foreign State, which preclude the punishability of the offence or of the offender, articles 280, second, seventh and eighth paragraphs, 281, 283, first and fourth paragraphs, 284 to 286, 287, 289 to 294, 297, third paragraph, 305, and 311, fifth paragraph, of the Code of Criminal Procedure shall also apply by analogy.

6. If, in accordance with article 26, second paragraph, the public prosecutor has refused to summon a certain witness, the sentenced person may again request the court to order the witness to be summoned. The court shall do so if it is of the opinion that the public prosecutor could not have arrived at his decision on reasonable grounds.

7. The articles mentioned in the third and fifth paragraphs shall not apply in so far as they relate to a witness whose identity has not been disclosed or only partially been disclosed.

8. The public prosecutor shall present a submission to the court, after reading it aloud. If the submission is to the effect that enforcement should be agreed to, it shall indicate the penalty or measure which in the opinion of the public prosecutor should be imposed instead of the foreign sanction. The public prosecutor shall also state which offence under Dutch law corresponds to the offence for which a foreign sanction has been imposed on the sentenced person.

Article 29

1. Upon the application of the public prosecutor the district court may at the hearing order that the sentenced person who has not been deprived of his liberty be remanded in custody in cases where provisional arrest is allowed under article 8.

2. Before the examination at the hearing is concluded, the district court shall give an ex officio ruling on remand in custody of a sentenced person who has been provisionally deprived of his liberty pursuant to this Act.

3. An order depriving a person of his liberty under one of the preceding paragraphs shall remain in force after the district court has given judgment until the judgment becomes final.

4. Such deprivation of liberty shall end, subject to the possibility of further deprivation of liberty on other grounds:
    a. as soon as this is ordered by the district court or by the public prosecutor ex officio or at the request of the sentenced person or his counsel or by the Supreme Court in a judgment on an appeal in cassation;
    b. if the duration of the deprivation of liberty has equalled that of the penalty or measure imposed by the Dutch court.

Article 30

1. The district court shall rule that enforcement is inadmissible if it finds:
    a. that the documents submitted do not satisfy the requirements laid down in the applicable treaty;
    b. that the sentenced person could have successfully invoked grounds which, under Dutch law but not under the law of the foreign State, preclude the punishability

of the offence or the offender, and that he does not require compulsory psychiatric treatment;

c. that enforcement in the Netherlands is not possible on the grounds of one of the provisions contained in articles 2, 3, 4, 6, or 7; or

d. in a case where enforcement may be refused under the applicable treaty, that after due consideration of all the interests involved it would not be reasonable to decide to enforce the judgment in the Netherlands.

The public prosecutor may withdraw his application at any time before the examination at the hearing is concluded. He shall inform the sentenced person immediately that the application has been withdrawn.

3. In cases other than those provided for in the preceding paragraphs the district court shall rule that enforcement is admissible, and shall state the provisions of the laws and treaties which are applicable. Articles 345, with the exception of the fourth paragraph, 346 and 347 of the Code of Criminal Procedure shall apply by analogy.

4. If the application is considered by a single-judge chamber of the court, articles 378 to 381 of the Code of Criminal Procedure shall apply by analogy, except in so far as they relate to a witness whose identity has not been disclosed or only partially been disclosed. If the application is considered by a full-bench chamber of the court, article 362 of that Code shall apply by analogy.

5. Articles 363 to 365 of Code of Criminal Procedure shall apply by analogy.

Article 31

1. If the district court deems enforcement admissible, it shall permit enforcement of the foreign judgment and impose, subject to the relevant provisions of the applicable treaty, the penalty or measure prescribed for the corresponding offence under Dutch law. The judgment of the court shall specify the grounds on which it is based. It shall also include any special reasons which have determined the penalty or measure and as far as possible the circumstances which played a role in determining the length or amount of the penalty. Articles 353 and 357 of the Code of Criminal Procedure shall apply by analogy.

2. In ordering a determinate prison sentence or detention the district court shall rule that the time during which the sentenced person was deprived of his liberty in the foreign State in enforcement of the sanction imposed upon him there, or with a view to his transfer to the Netherlands or pursuant to the provisions of this Act, shall be deducted in full from the said sentence. In ordering the payment of a fine the court may make a similar order. If it does so, it shall state in its judgment the criteria used to determine what has been deducted.

3. The district court shall immediately send Our Minister an authenticated copy of its judgment.

Article 31a

1. Permission to enforce a sanction imposed in a foreign State whose purpose is to confiscate the proceeds from crime may be limited to the enforcement of the

requirement to pay a sum of money to the State which represents only part of the proceeds.

2. If the purpose of the sanction imposed in the foreign State is to deprive an offender of the proceeds from crime, the district court shall order forfeiture if the foreign State has explicitly requested that the sanction be enforced only against property representing those proceeds. In that case the district court shall not be bound by the restrictions pursuant to article 33a, first paragraph under *a*, of the Penal Code.

3. Articles 552b, 552d, 552e and 552g of the Code of Criminal Procedure shall apply by analogy to orders of forfeiture.

4. Article 577b of the Code of Criminal Procedure shall apply by analogy to orders imposing the requirement to pay a sum of money to the State for the purpose of confiscation of proceeds from crime.

5. Article 13d shall apply by analogy.

Article 32

1. Both the public prosecutor and the sentenced person may lodge an appeal in cassation against the judgment of the district court.

2. Articles 431 tot 434, 436 to 440, 441, first paragraph, 442 to 444, 449, first paragraph, 450 to 455 and 456 of the Code of Criminal Procedure shall apply by analogy.

3. If the judgment against which an appeal has been lodged was given by a single-judge chamber, the appeal in cassation shall be heard by a three-judge chamber of the Supreme Court.

4. If the judgment of the district court is either wholly or partially quashed, the Supreme Court shall itself dispose of the case wherever possible. If the Supreme Court is itself unable to dispose of the case, it may at its discretion either refer the case back to the district court whose judgment was quashed or refer it to another district court. In that event articles 18 to 28, 29, second paragraph, 30 and 31 and the preceding paragraphs of this article shall again apply.

5. The Supreme Court shall immediately send Our Minister an authenticated copy of its judgment.

6. If the Supreme Court refers the case to another district court, an order for deprivation of liberty pursuant to article 29 shall, notwithstanding the final paragraph of that article, remain in force until such time as said court gives a ruling on the matter of remand in custody.

Article 33

As soon as the judgment concerning the admissibility of enforcement has become final, the registrar of the court which last dealt with the case shall inform Our Minister that it has become final. The enforcement of a penalty or measure imposed pursuant to article 31 shall take place with due regard to any provisions laid down by or pursuant to the Penal Code, the Code of Criminal Procedure or any special statutes relating to the enforcement of criminal judgments.

PART D

Extrajudicial procedures

Division 1. Fines

Article 34
1. If the sanction imposed in the foreign State involves the payment of a fine only, with or without the threat of an alternative sanction involving deprivation of liberty, it shall be enforced pursuant to a decision of the public prosecutor.
2. Before taking a decision as referred to in the preceding paragraph the public prosecutor shall give the sentenced person the opportunity to be heard.
3. In accordance with the provisions of the applicable treaty the public prosecutor shall in his decision express the amount of the fine in Dutch currency. If the treaty contains no rules on the matter, the public prosecutor shall determine the amount of the sum in question in accordance with the rate of exchange obtaining at the time the sentence was pronounced in the foreign State. The rate of exchange shall be the average quoted on the commodity exchange in Amsterdam.
4. In the case of currencies not having a daily quotation on the commodity exchange in Amsterdam the exchange rate employed shall be calculated on the basis of the value of the currency concerned in special drawing rights on the last working day of the month in which the sanction to be enforced was imposed in the foreign State.

Article 35
1. A decision taken pursuant to article 34 and the day on which the sum referred to therein must be paid shall be communicated to the sentenced person by the public prosecutor as soon as possible.
2. If the fine imposed exceeds the sum of fifty guilders, the sentenced person may lodge a notice of objection with the district court, provided he does this within fourteen days of the occurrence of a circumstance from which it is clear that he has been informed of the decision.
3. The notice of objection shall be dealt with by the judge of the district court responsible for trying minor offences. If the said judge rules that the application should be heard by a full-bench chamber of the district court he shall refer the case to such chamber.
4. If the notice of objection is lodged by a person as referred to in article 2 of the Military Justice Act it shall be heard by the military judge of the district court responsible for trying minor offences. If said judge rules that the application should be heard by a full-bench chamber of the district court he shall refer the case to the military chamber.
5. Articles 449, third paragraph, and 450 tot 454 of the Code of Criminal Procedure shall apply by analogy to the procedure for lodging and withdrawing a notice of objection.

6. Articles 25, 26, 27, 28 and 30 of the present Act shall apply by analogy to the hearing of a notice of objection.
7. If the court rules that a notice of objection is well-founded, it shall quash the public prosecutor's decision or supplement it, subject to the provisions of article 24a of the Penal Code. If, notwithstanding that the decision has been quashed, the court deems enforcement admissible it shall take the steps which should otherwise have been taken by the public prosecutor. In all cases in which the court declares enforcement of a fine admissible it shall also specify the length of the terms of alternative detention.
8. Articles 32 and 33 of the present Act shall apply by analogy.

Article 36
1. Decisions as referred to in article 34 may be enforced as soon as they have been taken unless the applicable treaty provides otherwise. Enforcement shall be suspended if a notice of objection is lodged within the prescribed period.
2. Decisions taken pursuant to article 34 shall be enforced subject to the provisions laid down by or pursuant to the Code of Criminal Procedure with regard to the enforcement of fines, with the exception of the third paragraph of article 575 of that Code.

Article 37
If the enforcement of alternative detention is necessary, the public prosecutor shall for this purpose lodge an application as referred to in article 18 unless the court has already determined the length of detention pursuant to article 35, seventh paragraph.

Division 2. Supervision of compliance with conditions

a. Transfer of supervision

Article 38
1. If a public prosecutor who, under the provisions of article 15, has received a request for transfer of supervision of compliance with conditions imposed upon a sentenced person in a foreign State, is of the opinion that the request or part of the request may not be granted or that there is reason to invoke one of the grounds provided for in the applicable treaty for refusing such request, he shall immediately give notice thereof and of his recommendations to Our Minister, who shall decide on the matter.
2. If the request or part of the request is granted, notification of this decision shall be served on the sentenced person personally. The public prosecutor shall inform Our Minister of his decision.

Article 39
If the public prosecutor deems that there are grounds for ordering that the sentenced person be provided with support or assistance, he shall designate the probation and after-care organisation to be charged with this. Before taking this decision, he shall obtain the advice of this organisation.

Article 40
1. Supervision shall not extend to compliance with special conditions imposed by the decision on which the request is based which are contrary to Dutch law.
2. Supervision shall be carried out subject to the provisions laid down by or pursuant to article 14b, fourth paragraph, article 14d, first paragraph, and article 16 of the Penal Code.
3. The date of commencement and the length of probation shall be determined by reference to the law of the requesting State. Such probation shall on no account be longer than it would have been under Dutch law.

Article 41
1. The public prosecutor shall immediately inform Our Minister of any serious breach of the conditions.
2. As soon as probation comes to an end the public prosecutor shall report to Our Minister on the compliance with the conditions.

b. Application of foreign suspended sentences

Article 42
The public prosecutor shall ensure, subject to the provisions of article 16, that the procedures laid down in part C of this chapter are followed in the event that he receives a request for the application of a decision by a foreign authority imposing conditions whose infringement may or must lead to the revocation of a suspended sentence.

Division 3. Immediate enforcement

Article 43
1. If this is expressly provided for in a treaty enforcement or further enforcement of a sanction involving deprivation of liberty imposed in a foreign State may, on the instruction of Our Minister, be carried out in the Netherlands without the application of part C of this chapter.
2. The instruction referred to in the preceding paragraph may be issued only if it is evident from a declaration signed by the sentenced person that he has given his consent to his transfer to the Netherlands with a view to enforcement or further enforcement of the sanction imposed upon him.
3. The instruction referred to in the first paragraph may be issued only after advice has been obtained of the special chamber of the court of appeals at Arnhem, as referred to in article 73 of the Judicial Organization Act.
4. Pending a decision on the issue of an instruction as referred to above, the sentenced person may be provisionally deprived of his liberty in accordance with articles 8 to 12.
5. The enforcement of a sanction as referred to in the first paragraph shall take place on the order of the public prosecutor who has received the documents in the case under the provisions of article 15 or article 17.

PART E

Enforcement of judgments rendered in absentia

Article 44
Requests as referred to in part D, division 2, relating to judgments pronounced in absentia may not be granted unless the judgment was given on appeal and the appeal was lodged by the sentenced person against a judgment rendered after a hearing of the accused.

Article 45
1. A request for enforcement of a judgment rendered in absentia in the requesting State may not be dealt with until the public prosecutor who received the request has served the judgment on the sentenced person. The judgment shall not be served if proceedings for the offence on which judgment was passed would have been precluded by lapse of time under Dutch law, provided always that acts performed in the requesting state which interrupt or suspend time-limitation in that state have the same effects in the Netherlands. The authorities of the State in which the request originated shall be notified in writing of such service.
2. Insofar as this is provided for in a treaty, the sentenced person may lodge an opposition to a judgment rendered in absentia as referred to in the preceding paragraph with the court of the district in which he has his place of residence or is actually staying, within such period of time after service as the applicable treaty may specify. If the sentenced person is a person as referred to in article 2 of the Military Justice Act he may lodge an opposition with the district court which has jurisdiction over him under that Act.
3. An opposition shall be made by means of a statement made at the office of the public prosecutor at the district court referred to in the preceding paragraph or by registered letter addressed to the said office and specifying – under penalty of inadmissibility – the place of residence or address of the sentenced person where he can be reached for service of judicial documents. If an opposition has been lodged by registered letter the date of the opposition shall be the date on which the office of the public prosecutor receives the letter. Articles 450 and 451a of the Code of Criminal Procedure shall apply by analogy.
4. The public prosecutor shall hand all statements made or letters received within the time limit to the registrar or the court, who will then act in accordance with the provisions of article 451 of the Code of Criminal Procedure.

Article 46
1. If the sentenced person has lodged a valid opposition in accordance with article 45 with a view to having the opposition heard in the requesting State, the registrar of the court shall promptly pass the notice of opposition to our Minister for transmission to the requesting State.

2. If the sentenced person has lodged a valid opposition in accordance with article 45 with a view to having the opposition heard in the Netherlands, the request for enforcement of the judgment given in absentia in the requesting State shall be deemed to be a request for taking proceedings granted by Our Minister and based on the provisions of a treaty.

Article 47
1. A sentenced person who has lodged a valid opposition in accordance with article 45 with a view to having the opposition heard in the Netherlands shall be summonsed as soon as possible either by registered letter or by service in person, to appear at the hearing of the court designated in the summons.
2. If he fails to appear in court on the appointed day, the opposition shall be dismissed and part C or part D of this Act shall apply, unless the court, in the event of non-appearance by the sentenced person, orders suspension of the hearing in order to allow the sentenced person, if he was unable to attend the hearing, a further opportunity to do so.
3. If a sentenced person who has lodged an opposition appears on the appointed day, the foreign judgment shall, for the purposes of Dutch law, be considered null and void and the case shall be dealt with in accordance with the Code of Criminal Procedure.

PART F

Special types of enforcement[1]

Article 48
The conditions laid down in articles 1 to 7 of this Act governing the admissibility of the enforcement of sanctions imposed by a judgment shall apply by analogy to the supplementation and enforcement of foreign judgments pursuant to division 5 of Chapter I of the Benelux Treaty on the enforcement of criminal judgments, concluded at Brussels on 26 September 1968 (*Trb.* 1969, 9).

Article 49
1. A sentenced person to whom a partial judgment as referred to in division 5 of Chapter I of the Treaty referred to in article 48 applies, and who is present in the Netherlands, may be provisionally arrested at the request of a State which is a party to the said treaty, provided there is good reason to expect that a request which is susceptible of being granted and which is for the supplementation and enforcement of a judgment given in that State will shortly be made in respect of offences for which remand in custody is allowed under Dutch law.

---

[1] Note of the editors: Articles 48-50 have not yet entered into force, since the Benelux Treaty is awaiting ratification by Luxembourg.

2. Articles 9 to 12 shall apply by analogy.

Article 50
1. Parts A, C and E shall apply by analogy to requests for the supplementation and enforcement of judgments as referred to in article 48, provided always:
    a. that the supplementation and enforcement of a judgment given in a foreign State to the effect that the sentenced person has committed the offence he was charged with and that therefore a punishment or a measure must be imposed upon him is deemed to be equivalent to the enforcement of a sanction imposed in a foreign State;
    b. that an application by the public prosecutor, as referred to in article 18, requests the court to supplement the foreign judgment:
    c. that appeal by the sentenced person and the public prosecutor against the judgment of the court lies to the court of appeal and that the provisions of article 33 relating to a judgment of the court apply by analogy to that of a court of appeal. Articles 407 tot 412, 413, first paragraph, and 414, first paragraph, of the Code of Criminal Procedure shall apply by analogy.
2. Proceedings before the court of appeal shall by analogy be governed by articles 28, 30 and 31 of the Code of Criminal Procedure and by articles 416 to 418, 423, first paragraph, 423a and 424, second paragraph, of that Code.

CHAPTER IV

Transfer of enforcement of Dutch judgments

PART A

Requests by the Netherlands

Article 51
If the public prosecutions department charged with the enforcement of a judgment deems it to be in the interest of a proper administration of justice that a foreign State enforces or further enforces a penalty or measure imposed by a Dutch court or supervises compliance with conditions laid down by Dutch courts, the said public prosecutions department shall issue a reasoned recommendation to Our Minister that enforcement or supervision of conditions be transferred to that State and shall at the same time supply Our Minister with the judgment of the court of first instance or court of appeal which is to be enforced and any other documents of importance for such enforcement.

Article 52
1. Subject to the provisions of the following paragraph, Our Minister shall take a decision on the matter as soon as possible after receipt of a recommendation as

referred to in the preceding article. In doing so, if the request for enforcement or supervision may be based on a treaty, he shall take into account the provisions of such treaty.

2. If the recommendation of the public prosecutions department concerns a sentenced person who is present in the Netherlands, on whom a sanction involving deprivation of liberty has been imposed, and who has not declared that he consents to transfer of enforcement of that sanction, Our Minister shall, if he intends to follow the recommendation, notify the sentenced person in writing of the recommendation before taking a decision. The sentenced person shall also be informed that he may, within fourteen days of receipt of such notification, lodge a notice of objection to the proposed action by Our Minister with the court of highest fact-finding instance which imposed the sanction involving the deprivation of his liberty.

3. As soon as possible after receipt of a notice of objection lodged within the prescribed period, the court referred to in the preceding paragraph shall examine whether it would be reasonable for Our Minister, after giving due consideration to all the interests involved, to take the proposed decision. The sentenced person shall be heard at the hearing, or in any case invited to do so. If it becomes apparent that the sentenced person has no counsel, the president of the court shall instruct the office for legal assistance to assign him counsel.

4. Articles 21 to 26 of the Code of Criminal Procedure shall apply by analogy.

5. The court shall inform Our Minister and the sentenced person in writing of its decision. If the court considers the objection to be well-founded, Our Minister shall disregard the recommendation made by the public prosecutions department for transfer of enforcement.

Article 53

1. Our Minister shall give written notification to the public prosecutions department which has made a recommendation as referred to in article 51 of his decision on the matter and of any communications he may have received concerning decisions of the authorities of the foreign State regarding the request for enforcement or supervision made on the recommendation of the public prosecutions department.

2. A request submitted to the authorities of a foreign State for enforcement or supervision may be withdrawn at any time before the notification regarding the decision taken in that State on such request is received, without prejudice to the provisions of article 36, second paragraph, of the Benelux Treaty on the enforcement of criminal judgments.

Article 54

A person against whom a judgment in absentia has been rendered in the Netherlands imposing a penalty or measure or a partial judgment as referred to in division 5 of Chapter I of the Benelux Treaty on the enforcement of criminal judgments may oppose that judgment if a request for enforcement or supplementation has been made to the authorities of a foreign State, even if the judgment has become final, such opposition being permitted until the expiration of a period of time laid down in the applicable treaty and running from the date on which the judgment was served on him personally by the authorities of that State. Such an opposition may be lodged only with the competent authorities of the requested State in accordance with the relevant rules of the law of that State.

Article 55
1. As soon as a document has been received from the authorities of the requested State showing that a valid opposition has been lodged, the person who lodged the opposition shall be personally served with a summons to appear before the court which rendered the judgment. A period of at least twenty-one days, or such lesser period as the applicable treaty may specify, shall be observed – on penalty of declaration of nullity – between the day on which the summons is served and the date of the trial. This period may be reduced with the consent of the person summonsed, provided such consent is given in writing. Voluntary appearance in response to a summons served in contravention of the provisions of this article shall preclude any declaration of nullity.
2. If the person summonsed fails to appear in court on the appointed day, the opposition shall be dismissed, unless the court, in the event of non-appearance, orders suspension of the hearing in order to allow the sentenced person, if the was unable to attend the hearing, a further opportunity to do so. The public prosecutions department shall notify the authorities of the requested State and Our Minister as soon as possible in writing that an opposition has been dismissed.
3. If the person who lodged the opposition appears in court on the appointed day, article 403 of the Code of Criminal Procedure shall apply.

PART B

Requests to the Netherlands

Article 56
Unless Our Minister is from the outset of the opinion that a request by a foreign authority for transfer of the enforcement of a sanction imposed in the Netherlands should be refused he shall, when considering the question whether it would be in conflict with the interests of a proper administration of justice to grant the request, seek the opimion of the court which imposed the sanction at the highest fact-finding instance and of the public prosecutions department charged with enforcement.

Article 57
1. As soon as possible after receipt of the opinion referred to in the preceding article, Our Minister shall decide whether the request referred to in that article is to be granted. Article 52 shall apply by analogy.
2. Our Minister shall give immediate notice of his decision to the court and the public prosecutions department which advised on the matter.

PART C

Transfer

Article 58
Regulations shall be laid down by Order in Council concerning the procedure for obtaining a statement by or on behalf of a sentenced person who is present in the Netherlands indicating his consent to transfer of enforcement of a sanction involving deprivation of liberty imposed on him.

Article 59
1. Transfer of enforcement of judgments under this Chapter shall take place only on the general condition that the penalty, measure or conditions imposed by the Dutch court shall not be amended to the detriment of the sentenced person and that account will be taken in this connection of such part of the penalty or measure as has already been enforced in the Netherlands.
2. A sentenced person who is serving or will be obliged to serve a sanction involving deprivation of liberty in the Netherlands shall, when agreement has been reached with a foreign State regarding the further enforcement of such sanction, be handed over as soon as possible to the authorities of the said State at a time and place to be determined by Our Minister after consultation with these authorities.
3. Transfer of a sentenced person who has not declared that he consents to transfer of enforcement shall take place only on the general condition that the express permission of Our Minister shall be required if he is:
   a. to be prosecuted, punished or in any way restricted in his personal freedom in respect of offences committed before his transfer and with regard to which enforcement has not been transferred; or
   b. to be surrendered to the authorities of a third State in respect of offences committed before his transfer, unless the sentenced person has since then been given the opportunity to leave the territory of the State to which he has been transferred.
4. As soon as a sentenced person is handed over to the authorities referred to in the second paragraph, enforcement in the Netherlands of the sanction imposed upon him shall be suspended ipso jure.
5. If the right to enforce the sanction revives, the part already enforced in a foreign State shall be deducted.

CHAPTER V

Final provisions

Article 60
Where it is stated in this Act that provisions of the Code of Criminal Procedure apply by analogy, such provisions shall, if they apply to a suspect, also apply by analogy to a sentenced person.

Article 61
Orders for detention in police custody, remand in custody or extensions of a period in custody issued pursuant to this Act shall be dated and signed. Orders shall state the grounds on which they are issued. The sentenced person to whom the order relates shall be given a copy forthwith.

Article 62
Orders for the deprivation of liberty referred to in the preceding article shall be enforceable forthwith. The officials referred to in article 141 of the Code of Criminal Procedure shall be authorized to execute orders for deprivation of liberty. Articles 564 to 568 of the Code of Criminal Procedure shall apply to the enforcement of orders and the instructions to that effect.

Article 63
Sentenced persons who are detained in police custody or remanded in custody in accordance with this Act shall be treated as suspects subjected to similar measures under the Code of Criminal Procedure.

Article 64
1. The provisions laid down by or pursuant to article 40 of the Code of Criminal Procedure shall apply by analogy in respect of a sentenced person detained in police custody pursuant to article 9 of this Act.
2. A person remanded in custody in accordance with article 10 or in respect of whom an application for remand in custody has been made under article 29 shall, if he has no counsel, be assigned counsel by the office for legal assistance on the instruction of the president of the court in the district where such person is present. The public prosecutor shall immediately inform the president of the court in writing that assignment of counsel is required.
3. The provisions laid down by or pursuant to article 42, third and fourth paragraphs, and articles 45 to 49 of the Code of Criminal Procedure and the provisions of the Code relating to the powers of counsel and access to the documents in the case shall apply by analogy.

Article 65

1. In cases where pursuant to this Act a decision relating to provisional deprivation of liberty of a sentenced person may or must be taken, it may also be ordered that such deprivation of liberty be conditionally postponed or suspended.
2. Articles 80 to 88 of the Code of Criminal Procedure shall apply by analogy to orders made by a court or by an examining magistrate pursuant to the preceding paragraph.
3. The period referred to in article 11, second paragraph under *b*, shall not run during the time that the sentenced person has evaded further execution of the order for remand in custody.

Article 66

Articles 73, 79, 569 and 570 of the Code of Criminal Procedure shall apply by analogy to orders made pursuant to this Act for termination of provisional deprivation of liberty and the execution of such orders.

Article 67

In cases in which a final decision has been taken that a foreign judgment should not be enforced in the Netherlands, the court which heard the case may, at the request of the sentenced person, award him a sum to be paid by the State for damage sustained and expenses incurred as a result of provisional deprivation of liberty ordered pursuant to this Act. Damage includes loss other than pecuniary loss. Article 89, third, fourth and sixth paragraphs, and articles 90, 91, 93, 591 and 591a of the Code of Criminal Procedure shall apply by analogy.

Article 68

Articles 585 to 590 of the Code of Criminal Procedure shall apply by analogy to the service of process, notifications and notices to appear in court given pursuant to this Act unless the Act provides otherwise.

Article 69

Articles 48 and 50 of the Extradition Act shall apply by analogy to requests for the transit over Dutch territory of persons who for the purpose of enforcement of a judgment are handed over by the authorities of a foreign State to the authorities of another State.

(...)

Article 75

The provisions of the foregoing chapters shall not apply to the enforcement of custodial sentences imposed by foreign judicial authorities pursuant to article 6 of the Act of 7 August 1953 (*Stb.* 438) approving and implementing the Treaty of London of 19 June 1951 between the States party to the North Atlantic Treaty regarding the status of their forces.

Article 76
1. This Act may be cited as Act on the transfer of enforcement of criminal judgments.

(...)

6 Act containing provisions relating to the establishment of the International Tribunal for the prosecution of persons responsible for serious violations of international humanitarian law committed in the territory of the former Yugoslavia since 1991

Act of 21 April 1994, *Staatsblad* 308

Article 1
For the purposes of this Act, the following definitions shall apply:
Tribunal: the international Tribunal for the prosecution of persons responsible for serious violations of international humanitarian law committed in the territory of the former Yugoslavia since 1991, established by resolution 827 of the United Nations Security Council of 25 May 1993, including the Prosecutor at the Tribunal;
Statute: the Statute of the Tribunal, included in the annex to resolution 827 of the United Nations Security Council of 25 May 1993:
surrender: placing a person at the Tribunal's disposal by the Netherlands for the purpose of a criminal investigation concerning that person being conducted by the Tribunal;
transit: the transport under escort through Dutch territory of a person in order for him to be placed at the disposal of the Tribunal by a foreign State or be placed at the disposal of a foreign State by the Tribunal;
Our Minister: Our Minister of Justice.

Article 2
At the request of the Tribunal, persons may be surrendered to the Tribunal for the purpose of a criminal investigation on account of criminal offences in respect of which the Tribunal has jurisdiction pursuant to its Statute.

Article 3
1. Persons whose arrest as suspects has been ordered by the Tribunal and who are found in the Netherlands may be provisionally arrested at the Tribunal's request.
2. All public prosecutors and assistant public prosecutors shall be empowered to order such provisional arrest.
3. The provision of article 14, second to fifth paragraph, article 15, article 16, first paragraph under *a*, and article 17 of the Extradition Act shall apply by analogy with the proviso that the person arrested be brought before the public prosecutor in The Hague without delay.

Article 4
1. Sole competence to deal with requests for surrender by the Tribunal shall rest with the district court in The Hague.
2. Articles 21 to 27 and article 28, first paragraph, of the Extradition Act shall apply by analogy.
3. If the district court which is to rule on whether the Tribunal's request may be granted holds either that it cannot be established that the person brought before it is the person whose surrender has been requested or that surrender has been requested on account of offences in respect of which the Tribunal has no jurisdiction under its Statute, it shall declare surrender inadmissible in its judgment.
4. In cases other than those provided for by the third paragraph, the district court shall declare surrender admissible in its judgment. The judgment shall be immediately enforceable.
5. Articles 29, 30, first sentence and second paragraph, 32, 33, first and second paragraphs, 36 and 52 to 60 of the Extradition Act shall apply by analogy.

Article 5
Once the request for surrender has been granted, the person to be surrendered shall be placed at the disposal of the Tribunal without delay. Remand in custody ordered pursuant to article 27 of the Extradition Act may be extended until that time.

Article 6
Persons in the Netherlands whom the Tribunal orders to be brought before it as witnesses or experts may be detained by order of the public prosecutor in The Hague and placed at the disposal of the Tribunal.

Article 7
1. The transit of persons being surrendered to the Tribunal as suspects by the authorities of a foreign State shall be conducted on the instructions of Our Minister by Dutch officials and under their guard.
2. The transit of persons being transferred to the Netherlands by the authorities of a foreign State as witnesses or experts in the execution of a subpoena issued by the Tribunal shall be conducted on the instructions of Our Minister by Dutch officials and under their guard.
3. Persons who have been detained by order of the Tribunal shall be transported outside the premises subject to the Tribunal's authority at the request of the Tribunal on the instructions of Our Minister by Dutch officials and under their guard.
4. The officials referred to in this article shall be empowered to take all appropriate measures for the security of the persons in question and to prevent their escape.

Article 8
Data from a police file as referred to in the Police Files Act (*Staatsblad* 1990, 414), may be communicated, with or without a request to that end, to the Prosecutor at the Tribunal if necessary for the proper performance of his duties. The data shall be com-

municated via the Central Criminal Intelligence Department in accordance with instructions given by Our Minister.

Article 9

1. Requests of the Tribunal for any type of legal assistance whatsoever addressed to any judicial or police body, named or otherwise, shall be complied with wherever possible.
2. Articles 552i, 552j, 552n, 552o to 552q of the Code of Criminal Procedure and article 51, first and fourth paragraphs, of the Extradition Act shall apply by analogy.
3. Permission shall be given if requested for representatives of the Tribunal to be present when requests as referred to in the first paragraph are executed and for them to have the appropriate questions put to persons involved in the execution.
4. The Dutch authorities responsible for executing requests for legal assistance shall be responsible for the security of persons involved therein and to that end shall be empowered to attach conditions to the way in which requests for legal assistance are executed.

Article 10

1. Without prejudice to the provisions of article 7, second paragraph, witnesses or experts, regardless of their nationality, who come to the Netherlands in answer to a summons or notice issued by the Tribunal, shall not be prosecuted, arrested or subjected to any measures to restrict their liberty on account of offences or convictions which preceded their arrival in the Netherlands.
2. The immunity referred to in the first paragraph shall lapse if the witness or expert, despite having been able to leave the Netherlands for fifteen consecutive days following the date on which his presence is no longer required by the Tribunal, remains in the Netherlands or returns there after his departure.

Article 11

1. Custodial sentences imposed by a final judgment of the Tribunal may be enforced in the Netherlands at the Tribunal's request.
2. The convicted person may be provisionally arrested to that end at the Tribunal's request.
3. The public prosecutor or assistant public prosecutor in The Hague shall be competent to order such provisional arrest.
4. Article 9, second to fifth paragraph, 10, 11, first and second paragraph under *a*, and article 12 of the Act on the transfer of enforcement of criminal judgments shall apply by analogy.

Article 12

1. Sole competence to deal with requests for enforcement by the Tribunal shall rest with the district court in The Hague. Cases shall be dealt with by a full-bench chamber.

2. Articles 18, first paragraph, 19 and 24 to 29 of the Act on the transfer of enforcement of criminal judgments shall apply by analogy.
3. Unless the district court holds that, after due consideration of all the interests involved, it would not be reasonable to decide to enforce the judgment in the Netherlands, it shall declare enforcement admissible, stating the applicable statutory provisions. Article 30, third paragraph, second sentence, and fourth an fifth paragraphs, and 31 of the Act on the transfer of enforcement of criminal judgments shall apply by analogy. The judgment of the district court shall be immediately enforceable.
4. The district court may in no case impose a sentence longer than that laid down by the Tribunal.
5. Articles 33, 60 to 66 and 68 of the Act on the transfer of enforcement of criminal judgments shall apply by analogy.

Article 13
1. The further enforcement of a custodial sentence imposed by the Tribunal which is being enforced in the Netherlands under article 11 and 12 may be transferred to a foreign State. Articles 51 to 53, 56, 57 and 59 of the Act on the transfer of enforcement of criminal judgments shall apply by analogy.
2. Before deciding on transfer of enforcement pursuant to the first paragraph, Our Minister shall seek the advice of the Tribunal. If the Tribunal advises against the transfer, Our Minister shall decide against it.

Article 14
Articles 2 to 7, 11 and 12 of the Pardons Act shall apply by analogy to petitions for reduction or remission of sentences imposed by the Tribunal which are being enforced in the Netherlands under articles 11 and 12. Pardons shall be granted by the President of the Tribunal in accordance with article 28 of the Statute.

Article 15
The transit of persons who have been convicted by the Tribunal and in respect of whom a custodial sentence is to be enforced in a foreign State shall be conducted on the instructions of Our Minister by Dutch officials and under their guard. The said officials shall be empowered to take all appropriate measures for the security of the persons in question and to prevent their escape.

Article 16
Persons who, in accordance with the Tribunal's Statute, may not claim immunity from the Tribunal's jurisdiction, shall not be able, for the purposes of this Act, to claim such immunity from the jurisdiction of the Dutch courts and the enforceability of their decisions.

Article 17
Dutch law shall not apply to deprivation of liberty ordered by the Tribunal in premises used by the Tribunal in the Netherlands.

Appendix II
Treaties concluded by
the Kingdom of the Netherlands

Explanatory Note

This index contains, in chronological order, the treaties concluded by the Kingdom of the Netherlands which are relevant in the field of criminal law. It mentions the languages in which an authentic text exists and refers to the source(s) of the text in English. In cases in which an authentic text in English or Dutch does not exist, the index may refer to a translation in those languages.

Throughout the index, the date of entry into force of the treaty refers to the entry into force of the treaty for the Kingdom of the Netherlands only. Some multilateral treaties, therefore, might have entered into force earlier than that date. The index specifies whether the treaty has entered into force for the Kingdom as a whole (expressed by Kingdom), or one of its constituent parts and mentions the exact date of entry into force for each. NL stands for the Netherlands, NA for the Netherlands Antilles and A for Aruba. The Index also includes treaties which have not entered into force but whose ratification by the Kingdom of the Netherlands can be expected.

The index contains all reservations and declarations made by the Kingdom of the Netherlands regarding the treaties. It is updated to include the 1996 volume of the Treaty Series of the Kingdom of the Netherlands *(Tractatenblad van het Koninkrijk der Nederlanden)*. The index contains the actual text of reservations and declarations only; it therefore does not refer to reservations and declarations that have been withdrawn. Where these texts have been amended, the index contains the text as amended only. Regarding objections, only objections made by other nations to reservations and declarations of the Kingdom of the Netherlands as well as objections made by the Kingdom of the Netherlands to reservations and declarations of other nations appear in this index.

Treaties concluded by the Kingdom of the Netherlands

1

Title:	Treaty between the Netherlands and Great Britain for the suppression of the Slave Trade
Date and place:	4 May 1818, The Hague
Authentic texts:	Dutch, English, French
English text:	Stb. 1848, 79
Dutch text:	Stb. 1848, 79
In force since:	19 May 1818 (NL)

2

Title:	Revised Rhine Navigation Act
Date and place:	17 October 1868, Mannheim
Authentic texts:	French, German (Stb. 1869, 75; Trb. 1955, 161)
Dutch translation:	Stb. 1869, 75; Trb. 1955, 161
In force since:	1 July 1869 (Kingdom)
Declaration:	of 8 September 1895 entered into force on 27 May 1898
Related to:	73

3

Title:	Convention for the Protection of Submarine Cables
Date and place:	14 March 1884, Paris
Authentic text:	French
Dutch translation:	Stb. 1888, 74
In force since:	1 May 1888 (NL), 18 August 1892 (NA, A)

4

Title:	International Agreement to combat abuses, resulting from the sale of spirituals among fishermen on the Northsea outside the territorial waters (with Protocol)
Date and place:	16 November 1887, The Hague
Authentic text:	French (Stb. 1894, 59)

| *Dutch translation:* | Stb. 1894, 59 |
| *In force since:* | 23 May 1894 (NL) |

5

Title:	Treaty on mutual extradition of criminals between the Netherlands and Argentina
Date and place:	7 September 1893, Buenos-Ayres
Authentic texts:	French, Spanish (Stb. 1898, 29)
Dutch translation:	Stb. 1898, 29
In force since:	20 February 1898 (Kingdom)

6

Title:	Treaty on mutual extradition of criminals between the Netherlands and Monaco
Date and place:	26 June 1894, The Hague
Authentic text:	French (Stb. 1894, 147)
Dutch translation:	Stb. 1894, 147
In force since:	8 October 1894 (NL)

7

Title:	Treaty on extradition of criminals between the Netherlands and Romania
Date and place:	9 October 1894, Bucharest
Authentic text:	French (Stb. 1895, 88)
Dutch translation:	Stb. 1895, 88
In force since:	8 July 1895 (NL)

8

Title:	Treaty between The Kingdom of the Netherlands and Liberia to deliver up criminals
Date and place:	2 February 1895, The Hague
Authentic texts:	Dutch, English
English text:	Stb. 1896, 143
Dutch text:	Stb. 1896, 143
In force since:	30 October 1896 (Kingdom)

9

Title:	Treaty regarding mutual extradition of criminals between the Netherlands and Serbia
Date and place:	28 February 1896/11 March 1896, Belgrado
Authentic text:	French (Stb. 1897, 42)
Dutch translation:	Stb. 1897, 42
In force since:	28 January 1897 (NL)

| *Editor's note:* | On August 31, 1972, the Supreme Court of the Netherlands held that the Treaty, contracted in 1896 between the Netherlands and the Kingdom of Serbia, since it came into force, has been and still is binding on the Netherlands and continues to be in force between the Netherlands and the Republic of Yugoslavia. See NYIL 1973, p. 391. |

10

Title:	Treaty for the extradition of criminals between the Kingdom of the Netherlands and the United Kingdom of Great Britain and Ireland
Date and place:	26 September 1898, London
Authentic texts:	Dutch, English
English text:	Stb. 1899, 15
Dutch text:	Stb. 1899, 15
In force since:	14 March 1899 (Kingdom)
	The treaty entered into force for the following British colonies and possessions: Ascension Island, Antigua, British Virgin Islands, Dominica, Montserrat, St. Christopher, St. Kitts, Nevis, Anguilla, Bermuda Islands, Grenada, St. Lucia, St. Vincent, British-French condominium of the New Hebrides, British Territories of the High Commissioner of the Western Pacific, Falkland Islands, Hong Kong, Gibraltar, Seychelles, St. Helena.
	The treaty entered into force on 20 February 1915 for the Gilbert and Ellice Islands, the Salomons Islands.
	The treaty ceased to be applicable on 14 May 1991 in the relation between the Netherlands and the United Kingdom of Great Britain and Northern Ireland, the Channel Islands and the Isle of Man.
Related to:	52, 77, 81, 82, 83, 92, 126, 130

11

Title:	Convention (I) for the pacific settlement of international disputes
Date and place:	29 July 1899, The Hague
Authentic text:	French
Dutch translation:	Stb. 1900, 163
In force since:	4 september 1900 (Kingdom)

12

Title:	Convention (II) with respect to the laws and customs of war on land
Date and place:	29 July 1899, The Hague
Authentic text:	French

Dutch translation:	Stb. 1900, 163
In force since:	4 September 1900 (Kingdom)

13
Title:	Convention (III) for the adaptation of the principles of the Convention of Geneva of August 22, 1864 to maritime warfare
Date and place:	29 July 1899, The Hague
Authentic text:	French
Dutch translation:	Stb. 1900, 163
In force since:	4 September 1900 (Kingdom)

14
Title:	Declaration prohibiting the discharge of projectiles and explosives from balloons or from other similar new methodes
Date and place:	29 July 1899, The Hague
Authentic text:	French
Dutch translation:	Stb. 1900, 163
In force since:	4 September 1900 - 4 September 1905 (Kingdom)
Editor's note:	Renewed by declaration prohibiting the discharge of projectiles and explosives from balloons

15
Title:	Declaration prohibiting the use of projectiles that aim only at distributing asphyxiating and poisonous gases
Date and place:	29 July 1899, The Hague
Authentic text:	French
Dutch translation:	Stb. 1900, 163
In force since:	4 September 1900 (Kingdom)

16
Title:	Declaration prohibiting the use of bullets which explode or mutilate the human body easily, like bullets with a rough shell, of which the shell does not cover the core or has indentations
Date and place:	29 July 1899, The Hague
Authentic text:	French
Dutch translation:	Stb. 1900, 163
In force since:	4 September 1900 (Kingdom)

17
Title:	Extradition Treaty between the Netherlands and San Marino
Date and place:	7 November 1902, Rome
Authentic text:	French

English translation: 36 Stat. 2351; TS 542; 1 Bevans 681
Dutch translation: Stb. 1910, 73
In force since: 26 January 1910 (Kingdom)

28

Title: Convention (X) for the adaptation to Maritime Warfare of the principles of the Geneva Convention of 1906
Date and place: 18 October 1907, The Hague
Authentic text: French
Dutch translation: Stb. 1910, 73
In force since: 26 January 1910 (Kingdom)

29

Title: Convention (XI) relative to certain restrictions with regard to the exercise of the right of capture in naval war
Date and place: 18 October 1907, The Hague
Authentic text: French
English translation: 36 Stat. 2396; TS 544; 1 Bevans 711
Dutch translation: Stb. 1910, 73
In force since: 26 January 1910 (Kingdom)

30

Title: Convention (XIII) concerning the rights and duties of neutral powers in naval war
Date and place: ` 18 October 1907, The Hague
Authentic text: French
English text: 36 Stat. 2415; TS 545; 1 Bevans 723
Dutch translation: Stb. 1910, 73
In force since: 26 January 1910 (Kingdom)

31

Title: Declaration prohibiting the discharge of projectiles and explosives from balloons
Date and place: 18 October 1907, The Hague
Authentic text: French
English translation: 36 Stat. 2439; TS 546; 1 Bevans 739
Dutch translation: Stb. 1910, 73
In force since: 27 November 1909 (Kingdom)

32

Title: Extradition Treaty between the Netherlands and the United Mexican States
Date and place: 16 December 1907, Mexico

Authentic texts:	Dutch, Spanish
Dutch text:	Stb. 1909, 118
In force since:	2 July 1909 (Kingdom)

33

Title:	Agreement for the Suppression of the Circulation of Obscene Publications
Date and place:	4 May 1910, Paris
Authentic text:	French
English translation:	7 Martens Nouveau Recueil (3d) 266; 37 Stat. 1511; TS 559
Dutch translation:	Stb. 1912, 217
In force since:	8 December 1912 (NL); 18 May 1922 (NA, A)

34

Title:	International Convention for the Suppression of the White Slave Traffic
Date and place:	4 May 1910, Paris
Authentic text:	French (Stb. 1912, 355)
English translation:	7 Martens Nouveau Recueil (3d) 252; 98 UNTS 101
Dutch translation:	Stb. 1912, 355
In force since:	8 February 1913 (NL); 14 November 1921 (NA, A)
Related to:	44

35

Title:	International Convention for the Suppression of the Traffic in Women and Children
Date and place:	30 September 1921, Geneva
Authentic texts:	English, French
English text:	Stb. 1923, 526; 9 LNTS 415; 53 UNTS 39
Dutch translation:	Stb. 1923, 526
In force since:	19 September 1923 (Kingdom)
Related to:	41

36

Title:	International Convention for the Suppression of the Circulation of and Traffic in Obscene Publications
Date and place:	12 September 1923, Geneva
Authentic texts:	English, French
English text:	27 LNTS 213
Dutch translation:	Stb. 1927, 329
In force since:	13 September 1927 (Kingdom), Denounced for the Netherlands (effective on 26 July 1986)

Declaration: ... That the Kingdom of the Netherlands hereby denounces for the part of the Kingdom in Europe the International Convention for the suppression of the circulation of and the traffic in obscene publications established (Geneva, 12 September 1923) as well as the Protocol amending the said Convention (New York, 12 November 1947) in accordance with Article XII of the Convention. For the Kingdom of the Netherlands the Convention and the Protocol will therefore only remain in force in the Netherlands Antilles.

The reason for the denunciation of the Convention for the part of the Kingdom in Europe is that under the Act of 3 July 1985 (Bulletin of Acts, Orders and Decrees No. 385) the provisions of the Dutch Criminal Code were amended in such a way that it is no longer possible for the Netherlands fully to comply with the international obligations it assumed under the Convention. Article I of the Convention contains – inter alia – the obligation to make it a punishable offence to make or produce or have in possession, to import, convey or export obscene publications or any other objects for the purposes of distribution or public exhibition.

The new provisions of the Dutch Criminal Code fulfil this requirement only with regard to the portrayal of – or to any medium of information which portrays – sexual activity involving persons under the age of sixteen (i.e. child pornography). As regards the other forms of pornography, the only offences will be to display obscene images or objects in shop windows, to send such images or objects unsolicited through the mail or to supply, offer or show them to children. Since the Convention does not contain any provision which would allow the Netherlands to make punishable only those offences included in the amended Criminal Code, the Government of the Kingdom of the Netherlands has no other choice than to denounce the Convention for the Netherlands.

Related to: 42

37

Title: Protocol for the prohibition of the use in war of asphyxiating poisonous or other gases, and of bacteriological methodes of warfare

Date and place: 17 June 1925, Geneva

Authentic texts: English, French

English text: Stb. 1930, 422; 94 LNTS 65

Dutch translation: Stb. 1930, 422

In force since: 31 October 1930 (Kingdom)

38

Title:	Convention to Suppress Slave Trade and Slavery
Date and place:	25 September 1926, Geneva
Authentic texts:	English, French
English text:	Stb. 1928, 26; 60 LNTS 253; 46 Stat. 2183; TS 778; 212 UNTS 17
Dutch translation:	Stb. 1928, 26
In force since:	7 January 1928 (Kingdom)
Related to:	55, 59

39

Title:	International Convention for the Suppression of Counterfeiting Currency and Protocol
Date and place:	20 April 1929, Geneva
Authentic texts:	English, French
English text:	Stb. 1932, 285; 112 LNTS 371
Dutch translation:	Stb. 1932, 285
In force since:	29 July 1932 (NL); 22 March 1954 (NA, A)

40

Title:	International Convention for the Suppression of the Traffic in Women of Full Age
Date and place:	11 October 1933, Geneva
Authentic texts:	English, French
English text:	150 LNTS 431; 53 UNTS 49; Stb. 1935, 598
Dutch translation:	Stb. 1935, 598
In force since:	19 November 1935 (Kingdom)
Related to:	41

41

Title:	Protocol to Amend the Convention for the Suppression of the Traffic in Women and Children, concluded at Geneva on 30 September 1921, and the Convention for the Suppression of Traffic in Women of Full Age, Concluded at Geneva on 11 October 1933 (+Annex)
Date and place:	12 November 1947, Lake Success, New York
Authentic texts:	Chinese, English, French, Russian, Spanish
English text:	Stb. 1949, J 188; 53 UNTS 13
Dutch translation:	Stb. 1949, J 188
In force since:	7 March 1949 (Kingdom)
Related to:	35, 40

42

Title:	Protocol to amend the Convention for the Suppression of the Circulation of and Traffic in Obscene Publications, concluded at Geneva on 12 September 1923
Date and place:	12 November 1947, Lake Success, New York
Authentic texts:	Chinese, English, French, Russian, Spanish
English text:	Stb. 1949, J 188; 46 UNTS 170
Dutch translation:	Stb. 1949, J 188
In force since:	7 March 1949 (Kingdom), denounced for the Netherlands (effective on 26 July 1986)
Declaration:	see 36
Related to:	36

43

Title:	Convention on the Prevention and Punishment of the Crime of Genocide
Date and place:	9 December 1948, Paris
Authentic texts:	Chinese, English, French, Russian, Spanish
English text:	Trb. 1960, 32; 78 UNTS 277; 317 UNTS 319
Dutch translation:	Trb. 1960, 32
In force since:	18 September 1966 (Kingdom)
Objections:	the Government of the Kingdom of the Netherlands declares that it considers the reservations made by Albania, Algeria, Bulgaria, the Byelorussian Soviet Socialist Republic, Czechoslovakia, Hungary, India, Morocco, Poland, Rumania, the Ukrainian Soviet Socialist Republic and the Union of Soviet Socialist Republics in respect of Article IX of the Convention on the Prevention and Punishment of the Crime of Genocide, opened for signature at Paris on 9 December 1948, to be incompatible with the object and purpose of the Convention. The Government of the Kingdom of the Netherlands therefore does not deem any State which has made or which will make such reservation a party to the Convention.

to reservations of the United States:
... As concerns the first reservation, the Government of the Kingdom of the Netherlands recalls its declaration, made on 20 June 1966 on the occassion of the accession of the Kingdom of the Netherlands to the Convention (circulated 21 July 1966 with reference C.N. 99.1966, Treaties-1) stating that in its opinion the reservations in respect of article IX of the Convention, made at the time by a number of states, were incompatible with the object and purpose of the Convention and that Government of the Kingdom

of the Netherlands did not consider states making such reservations parties to the Convention. Accordingly, the Government of
the Kingdom of the Netherlands does not consider the United
States of America a party to the Convention. Similarly, the
Government of the Kingdom of the Netherlands does not consider
parties to the Convention other states which have made such
reservation, i.e. in addition to the States mentioned in the aforementioned declaration, the People's Republic of China, Democratic Yemen, the German Democratic Republic, the Mongolian
People's Republic, the Philippines, Rwanda, Spain, Venezuela, and
Vietnam. On the other hand, the Government of the Kingdom of
the Netherlands does consider parties to the Convention those
states that have since withdrawn their reservations, i.e. the Union
of Soviet Socialist Republics, the Byelorussian Soviet Socialist
Republic, and the Ukrainian Soviet Socialist Republic. As the
Convention may come into force between the Kingdom of the
Netherlands and the United States of America as a result of the
latter withdrawing its reservation in respect of article IX, the
Government of the Kingdom of the Netherlands deems it useful
to express the following position on the second reservation of the
United States of America:
The Government of the Kingdom of the Netherlands objects to
this reservation on the ground that it creates uncertainty as to the
extent of the obligations the Government of the United States of
America is prepared to assume with regard to the Convention.
Moreover, any failure by the United States of America to act upon
the obligations contained in the Convention on the ground that
such action would be prohibited by the constitution of the United
States would be contrary to the generally accepted rule of international law, as laid down in article 27 of the Vienna Convention
on the law of treaties (Vienna, 23 May 1969).

44

Title:	Protocol Amending the International Agreement for the Suppres-sion of the White Slave Traffic, Signed at Paris, on 18 May 1904, and the International Convention for the Supression of the White Slave Traffic, Signed at Paris, on 4 May 1910
Date and place:	4 May 1949, Lake Success, New York
Authentic texts:	Chinese, English, French, Russian, Spanish
English text:	30 UNTS 23; 2 UST 1997; TIAS 2332
Dutch translation:	Stb. 1949, K 257
In force since:	26 September 1950 (Kingdom)
Related to:	18, 34

45

Title:	Convention (I) for the Amelioration of the Condition of the Wounded and Sick in Armed Forces in the Field
Date and place:	12 August 1949, Geneva
Authentic texts:	English, French
English text:	Stb. 1954, 246; 75 UNTS 31; 6 UST 3114; TIAS 3362
Dutch translation:	Trb. 1951, 72
In force since:	3 February 1955 (Kingdom)
Related to:	110, 111

46

Title:	Convention (II) for the Amelioration of the Condition of the Wounded, Sick, and Shipwrecked Members of Armed Forces at Sea
Date and place:	12 August 1949, Geneva
Authentic texts:	English, French
English text:	Stb. 1954, 247; 75 UNTS 85; 6 UST 3217: TIAS 3363
Dutch translation:	Trb. 1951, 73
In force since:	3 February 1955 (Kingdom)
Related to:	110, 111

47

Title:	Convention (III) Relative to the Treatment of Prisoners of War
Date and place:	12 August 1949, Geneva
Authentic texts:	English, French
English text:	Stb. 1954, 248; 75 UNTS 135; 6 UST 3316; TIAS 3364
Dutch translation:	Trb. 1951, 74
In force since:	3 February 1955 (Kingdom)
Related to:	110, 111

48

Title:	Convention (IV) Relative to the Protection of Civilian Persons in Time of War
Date and place:	12 August 1949, Geneva
Authentic texts:	English, French
English text:	Stb. 1954, 249; 75 UNTS 287; 6 UST 3516; TIAS 3365
Dutch text:	Trb. 1951, 75
In force since:	3 February 1955 (Kingdom)
Related to:	110, 111

49

Title:	Convention on Road Traffic and Protocol on Road Signs and Signals

Date and place:	19 September 1949, Geneva
Authentic texts:	English, French
English text:	Trb. 1951, 81
Dutch translation:	Trb. 1951, 81
In force since:	Convention: 19 October 1952 (NL); Protocol: 20 December 1953 (NL) Convention and Protocol 8 June 1957 (NA, A)
Reservation:	Annex 2 is excluded from application to the Netherlands Annex 1 and 2 are excluded from application to the Netherlands Antilles and Aruba.
Objection:	...while regretting the reservation to article 33 made by the Sovjet Union, the Netherlands Government does not oppose the accession of the Sovjet Union to the Convention on Road Traffic, it being understood that the Netherlands Government likewise does not consider itself bound by the provision to which a reservation was made as far as the Sovjet Union is concerned.

50

Title:	European Convention for the Protection of Human Rights and Fundamental Freedoms
Date and place:	4 November 1950, Rome
Authentic texts:	English, French
English text:	Trb. 1951, 154; ETS 5; 213 UNTS 221
Dutch translation:	Trb. 1990, 156
In force since:	31 August 1954 (NL); 31 December 1955 (NA, A)
Declaration:	(Translation (original French))

The Minister of Foreign Affairs of the Kingdom of the Netherlands, declares that, in accordance with Article 25 of the Convention for the Protection of Human Rights and Fundamental Freedoms, signed at Rome on 4 November, 1950, the Government of the Kingdom of the Netherlands recognizes, for the Kingdom in Europe and the Netherlands Antilles, from 1 September, 1979 until denunciation, the competence of the European Commission of Human Rights to receive requests adressed to the Secretary General of the Council of Europe from any person, non-governmental organisation or group of individuals claiming to be the victim of a violation by one of the High Contracting Parties of rights set forth in the said Convention.

The Minister of Foreign Affairs of the Kingdom of the Netherlands declares that the Government of the Kingdom of the Netherlands recognizes, from 1 September, 1979 until denunciation, for the Kingdom in Europe and the Netherlands Antilles, as compulsory ipso facto and without special agreement, vis-à-vis any other

High Contracting Party to the Convention mentioned below accepting the same obligation, on condition of reciprocity, the jurisdiction of the European Court of Human Rights in accordance with Article 46 of the Convention for the Protection of Human Rights and Fundamental Freedoms, Convention signed at Rome on 4 November, 1950, in all matters concerning the interpretation and application of the said Convention.

Related to: 53, 72, 133, 137

51

Title:	Agreement between the Parties to the North Atlantic Treaty regarding the Status of their Forces
Date and place:	19 June 1951, London
Authentic texts:	English, French
English text:	Trb. 1951, 114; 199 UNTS 67
Dutch translation:	Trb. 1953, 10
In force since:	18 December 1953 (NL)
Declaration:	On signing the Agreement of to-day's date regarding the Status of the Forces of the North Atlantic Treaty Countries, the Plenipotentiaries of the Kingdom of Belgium, the Grand Duchy of Luxembourg and the Kingdom of the Netherlands make the following Declaration: The forces of the Kingdom of Belgium, the Grand Duchy of Luxembourg and the Kingdom of the Netherlands, their civilian components and their members may not avail themselves of the provisions of the present Agreement to claim in the territory of one of the afore-mentioned Powers any exemption which they do not enjoy in their own territory, with respect to duties, taxes and other dues,which have been or will be standardized under the terms of conventions which have been or will be concluded for the purpose of bringing about the Economic Union of Belgium, Luxembourg, and the Netherlands.
Related to:	54, 67

52

Title:	Letters of Understanding between the Government of the Netherlands and the Government of Pakistan on the Applicability of the Treaty for the Extradition of Criminals between the Kingdom of the Netherlands and the United Kingdom of Great Britain and Ireland, signed at London, 26 September 1898
Date and place:	11 March/24 June 1952, The Hague
Authentic text:	English
English text:	Trb. 1971, 211

In force since:	The respective governments consider the Treaty of 26 September 1898 still to be in force between the Netherlands and Pakistan (Kingdom)
Related to:	10

53

Title:	Protocol to the Convention for the Protection of Human Rights and Fundamental Freedoms
Date and place:	20 March 1952, Paris
Authentic texts:	English, French
English text:	Trb. 1952, 80; 213 UNTS 262; ETS 9
Dutch translation:	Trb. 1990, 157
In force since:	31 August 1954 (NL); 31 December 1955 (NA, A)
Related to:	50, 72, 133, 137

54

Title:	Protocol on the status of international military Headquaters set up pursuant to the North Atlantic Treaty
Date and place:	28 August 1952, Paris
Authentic texts:	English, French
English text:	Trb. 1953, 11
Dutch translation:	Trb. 1953, 11
In force since:	22 July 1954 (NL)
Declaration:	(Translation (original French))
	Nationals of the Kingdom of Belgium, of the Grand Duchy of Luxembourg and of the Kingdom of the Netherlands cannot invoke the prevalence of provisions of the present Protocol for claims within the territory of one of these powers, an exemption to which they are not entitled when they exercise their functions in their own country, with respect to duties, taxes and other levies of which the unification has been or will be achieved by virtue of conventions that aim at the realization of a Belgian-Luxembourg-Dutch Economic Union.
Related to:	51

55

Title:	Protocol Amending the Slavery Convention Signed at Geneva on 25 September 1926
Date and place:	7 December 1953, New York
Authentic texts:	Chinese, English, French, Russian, Spanish
English text:	Trb. 54, 84; 182 UNTS 51; 7 UST 479; TIAS 3532
Dutch translation:	Trb. 1955, 33

In force since:	7 July 1955 (Kingdom)
Related to:	38, 59

56

Title:	Convention for the Protection of Cultural Property in the Event of Armed Conflict
Date and place:	14 May 1954, The Hague
Authentic texts:	English, French, Russian, Spanish
English text:	Trb. 1955, 47
Dutch translation:	Trb. 1955, 47
In force since:	14 January 1959 (NL)

57

Title:	Exchange of Notes between the United States Government and The Netherlands Government Regarding the Status of the United States Armed Forces in the Netherlands
Date and place:	13 August 1954, The Hague
Authentic text:	English
English text:	Trb. 1954, 120
Dutch translation:	Trb. 1954, 120
In force since:	16 november 1954 (NL)

58

Title:	Exchange of Letters between the Government of the Netherlands and the Government of Indonesia relative to permitting the mutual presence of Judicial authorities at the hearing of witnesses
Date and place:	28 August 1954, 12 January 1955, 14 April 1955, 6 May 1955, 28 July 1955, The Hague
Authentic text:	Dutch
Dutch text:	Parliamentary Proceedings (II), 1954-1955, 4039, nr. 1
In force since:	28 July 1955 (NL)

59

Title:	Supplementary Convention on the Abolition of Slavery, the Slave Trade, and Institutions and Practices Similar to Slavery
Date and place:	7 September 1956, Geneva
Authentic texts:	Chinese, English, French, Russian, Spanish
English text:	Trb. 1957, 118; 266 UNTS 3; 18 UST 3201; TIAS 6418
Dutch translation:	Trb. 1957, 118
In force since:	3 December 1957 (Kingdom)
Related to:	38, 55

60

Title:	European Convention on Extradition
Date and place:	13 December 1957, Paris
Authentic texts:	English, French
English text:	Trb. 1965, 9; ETS 24
Dutch translation:	Trb. 1965, 9
In force since:	15 May 1969 (NL)

The application of the Convention has been extended in the relation between the Netherlands and France with regard to Polynésie Française, de Nouvelle Calédonie, Wallis et Futuna, Mayotte, Saint Pierre et Miquelon (since 1 July 1991)

The application of the Convention has been extended to the Netherlands Antilles and Aruba in the relations between the Kingdom and Sweden (1 October 1993), Liechtenstein (1 December 1993), Italy (30 December 1993), Switzerland (1 January 1994), Luxemburg (1 February 1994), France (1 March 1994), Turkey (1 May 1994), Denmark (1 May 1994), Norway (1 May 1994), Czech Republic (1 June 1994), Cyprus (1 June 1994), Greece (1 September 1994), Slovak Republic (1 September 1994), Spain (1 February 1995), United Kingdom (to be determined), Israel (1 November 1995), Portugal (1 December 1995), Austria (1 January 1996), Croatia (1 May 1996), Slovenia (to be determined), Hungary (1 July 1996), Finland (1 October 1996), Bulgaria (1 October 1996).

Reservation: to Article 1:

The Netherlands Government reserves the right not to grant extradition requested for the purpose of executing a judgment pronounced by default against which no remedy remains open, if such extradition might have the effect of subjecting the person claimed to a penalty without his having been enabled to exercise the rights of defence prescribed in Article 6 (3) (c) of the Convention for the Protection of Human Rights and Fundamental Freedoms signed at Rome on 4 November 1950.

The Netherlands Government reserves the right to refuse extradition on humanitarian grounds if it would cause particular hardship to the person claimed, for example, because of his youth, advanced age or state of health.

to Article 7:

The Netherlands Government reserves the right not to grant extradition when, in accordance with Article 7 (2), the requesting State would be authorised to refuse extradition in like cases.

to Article 9:

The Netherlands Government will not grant extradition if it is satisfied that final judgment for the offence for which extradition is requested has been passed on the person claimed by the competent authorities of a third State and, in the event of conviction for that offence, the convicted person is serving his sentence, has already served it or has been dispensed from serving it.

to Article 28:

By reason of the special arrangements between the Benelux countries, the Netherlands Government does not accept Article 28 (1) and (2) in respect of its relations with the Kingdom of Belgium and the Grand Duchy of Luxembourg. The Netherlands Government reserves the right to derogate from these provisions in respect of its relations with other member States of the European Economic Community.

Declarations: concerning Articles 6 and 21:

The government of the Kingdom of the Netherlands will not permit the transit of Netherlands nationals nor their extradition for the purposes of the enforcement of penalties or other measures. However Netherlands nationals may be extradited for purposes of prosecution if the requesting State provides a guarantee that the person claimed may be returned, to the Netherlands to serve his sentence there if, following his extradition, a custodial sentence other than a suspended sentence or a measure depriving him of his liberty is imposed upon him.

As regards the Netherlands, 'nationals' for the purposes of the Convention are to be understood as meaning persons of Netherlands nationality as well as foreigners integrated into the Netherlands community in so far as they can be prosecuted within the Kingdom of the Netherlands for the act in respect of which extradition is requested and in so far as such foreigners are not expected to lose their right of residence in the Kingdom as a result of the imposition of a penalty or measure subsequent to their extradition.

concerning Article 19:

The Netherlands Government will not grant temporary extradition under Article 19 (2) save of a person who is serving a sentence in its territory and if necessitated by special circumstances.

concerning Article 21(5):
The Netherlands Government reserves the right not to grant transit except on the same conditions on which it grants extradition.

Related to: 106, 114, 118, 213

61
Title: Convention on the Territorial Sea and the Contiguous Zone
Date and place: 29 April 1958, Geneva
Authentic texts: Chinese, English, French, Russian, Spanish
English text: Trb. 1959, 123
Dutch translation: Trb. 1959, 123
In force since: 20 March 1966 (Kingdom)
Objections: In depositing their instrument of ratification regarding the Convention on the Territorial Sea and the Contiguous Zone concluded at Geneva on April 29th 1958, the Government of the Kingdom of the Netherlands declare that they do not find acceptable:
the reservations made by the Government of Czechoslovakia to article 19, by the Governments of Bulgaria, the Byelorussian Soviet Socialist Republic, Czechoslovakia, Romania, The Ukrainian Soviet Socialist Republic and the Union of Soviet Socialist Republics to article 20, and by the Governments of Hungary and Czechoslovakia to article 21;
the reservations made by the Iranian Government to article 14;
the declaration by the Government of Colombia as far as it amounts to a reservation on article 14;
the reservation made by the Government of the Tunisian Republic to article 16, paragraph 4;
the declarations made by the Governments of Bulgaria, the Byelorussian Soviet Socialist Republic, Romania, the Ukrainian Soviet Socialist Republic and the Union of Soviet Socialist Republics on article 23, and the declaration made by the Governments of Czechoslovakia and Hungary on the articles 14 and 23 as far as these declarations amount to a reservation to the said articles;
the reservation made by the Government of the Republic of Italy to article 24, paragraph 1.
The Government of the Kingdom of the Netherlands reserve all rights regarding the reservations made by the Government of Venezuela on ratifying the present Convention in respect of article 12 and article 24, paragraphs 2 and 3.

62
Title: Convention on the High Seas
Date and place: 29 April 1958, Geneva

Authentic texts:	Chinese, English, French, Russian, Spanish
English text:	Trb. 1959, 124
Dutch translation:	Trb. 1959, 124
In force since:	20 March 1966 (Kingdom)
Objections:	In depositing their instrument of ratification regarding the Convention on the High Seas concluded at Geneva on April 29th 1958, the Government of the Kingdom of the Netherlands declare that they do not find acceptable the reservations to article 9 made by the Governments of Albania, Bulgaria, the Byelorussian Soviet Socialist Republic, Czechoslovakia, Hungary, Poland, Romania, the Ukrainian Soviet Socialist Republic, and the Union of Soviet Socialist Republics;
	the declarations made by the Governments of Albania, Bulgaria, the Byelorussian Soviet Socialist Republic, Czechoslovakia, Hungary, Poland, Romania, the Ukrainian Soviet Socialist Republic and the Union of Soviet Socialist Republics on the definition of piracy given in the Convention, as far as these declarations amount to a reservation;
	the reservations made by the Iranian Government to articles 2, 3 and 4, and to articles 2, paragraph 3, and 26, paragraphs 1 and 2;
	the declaration made by the Government of Iran on article 2 as far as it amounts to a reservation to the said article;
	the reservation made by Government of Indonesia.

63

Title:	Convention on Fishing and Conservation of the Living Resources of the High Seas
Date and place:	29 April 1958, Geneva
Authentic texts:	Chinese, English, French, Russian, Spanish
English text:	Trb. 1959, 125
Dutch translation:	Trb. 1959, 125
In force since:	20 March 1966 (Kingdom)

64

Title:	Convention on the Continental Shelf
Date and place:	29 April 1958, Geneva
Authentic texts:	Chinese, English, French, Russian, Spanish
English text:	Trb. 1959, 126
Dutch translation:	Trb. 1959, 126
In force since:	20 March 1966 (Kingdom)
Objections:	In depositing their instrument of ratification regarding the Convention on the Continental Shelf concluded at Geneva on April 29th 1958, the Government of the Kingdom of the Netherlands declare

that they do not find acceptable the reservations made by the
Iranian Government to Article 4;
the reservations made by the Government of the French Republic
to Articles 5, paragraph 1, and 6, paragraphs 1 and 2.
The Government of the Kingdom of the Netherlands reserve all
rights regarding the reservations in respect of Article 6 made by
the Government of Venezuela when ratifying the present Convention.

65

Title:	Optional Protocol of Signature concerning the compulsory settle-ment of disputes
Date and place:	29 April 1958, Geneva
Authentic texts:	Chinese, English, French, Russian, Spanish
English text:	Trb. 1959, 127
Dutch translation:	Trb. 1959, 127
In force since:	18 February 1966 (Kingdom)
Related to:	61, 62, 63, 64

66

Title:	European Convention on Mutual Assistance in Criminal Matters
Date and place:	20 April 1959, Strasbourg
Authentic texts:	English, French
English text:	Trb. 1965, 10; ETS 30; 472 UNTS 185
Dutch translation:	Trb. 1965, 10
In force since:	15 May 1969 (NL), 1 January 1986 (A), 21 July 1993 (NA) 1 July 1991, applicable in relation with France with regard to Territoires Français d'Outre Mer, de Polynésie Française, de Nou-velle Calédonie, Wallis et Futuna, collectivités territoriales de Mayotte, Saint Pierre et Miquelon
Reservations:	(Translation (original French)) to Article 2: The Netherlands Government reserve the right not to comply with a request for assistance (a) if there are good grounds for believing that it concerns an inquiry instituted with a view to prosecuting, punishing or other-wise interfering with an accused person because of his religion or political convictions, his nationality, his race or the population group to which he belongs; (b) in so far as it concerns a prosecution or proceedings incom-patible with the principle 'non bis in idem'; (c) in so far as it concerns an inquiry into acts for which the accused person is being procecuted in the Netherlands.

to Article 11:
The Netherlands Government will not grant temporary transit, as provided for in Article 11, save where the person concerned is serving a sentence in its territory and where there are no special considerations opposed thereto.

to Article 22:
The Netherlands Government will not notify the subsequent measures referred to in Article 22 except in so far as the organisation of its judicial records allows of so doing.

to Article 26:
By reason of the special arrangements between the Benelux countries, the Netherlands Government does not accept Article 26 (1) and (3) in respect of its relations with the Kingdom of Belgium and the Grand Duchy of Luxembourg.

The Netherlands Government reserves the right to derogate from these provisions in respect of its relations with other member States of the European Economic Community.

Declarations:
(Translation (original French))
Having regard to the equality under public law which exists between the Netherlands, Surinam and the Netherlands Antilles, the term 'metropolitan territories', used in paragraph 1 of Article 25 of this Convention, loses its initial meaning in respect of the Kingdom of the Netherlands and, as a consequence, in its application to the Kingdom, shall be considered to mean 'territory in Europe'. In respect of paragraph 4 of Article 25 of this Convention, it is important to note that since 1 October, 1962, the government of the Kingdom of the Netherlands is no longer responsible for the international relations of West-Guinea.

concerning Article 5:
The Netherlands Government declares that letters rogatory for search or seizure within the Netherlands will not be executed save for extraditable offences within the meaning of the European Convention on Extradition, and provided that the Netherlands court has authorised execution in accordance with its municipal law.

concerning Article 24:
The Netherlands Government declares that, as regards the Netherlands, judicial authorities for the purposes of the Convention are to be understood as meaning members of the judiciary responsible

for administering the law, examining magistrates and members of the Department of Public Prosecution.

concerning Article 25 (4):
In the event of the Netherlands Government making a declaration extending to the application of the Convention to Surinam and/or the Netherlands Antilles, it may qualify such declarations by conditions relating to local needs and, in particular, may declare that the Convention can be denounced separately in respect of those countries.

With regard to the Netherlands Antilles and Aruba
The Government of the Kingdom of the Netherlands declares having regard to Article 16, that the Kingdom of the Netherlands will require requests for legal assistance regarding the Netherlands Antilles and Aruba to be accompanied by an English translation: declares in accordance with the declaration of the Netherlands Government concerning Article 25, paragraph 4, that the Convention may be denounced separately in respect of the Netherlands Antilles and Aruba.

Related to:	115, 119

67

Title:	Agreement to Supplement the Agreement (of June 19, 1951) between the Parties of the North Atlantic Treaty regarding the Status of their Forces with Respect to Foreign Forces Stationed in the Federal Republic of Germany
Date and place:	3 August 1959, Bonn
Authentic texts:	German, English, French
English text:	14 UST 531; TIAS 5351; 481 UNTS 262; Trb. 1960, 37
Dutch translation:	Trb. 1961, 119
In force since:	1 July 1963 (NL)
related to:	51, 94, 128, 174, 175, 176

68

Title:	Single Convention on Narcotic Drugs, 1961
Date and place:	30 March 1961, New York
Authentic texts:	Chinese, English, French, Russian, Spanish
English text:	Trb. 1962, 30; 520 UNTS 151; 18 UST 1407; TIAS 6298
Dutch translation:	Trb. 1963, 81
In force since:	15 August 1965 (Kingdom)
Related to:	95, 105

69

Title:	Treaty between the Kingdom of Belgium, the Grand Duchy of Luxembourg and the Kingdom of the Netherlands, on extradition and mutual assistance in criminal matters
Date and place:	27 June 1962, Brussels
Authentic texts:	Dutch, French
English translation:	616 UNTS 79
Dutch text:	Trb. 1962, 97
In force since:	11 December 1967 (NL)
Declaration:	(Translation (original Dutch))

As a result of the entry into force of the Police Act 1993 on 1 April 1994, the difference between *Rijkspolitie* and *Gemeentepolitie* was abolished. Consequently, the third and the fourth part of paragraph 4 of Article 27 of this Treaty, must be read as: concerning the Netherlands, the officials appointed to exercise police tasks.
concerning Belgium and Luxembourg, the members of the municipal police of the municipalities of which the territories are located at a distance of less than ten kilometers from the border.

Related to: 102, 213

70

Title:	Convention on Consular Relations
Date and place:	24 April 1963, Vienna
Authentic texts:	Chinese, English, French, Russian, Spanish
English text:	Trb. 1965, 40; 21 UST 77; TIAS 6820; 596 UNTS 261
Dutch translation:	Trb. 1981, 143
In force since:	16 January 1986 (Kingdom)
Declaration:	

On the occasion of the accession of the Kingdom of the Netherlands to the Vienna Convention on Consular Relations, the Kingdom of the Netherlands declares the following:

– The Kingdom of the Netherlands interprets Chapter II of the Convention as applying to all career consular officers and employees, including those assigned to a consular post headed by a honorary consular officer.

– The Kingdom of the Netherlands interprets the words 'not, solely by the operation of the law of the receiving State' in article II of the Optional Protocol concerning Acquisition of Nationality as meaning that acquisition of nationality solely by the operation of this law.

On the same occasion the Kingdom of the Netherlands further declares as follows:

1. The Kingdom of the Netherlands does not regard as valid the reservations to the Articles 46, 49 and 62 of the Convention made by the United Arab Republic. This declaration should not be regarded as an obstacle to the entry into force of the Convention between the Kingdom of the Netherlands and the United Arab Republic.
2. The Kingdom of the Netherlands does not regard as valid the reservation to Article 62 of the Convention made by the Kingdom of Morocco. This declaration should not be regarded as an obstacle to the entry into force of the Convention between the Kingdom of the Netherlands and the Kingdom of Morocco.

Objection: The Kingdom of the Netherlands accepts the reservation made by the Yemen Arab Republic concerning the Articles 46, paragraph 1, and 49 of the Convention only in so far it does not purport to exclude the husbands of female members of the consular posts from enjoying the same privileges and immunities under the present Convention.

Response of the Yemen Arab Republic of 28 May 1987:
We should like to make clear in this connection that it was our country's intention in making that reservation that the expression 'family of a member of the consular post' should, for the purposes of enjoyment of the priviliges and immunities specified in the Convention, be understood to mean the member of the consular post, his spouse and minor children only.
We should like to make it clear that this reservation is not intended to exclude the husbands of female members of the consular posts, as was suggested in the Netherlands interpretation, since it is natural that husbands should in cases enjoy the same privileges and immunities.

71
Title: Convention on Offences and Certain Other Acts Committed on Board Aircraft
Date and place: 14 September 1963, Tokyo
Authentic texts: English, French, Spanish
English text: Trb. 1964, 115; 704 UNTS 219; 20 UST 2941; TIAS 6768
Dutch translation: Trb. 1964, 186
In force since: 12 February 1970 (NL), 2 September 1974 (NA, A)

72
Title: Protocol No. 4 to the Convention for the Protection of Human Rights and Fundamental Freedoms securing certain rights and

freedoms other than those already included in the convention and in the first protocol thereto

Date and place: 16 September 1963, Strasbourg
Authentic texts: English, French
English text: Trb. 1964, 15; ETS 46
Dutch translation: Trb. 1990, 159
In force since: 23 June 1982 (Kingdom)
Declaration: (Translation (original French))

As Protocol No. 4 to the Convention for the Protection of Human Rights and Fundamental Freedoms, securing certain rights and freedoms other than those already included in the Convention and in the first Protocol thereto, applies to the Netherlands and to the Netherlands Antilles by virtue of its ratification by the Netherlands, the Netherlands and the Netherlands Antilles are considered as separate territories for the application of Articles 2 and 3 of the Protocol, in accordance with the provisions of Article 5, paragraph 4. According to Article 3 no one shall be expelled from the territory of the State of which he is a national and no one shall be deprived of the right to enter that territory. However, only one Netherlands nationality exists for the Kingdom as a whole. Nationality shall therefore not be a criterion to distinguish between 'nationals' of the Netherlands and of the Netherlands Antilles, a distinction which is inevitable, because there is a different application of Article 3 in each of the constituent parts of the Kingdom. For these reasons, the Netherlands reserve the possibility to make a distinction based on law in the application of Article 3 of the Protocol between Netherlands nationals according to their origin, whether it be the Netherlands, or the Netherlands Antilles.

The Minister of Foreign Affairs of the Kingdom of the Netherlands declares that, in accordance with paragraph 2 of Article 6 of Protocol No. 4 to the Convention for the Protection of Human Rights and Fundamental Freedoms, and Article 25 of the said Convention, the Government of the Kingdom of the Netherlands recognizes, until denunciation, for the Kingdom in Europe and the Netherlands Antilles, the competence of the European Commission of Human Rights to receive requests addressed to the Secretary General of the Council of Europe from any person, non-governmental organisation or group of individuals claiming to be the victim of a violation by one of the High Contracting Parties of Rights set forth in this Protocol.

The Minister of Foreign Affairs of the Kingdom of the Netherlands declares that, in accordance with paragraph 2 of Article 6 of Protocol No. 4 to the Convention for the Protection of Human Rights and Fundamental Freedoms, and Article 46 of the said Convention, the Government of the Kingdom of the Netherlands recognizes, until denunciation, for the Kingdom in Europe and the Netherlands Antilles, as compulsory ipso facto and without special agreement, vis-à-vis any other Contracting Party to the Protocol accepting the same obligation, on condition of reciprocity, the jurisdiction of the European Court of Human Rights, in all matters concerning the interpretation and application of this Protocol.

Related to: 50, 53, 133, 137

73

Title: Agreement to amend the Revised Rhine Navigation Act, signed at Mannheim, October 17, 1868
Date and place: 20 November 1963, Strasbourg
Authentic texts: Dutch, German, French
Dutch text: Trb. 1964, 83
In force since: 14 April 1967 (NL)
Related to: 2

74

Title: European Convention on the Supervision of Conditionally Sentenced or Conditionally Released Offenders
Date and place: 30 November 1964, Strasbourg
Authentic texts: English, French
English text: Trb. 1965, 55; ETS 51
Dutch translation: Trb. 1982, 53
In force since: 1 January 1988 (NL)
Reservation: a. The Kingdom of the Netherlands declares with regard to article 7 of the Convention that complete application will not be accepted of the person to whom the decision relates has already been irrevocably tried by the competent authorities of a third state in respect of the same offence and if, in the event of conviction for this offence, the offender is serving or has already served his sentence or has been exempted from doing so.
b. The Kingdom of the Netherlands does not accept the provisions contained in Part III of the Convention.
c. By reason of the special regime between the Benelux countries, the Kingdom of the Netherlands does not accept the provisions of paragraph 2 of article 37 of the Convention.

Declaration:	1. With regard to Article 37, paragraph 2 (c) of the Convention: The provisions contained in Parts II and IV of the Convention will not be applied in the case of convictions in absentia. 2. With regard to Article 29, paragraph 2 of the Convention: The Kingdom of the Netherlands requires a translation in Dutch, French, English or German of any documents not drawn up in one of the above four languages.

75

Title:	European Agreement for the prevention of broadcasts transmitted from stations outside national territories
Date and place:	22 January 1965, Strasbourg
Authentic texts:	English, French
English text:	Trb. 1965, 92
Dutch translation:	Trb. 1965, 92
In force since:	27 September 1974 (NL)

76

Title:	International Convention on the Elimination of All forms of Racial Discrimination
Date and place:	7 March 1966, New York
Authentic texts:	Chinese, English, French, Russian, Spanish
English text:	Trb. 1966, 237; 660 UNTS 195
Dutch translation:	Trb. 1967, 48
In force since:	9 January 1972 (Kingdom)
Declaration:	(Translation (original French))

(The government of the Kingdom of the Netherlands) declares that, in accordance with Article 14, paragraph 1 of the International Convention on the Elimination of All Forms of Racial Discrimination concluded at New York on 7 March, 1966, the Kingdom of the Netherlands recognizes, for the Kingdom in Europe, Surinam and the Netherlands Antilles, the competence of the Committee on the Elimination of Racial Discrimination to receive and consider communications from individuals or groups of individuals within its jurisdiction claiming to be victims of a violation by the Kingdom of the Netherlands of any of the rights set forth in this Convention.

– With regard to Article 14, paragraph 1

The Government of the Kingdom of the Netherlands declares that it recognizes the competence of the Committee.

77

Title: Exchange of Notes between the Government of the Netherlands and the Government of Uganda on the Applicability of the Treaty for the Extradition of Criminals between the Kingdom of the Netherlands and the United Kingdom of Great Britain and Ireland signed at London, September 26, 1898

Date and place: 30 September 1966/27 January 1967, Nairobi/Entebbe

Authentic text: English

English text: Trb. 1967, 132

In force since: 27 January 1967 (NL)

Related to: 10

78

Title: International Covenant on Civil and Political Rights with Optional Protocol

Date and place: 19 December 1966, New York

Authentic texts: Chinese, English, French, Russian, Spanish

English text: Trb. 1969, 99

Dutch translation: Trb. 1978, 177

In force since: 11 March 1979 (Kingdom)

The provisions of article 41 of the Convention entered into force for the Kingdom of the Netherlands on 28 March 1979

Reservations: Clarify that although the reservations stated below are partly of an interpretational nature, the Kingdom of the Netherlands has preferred reservations to interpretational declarations in all cases, since if the latter form were used doubt might arise concerning whether the text of the Covenant allows for the interpretation put upon it. By using the reservation form the Kingdom of the Netherlands wishes to ensure in all cases that the relevant obligations arising out of the Covenant will not apply to the Kingdom, or will apply only in the way indicated.

Article 10
The Kingdom of the Netherlands subscribes to the principle set out in paragraph 1 of this article, but it takes the view that ideas about the treatment of prisoners are so liable to change; that it does not wish to be bound by the obligations set out in paragraph 2 and paragraph 3 (second sentence) of this Article.

Article 12, paragraph 1
The Kingdom of the Netherlands regards the Netherlands and the Netherlands Antilles as separate territories of a State for the purpose of this provision.

Article 12, paragraphs 2 and 4
The Kingdom of the Netherlands regards the Netherlands and the Netherlands Antilles as separate countries for the purpose of these provisions.

Article 14, paragraph 3 (d)
The Kingdom of the Netherlands reserve the statutory option of removing a person charged with a criminal offence from the court-room in the interests of the proper conduct of the proceedings.

Article 14, paragraph 5
The Kingdom of the Netherlands reserves the statutory power of the Supreme Court of the Netherlands to have sole jurisdiction to try certain categories of persons charged with serious offences committed in the discharge of a public office.

Article 14, paragraph 7
The Kingdom of the Netherlands accepts this provision only insofar as no obligations arise from it further to those set out in Article 68 of the Criminal Code of the Netherlands and Article 70 of the Criminal Code of the Netherlands Antilles as they now apply. They read:
1. Except in cases where court decisions are eligible for review, no person may be prosecuted again for an offence in respect of which a court in the Netherlands or the Netherlands Antilles has delivered an irrevocable judgement.
2. If the judgement has been delivered by some other court, the same person may not be prosecuted for the same offence in the case of (I) acquittal or withdrawal of proceedings or (II) conviction followed by complete execution, remission or lapse of the sentence.

Article 19, paragraph 2
The Kingdom of the Netherlands accepts the provision with the proviso that it shall not prevent the Kingdom from requiring the licensing of broadcasting, television or cinema enterprises.

Article 20, paragraph 1
The Kingdom of the Netherlands does not accept the obligation set out in this provision in the case of the Netherlands.

Declaration: The Kingdom of the Netherlands declares under article 41 of the International Covenant on Cival and Political Rights that it recognizes the competence of the Human Rights committee referred to in article 28 of the Covenant to receive and consider

Objections:

communications to the effect that a State Party claims that another State Party is not fulfilling its obligations under the Covenant. (Algeria) In the opinion of the Government of the Kingdom of the Netherlands, the interpretative declaration concerning article 13, paragraphs 3 and 4 of the International Covenant on Economic, Social and Cultural Rights (adopted by the General Assembly of the United Nations on 16 December 1966) must be regarded as a reservation to the Covenant. From the text and history of the Covenant it follows that the reservation with respect to article 13, paragraphs 3 and 4 made by the Government of Algeria is incompatible with the object and purpose of the Covenant. The Government of the Kingdom of the Netherlands therefore considers the reservation unacceptable and formally raises an objection to it. (This objection is) not an obstacle to the entry into force (the Covenant) between the Kingdom of the Netherlands and Algeria.

(United States) The Government of the Kingdom of the Netherlands objects to the reservation with respect to capital punishment for crimes committed by persons below eighteen years of age, since it follows from the text and history of the Covenant that the said reservation is incompatible with the text, the object and purpose of Article 6 of the Covenant, which according to Article 4 lays down the minimum standard for the protection of the right of life.
The Government of the Kingdom of the Netherlands objects to the reservation with respect to article 7 of the Covenant, since it follows from the text and the interpretation of this Article that the said reservation is incompatible with the object and purpose of the Convenant.
In the opinion of the Government of the Kingdom of the Netherlands this reservation has the same effect as a general derogation from this Article, while according to Article 4 of the Covenant, no derogations, not even in times of public emergency, are permitted.
It is the understanding of the Government of the Kingdom of the Netherlands that the understanding and declarations of the United States do not exclude or modify the legal effect of provisions of the Covenant in their application to the United States, and do not in any way limit the competence of the Human Rights Committee to interpret these provisions in their applications to the United States.
Subject to the provision of Article 21, paragraph 3 of the Vienna Convention of the Law of Treaties, these objections do not constitute an obstacle to the entry into force of the Covenant between the Kingdom of the Netherlands and the United States.

(Republic of Korea) In the opinion of the Government of the Kingdom of the Netherlands it follows from the text and the history of the International Covenant on Civil and Political Rights that the reservations with respect to articles 14, paragraphs 5 and 7 and 22 of the Covenant made by the Government of the Republic of Korea are imcompatible with the object and purpose of the Covenant. The Government of the Kingdom of the Netherlands therefore considers the reservation unacceptable and formally raises objection to it, this objection is not an obstacle to the entry into force of this Covenant between the Kingdom of the Netherlands and the Republic of Korea.

(Translation (original French))
(Congo) The Belgian Government/the Government of the Kingdom of the Netherlands wishes to note that the scope of application of Article 11 is particularly limited. In fact, Article 11 prohibits imprisonment in cases in which there is no other reason to resort to such means, than the ground that the debtor is unable to fulfil a contractual obligation. Imprisonment is not incompatible with Article 11 if other reasons to impose such a penalty exist, for example in cases where the debtor used bad faith or fraudulent manouvres to avoid fulfilling his obligations. A similar interpretation of Article 11 was confirmed in reading the travaux preparatoires (Cf. Document A/2929 of July 1, 1955).
After having examined the explanations given by the Congo concerning the issued reservation, the (Belgian Government/ Government of the Kingdom of the Netherlands), provisionally reached the conclusion that Congolese legislation authorises imprisonment for financial debts in cases where other forms of coercion fail, when debts of more than 20,000 francs CFA are concerned and when the debtor is between 18 and 60 years old and when he has become insolvent through bad faith. The latter condition demonstrates sufficiently that there is no contradiction between Congolese legislation and the text and purpose of Article 11 of the Covenant.
By virtue of the provisions of Article 4, paragraph 2 of the said Covenant, Article 11 is excluded from the scope of application of a regulation that provides that in times of public emergency, the States Parties to the present Covenant may, under certain circumstances, take measures derogating from their obligations under the Covenant. Article 11 is one of those articles containing a provision that no derogation may be made under any circumstances. Any reservation concerning that article nullifies its effect and is accordingly imcompatible with the text and purpose of the Covenant.

Consequently, and without prejudice to its firm opinion, according to which Congolese law is in perfect conformity with the provision of Article 11 of the Covenant, the (Belgian Government/ Government of the Kingdom of the Netherlands), fear that the reservation issued by Congo could, in principle, constitute a precedent which could have considerable effects on the international level.

(The Belgian Government/Government of the Kingdom of the Netherlands), hopes therefore that the reservation will be withdrawn and, for the time being, wishes to raise an objection to this reservation.

(Australia) I. *Reservation by Australia regarding articles 2 and 50*
The reservation that article 2, paragraphs 2 and 3, and article 50 shall be given effect consistently with and subject to the provisions in article 2, paragraph 2 is acceptable to the Kingdom on the understanding that it will in no way impair Australia's basic obligation under international law, as laid down in article 2, paragraph 1, to respect and to ensure to all individuals within its territory and subject to its jurisdiction the rights recognized in the International Covenant on Civil and Political Rights.

II. *Reservation by Australia regarding article 10*
The Kingdom is not able to evaluate the implications of the first part of the reservation regarding article 10 on its merits, since Australia has given no further explanation on the laws and lawful arrangements, as referred to in the text of the reservation. In expectation of further clarification by Australia, the Kingdom for the present reserves the right to raise objection to the reservation at a later stage.

III. *Reservation by Australia regarding 'Convicted Persons'*
The Kingdom finds it difficult, for the same reasons as mentioned in its commentary on the reservation regarding article 10, to accept the declaration by Australia that it reserves the right not to seek amendment of laws now in force in Australia relating to the rights of persons who have been convicted of serious criminal offences. The Kingdom expresses the hope it will be possible to gain a more detailed insight in the laws now in force in Australia, in order to facilitate a definitive opinion on the extent of this reservation.

(India) The Government of the Kingdom of the Netherlands objects to the declaration made by the Government of the Republic of India in relation to article 1 of the International Covenant on Civil and Political Rights and article 1 of the International Covenant on Economics, Social and Cultural Rights, since the right of self-determination as embodied in the Covenants is conferred upon all peoples. This follows not only from the very language of article 1 common to the two Covenants but as well from the most authoritive statement of the law concerned i.e.. the Declaration on Principles of International Law concerning Friendly Relations and Co-operation among States in accordance with the Charter of the United Nations. Any attempt to limit the scope of this right or to attach conditions not provided for in the relevant instruments would undermine the concept of self-determination itself and would thereby seriously weaken its universally acceptable character.

Related to: 160

79

Title: Convention on Conduct of Fishing Operations in the North Atlantic

Date and place: 1 June 1967, London

Authentic texts: English, French

English text: Trb. 1968, 54

Dutch translation: Trb. 1968, 54

In force since: 26 September 1976 (NL)

80

Title: Agreement between Belgium, the Federal Republic of Germany, France, Italy, Luxembourg and the Netherlands on mutual assistance between the respective customs administrations

Date and place: 7 September 1967, Rome

Authentic texts: Dutch, French, German, Italian

Dutch text: Trb. 1968, 172

In force since: 1 June 1970 (NL)

81

Title: Exchange of Notes between the Government of the Netherlands and the Government of Kenya on the Applicability of the Treaty for the Extradition of Criminals between the Kingdom of the Netherlands and the United Kingdom of Great Britain and Ireland, signed at London, 26 September 1898

Date and place: 10 November 1967, Nairobi

Authentic text: English

English text: Trb. 1968, 1

Dutch translation: Trb. 1968, 1

In force since:	15 May 1968 (NL)
Related to:	10

82

Title:	Exchange of Notes between the Government of the Netherlands and the Government of Malawi on the Applicability of the Treaty for the Extradition of Criminals between the Kingdom of the Netherlands and the United Kingdom of Great Britain and Ireland, signed at London, 26 September 1898
Date and place:	21 November 1967/28 June 1968, Lusaka/Blantyre
Authentic text:	English
English text:	Trb. 1968, 121
Dutch translation:	Trb. 1968, 121
In force since:	8 January 1969 (NL)
Related to:	10

83

Title:	Exchange of Notes between the Government of the Netherlands and the Government of Tanzania on the Applicability of the Treaty for the Extradition of Criminals between the Kingdom of the Netherlands and the United Kingdom of Great Britain and Ireland, signed at London, 26 September 1898
Date and place:	2 April/9 May 1968, Dar es Salaam
Authentic text:	English
English text:	Trb. 1968, 109
Dutch translation:	Trb. 1968, 109
In force since:	27 December 1968 (NL)
Related to:	10

84

Title:	European Convention on Information on Foreign Law
Date and place:	7 June 1968, London
Authentic texts:	English, French
English text:	Trb. 1968, 142; ETS 62
Dutch translation:	Trb. 1968, 142
In force since:	2 March 1977 (NL)
Declaration:	With reference to Article 2 the Government of the Kingdom of the Netherlands designates as the National Liaison body: Ministry of Justice (receiving and transmitting agency) Main Division of Private Law Schedeldoekshaven 100 The Hague
Related to:	113

85

Title:	Treaty between the Kingdom of Belgium, the Grand Duchy of Luxembourg and the Kingdom of the Netherlands on the enforcement of criminal judgments
Date and place:	26 September 1968, Brussels
Authentic texts:	Dutch, French
Dutch text:	Trb. 1969, 9
Editor's note:	The Treaty was ratified by the Netherlands, it has however not entered into force yet, because the condition of three ratifications has not been fulfilled

86

Title:	Agreement regarding the Status of Personnel of Sending States attached to an International Military Headquarter of NATO in the Federal Republic of Germany
Date and place:	7 February 1969, Bonn
Authentic texts:	English, French, German
English text:	Trb. 1969, 86
Dutch translation:	Trb. 1969, 86
In force since:	21 December 1969 (NL)

87

Title:	Agreement on cooperation between administrative and judicial authorities in matters pertaining to the Benelux Economic Union, with additional protocols
Date and place:	29 April 1969, The Hague
Authentic texts:	Dutch, French
Dutch text:	Trb. 1969, 124
In force since:	1 February 1971 (NL)

88

Title:	European Agreement relating to persons participating in proceedings of the European Commission and Court of Human Rights
Date and place:	6 May 1969, London
Authentic texts:	English, French
English text:	Trb. 1971, 47; ETS 67
Dutch translation:	Trb. 1971, 47
In force since:	29 February 1972 (Kingdom)

89

Title:	European Convention on the International Validity of Criminal Judgments
Date and place:	28 May 1970, The Hague

Authentic texts:	English, French
English text:	Trb. 1971, 137; ETS 70
Dutch translation:	Trb. 1971, 137
In force since:	1 January 1988 (NL)
Reservations:	a. The Kingdom of the Netherlands declares that it reserves the right to refuse to enforce an 'ordonnance penale' (penal order) or a judgement in absentia rendered by the authorities of the requesting State at a time when the right to institute criminal proceedings for the offence to which the 'ordonnance penale' (penal order) or judgement relates would have been precluded under Dutch criminal law for reasons of lapse of time.

b. The Kingdom of the Netherlands accepts the application of Part III of the Convention only in respect of Section I thereof.

Declarations: 1. With regard to Articles 37 and 41 of the Convention:

The Netherlands Government does not believe that it is the intention that a person sentenced abroad should have more extensive rights of appeal than would be applicable under Netherlands law in the case of persons prosecuted and sentenced in the first instance in the Netherlands.

2. With regard to Article 45, paragraph 1 of the Convention:

Fines or confiscation of sums of money imposed in a currency of which rate of exchange against the Dutch guilder is not registered daily at the Amsterdam foreign exchange, shall be expressed in terms of special drawing rights of the currency in question on the last working day of the month in which the requesting State imposed the sanction to be implemented.

3. With regard to Article 19, paragraph 2 of the Convention:

Documents submitted to the Kingdom of the Netherlands, where not drawn up in Dutch, French, English or German, should be accompanied by a translation into one of the above four languages.

4. With regard to Article 64, paragraph 4 of the Convention:

Once the Convention on the enforcement of criminal judgements concluded in Brussels on 26 September 1968 between the Kingdom of the Netherlands, the Kingdom of Belgium and the Grand Duchy of Luxembourg comes into force it will preclude application of the present European Convention as regards relations between the Kingdom of the Netherlands, the Kingdom of Belgium and the Grand Duchy of Luxembourg.

90

Title:	Convention for the Suppression of Unlawful Seizure of Aircraft
Date and place:	16 December 1970, The Hague

Authentic texts:	English, French, Russian, Spanish
English text:	Trb. 1971, 50; 860 UNTS 105; 22 UST 1641; TIAS 7192
Dutch translation:	Trb. 1971, 50
In force since:	26 September 1973 (NL); 11 July 1974 (NA, A)

91

Title:	Convention on Psychotropic Substances
Date and place:	21 February 1971, Vienna
Authentic texts:	Chinese, English, French, Russian, Spanish
English text:	Trb. 1989, 129; 1019 UNTS 175; TIAS 9725; 32 UST 543
Dutch translation:	Trb. 1989, 129
In force since:	7 December 1993 (NL)

92

Title:	Letters of Understanding between the Government of the Netherlands and the Government of India on the Applicability of the Treaty for the Extradition of Criminals between the Kingdom of the Netherlands and the United Kingdom of Great Britain and Ireland, signed at London, 26 September 1898
Date and place:	6/27 August 1971, The Hague
Authentic text:	English
English text:	Trb. 1971, 198
In force since:	The treaty of 26 September 1898 has continued without interruption to be binding upon India and the Kingdom of the Netherlands
Related to:	10

93

Title:	Convention for the Suppression of Unlawful Acts against the Safety of Civil Aviation
Date and place:	23 September 1971, Montreal
Authentic texts:	English, French, Russian, Spanish
English text:	Trb. 1971, 218; 974 UNTS 177; 24 UST 564; TIAS 7570
Dutch translation:	Trb. 1971, 218
In force since:	26 September 1973 (NL); 11 July 1974 (NA, A)
Related to:	148

94

Title:	Agreement to amend the Agreement of 3 August 1959 to Supplement the Agreement between the Parties to the North Atlantic Treaty regarding the Status of their Forces with respect to Foreign Forces Stationed in the Federal Republic of Germany.
Date and place:	21 October 1971, Bonn
Authentic texts:	English, French, German

English text:	Trb. 1972, 45
Dutch translation:	Trb. 1972, 45
In force since:	18 January 1974 (NL)
Related to:	67, 128, 174, 175, 176

95

Title:	Protocol Amending the Single Convention on Narcotic Drugs, 1961
Date and place:	25 March 1972, Geneva
Authentic texts:	Chinese, English, French, Russian, Spanish
English text:	Trb. 1980, 184; 976 UNTS 3; 26 UST 1439; TIAS 8118
Dutch translation:	Trb. 1980, 184
In force since:	28 June 1987 (Kingdom)
Related to:	68, 105

96

Title:	Convention on the prohibition of the development, production and stockpiling of bacteriological (biological) and toxin weapons and on their destruction
Date and place:	10 April 1972, London, Moscow, Washington
Authentic texts:	English, French, Chinese, Russian, Spanish
English text:	Trb. 1972, 142
Dutch translation:	Trb. 1972, 142
In force since:	22 June 1981 (Kingdom)

97

Title:	European Convention on the Transfer of Proceedings in Criminal Matters
Date and place:	15 May 1972, Strasbourg
Authentic texts:	English, French
English text:	Trb. 1973, 84; ETS 73
Dutch translation:	Trb. 1973, 84
In force since:	19 July 1985 (Kingdom)
Declarations:	1. With reference to Article 18: The Kingdom of the Netherlands requires that the documents relating to the application of the above-mentioned Convention be accompanied by a translation, unless they are drawn up in the Dutch, German, French or English language; 2. with reference to article 21, second paragraph, subparagraph d: The Kingdom of the Netherlands understands that the decision to institute proceedings includes the conditional decision not to prosecute, in so far as the conditions imposed have been met;

3. with reference to Article 43, fourth paragraph: With regard to its relations with Belgium and Luxembourg concerning the transfer of proceedings in criminal matters, the Kingdom of the Netherlands will not apply the above-mentioned Convention, but the Treaty between the Kingdom of Belgium, the Grand Duchy of Luxembourg and the Kingdom of the Netherlands on the Transfer of Proceedings in Criminal Matters, signed at Brussels on 11 May 1974.

Declaration with reference to Article 42, first paragraph ' – in the Netherlands: any unlawful behaviour to which the Traffic Regulations (Administrative Enforcement) Act *(Wet administratiefrechtelijke handhaving verkeersvoorschriften)* of 3 July 1989 (Bulletin of Acts, Orders and Decrees, 300) is applicable.'

98

Title:	Convention on International Trade in Endangered Species of Wild Fauna and Flora
Date and place:	3 March 1973, Washington
Authentic texts:	Chinese, English, French, Russian, Spanish
English text:	Trb. 1975, 23
Dutch translation:	Trb. 1975, 23
In force since:	18 July 1984 (NL), 29 March 1995 (A)

99

Title:	International Convention for the Prevention of Pollution from Ships, 1973
Date and place:	2 November 1973, London
Authentic texts:	English, French, Russian, Spanish
English text:	Trb. 1975, 147
Dutch translation:	Trb. 1978, 187
In force since:	2 October 1983 (Kingdom) as amended by the Protocol of 17 February 1978
Declaration:	1. Since the Government of the Kingdom of The Netherlands acknowledges that full compliance with the discharge requirements of Annex I by ships in contingent upon tha availability of adequate facilities for oily wastes as called for by the said Annex, it expresses its deep concerning regarding the present inadequacy of such facilities in many ports of the world;
	2. The provisions of Annex I will be implemented in compliance with the recommendations as contained in the circulars issued by the Marine Environment Protection Committee of the International

Maritime Organization, under numbers MEPC/circ. 97 and
MEPC/circ. 99.

Related to: 112

100

Title: Convention on the Prevention and Punishment of Crimes against
                            Internationally Protected Persons, Including Diplomatic Agents
Date and place: 14 December 1973, New York
Authentic texts: Chinese, English, French, Russian, Spanish
English text: Trb. 1981, 69; 28 UST 1975; TIAS 8532
Dutch translation: Trb. 1981, 69
In force since: 5 January 1989 (Kingdom)
Reservation: With regard to Article 7:
                            In cases where the judicial authorities of either the Netherlands,
                            the Netherlands Antilles or Aruba cannot exercise jurisdiction
                            pursuant to one of the principles mentioned in Article 3, paragraph
                            1, the Kingdom accepts the aforesaid obligation subject to the
                            condition that it has received and rejected a request for extradition
                            from another State Party to the Convention;
Declaration: In the view of the Government of the Kingdom of the Netherlands
                            Article 12 of the Convention, and in particular the second sentence
                            of that Article, in no way affects the applicability of Article 33 of
                            the Convention of 28 July 1951 relating to the Status of Refugees.

101

Title: European Convention on the Non-Applicability of Statutory
                            Limitations to Crimes against Humanity and War Crimes
Date and place: 25 January 1974, Strasbourg
Authentic texts: English, French
English text: Trb. 1979, 69; ETS 82
Dutch translation: Trb. 1979, 69
Editor's note: The Netherlands ratified the Convention on November 25, 1981.
                            The Convention has not entered into force yet, because the
                            condition of three ratifications has not been fulfilled.
Declaration: The offences specified in Article 85 of the Additional Protocol to
                            the Geneva Conventions of 12 August 1949, and relating to the
                            protection of victims of international armed conflicts (Protocol I)
                            of 12 December 1977 are, for the purposes of Article 1, paragraph
                            3, to be regarded as violations of a nature comparable to those
                            referred to in Article 1, paragraph 2 where these offences are
                            particularly serious in view of the actual circumstances and
                            measure of intent on the part of the perpetrator, and of the extent
                            of the foreseeable consequences.

102

Title:	Protocol to supplement and to amend the Benelux Treaty on extradition and mutual assistance in criminal matters
Date and place:	11 May 1974, Brussels
Authentic texts:	Dutch, French
Dutch text:	Trb. 1974, 161
In force since:	1 March 1982 (NL)
Related to:	69

103

Title:	Treaty between the Kingdom of the Netherlands, the Kingdom of Belgium and the Grand Duchy of Luxemburg on the transfer of proceedings in criminal matters
Date and place:	11 May 1974, Brussels
Authentic texts:	Dutch, French
Dutch text:	Trb. 1974, 184
Editor's note:	The Treaty was ratified by the Netherlands. It has however not entered into force yet, because the condition of two ratifications has not been fulfilled

104

Title:	Convention for the Prevention of Marine Pollution from Land-Based Sources
Date and place:	4 June 1974, Paris
Authentic texts:	English, French
English text:	Trb. 1975, 29
Dutch translation:	Trb. 1975, 29
In force since:	6 May 1978 (NL)
Related to:	143

105

Title:	Single Convention on Narcotic Drugs, 1961, as amended by the Protocol amending the Single Convention on Narcotic Drugs, 1961
Date and place:	8 August 1975, New York
Authentic texts:	Chinese, English, French, Russian, Spanish
English text:	Trb. 1987, 90; 976 UNTS 105
Dutch translation:	Trb. 1963, 81 and Trb. 1980, 184
In force since:	28 June 1987 (Kingdom)
Related to:	68, 95

106

Title:	Additional Protocol to the European Convention on Extradition
Date and place:	15 October 1975, Strasbourg
Authentic texts:	English, French
English text:	Trb. 1979, 119; ETS 86
Dutch translation:	Trb. 1979, 119
In force since:	12 April 1982 (NL); 21 July 1993 (NA, A)
Declaration:	The Government of the Kingdom of the Netherlands declare, in accordance with Article 6 of the aforementioned Protocol, that it does not accept Chapter I of the Protocol.
	Although Dutch legislation is fully in accordance with Article 1 (opening words and a and b) and does not contain any provisions contrary to Article 1 (opening words and c) in the case of acts committed during an international armed conflict, the Government of the Kingdom of the Netherlands wishes to reserve for itself the right to refuse extradition under Article 3 of the European Convention on Extradition in cases of violations of laws and customs of war which have been committed during a non-international armed conflict.
Related to:	60, 114

107

Title:	Agreement on Procedures for Mutual Assistance between the United States Department of Justice and the Netherlands Commisssion of Three
Date and place:	29 March 1976, Washington
Authentic text:	English
English text:	27 UST 1064; TIAS 8245; Parliamentary Proceedings (II), 1975-1976, 13787, nrs. 4-5, p. 43.
Dutch translation:	Parliamentary Proceedings (II), 1975-1976, 13787, nrs. 4-5, p. 44
In force since:	29 March 1976

108

Title:	Agreement between the Netherlands and the Republic of Suriname on Extradition and Mutual Assistance in Criminal Matters
Date and place:	27 August 1976, The Hague
Authentic text:	Dutch
Dutch text:	Trb. 1976, 143
In force since:	19 June 1981 (NL), suspended 16 December 1982, reinforced 1 October 1995 (NL) and 1 December 1995 (A)
Related to:	178

109

Title:	European Convention on the Suppression of Terrorism
Date and place:	27 January 1977, Strasbourg
Authentic texts:	English, French
English text:	Trb. 1977, 63; ETS 90
Dutch translation:	Trb. 1977, 63
In force since:	19 July 1985 (NL)
Reservation:	With due observance of Article 13, first paragraph, of the Convention, the Kingdom of the Netherlands reserves the right to refuse extradition in respect of any offence mentioned in Article 1 of the Convention including the attempt to commit or participation in one of these offences, which it considers to be a political offence or an offence connected with a political offence.
Related to:	120

110

Title:	Protocol Additional to the Geneva Conventions of 12 August 1949, and Relating to the Protection of Victims of International Armed Conflicts (Protocol I)
Date and place:	12 December 1977, Bern
Authentic texts:	Arabic, Chinese, English, French, Russian, Spanish
English text:	Trb. 1978, 41
Dutch translation:	Trb. 1980, 87
In force since:	26 December 1987 (Kingdom)
Declaration:	With regard to Article 90 paragraph 2:

The Government of the Kingdom of the Netherlands recognizes ipso facto and without special agreement in relation to any other High Contracting Party accepting the same obligation, the competence of the Commission to enquire into allegations by such other Party as authorized by this Article.

With regard to Protocol I as a whole:

It is the understanding of the Government of the Kingdom of the Netherlands that the rules introduced by Protocol I relating to the use of weapons were intended to apply and consequently do apply solely to conventional weapons, without prejudice to any other rules of international law applicable to other types of weapons.

With regard to Article 41, paragraph 3, Article 56, paragraph 2, Article 57, paragraph 2, Article 58, Article 78, paragraph 1, and Article 86, paragraph 2 of Protocol I:

It is the understanding of the Government of the Kingdom of the Netherlands that the word 'feasible' means that which is practible or practically possible, taking into account all circumstances ruling at the time, including humanitarian and military considerations;

With regard to Article 44, paragraph 3 of Protocol I:
It is the understanding of the Government of the Kingdom of the Netherlands that the words 'engaged in a military deployment' mean 'any movement towards a place from which an attack may be launched';
With regard to Article 47 of Protocol I:
It is the understanding of the Government of the Kingdom of the Netherlands that Article 47 in no way prejudices the applications of Articles 45 and 75 of Protocol I to mercenaries as defined in this Article;
With regard to Article 51, paragraph 5 and Article 57, paragraphs 2 and 3 of Protocol I:
It is the understanding of the Government of the Kingdom of the Netherlands that military advantage refers to the advantage anticipated from the attack considered as a whole and not only from isolated or particular parts of the attack;
With regard to Articles 51 to 58 inclusive of Protocol I:
It is the understanding of the Government of the Kingdom of the Netherlands that military commanders, and other responsible for planning, deciding upon or executing attacks necessarily have to reach decisions on the basis of their assessment of the information from all sources which is available to them at the relevant time;
With regard to Article 52, paragraph 2 of Protocol I:
It is the understanding of the Government of the Kingdom of the Netherlands that a specific area of land may also be a military objective if, because of its location or other reasons specified in paragraph 2, its total or partial destruction, capture, or neutralization in the circumstances ruling at the time, offers a definite military advantage;
With regard to Article 53 of Protocol I:
It is the understanding of the Government of the Kingdom of the Netherlands that if and for so long as the objects and places protected by this Article, in violation of paragraph (b), are used in support of the military effort they will thereby lose such protection.

Related to: 45, 46, 47, 48

111

Title: Protocol Additional to the Geneva Conventions of 12 August 1949, and Relating to the Protection of Victims of Non-International Armed Conflicts (Protocol II)

Date and place: 12 December 1977, Bern
Authentic texts: Arabic, Chinese, English, French, Russian, Spanish

English text:	Trb. 1978, 42
Dutch translation:	Trb. 1980, 88
In force since:	26 December 1987 (Kingdom)
Related to:	45, 46, 47, 48

112

Title:	Protocol of 1978 relating to the International Convention for the Prevention of Pollution from Ships, 1973
Date and place:	17 February 1978, London
Authentic texts:	English, French, Russian, Spanish
English text:	Trb. 1978, 188
Dutch translation:	Trb. 1978, 188
In force since:	2 October 1983 (Kingdom)
Declaration:	1. Since the Government of the Kingdom of the Netherlands acknowledges that full compliance with the discharge requirements of Annex I by ships is contingent upon the availability of adequate facilities for oily wastes as called for by the said Annex, it expresses its deep concern regarding the present inadequacy of such facilities in many ports of the world;
	2. The provisions of Annex I will be implemented in compliance with the recommendations as contained in the circulars issued by the Marine Environment Protection Committee of the International Maritime Organization, under numbers MEPC/circ.97 and MEPC/circ.99.
Objection:	(Canada) The Government refers to the declaration made by Canada at the time of its accession to the Protocol of 1978 to the International Convention for the Prevention of Pollution from Ships (MARPOL 1973) relating to Article 234 of the United Nations Convention on the Law of the Sea of 10 December 1982. The Government takes note of this declaration by Canada and considers that it should be read in conformity with Articles 57, 234 and 236 of the United Nations Convention on the Law of the Sea.
	In particular, the Government recalls that Article 234 of that Convention applies within the limits of the exclusive economic zone or of a similar zone delimited in conformity with Article 57 of the Convention and that the laws and regulations contemplated in Article 234 shall have due regard to navigation and the protection and preservation of the marine environment based on the best available scientific evidence.
Related to:	99

113

Title:	Additional Protocol to the European Convention on Information on Foreign Law
Date and place:	15 March 1978, Strasbourg
Authentic texts:	English, French
English text:	Trb. 1979, 165; ETS 97
Dutch translation:	Trb. 1979, 165
In force since:	4 September 1980 (NL); 1 January 1986 (A)
Declaration:	with regard to Article 5, paragraph 1:
	The Government of the Kingdom of the Netherlands declares that it will only be bound by Chapter I of this Protocol.
Related to:	84

114

Title:	Second Additional Protocol to the European Convention on Extradition
Date and place:	17 March 1978, Strasbourg
Authentic texts:	English, French
English text:	Trb. 1979, 120; ETS 98
Dutch translation:	Trb. 1979, 120
In force since:	5 June 1983 (NL); 21 July 1993 (NA, A)
Related to:	60, 106

115

Title:	Additional Protocol to the European Convention on Mutual Assistance in Criminal Matters
Date and place:	17 March 1978, Strasbourg
Authentic texts:	English, French
English text:	Trb. 1979, 121; ETS 99
Dutch translation:	Trb. 1979, 121
In force since:	12 April 1982 (NL); 1 January 1986 (A); 6 January 1994 (NA)
Declaration:	with regard to Article 8, paragraph 2a:
	The Government of the Kingdom of the Netherlands accepts Chapter I of the Additional Protocol, with respect to the Netherlands Antilles, only in respect of relations with States with which the Kingdom of the Netherlands, in respect of the Netherlands Antilles, has concluded a treaty on the avoidance of double taxation, that is fully in force.
Related to:	66

116

Title:	European Convention on the Control of the Acquisition and Possession of Firearms by Individuals

Date and place:	28 June 1978, Strasbourg
Authentic texts:	English, French
English text:	Trb. 1980; 123 ETS 101
Dutch translation:	Trb. 1980, 123
In force since:	1 July 1982 (Kingdom)
Reservation:	(Translation (original French))

... that the Government of the Netherlands accepts the said Convention for the Kingdom in Europe and for the Netherlands Antilles, and that the Convention so accepted shall be observed, under the reservation, provided for in Article 15, paragraph 1 of the Convention and in Annex II under A, that the Kingdom shall not apply Chapter II of the Convention concerning the objects meant under A, paragraph 1, letters j to n of Annex I of the Convention, and under the reservation, provided for in Article 15, paragraph 1 of the Convention and in Annex II, under b, that the Kingdom shall not apply Chapter III of the Convention.

Declaration: In application of the provisions of Article 9, paragraph 3 of the European Convention on the Control of the Acquisition and Possession of Firearms by Individuals, the Government of the Kingdom of the Netherlands declare to designate as the authority to which notifications as provided in that article may be sent:

– for the Netherlands: the National Bureau of Firearms *(Landelijke Vuurwapencentrale)* of the Central Investigation Service *(Centrale recherche Informatiedienst)*, and

– for the Netherlands Antilles: the Attorney-General at the Court of Justice of the Netherlands Antilles.

117

Title:	Agreement on Procedures for Mutual Assistance between the United States Department of Justice and the Ministry of Justice of the Kingdom of the Netherlands in Connection with Matters relating to the McDonnell Douglas Corporation
Date and place:	21 March 1979, Washington DC
Authentic text:	English
English text:	30 UST 2500; TIAS 9348
In force since:	21 March 1979

118

Title:	Agreement between the Kingdom of the Netherlands and the Federal Republic of Germany to supplement and to facilitate the application of the European Convention on Extradition of December 13, 1957
Date and place:	30 August 1979, Wittem

Authentic texts: Dutch, German
Dutch text: Trb. 1979, 142 and Trb. 1995, 89 (amendments)
In force since: 30 January 1983 (NL)
Related to: 60

119

Title: Agreement between the Kingdom of the Netherlands and the
                       Federal Republic of Germany to supplement and facilitate the
                       application of European Convention on Mutual Assistance in
                       Criminal Matters of April 20, 1959
Date and place: 30 August 1979, Wittem
Authentic texts: Dutch, German
Dutch text: Trb. 1979, 143 and Trb. 1995, 88 (amendments)
In force since: 30 January 1983 (NL)
Related to: 66

120

Title: Agreement concerning the application of the European Convention
                       on the Suppression of Terrorism between the Member States of
                       the European Communities
Date and place: 4 December 1979, Dublin
Authentic texts: Danish, Dutch, English, French, German, Irish, Italian
Dutch text: Trb. 1980, 14
Editor's note: The Agreement was ratified by the Netherlands, it has however
                       not entered into force yet, because the requirement that all Mem-
                       ber States of the European Communities have ratified the Conven-
                       tion, has not been fulfilled.
Related to: 109

121

Title: International Convention Against the Taking of Hostages
Date and place: 17 December 1979, New York
Authentic texts: Arabic, Chinese, English, French, Russian, Spanish
English text: Trb. 1981, 53
Dutch translation: Trb. 1981, 53
In force since: 5 January 1989 (Kingdom)
Reservation: with regard to Article 8:
                       In cases where the judicial authorities of either the Netherlands,
                       the Netherlands Antilles or Aruba cannot exercise jurisdiction
                       pursuant to one of the principles mentioned in Article 5, paragraph
                       1, the Kingdom accepts the aforesaid obligation subject to the
                       condition that it has received and rejected a request for extradition
                       from another State Party to the Convention.

Declaration:	In the view of the Government of the Kingdom of the Netherlands Article 15 of the Convention, and in particular the second sentence of that Article, in no way affects the applicability of Article 33 of the Convention of 28 July 1951 relating to the Status of Refugees.

122

Title:	Convention on the Elimination of All Forms of Discrimination against Women
Date and place:	18 December 1979, New York
Authentic texts:	Arabic, Chinese, English, French, Russian, Spanish
English text:	Trb. 1980, 146
Dutch translation:	Trb. 1981, 61
In force since:	22 August 1991 (Kingdom)
Declaration:	During the preparatory stages of the present Convention and in the course of debates on it in General Assembly the position of the Government of the Kingdom of the Netherlands was that it was not desirable to introduce political considerations such as those contained in paragraphs 10 and 11 of the preamble in a legal instrument of this nature. Moreover, the considerations are not directly related to the achievement of total equality between men and women. The Government of the Kingdom of the Netherlands considers that it must recall its objections to the said paragraphs in the preamble at this occassion.
Objections:	The Government of the Kingdom of the Netherlands objects to the following declarations and reservations: The Government of the Kingdom of the Netherlands considers that the reservations made by Bangladesh regarding article 2, article 13 (a) and article 16, paragraph 1 (c) and (f), by Egypt regarding article 2, article 9 and article 16, by Brazil regarding article 15, paragraph 4, and article 16, paragraph 1 (a), (c), (g) and (h), by Iraq regarding article 2, paragraphs (f) and (g), article 9 and article 16, by Mauritius regarding article 11, paragraph 1 (b) and (d) and article 16, paragraph 1 (g), by Jamaica regarding article 9, paragraph 2, by the Republic of Korea, regarding article 9 and article 16, paragraph 1 (c), (d), (f) and (g) by Thailand regarding article 9, paragraph 2, article 15, paragraph 3 and article 16, by Tunisia regarding article 9, paragraph 2, article 15, paragraph 4, and article 16, paragraph 1 (c), (d), (f), (g) and (h), by Turkey regarding article 15, paragraphs 2 and 4, and article 16, paragraph 1 (c), (d), (f) and (g), are incompatible with the object and purpose of the Convention (article 28, paragraph 2). The Government of the Kingdom of the Netherlands has examined the contents of the reservation made by the Libyan Arab Jama-

hiriya, by which the accession 'is made subject to the general reservation that such accession cannot conflict with the laws on personal status derived from the Islamic Shariah', and considers the said reservation imcompatible with the object and purpose of the Convention.

The Government of the Kingdom of the Netherlands has also examined the reservations made by the Republic of Malawi, by which 'owing to the deep-rooted nature of some traditional customs and practices of Malawians, the Government of the Republic of Malawi shall not, for the time being, consider itself bound by such provisions of the Convention as require immediate eradication of such traditional customs and practices', and considers the said reservations imcompatible with the object and purpose of the Convention.

The Government of the Kingdom of the Netherlands therefore objects to the abovementioned reservations.

These objections shall not preclude the entry into force of the Convention as between Bangladesh, Egypt, Brazil, Iraq, Mauritius, Jamaica, the Republic of Korea, Thailand, Tunisia, Turkey, Libyan, Arab Jamahiriya, Malawi and the Kingdom of the Netherlands.

The Government of the Kingdom of the Netherlands considers that the declarations made by India regarding Article 5 (a) and Article 16, paragraph 1, of the Convention are reservations incompatible with the object and purpose of the Convention (Article 28, paragraph 2).

The Government of the Kingdom of the Netherlands considers that the declaration made by India regarding Article 16, paragraph 2, of the Convention is a reservation incompatible with the object and purpose of the Convention (Article 28, paragraph 2).

The Government of the Kingdom of the Netherlands considers that the declaration made by Morocco expressing the readiness of Morocco to apply the provisions of Article 2 provided that they do not conflict with the provisions of the Islamic Shariah, is a reservation incompatible with the object and purpose of the Convention (Article 28, paragraph 2).

The Government of the Kingdom of the Netherlands considers that the declaration made by Morocco regarding Article 15, paragraph 4, of the Convention is a reservation incompatible with the object and purpose of the Convention (Article 28, paragraph 2).

The Government of the Kingdom of the Netherlands considers that the reservations made by Morocco regarding Article 9, paragraph 2, and Article 16 of the Convention are reservations incompatible with the object and purpose of the Convention (Article 28, paragraph 2).

The Government of the Kingdom of the Netherlands has examined the reservations made by the Maldives,.....The Government of the Kingdom of the Netherlands considers the said reservations incompatible with the object and purpose of the Convention.

The Government of the Kingdom of the Netherlands objects to the abovementioned declarations and reservations.

These objections shall not preclude the entry into force of the Convention as between India, Morocco, the Maldives and the Kingdom of the Netherlands.

123

Title:	Convention on the Physical Protection of Nuclear Material
Date and place:	3 March 1980, Vienna/New York
Authentic texts:	Arabic, Chinese, English, French, Russian, Spanish
English text:	Trb. 1980, 166; TIAS 11080
Dutch translation:	Trb. 1981, 7
In force since:	6 October 1991 (NL)
Reservation:	... the Kingdom of the Netherlands makes the reservation, that in cases where the judicial authorities of the Netherlands are unable to exercise jurisdiction on the grounds of one of the principles referred to in Article 8, paragraph 1, of the Convention, the Kingdom shall be bound by this obligation only if it has received an extradition request from a Party to the Convention and the said request has been rejected.

124

Title:	Extradition Treaty between the Kingdom of the Netherlands and the United States of America
Date and place:	24 June 1980, The Hague
Authentic texts:	Dutch, English
English text:	Trb. 1980, 111; TIAS 10733
Dutch text:	Trb. 1980, 111
In force since:	15 September 1983 (Kingdom)

125

Title:	Convention on Prohibitions or Restrictions on the Use of Certain Conventional Weapons which may be deemed to be Excessively Injurious or to have Indiscriminate Effects
Date and place:	10 October 1980, Geneva
Authentic texts:	Arabic, Chinese, English, French, Russian, Spanish
English text:	Trb. 1981, 154

Dutch translation:	Trb. 1982, 52
In force since:	18 December 1987 (NL)
Declarations:	With regard to Article 2, paragraph 4, of Protocol II; It is the understanding of the Government of the Kingdom of the Netherlands that a specific area of land may also be a military objective if, because of its location or other reasons specified in paragraph 4, its total or partial destruction, capture, or neutralization in the circumstances ruling at a time, offers a definitive military advantage;
	With regard to Article 3, paragraph 3, under C, of Protocol II: It is the understanding of the Government of the Kingdom of the Netherlands that military advantage refers to the advantage anticipated from the attack considered as a whole and not only from isolated or particular parts of the attack;
	With regard to Article 8, paragraph 1, of Protocol II: It is the understanding of the Kingdom of the Netherlands that the words 'as far as it is able' mean 'as far as it is technically able'.
	With regard to Article 1, paragraph 3, of Protocol III: It is the understanding of the Government of the Kingdom of the Netherlands that a specific area of land may also be a military objective if, because of its location or other reasons specified in paragraph 3, its total or partial destruction, capture, or neutralization in the circumstances ruling at the time, offers a definitive military advantage.
Related to:	205, 209

126

Title:	Exchange of letters between the Government of the Kingdom of the Netherlands and the Bahamas regarding the applicability of the Extradition Treaty between the Kingdom of the Netherlands and the United Kingdom of Great Britain and Ireland, signed at London on 26th September 1898
Date and place:	18 November 1980/28 May 1985, Kingston/Nassau
Authentic text:	English
English text:	Trb. 1986, 119
Dutch translation:	Trb. 1986, 119
In force since:	28 June 1988 (Kingdom)
Related to:	10

127

Title:	Convention for the Protection of Individuals with Regard to Automatic Processing of Personal Data
Date and place:	28 January 1981, Strasbourg

Authentic texts:	English, French
English text:	Trb. 1988, 7; ETS 108
Dutch translation:	Trb. 1988, 7
In force since:	1 December 1993 (NL)
Declarations:	In accordance with article 24, first paragraph, the Convention shall apply to the Kingdom in Europe.

Pursuant to article 3, second paragraph, under a, of the Convention, the Kingdom of the Netherlands (for the Kingdom in Europe) declares that:

I. the Convention shall not apply to the following personal data files:

– personal data files which are by their nature intended for personal or domestic use;

– personal data files kept exclusively for public informations purposes by the press, radio or television;

– books and other written publications, or index systems pertaining to them;

– personal data files kept in archives repositories designated for that purpose by law;

– personal data files which are established and to which public access is required by law;

– personal data files kept for the purpose of implementing the Elections Act *(Kieswet)*;

II. the Convention shall as yet not apply to the following personal data files:

– personal data files established under or pursuant to the Criminal Records and Certificates of Good Behaviour Act *(Wet op de justitiële documentatie en op de verklaringen omtrent het gedrag)*;

– personal data files established pursuant to the Population and Residence Registers Act *(Wet bevolkings- en verblijfsregisters)*;

– the central register of students in higher education, established under the University Education Act, the Higher Vocational Education Act and the Open University Act *(Wet op het wetenschappelijk onderwijs, Wet op het hoger beroepsonderwijs, Wet op de open universiteit)*; and

– files of registered vehicle registration marks and of issued driving licences, established pursuant to the Road Traffic Act *(Wegenverkeerswet)*.

In accordance with article 13, second paragraph, under a, of the Convention the authority designated by the Kingdom of the Netherlands (for the Kingdom in Europe) is:

Registratiekamer

Postbus 3011

NL-2280 GA Rijswijk
The Netherlands
tel: + (70) 3190190
tel: + (70) 3940460

128

Title: Agreement to amend the Protocol of Signature to the Agreement
                     of 3 August 1959 to Supplement the Agreement between the
                     Parties to the North Atlantic Treaty regarding the Status of their
                     Forces with respect to Foreign Forces stationed in the Federal
                     Republic of Germany as amended by the Agreement of 21 Octo-
                     ber 1971
Date and place: 18 May 1981, Bonn
Authentic texts: English, French, German
English text: Trb. 1981, 168
Dutch translation: Trb. 1981, 168
In force since: 8 August 1982 (NL)
Related to: 67, 94, 174, 175, 176

129

Title: Treaty between the Kingdom of the Netherlands and the United
                     States of America on Mutual Assistance in Criminal Matters
Date and place: 12 June 1981, The Hague
Authentic texts: Dutch, English
English text: Trb. 1981, 188
Dutch text: Trb. 1981, 188
In force since: 15 September 1983 (Kingdom)
Declaration: with reference to Article 20, second paragraph:
                     (...) this Treaty shall not apply to requests for assistance relating
                     to fiscal offences addressed to the Netherlands Antilles. With-
                     drawn with regard to Aruba on 16 June 1993

130

Title: Letters of understanding between the Government of the Nether-
                     lands and the Government of New Zealand on the Applicability of
                     the Treaty for the Extradition of Criminals between the Kingdom
                     of the Netherlands and the United Kingdom of Great Britain and
                     Ireland, signed at London, 26 September 1898
Date and place: 9 June 1982, Wellington
Authentic text: English
English text: Trb. 1982, 103

In force since: The Treaty of 26 September 1898 has continued without interruption to be binding upon New Zealand and the Netherlands
Related to: 10

131

Title: United Nations Convention on the Law of the Sea
Date and place: 10 December 1982, Montego Bay
Authentic texts: Arabic, Chinese, English, French, Russian, Spanish
English text: Trb. 1983, 83
Dutch translation: Trb. 1984, 55
In force since: 28 July 1996 (NL)
Declaration: in respect of article 287 of the Convention:
                       The Kingdom of the Netherlands hereby declares that, having regard to Article 287 of the Convention, it accepts the jurisdiction of the International Court of Justice in the settlement of disputes concerning the interpretation and application of the Convention with States Parties to the Convention which have likewise accepted the said jurisdiction.
Objections: The Kingdom of the Netherlands objects to any declaration or statement excluding or modifying the legal effect of the provisions of the United Nations Convention on the Law of the Sea.
                       This is particularly the case with regard to the following matters:
                       I. Innocent passage in the territorial sea
                       The Convention permits innocent passage in the territorial sea for all ships, including foreign warships, nuclear-powered ships and ships carrying nuclear or hazardous waste, without any prior consent or notification, and with due observance of special precautionary measures established for such ships by international agreements.
                       II. Exclusive economic zone
                       1. Passage through the Exclusive Economic Zone
                       Nothing in the Convention restricts the freedom of navigation of nuclear-powered ships or ships carrying nuclear of hazardous waste in the Exclusive Economic Zone, provided such navigation is in accordance with the applicable rules of international law. In particular, the Convention does not authorize the coastal state to make the navigation of such ships in the EEZ dependent on prior consent or notification.
                       2. Military exercises in the Exclusive Economic Zone
                       The Convention does not authorize the coastal state to prohibit military exercises in its EEZ. The rights of the coastal state in its EEZ are listed in article 56 of the Convention, and no such authority is given to the coastal state. In the EEZ all states enjoy

the freedoms of navigation and overflight, subject to the relevant provisions of the Convention.

3. Installations in the Exclusive Economic Zone

The coastal state enjoys the right to authorize, operate and use installations and structures in the EEZ for economic purposes. Jurisdiction over the establishment and use of installations and structures is limited to the rules contained in article 56 paragraph 1, and is subject to the obligations contained in article 56 paragraph 2, article 58 and article 60 of the Convention.

4. Residual rights

The coastal state does not enjoy residual rights in the EEZ. The rights of the coastal state in its EEZ are listed in article 56 of the Convention, and can not be extended unilaterally.

III. Passage through straits

Routes and sealanes through straits shall be established in accordance with the rules provided for in the Convention. Considerations with respect to domestic security and public order shall not affect navigation in straits used for international navigation. The application of other international instruments to straits is subject to the relevant articles of the Convention.

IV. Archipelagic States

The application of Part IV of the Convention is limited to a state constituted wholly by one or more archipelagos, and may include other islands. Claims to archipelagic status in contravention of article 46 are not acceptable.

The status of archipelagic state, and the rights and obligations deriving from such status, can only be invoked under the conditions of part IV of the Convention.

V. Fisheries

The Convention confers no jurisdiction on the coastal state with respect to the exploitation, conservation and management of living marine resources other than sedentary species beyond the Exclusive Economic Zone.

The Kingdom of the Netherlands considers that the conservation and management of straddling fish stocks and highly migratory species should, in accordance with articles 63 and 64 of the Convention, take place on the basis of international cooperation in appropriate subregional and regional organizations.

VI. Underwater cultural heritage

Jurisdiction over objects of an archaeological and historical nature found at sea is limited to articles 149 and 303 of the Convention. The Kingdom of the Netherlands does however consider that there may be a need to further develop, in international cooperation, the international law on the protection of underwater cultural heritage.

VII. Baselines and delimitation

A claim that the drawing of baselines or the delimitation of maritime zones is in accordance with the Convention will only be acceptable if such lines and zones have been established in accordance with the Convention.

VIII. National legislation

As a general rule of international law, as stated in articles 27 and 46 of the Vienna Convention on the Law of Treaties, states may not rely on national legislation as a justification for a failure to implement the Convention.

IX. Territorial claims

Ratification by the Kingdom of the Netherlands does not imply recognition or acceptance of any territorial claim made by a State Party to the Convention.

X. Article 301

Article 301 must be interpreted,in accordance with the Charter of the United Nations, as applying to the territory and the territorial sea of a coastal state.

XI. General declaration

The Kingdom of the Netherlands reserves its right to make further declarations relative to the Convention and to the Agreement, in response to future declarations and statements.

C. Declaration in accordance with Annex IX of the Convention
Upon depositing its instrument of ratification the Kingdom of the Netherlands recalls that, as Member State of the European Community, it has transferred competence to the Community with respect to certain matters governed by the Convention. A detailed declaration on the nature and extent of the competence transferred to the European Community will be made in due course in accordance with the provisions in Annex IX of the Convention.

132

Title:	European Convention on the Transfer of Sentenced Persons
Date and place:	21 March 1983, Strasbourg
Authentic texts:	English, French
English text:	Trb. 1983, 74; ETS 112; TIAS 10824
Dutch translation:	Trb. 1983, 74
In force since:	1 January 1988 (NL), 1 June 1996 (NA/A)
Declaration:	With regard to Article 3, paragraph 4, of the Convention:

As far as The Kingdom of the Netherlands is concerned, the term 'national' should include all those who fall under the provisions of the Act governing the position of Moluccans of 9 September 1976, (Bulletins of Acts, Orders and Decrees 468), as well as

aliens or stateless persons whose only place of ordinary residence (résidence habituelle) is within the Kingdom and who, according to a statement to this effect issued to the government of the sentencing State by the Netherlands government, do not, under the terms of the present Convention, lose their right of residence in the Kingdom as a result of the execution of a punishment or measures.
With regard to Article 17, paragraph 3, of the Convention:
Documents submitted to the Kingdom should be drawn up in Dutch, French, English or German, or accompanied by a translation in one of the above four languages.

Related to: 145

133
Title: Protocol No. 6 to the Convention for the protection of Human Rights and Fundamental Freedoms concerning the abolition of the death penalty
Date and place: 28 April 1983, Strasbourg
Authentic texts: English, French
English text: Trb. 1983, 86; ETS 114
Dutch translation: Trb. 1990, 160
In force since: 1 May 1986 (Kingdom)
Declaration: On the occasion of the deposit today of the instrument of acceptance by the Kingdom of the Netherlands of Protocol No. 6 to the Convention for the Protection of Human Rights and Fundamental Freedoms concerning the abolition of the death penalty, done at Strasbourg on 28 April 1983, I have the honour to state, on behalf of the Government of the Kingdom of the Netherlands that the bills for the abolition of capital punishment, insofar as it is still provided for under Dutch military law and Dutch regulations governing wartime offences, have been before Parliament since 1981. It should be noted, however, that under the provisions of the Constitution of the Netherlands, which came into force on 17 February 1983, capital punishment may not be imposed. Futhermore, I have the honour to communicate herewith, in accordance with Article 2 of the said Protocol, the sections 103 and 108 of the criminal code of the Netherlands Antilles and Aruba.

Sections 103 and 108 of the Criminal Code of the Netherlands Antilles and Aruba
103. Any person who enters into an understanding with a foreign power with a view to inducing that power to engage in hostilities or wage war against the State, to strengthening its resolve to do

so, or to promising or providing assistance in the preparation of such acts, shall be liable to a prison sentence of a maximum of fifteen years.

If the hostilities are carried out or a state of war occurs, the death sentence, life imprisonment, or a determinate prison sentence of a maximum of twenty years shall be imposed:

108. Any person who in time of war intentionally aids an enemy of the State or disadvantages the State in relation to an enemy, shall be liable to a determinate prison sentence of a maximum of fifteen years. Life imprisonment or a determinate prison sentence of a maximum of twenty years shall be imposed if the offender:

1° informs or gives the enemy possession of any maps, plans, drawings or descriptions of military facilities or supplies any information relating to military operations or plans; or

2° acts as a spy for the enemy or assists, shelters or conceals an enemy spy.

The death penalty, life imprisonment or a determinate prison sentence of a maximum of twenty years shall be imposed if the offender:

1° destroys, renders unusable or betrays to the enemy or puts the enemy in possession of any fortified or manned location or post, any means of communication, any military supplies, any war funds, any resticted area (PB 1965, 69), or the navy or army of any part thereof, or if he hinders, impedes or sabotages any defensive or offensive flooding operations, whether planned or executed, or any other military operation.

2° causes or incites insurrection, mutiny or desertion among service personnel.

Related to: 50, 53, 72, 137

134

Title:	European Convention on the Compensation of Victims of Violent Crimes
Date and place:	24 November 1983, Strasbourg
Authentic texts:	English, French
English text:	Trb. 1984, 2; ETS 116
Dutch translation:	Trb. 1984, 2
In force since:	1 February 1988 (NL)
Declaration:	with reference to Article 12:

The Kingdom of the Netherlands designated as the central authority: Secretaris van de Commissie tot beheer van het schadefonds geweldsmisdrijven, Postbus 20303, 2500 EH 's-Gravenhage.

135

Title:	Agreement between the Kingdom of the Netherlands and the Kingdom of Norway on mutual administrative assistance in customs matters
Date and place:	20 December 1983, Oslo
Authentic texts:	Dutch, English, Norwegian
English text:	Trb. 1984, 8
Dutch text:	Trb. 1984, 8
In force since:	18 April 1984 (NL)

136

Title:	Agreement between the Kingdom of the Netherlands and the Republic of Finland on mutual assistance in customs matters
Date and place:	4 April 1984, The Hague
Authentic text:	English
English text:	Trb. 1984, 39
Dutch translation:	Trb. 1984, 39
In force since:	19 June 1985 (NL)

137

Title:	Protocol No. 7 to the Convention for the Protection of Human Rights and Fundamental Freedoms
Date and place:	22 November 1984, Strasbourg
Authentic texts:	English, French
English text:	Trb. 1985, 2: ETS 117
Dutch translation:	Trb. 1990, 161
Declaration:	The Netherlands Government interprets paragraph 1 of Article 2 thus that the right conferred to everyone convicted of a criminal offence to have conviction or sentence reviewed by a higher tribunal relates only to convictions or sentences given in the first instance by tribunals which according to Netherlands law are in charge of jurisdiction in criminal matters.
Related to:	50, 53, 72, 133

138

Title:	Convention against Torture and Other Cruel, Inhuman or Degrading Treatment or Punishment
Date and place:	10 December 1984, New York
Authentic texts:	Arabic, Chinese, English, French, Russian, Spanish
English text:	Trb. 1985, 69
Dutch translation:	Trb. 1985, 69
In force since:	20 January 1989 (Kingdom)

Declaration: It is the understanding of the Government of the Kingdom of the Netherlands that the term 'lawful sanctions' in Article 1, paragraph 1, must be understood as referring to those sanctions which are lawful not only under national law but also under international law.

The Government of the Kingdom of the Netherlands hereby declares that it recognizes the competence of the Committee against Torture, under the conditions laid down in Article 21, to receive and consider communications to the effect that another State Party claims that the Kingdom is not fulfilling its obligations under this convention.

The Government of the Kingdom of the Netherlands hereby declares that it recognizes the competence of the Committee against Torture, under the conditions laid down in Article 22, to receive and consider communications from or on behalf of individuals subject to its jurisdiction who claim to be victims of a violation by the Kingdom of the provisions of the Convention.

On 24 January 1995 the Kingdom of the Netherlands accepted the Secretary General's proposal of 28 February 1992 (text in English, Trb. 1993, 42) to change Articles 17 and 18 of the Treaty.

139

Title: Agreement between the Kingdom of the Netherlands and the Kingdom of Sweden on mutual assistance in customs matters
Date and place: 20 March 1985, Stockholm
Authentic text: English
English text: Trb. 1985, 64
Dutch translation: Trb. 1985, 64
In force since: 19 January 1986 (NL)

140

Title: Agreement between the Governments of the States of the Benelux Economic Union, the Federal Republic of Germany and the French Republic, on the Gradual Abolition of Checks at their Common Borders
Date and place: 14 June 1985, Schengen
Authentic texts: Dutch, French, German
Dutch text: Trb. 1985, 102
In force since: 2 March 1986 (NL)
Related to: 161

141
Title: European Convention on Spectator Violence and Misbehaviour at
                            Sport Events in Particular at Football Matches
Date and place: 19 August 1985, Strasbourg
Authentic texts: English, French
English text: Trb. 1985, 133; ETS 120
Dutch translation: Trb. 1985, 133
In force since: 1 February 1989 (NL)

142
Title: Treaty on Extradition between the Kingdom of the Netherlands
                            and Australia
Date and place: 5 September 1985, The Hague
Authentic texts: Dutch, English
English text: Trb. 1985, 137
Dutch text: Trb. 1985, 137
In force since: 1 February 1988 (Kingdom)

143
Title: Protocol amending the Convention for the Prevention of Marine
                            Pollution from Land-Based Sources
Date and place: 26 March 1986, Paris
Authentic texts: English, French
English text: Trb. 1986, 87
Dutch translation: Trb. 1986, 87
In force since: 1 September 1989 (NL)
Related to: 104

144
Title: Convention between the Member States of the European Com-
                            munities on Double Jeopardy
Date and place: 25 May 1987, Brussels
Authentic texts: Dutch, English, French, German, Greek, Irish, Italian, Portuguese,
                            Spanish
English text: Trb. 1987, 167
Dutch text: Trb. 1987, 167
In force since: Provisional application accepted by the Netherlands as of 6
                            January 1994 (Kingdom)
Declaration: Designated authority as meant in Article 4, paragraph 3:
                            For the Netherlands:
                            The Ministry of Justice in The Hague
                            For the Netherlands Antilles:
                            The Ministry of Justice in Willemstad, Curaçao

For Aruba:
The Ministry of Justice in Oranjestad, Aruba

145

Title:	Agreement on the Application among the Member States of the European Communities of the Council of Europe Convention on the Transfer of Sentenced Persons
Date and place:	25 May 1987, Brussels
Authentic texts:	Danish, Dutch, English, French, German, Greek, Irish, Italian, Portuguese, Spanish
English text:	Trb. 1987, 168
Dutch text:	Trb. 1987, 168
Related to:	132

146

Title:	European Convention for the Prevention of Torture and Inhuman or Degrading Treatment or Punishment
Date and place:	26 November 1987, Strasbourg
Authentic texts:	English, French
English text:	Trb. 1988, 19; ETS 126
Dutch translation:	Trb. 1988, 19
In force since:	1 February 1989 (Kingdom)
Declaration:	with reference to Article 15: The Kingdom of the Netherlands informed the Committee of the name and address of the authority: Ministerie van Buitenlandse Zaken, Directie Raad van Europa en Wetenschappelijke Samenwerking, Bureau Raad van Europa, Bezuidenhoutseweg 67, 2594 AC 's-Gravenhage.

147

Title:	Convention on Mutual Administrative Assistance in Tax Matters
Date and place:	25 January 1988, Strasbourg
Authentic texts:	English, French
English text:	Trb. 1991, 4; ETS 127
Dutch translation:	Trb. 1991, 4
In force since:	1 February 1997 (Kingdom)
Reservation:	The Kingdom of the Netherlands (for the Netherlands) declares in accordance with Article 30, paragraph 1 (a), (b), (c) and (d) of the Convention that it reserves the right: – not to provide assistance in relation to the taxes of other Parties listed in Article 2, paragraph 1, (b), (i), (iii), letters B, C, D, E, F and G, and (iv);

– not to provide assistance in respect of any tax claim which is in existence on the date of entry into force of the Convention for the Kingdom of the Netherlands (for the Netherlands);

– not to provide assistance in the service of documents for all taxes.

The Kingdom of the Netherlands (for the Netherlands Antilles and Aruba) declares in accordance with Article 30, paragraph 1 (a), (b), (c), (d) and (e) of the Convention that it reserves the right:

– not to provide assistance in relation to the taxes of other Parties listed in Article 2, paragraph 1, (b);

– not to provide assistance in the recovery of any tax claim, or in the recovery of an administrative fine, for all taxes;

– not to provide assistance in respect of any tax claim which is in existence on the date of entry into force of the Convention for the Kingdom of the Netherlands (for the Netherlands Antilles and Aruba);

– not to provide assistance in the service of documents for all taxes;

– not to permit the service of documents through the post as provided for in paragraph 3 of Article 17.

Declarations: The Kingdom of the Netherlands (for the Netherlands) declares:

– in accordance with Article 4, paragraph 3, that its authorities may inform its resident or national before transmitting information concerning him, in conformity with Articles 5 and 7;

– in accordance with Article 9, paragraph 3, that it will not accept, as a general rule, the requests as referred to in Article 9, paragraph 1, of the Convention, in sofar as these requests concern social security contributions.

The Kingdom of the Netherlands (for the Netherlands Antilles and Aruba) declares:

– in accordance with Article 4, paragraph 3, that its authorities may inform its resident or national before transmitting information concerning him, in conformity with Articles 5 and 7;

– in accordance with Article 9, paragraph 3, that it will not accept, as a general rule, the requests as referred to in Article 9, paragraph 1, of the Convention.

The Kingdom of the Netherlands will apply the Convention to the Netherlands Antilles and Aruba only in respect of Parties to this Convention with which the Kingdom of the Netherlands has concluded a convention for the avoidance of double taxation which is applicable to the Netherlands Antilles and/or Aruba and which contains a provision concerning exchange of information.

Article 30, paragraph 2, of the Convention prohibits other reservations than those explicitly allowed under paragraph 1 of Article

30. In the present context, this means that all reservations further limiting the application of provisions of the Convention are prohibited. The declaration made in respect to the Netherlands Antilles and Aruba, however, is of a different nature as it refers to territorial application and does not, in the view of the Netherlands Government, constitute a reservation prohibited under Article 30 of the Convention. The Netherlands Antilles and Aruba will observe the Convention in relation to those Parties to the Convention with which a convention for the avoidance of double taxation has been concluded.

Annex A
Taxes to which the Convention applies:
for the Netherlands:
Article 2, paragraph 1 (a)
– Income Tax *(Inkomstenbelasting)*
– Salaries Tax *(Loonbelasting)*
– Corporation Tax *(Vennootschapsbelasting)*
– Dividend Tax *(Dividendbelasting)*
– Wealth Tax *(Vermogensbelasting)*
Article 2, paragraph 1 (b)
– Social Security Contributions *(Premies sociale verzekering)*
Article 2, paragraph 1 (c)
– Inheritance, Transfer or Gift Tax *(Rechten van successie, overgang of schenking)*
for the Netherlands Antilles:
Article 2, paragraph 1 (a)
– Income Tax *(Inkomstenbelasting)*
– Salaries Tax *(Loonbelasting)*
– Corporation Tax *(Winstbelasting)*
for Aruba:
Article 2, paragraph 1 (a)
– Income Tax *(Inkomstenbelasting)*
– Salaries Tax *(Loonbelasting)*
– Corporation Tax *(Winstbelasting)*

Annex B
Competent Authorities for the Netherlands:
– For tax purposes: the Minister of Finance or his authorised representative
– For social security purposes: the State Secretary for Social Affairs and Employment or his authorised representative

Competent Authorities for the Netherlands Antilles:
The Minister of Finance or his authorised representative
Competent Authorities for Aruba:
The Minister of Finance or his authorised representative

Annex C
Definition of the term 'national' for the purpose of the Convention:
The term 'national' means for the Netherlands:
1. all individuals possessing the Dutch nationality;
2. all legal persons, companies and associations deriving their status as such from the laws in force in the Netherlands.
The term 'national' means for the Netherlands Antilles:
1. all individuals possessing the Dutch nationality;
2. all legal persons, companies and associations deriving their status as such from the laws in force in the Netherlands Antilles.
The term 'national' means for Aruba:
1. all individuals possessing the Dutch nationality and having a legally valid title of residence for Aruba;
2. all legal persons, companies and associations deriving their status as such from the laws in force in Aruba.

148

Title: Protocol for the Suppression of Unlawful Acts of Violence at Airports Serving International Civil Aviation, Supplementary to the Convention for the Suppression of Unlawful Acts against the Safety of Civil Aviation, Done at Montreal on 23 September 1971

Date and place: 24 February 1988, Montreal
Authentic texts: English, French, Russian, Spanish
English text: Trb. 1988, 88
Dutch translation: Trb. 1988, 88
In force since: 10 August 1995 (NL)
Declaration: The Government of the Kingdom of the Netherlands hereby declares that, in the light of the preamble, it understands the provisions laid down in Article II and III of the Protocol to signify the following:
— only those acts which, in view of the nature of the weapons used and the place where they are committed, cause or are likely to cause incidental loss of life or serious injury among the general public or users of international civil aviation in particular, shall be classed as acts of violence within the meaning of the new paragraph 1 *bis* (a), as contained in Article II of the Protocol;

– only those acts which, in view of the damage which they cause to buildings or aircraft at the airport or their disruption of the services provided by the airport, endanger or are likely to to endanger the safe operation of the airport in relation to international civil aviation, shall be classed as acts of violence within the meaning of the new paragraph 1 *bis* (b), as contained in Article II of the Protocol.

Editor's note: The Act of 30 March 1995 (Stb. 194), approving the Protocol contained the following reservation which was not published in the Trb.

(Translation (original Dutch))

The Kingdom of the Netherlands will be bound by the obligation to exercise jurisdiction, as laid down in Article III of the Protocol, only after it has received and rejected a request for extradition from the Contracting State on whose territory the offence was committed.

Related to: 93

149

Title: Convention for the Suppression of Unlawful Acts against the Safety of Maritime Navigation

Date and place: 10 March 1988, Rome

Authentic texts: Arabic, Chinese, English, French, Russian, Spanish

English text: Trb. 1989, 17

Dutch translation: Trb. 1989, 17

In force since: 3 June 1992 (Kingdom)

Reservation: With regard to the obligation laid down in article 1 of the Protocol in conjunction with article 10 of the Convention for the Suppression of Unlawful Acts against the Safety of Maritime Navigation to exercise jurisdiction in cases where the judicial authorities of the Netherlands cannot exercise jurisdiction on any of the grounds referred to in article 3, paragraph 1, of the Protocol, the Government of the Kingdom of the Netherlands reserves the right to be bound to exercise such jurisdiction only after the Kingdom has received and rejected a request for extradition from a State Party.

Related to: 150

150

Title: Protocol for the Suppression of Unlawful Acts against the Safety of Fixed Platforms located on the Continental Shelf

Date and place: 10 March 1988, Rome

Authentic texts: Arabic, Chinese, English, French, Russian, Spanish

English text:	Trb. 1989, 18
Dutch translation:	Trb. 1989, 18
In force since:	3 June 1992 (Kingdom)
Reservation:	With regard to the obligation laid down in article 1 of the Protocol in conjunction with article 10 of the Convention for the Suppression of Unlawful Acts against the Safety of Maritime Navigation to exercise jurisdiction in cases where the judicial authorities of the Netherlands cannot exercise jurisdiction on any of the grounds referred to in article 3, paragraph 1, of the Protocol, the Government of the Kingdom of the Netherlands reserves the right to be bound to exercise such jurisdiction only after the Kingdom has received and rejected a request for extradition from a State Party.
Related to:	149

151

Title:	Agreement between the Kingdom of the Netherlands and the Republic of Venezuela on prevention, control and suppression of the abuse of illicit traffic in and the illicit production of narcotic drugs, psychotropic substances and related chemical substances thereto, with annex
Date and place:	29 August 1988, Oranjestad
Authentic texts:	Dutch, Spanish
Dutch text:	Trb. 1988, 136
In force since:	2 August 1989 (Kingdom)

152

Title:	Treaty between the Kingdom of the Netherlands and Australia on Mutual Assistance in Criminal Matters
Date and place:	26 October 1988, Canberra
Authentic texts:	Dutch, English
English text:	Trb. 1989, 13
Dutch text:	Trb. 1989, 13
In force since:	1 June 1991 (Kingdom)
Editor's note:	Article 18 is not applicable to Aruba and Netherlands Antilles

153

Title:	United Nations Convention against Illicit Traffic in Narcotic Drugs and Psychotropic Substances
Date and place:	20 December 1988, Vienna
Authentic texts:	Arabic, Chinese, English, French, Russian, Spanish
English text:	Trb. 1989, 97
Dutch translation:	Trb. 1990, 94

In force since:	7 December 1993 (NL)
Reservation:	The Government of the Kingdom of the Netherlands accepts the provisions of Article 3, paragraph 6, 7 and 8 only in so far as the obligations under these provisions are in accordance with Dutch criminal legislation and Dutch policy on criminal matters.
Declarations:	With reference to Article 7, paragraph 9, of the Convention: Requests for mutual assistance which are not made in Dutch, English, French or German shall be accompanied by a translation in one of these languages.

with reference to Article 5, paragraph 4 (d), of the Convention: The declarations made for the Netherlands under Article 7, paragraph 8 and 9, are applicable.

With reference to Article 7, paragraph 8:
The Kingdom of the Netherlands designated the authority:
Het Hoofd van de Afdeling Internationale rechtshulp
Ministerie van Justitie
Postbus 20301
2500 EH 's Gravenhage
Nederland

With reference to Article 17, paragraph 7: The Kingdom of the Netherlands designated the authority:
de Centrale Recherche Informatiedienst
t.a.v. Landelijke Officier van Justitie
Stafbureau Openbaar Ministerie
Postbus 20302
2500 EH 's-Gravenhage
Nederland
telefoon: (31)703600846 of (31)79459888
telex: 31152
telefax: (31)703658915 of (31)79458754

Objection:	(Brazil) The Kingdom of the Netherlands, Member State of the European Community, attached to the principle of freedom of navigation, notably in the exclusive economic zone, considers that the declaration of Brazil concerning paragraph 11 of article 17 of the United Nations Convention against Illicit Traffic in Narcotic Drugs and Psychotropic Substances, adopted in Vienna on 20 December 1988, goes further than the rights according to coastal states by international law.

154

Title:	Convention on Insider Trading

Date and place:	20 April 1989, Strasbourg
Authentic texts:	English, French
English text:	Trb. 1993, 111; ETS 130
Dutch translation:	Trb. 1993, 111
In force since:	1 November 1994 (NL)
Declarations:	In accordance with Article 3 of the Convention on Insider Trading, the Government of the Netherlands declares that it undertakes to provide other Parties, subject to reciprocity, with the greatest possible measure of mutual assistance in the exchange of information necessary for the surveillance of operations carried out in the organised stock markets which could adversely affect equal access to information for all users of the stock market or the quality of the information supplied to investors in order to ensure honest dealing.

In accordance with Article 4 of the Convention, the following authority is designated for the Netherlands to be actually responsible for submitting any request for assistance, and for receiving and taking action on request for assistance from the corresponding authorities designated by each party:

The Securities Board of the Netherlands *(Stichting Toezicht Effectenverkeer)*, P.O. Box 11723, 1001 GS Amsterdam.

Contact officer of the Securities Board is Mr. Paul Mulder, Secretary Legal Affairs, tel. (31)20 6206549, fax. (31) 206206649.

In accordance with Article 6, Section 5 of the Convention, the Government of the Netherlands declares the following derogations:

– In accordance with national law, the Dutch authority as requested authority may be ordered by a judicial authority to disclose information gathered within the framework of the request for the purpose of court proceedings if the court deems that the disclosure of that information is of greater importance than the confidentiality requirement of the requested authority;

– In accordance with national law, the Dutch authority as requested authority may, provided the requesting authority has been informed, wish to provide the competent Dutch authorities the information gathered within the framework of the request, to investigate violations of national law or to secure compliance with national law.

– In accordance with national law, the Dutch authority as requested authority may, provided the requesting authority has been informed, wish to disclose information gathered within the framework of the request, if necessary to fulfil its tasks and duties.

Related to:	156

155

Title:	Agreement between the Member States of the European Communities on the Simplification and Modernization of Methods of Transmitting Extradition Requests
Date and place:	26 May 1989, Donostia-San Sebastian
Authentic texts:	Danish, Dutch, English, French, German, Irish, Italian, Portuguese, Spanish
English text:	Trb. 1990, 97
Dutch text:	Trb. 1990, 97
Editor's note:	Provisional application between the states that ratified and declared as referred to in article 5 (Kingdom)
Declaration:	(Translation (original Dutch))

The Kingdom of the Netherlands designates as central authorities, responsible for transmitting and receiving extradition requests and the necessary supporting documents, as well as any other official correspondence relating to an extradition request:
– for the Netherlands: the Ministry of Justice in The Hague,
– for the Netherlands Antilles: the Ministry of Justice in Willemstad, Curaçao,
– for Aruba: the Ministry of Justice in Oranjestad, Aruba.

156

Title:	Protocol to the Convention on Insider Trading
Date and place:	11 September 1989, Strasbourg
Authentic texts:	English, French
English text:	Trb. 1993, 112; ETS 133
Dutch translation:	Trb. 1993, 112
In force since:	1 November 1994 (NL)
Related to:	154

157

Title:	Treaty between the Kingdom of the Netherlands and Canada on Extradition
Date and place:	13 October 1989, Montreal
Authentic texts:	Dutch, English, French
English text:	Trb. 1989, 169
Dutch text:	Trb. 1989, 169
In force since:	1 December 1991 (Kingdom)

158

Title:	Convention on the Rights of the Child
Date and place:	20 November 1989, New York
Authentic texts:	Arabic, Chinese, English, French, Russian, Spanish

English text:	Trb. 1990, 46
Dutch translation:	Trb. 1990, 170
In force since:	8 March 1995 (NL)
Reservations:	Article 26

The Kingdom of the Netherlands accepts the provisions of article 26 of the Convention with the reservation that these provisions shall not imply an independent entitlement of children to social security, including social insurance.

Article 37

The Kingdom of the Netherlands accepts the provisions of article 37 (c) of the Convention with the reservation that these provisions shall not prevent the application of adult penal law to children of sixteen years and older, provided that certain criteria laid down by law have been met.

Article 40

The Kingdom of the Netherlands accepts the provisions of article 40 of the Convention with the reservation that cases involving minor offences may be tried without the presence of legal assistance and with respect to such offences the position remains that no provision is made in all cases for a review of the facts or of measures imposed as a consequence.

Declarations: Article 14

It is the understanding of the Government of the Kingdom of the Netherlands that article 14 of the Convention is in accordance with the provisions of article 18 of the International Covenant on Civil and Political Rights of 19 December 1966 and that this article shall include the freedom of a child to have or adopt a religion or belief of his or her choice as soon as the child is capable of making such choice in view of his or her age or maturity.

Article 22

With regard to article 22 of the convention, the Government of the Kingdom of the Netherlands declares:

a) that it understands the term 'refugee' in paragraph 1 of this article as having the same meaning as in article 1 of the Convention relating to the Status of Refugees of 28 July 1951; and

b) that it is of the opinion that the obligation imposed under the terms of this article does not prevent

– the submission of a request for admission from being made subject to certain conditions, failure to meet such conditions resulting in inadmissibility;

– the referral of a request for admission to a third State, in the event that such a State is considered to be primarily responsible for dealing with the request for asylum.

Article 38

With regard to article 38 of the Convention, the Government of the Kingdom of the Netherlands declares that it is of the opinion that States should not be allowed to involve children directly or indirectly in hostilities and that the minimum age for the recruitment or incorporation of children in the armed forces should be above fifteen years.

In times of armed conflict, provisions shall prevail that are most conducive to guaranteeing the protection of children under international law, as referred to in article 41 of the Convention.

Objections: With regard to the reservations made by Djibouti, Indonesia, Pakistan, the Syrian Arab Republic and Iran upon rafication:

The Government of the Kingdom of the Netherlands considers that such reservations, which seek to limit the responsibilities of the reserving State under the Convention by invoking general principles of national law, may raise doubts as to the commitment of these States to the object and purpose of the Convention and, moreover, contribute to undermining the basis of international treaty law, It is in the common interest of States that treaties to which they have chosen to become parties should be respected, as to object and purpose, by all parties. The Government of the Kingdom of the Netherlands therefore objects to these reservations. This objection does not constitute an obstacle to the entry into force of the Convention between the Kingdom of the Netherlands and the aforementioned States.

The Government of the Kingdom of the Netherlands considers, with regard to the reservation made by Qatar relating to the Convention on the Rights of the child, that such reservation, which seek to limit the responsibilities of the reserving State under the Convention by invoking general principles of national law, may raise doubts as to the commitment of this State to the object and purpose of the Convention and, moreover, contribute to undermining the basis of international treaty law. It is in the common interest of States that treaties to which they have chosen to become parties should be respected, as to object and purpose, by all parties. The Government of the Kingdom of the Netherlands therefore objects to this reservation.

This objection shall not preclude the entry into force of the Convention between the Kingdom of the Netherlands and Qatar.

The Government of the Kingdom of the Netherlands considers, with regard to the reservation made by the Republic of Turkey relating to the Convention on the Rights of the Child, that such reservations, which seek to limit the responsibilities of the reserving State under the Convention by invoking national law, may raise doubts as to the commitment of this State to the object and purpose of the Convention and, moreover, contribute to undermining the basis of international treaty law. It is in the common interest of States that treaties to which they have chosen to become parties should be respected, as to object and purpose, by all parties. The Government of the Kingdom of the Netherlands therefore objects to this reservation.

This objection shall not preclude the entry into force of the Convention between the Kingdom of the Netherlands and the Republic of Turkey.

The Government of the Kingdom of the Netherlands considers, with regard to the reservation made by Botswana relating to the Convention on the Rights of the Child, that such reservations, which seek to limit the responsibilities of the reserving State under the Convention by invoking general principles of national law, may raise doubts as to the commitment of this State to the object and purpose of the Convention and, moreover, contribute to undermining the basis of international treaty law. It is in the common interest of States that treaties to which they have chosen to become parties should be respected, as to object and purpose, by all parties. The Government of the Kingdom of the Netherlands therefore objects to this reservation.

This objection shall not preclude the entry into force of the Convention between the Kingdom of the Netherlands and Botswana.

The Government of the Kingdom of the Netherlands considers, with regard to the reservation made by Malaysia relating to the Convention on the Rights of the Child, that such reservations, which seek to limit the responsibilities of the reserving State under the central provisions of the Convention by invoking the Constitution, national laws and national policies, raise serious doubts as to the commitment of this State to the object and purpose of the Convention and, moreover, contribute to undermining the basis of international treaty law. It is in the common interest of States that treaties to which they have chosen to become parties should be respected, as to object and purpose, by all parties. The Government of the Kingdom of the Netherlands therefore objects to these reservations.

This objection shall not preclude the entry into force of the Convention between the Kingdom of the Netherlands and Malaysia.

159

Title:	Agreement between the Kingdom of the Netherlands and the United States of America on Mutual Administrative Assistance in the Exchange of Information in Security Matters
Date and place:	11 December 1989, The Hague
Authentic text:	English
English text:	Trb. 1990, 11
Dutch translation:	Trb. 1990, 61
In force since:	1 July 1992 (NL)

160

Title:	Second Optional Protocol to the International Convenant on Civil and Political Rights, aiming at the Abolition of the Death Penalty
Date and place:	15 December 1989
Authentic texts:	Arabic, Chinese, English, French, Russian, Spanish
English text:	Trb. 1990, 125
Dutch translation:	Trb. 1990, 125
In force since:	11 July 1991 (Kingdom)
Related to:	78

161

Title:	Convention applying the Schengen Agreement of 14 June 1985 between the Governments of the States of the Benelux Economic Union, the Federal Republic of Germany and the French Republic, on the Gradual Abolition of Checks at their Common Borders
Date and place:	19 June 1990, Schengen
Authentic texts:	Dutch, French, German
Dutch text:	Trb. 1990, 145
In force since:	1 September 1993 (NL), postponed until 26 March 1995
Declarations:	(Translation (original Dutch))

With regard to the common border of the Kingdom of the Netherlands and the Kingdom of Belgium:

On the territory of the Netherlands, the competent officers of the Kingdom of Belgium shall exercise the right to pursue – as far as the application of the right to apprehend, the territorial application of this and the offences for which this right can be applied are concerned – in accordance with the corresponding provisions in Article 27 of the Benelux Treaty on Extradition and Mutual Legal Assistance in Criminal Matters of 27 June 1962, as amended by the Protocol of 11 May 1974.

With regard to the common border of the Kingdom of the Netherlands and the Federal Republic of Germany:

On the territory of the Netherlands, the competent officers of the Federal Republic of Germany shall exercise the right to pursue within a zone of 10 kilometers parallel to the common border, in which they may apprehend the pursued person on the public road and in public places, provided that there is a suspicion of, or a conviction for a crime, that on the basis of Article 2, paragraph 1, of the European Convention on Extradition of 13 December 1957, could lead to extradition. The foregoing does not preclude, that on the basis of additional agreements, as provided for in paragraph 10 of Article 41, the zone in which the right to pursue can be exercised, may be further determined according to local circumstances.

By Memorandum of 25 November 1994, the Kingdom of the Netherlands has submitted two declarations to the Government of Luxembourg. The text of a declaration pursuant to Article 57, third paragraph, of the present Agreement, reads as follows:
By virtue of Article 57, third paragraph, of the Agreement of 19 June 1990, concluded at Schengen, implementing the Accord concluded between the governments of the States of the Benelux Economic Union, the Federal Republic of Germany and the French Republic on 14 June 1985 at Schengen, concerning the gradual abolition of checks at their common borders, as amended by the Agreements of 27 November 1990, 25 June 1991, and 6 November 1992, concerning the accession of the Italian Republic, the Kingdom of Spain, the Republic of Portugal and the Hellenic Republic, the Kingdom of the Netherlands designates as authorities to request and receive information:
The Ministry of Justice
Postbus 20301
2500 EH The Hague

Declaration of the Kingdom of the Netherlands with regard to the provisions concerning the Kingdom of the Netherlands in Article 40, fourth paragraph, and in Article 41, seventh paragraph, of the Agreement of 19 June 1990, concluded at Schengen, implementing the Accord concluded between the governments of the States of the Benelux Economic Union, the Federal Republic of Germany and the French Republic on 14 June 1985 at Schengen, concerning the gradual abolition of checks at their common borders, as amended by the Agreements of 27 November 1990, 25 June 1991, and 6 November 1992, concerning the accession of the Italian Republic, the Kingdom of Spain, the Republic of Portugal and the Hellenic Republic. As a result of the entry into force of the Police Act 1993 on 1 April 1994 the difference between *Rijkspolitie* and

Gemeentepolitie was abolished. Consequently, the words *ambtenaren van de Rijkspolitie en de Gemeentepolitie* must be read as: 'the officials appointed to exercise police tasks'.

Related to: 140, 213

162

Title: Convention on Laundering, Search, Seizure and Confiscation of the Proceeds from Crime

Date and place: 8 November 1990, Strasbourg

Authentic texts: English, French

English text: Trb. 1990, 172; ETS 141

Dutch translation: Trb. 1990, 172

In force since: 1 September 1993 (NL)

Reservation: In accordance with Article 2, paragraph 2, of the Convention the Kingdom of the Netherlands declares that it reserves the right not to apply Article 2, paragraph 1, of the Convention with regard to the confiscation of the proceeds from offences punishable under legislation on taxation or on customs and excise.

Declarations: In accordance with Article 6, paragraph 4, of the Convention the Kingdom of the Netherlands declares that Article 6, paragraph 1, of the Convention will only be applied to predicate offences that qualify as *misdrijven* (crimes) under the domestic law of the Netherlands (Kingdom in Europe).

In accordance with Article 23, paragraph 2, of the Convention the Central authority, referred to in Article 23, paragraph 1, designated for the Netherlands (the Kingdom in Europe) is:

Het Ministerie van Justitie, Afdeling Internationale Rechtshulp, Postbus 20301, 2500 EH 's Gravenhage, Nederland.

In accordance with Article 25, paragraph 3, of the Convention the Kingdom of the Netherlands declares that requests made to the Netherlands (the Kingdom as Europe) and documents supporting such requests in a language other than Dutch, French, English or German be accompanied by a translation into one of these languages.

In accordance with Article 38, paragraph 1, of the Convention the Kingdom of the Netherlands declares that the Convention shall apply to the Netherlands (the Kingdom in Europe).

Related to: 179

163

Title: Treaty between the Kingdom of the Netherlands and Canada on Mutual Assistance in Criminal Matters

Date and place: 1 May 1991, The Hague

Authentic texts:	Dutch, English, French
English text:	Trb. 1991, 85
Dutch text:	Trb. 1991, 85
In force since:	1 May 1992 (NL, A)

164

Title:	Convention between the Member States of the European Communities on the Enforcement of Foreign Criminal Sentences
Date and place:	13 November 1991, Brussels
Authentic texts:	Danish, Dutch, English, French, German, Greek, Irish, Italian, Portuguese, Spanish
English text:	Trb. 1992, 39
Dutch text:	Trb. 1992, 39
Editor's note:	The Convention has been ratified by the Netherlands. It has however not entered into force yet, because the requirement that all Member States of the European Communities have ratified the Convention has not been fulfilled.

165

Title:	Europe Agreement establishing an association between the European Communities and their Member States, of the one part, and the Republic of Poland, of the other part
Date and place:	16 December 1991, Brussels
Authentic texts:	Danish, German, English, French, Greek, Italian, Dutch, Portuguese, Spanish, Polish
English text:	1993 OJ L 348/2
Dutch text:	Trb. 1992, 184; 1993 PB L 348/2
In force since:	1 February 1994 (NL)

166

Title:	Europe Agreement between the European Communities and their Member States, of the one part, and the Republic of Hungary, of the other part
Date and place:	16 December 1991, Brussels
Authentic texts:	Danish, German, English, French, Greek, Italian, Dutch, Portuguese, Spanish, Hungarian
English text:	1993 OJ L 347/1
Dutch text:	Trb. 1992, 185; 1993 PB L 347/1
In force since:	1 February 1994 (NL)

167

Title:	Treaty on European Union
Date and place:	7 February 1992, Maastricht

Authentic texts:	Danish, Dutch, English, French, German, Greek, Irish, Italian, Portuguese, Spanish
Dutch text:	Trb. 1992, 74
In force since:	1 November 1993 (NL)

168

Title:	Treaty providing a Framework for friendship and closer cooperation between the Kingdom of the Netherlands and the Republic of Suriname
Date and place:	18 June 1992, The Hague
Authentic text:	Dutch
Dutch text:	Trb. 1992, 103
In force since:	1 May 1995 (Kingdom)

169

Title:	Agreement between the Government of the Kingdom of the Netherlands and the Government of Hong Kong for the Surrender of Fugitive Offenders
Date and place:	2 November 1992, Hong Kong
Authentic texts:	Chinese, Dutch, English
English text:	Trb. 1992, 198
Dutch text:	Trb. 1992, 198

170

Title:	Agreement between the Government of the Kingdom of the Netherlands and the Government of the United States of America regarding Mutual Cooperation in the Tracing, Freezing, Seizure, and Forfeiture of Proceeds and Instrumentalities of Crime and the Sharing of Forfeited Assets
Date and place:	20 November 1992, Washington
Authentic texts:	Dutch, English
English text:	Trb. 1993, 5
Dutch text:	Trb. 1993, 5
In force since:	31 July 1994 (NL)

171

Title:	Convention on the Prohibition of the Development, Production Stockpiling and Use of Chemical Weapons and on their Destruction
Date and place:	13 January 1993, Paris
Authentic texts:	Arabic, Chinese, English, French, Russian, Spanish
English text:	Trb. 1993, 162
Dutch translation:	Trb. 1993, 162

172

Title:	Europe Agreement establishing an association between the European Communities and their Member States, of the one part, and Romania, of the other part
Date and place:	1 February 1993, Brussels
Authentic texts:	Danish, Dutch, English, French, German, Italian, Spanish, Greek, Portuguese, Romanian
English text:	1994 OJ L 368/1
Dutch text:	Trb. 1994, 16; 1994 PB L 368/1
In force since:	1 February 1995 (NL)

173

Title:	Europe Agreement establishing an association between the European Communities and their Member States, of the one part, and the republic of Bulgaria, of the other part
Date and place:	8 March 1993, Brussels
Authentic texts:	Danish, Dutch, English, French, German, Italian, Spanish, Greek, Portuguese, Bulgarian
English text:	1994 OJ L 368/5
Dutch text:	Trb. 1994, 17; 1994 PB L 368/5
In force since:	1 February 1995 (NL)

174

Title:	Agreement to amend the Agreement of 3 August 1959, as amended by the Agreements of 21 October 1971 and 18 May 1981, to Supplement the Agreement between the Parties of the North Atlantic Treaty regarding the Status of their Forces with respect to Foreign Forces stationed in the Federal Republic of Germany
Date and place:	18 March 1993, Bonn
Authentic texts:	English, French, German
English text:	Trb. 1993, 121
Dutch translation:	Trb. 1995, 43
Related to:	67, 94, 128, 175, 176

175

Title:	Agreement to implement paragraph 1 of article 45 of the Agreement of 3 August 1959, as amended by the Agreements of 21 October 1971, 18 May 1981 and 18 March 1993, to Supplement the Agreement between the Parties to the North Atlantic Treaty regarding the Status of their Forces with respect to Foreign Forces stationed in the Federal Republic of Germany
Date and place:	18 March 1993, Bonn
Authentic texts:	German, English, French

English text:	Trb. 1993, 151
Dutch translation:	Trb. 1995, 44
Related to:	67, 94, 128, 174, 176

176

Title:	Administrative Agreement to implement Article 60 of the Agreement of 3 August 1959, as amended by the Agreements of 21 October 1971, 18 May 1981 and 18 March 1993, to supplement the Agreement between the Parties to the North Atlantic Treaty regarding the Status of their Forces with respect to Foreign Forces stationed in the Federal Republic of Germany
Date and place:	18 March 1993, Bonn
Authentic texts:	English, French, German
English text:	Trb. 1994, 18
Dutch translation:	Trb. 1995, 93
Related to:	67, 94, 128, 174, 175

177

Title:	Agreement between the Government of the Kingdom of the Netherlands and the Government of the United States of America on Mutual administrative assistance in the exchange of information in futures matters
Date and place:	29 April 1993, Washington
Authentic text:	English
English text:	Trb. 1993, 86
Dutch translation:	Trb. 1993, 183
In force since:	1 February 1994 (NL)

178

Title:	Protocol containing special arrangements regarding the Agreement, concluded on August 29, 1976 in The Hague, between the Kingdom of the Netherlands and the Republic of Suriname concerning Extradition and Mutual Assistance in Criminal Matters
Date and place:	18 May 1993, The Hague
Authentic text:	Dutch
Dutch text:	Trb. 1993, 87
In force since:	28 February 1995 (NL), 1 December 1995 (A)
Related to:	108

179

Title:	Agreement between the Government of the Kingdom of the Netherlands and the Government of the Kingdom of Great Britain and Northern Ireland to supplement and facilitate the Operation of

	the Convention of the Council of Europe on Laundering, Search, Seizure and Confiscation of the Proceeds from Crime, concluded at Strasbourg on 8 November 1990
Date and place:	15 September 1993, London
Authentic texts:	Dutch, English
English text:	Trb. 1993, 150
Dutch text:	Trb. 1993, 150
In force since:	2 June 1994 (NL)
Related to:	162

180

Title:	Europe Agreement establishing an association between the European Communities and their Member States, of the one part, and the Slovak Republic, of the other part
Date and place:	4 October 1993, Luxembourg
Authentic texts:	Danish, German, English, French, Dutch, Greek, Italian, Portuguese, Spanish, Slovakian
English text:	1994 OJ L 341/17
Dutch text:	Trb. 1994, 72
In force since:	1 February 1995 (NL)

181

Title:	Europe Agreement establishing an association between the European Communities and their Member States, of the one part, and the Czech Republic, of the other part
Date and place:	4 October 1993, Luxembourg
Authentic texts:	Danish, Dutch, English, French, German, Greek, Italian, Portuguese, Spanish, Czech
English text:	1994 OJ L 341/14
Dutch text:	Trb. 1994, 73
In force since:	1 February 1995 (NL)

182

Title:	Treaty between the Kindom of the Netherlands and the French Republic concerning the checks of persons on the airports of Sint Maarten
Date and place:	17 May 1994, Paris
Authentic texts:	Dutch, French
Dutch text:	Trb. 1994, 144

183

| *Title:* | Agreement between the Kingdom of the Netherlands and the United Nations concerning the Headquarters of the International |

	Tribunal for the Prosecution of Persons Responsible for Serious Violations of International Humanitarian Law Committed in the Territory of the Former Yugoslavia since 1991
Date and place:	29 July 1994, New York
Authentic text:	English
English text:	Trb. 1994, 189
In force since:	provisional application from the date of signature (NL)
Related to:	208

184

Title:	Agreement between the government of the Kingdom of the Netherlands and the Government of the Federal Republic of Germany on privileges and immunities of liaison officers and other members of staff who are employed at the Europol Drugs Unit in The Hague on behalf of the Government of the Federal Republic of Germany
Date and place:	30 November/22 December 1994, Bonn
Authentic texts:	Dutch, German
Dutch text:	Trb. 1995, 24
In force since:	7 January 1995 (NL). Exchange of letters of 8 December 1995 and 11 January 1996, prolongation for an indefinite period from 31 January 1996

185

Title:	Agreement between the Government of the Kingdom of the Netherlands and the Government of Denmark on Privileges and immunities of liaison officers and other members of staff who are employed at the Europol Drugs Unit in the Hague on behalf of the Government of Denmark
Date and place:	30 November 1994/6 January 1995, Copenhague
Authentic text:	English
English text:	Trb. 1995, 47
In force since:	24 January 1995 (NL). Exchange of letters of 6 February and 28 May 1996, prolongation for an indefinite period from 24 January 1996

186

Title:	Agreement between the Government of the Kingdom of the Netherlands and the Government of Greece on privileges and immunities of liaison officers and other members of staff who are employed at the Europol Drugs Unit in the Hague on behalf of the Government of Greece
Date and place:	30 November 1994/20 January 1995, Athens

Authentic text:	English
English text:	Trb. 1995, 59
In force since:	10 February 1995 (NL). Exchange of letters of 7 February 1996, prolongation for an indefinite period from that date

187

Title:	Agreement between the Government of the Kingdom of the Netherlands and the Government of the Kingdom of Great Britain and Nothern Ireland on privileges and immunities of liaison officers and other members of staff who are employed at the Europol Drugs Unit in the Hague on behalf of the Government of the Kingdom of Great Britain and Northern Ireland
Date and place:	30 November 1994/27 January 1995, London
Authentic text:	English
English text:	Trb. 1995, 60
In force since:	16 February 1995 (NL). Exchange of letters 6 and 14 February 1996, prolongation for an indefinite period from 14 February 1996

188

Title:	Agreement between the Government of the Kingdom of the Netherlands and the Government of Portugal on privileges and immunities of liaison officers and other members of staff who are employed at the Europol Drugs Unit in the Hague on behalf of the Government of Portugal
Date and place:	30 November 1994/1 February 1995, Lisbon
Authentic texts:	French, Portuguese, (Trb. 1995, 56)
In force since:	24 February 1995 (NL)

189

Title:	Agreement between the Government of the Kingdom of the Netherlands and the Government of Luxembourg on Privileges and immunities of liaison officers and other members of staff who are employed at the Europol Drugs Unit in the Hague on behalf of the Government of Luxembourg
Date and place:	30 November 1994/16 March 1995, Luxembourg
Authentic text:	French (Trb. 1995, 97)
In force since:	1 April 1995 (NL). Exchange of letters 18 and 31 July 1996, prolongation of the treaty for a year from 1 April 1996

190

Title:	Agreement between the Government of the Kingdom of the Netherlands and the Government of Eire on Privileges and immunities of liaison officers and other members of staff who are

employed at the Europol Drugs Unit in the Hague on behalf of the Government of Eire

Date and place:	30 November 1994/14 June 1995, Dublin
Authentic text:	English˙
English text:	Trb. 1995, 157
In force since:	30 June 1995 (NL)

191

Title:	Agreement between the Government of the Kingdom of the Netherlands and the Italian Government on Privileges and immunities of liaison officers and other members of staff who are employed at the Europol Drugs Unit in the Hague on behalf of the Government of Italy
Date and place:	1 December 1994/24 January 1995, Rome
Authentic text:	English
English text:	Trb. 1995, 53
In force since:	9 February 1995 (NL). Exchange of letters 8 February and 19 March 1996 for an indefinite period from 9 February 1996

192

Title:	Agreement between the Government of the Kingdom of the Netherlands and the French Government on Privileges and immunities of liaison officers and other members of staff who are employed at the Europol Drugs Unit in the Hague on behalf of the Government of France
Date and place:	1 December 1994/15 February 1995, Paris
Authentic text:	French (Trb. 1995, 69)
In force since:	7 March 1995 (NL). Exchange of letters 25 June and 7 August 1996. The treaty continues to be in force from 7 March 1996 until the entry into force of the Europol Convention

193

Title:	Convention on the Safety of United Nations and Associated Personnel
Date and place:	9 December 1994, New York
Authentic texts:	Arabic, Chinese, English, French, Russian, Spanish
English text:	Trb. 1996, 62; 34 ILM 482 (1995)
Dutch translation:	Trb. 1996, 62

194

Title:	Agreement between the Government of the Kingdom of the Netherlands and the Government of Belgium on Privileges and immunities of liaison officers and other members of staff who are

	employed at the Europol Drugs Unit in the Hague on behalf of the Government of Belgium
Date and place:	9/13 February 1995, Brussels
Authentic text:	Dutch
Dutch text:	Trb. 1995, 74
In force since:	Provisional application from 1 March 1995 (NL). Exchange of letters 28 and 29 February 1996, prolongation for an indefinite period from 1 March 1996

195

Title:	Convention Drawn Up on the Basis of Article K.3 of the Treaty on European Union, on Simplified Extradition Procedure between the Member States of the European Union
Date and place:	10 March 1995, Brussels
Authentic texts:	Danish, Dutch, English, Finnish, French, German, Greek, Irish, Italian, Portuguese, Spanish, Swedish
English text:	Trb. 1995, 110; 1995 OJ C 78/1
Dutch text:	Trb. 1995, 110; 1995 PB C 78/1

196

Title:	Agreement between the Government of the Kingdom of the Netherlands and the Government of the Kingdom of Sweden on Privileges and immunities of liaison officers and other members of staff who are employed at the Europol Drugs Unit in the Hague on behalf of the Government of Sweden.
Date and place:	12 April/28 August 1995
Authentic text:	English
English text:	Trb. 1995, 226
In force since:	14 September 1995 (NL). Exchange of letters of 20 August and 23 October 1996, prolongation for an indefinite period from 14 September 1996.

197

Title:	Agreement between the Government of the Kingdom of the Netherlands and the Government of Finland on Privileges and immunities of liaison officers and other members of staff who are employed at the Europol Drugs Unit in the Hague on behalf of the Government of Finland
Date and place:	20 April/12 May 1995, Helsinki
Authentic text:	English
English text:	Trb. 1995, 148
In force since:	30 May 1995 (NL). Exchange of letters 15 May and 24 June 1996, prolongation for an indefinite period from 30 May 1996

198

Title:	Agreement among the States Parties to the North Atlantic Treaty and the other States participating in the Partnership for Peace regarding the Status of their Forces
Date and place:	19 June 1995, Brussels
Authentic texts:	English, French
English text:	Trb. 1996, 74
Dutch translation:	Trb. 1996, 74

199

Title:	Unidroit Convention on stolen or illegally exported cultural objects
Date and place:	24 June 1995, Rome
Authentic texts:	English, French
English text:	Trb. 1996, 227
Declarations:	The Kingdom of the Netherlands declares that under article 3, paragraph 5, of the Convention, it will consider a claim, subject to a time limitation of 75 years.
	Furthermore the Kingdom of the Netherlands, being a Member of the European Union, declares that under article 13, paragraph 3, of the Convention, it will apply in its relations with other Contracting States which are Members of the European Union the internal rules of the European Union and will not therefore apply in its relations with these Contracting States the provisions of this Convention the scope of application of which coincides with that of those rules.

200

Title:	Convention drawn up on the basis of Article K.3 of the Treaty on European Union, on the establishment of a European Police Office (Europol Convention)
Date and place:	26 July 1995, Brussels
Authentic texts:	Danish, Dutch, English, Finnish, French, German, Greek, Irish, Italian, Portuguese, Spanish, Swedish
English text:	Trb. 1995, 282; 1995 OJ C 316/1
Dutch text:	Trb. 1995, 282; 1995 PB C 316/1
Declarations:	The Federal Republic of Germany, the Republic of Austria and the Kingdom of the Netherlands will transmit data under this Convention on the understanding that, for the non-automated processing and use of such data, Europol and the Member States will comply with the spirit of the data protection provisions of this Convention.

Article 40(2)

The following Member States agree that in such cases they will systematically submit the dispute in question to the Court of Justice of the European Communities:

– Kingdom of Belgium
– Kingdom of Denmark
– Federal Republic of Germany
– Hellenic Republic
– Kingdom of Spain
– French Republic
– Ireland
– Italian Republic
– Grand Duchy of Luxembourg
– Kingdom of the Netherlands
– Republic of Austria
– Portuguese Republic
– Republic of Finland
– Kingdom of Sweden.

The governments of the Netherlands, Luxembourg and Belgium call upon the need to find a satisfactory solution before June 1996 with regard to the competence of the Court of Justice of the European Communities in prejudicial questions before having the Convention on the use of information technology for custom purposes entering into force.

Related to: 212

201

Title: Convention drawn up on the basis of Article K.3 of the Treaty on European Union, on the use of information technology for customs purposes

Date and place: 26 July 1995, Brussels

Authentic texts: German, English, Danish, Spanish, Finish, French, Greek, Irish, Italian, Dutch, Portuguese, Swedish

English text: Trb. 1995, 287; 1995 OJ C 316/33

Dutch text: Trb. 1995, 287; 1995 PB C 316/33

Declaration: The governments of the Netherlands, Luxembourg and Belgium call upon the need to find a satisfactory solution before June 1996 with regard to the competence of the Court of Justice of the European Communities in prejudicial questions before having the Convention on the use of information technology for custom purposes entering into force.

Related to: 202

202

Title:	Agreement on provisional application between certain Member States of the European Union of the Convention drawn up on the basis of Article K.3 of the Treaty on European Union on the use of information technology for customs purposes
Date and place:	26 July 1995, Brussels
Authentic texts:	Danish, Dutch, English, Finnish, French, German, Greek, Irish, Italian, Portuguese, Spanish, Swedish
English text:	Trb. 1995, 288; 1995 OJ C 316/58
Dutch text:	Trb. 1995, 288; 1995 PB C 316/58
Related to:	201

203

Title:	Convention drawn up on the basis of Article K.3 of the Treaty on European Union, on the protection of the European Communities' financial interests
Date and place:	26 July 1995, Brussels
Authentic texts:	Danish, Dutch, English, Finnish, French, German, Greek, Irish, Italian, Portuguese, Spanish, Swedish
English text:	Trb. 1995, 289; 1995 OJ C 316/48
Dutch text:	Trb. 1995, 289; 1995 PB C 316/48
Declaration:	The governments of the Netherlands, Luxembourg and Belgium call upon the need to find a satisfactory solution before June 1996, with regard to the competence of the Court of Justice of the European Communities in prejudicial questions, before having the Convention on the protection of the European Communities' financial interests into force.
Related to:	214

204

Title:	Agreement on mutual administrative assistance for the proper application of customs law and for the prevention, investigation and combating of customs offences between the Kingdom of the Netherlands and the Republic of Estonia
Date and place:	11 October 1995, The Hague
Authentic texts:	Dutch, Estonian, English
English text:	Trb. 1995, 262
Dutch text:	Trb. 1995, 262

205

Title:	Additional Protocol to the Convention on prohibitions or restrictions on the use of certain conventional weapons which may be

deemed to be excessively injurious or to have indiscriminate
effects

Date and place: 13 October 1995, New York
Authentic texts: Arabic, Chinese, English, French, Russian, Spanish
English text: Trb. 1996, 261
Dutch translation: Trb. 1996, 261
Related to: 125

206

Title: Exchange of letters containing a treaty between the Kingdom of
the Netherlands and the Swiss Confederacy regarding articles 7
and 15 of the European Convention on Mutual Assistance in
Criminal Matters
Date and place: 4 December 1995/12 February 1996 The Hague
Authentic texts: German, French, Italian, Dutch
Dutch text: Trb. 1996, 49
In force since: 12 February 1996 (NL)

207

Title: European Agreement relating to persons participating in proceed-
ings of the European Court of Human Rights
Date and place: 5 March 1996, Strasbourg
Authentic texts: English, French
English text: Trb. 1996, 130
Dutch translation: Trb. 1996, 130

208

Title: Exchange of letters between the Kingdom of the Netherlands and
the United Nations constituting a treaty regarding the applicability
of the Agreement between the United Nations and the Kingdom
of the Netherlands concerning the Headquarters of the International Tribunal for the former Yugoslavia to the activities and
proceedings of the International Tribunal for Rwanda
Date and place: 22/24 April 1996, New York
Authentic text: English
English text: Trb. 1996, 143
In force since: 1 June 1996 (NL)
Related to: 183

209

Title: Protocol on Prohibitions or Restrictions on the Use of Mines,
Boobytraps and Other Devices as Amended on 3 May 1996
(Protocol II as amended on 3 May 1996) annexed to the Conven-

tion on prohibitions or restrictions on the use of certain conventional weapons which may be deemed to be excessively injurious or to have indiscriminate effects

Date and place: 3 May 1996, Geneva
Authentic texts: Arabic, Chinese, English, French, Russian, Spanish
English text: Trb. 1996, 260
Related to: 125

210

Title: Agreement between the Government of the Kingdom of the Netherlands and the Government of the State of Israel on mutual administrative assistance in customs matters
Date and place: 21 May 1996, Oegstgeest
Authentic texts: Dutch, English, Hebrew
English text: Trb. 1996, 155
Dutch text: Trb. 1996, 155

211

Title: Exchange of letters between the Registrar of the International Criminal Tribunal for the former Yugoslavia, and the Government of the Netherlands on the assigned residence of general Blaskic
Date and place: 12/17 June 1996, The Hague
Authentic text: English
English text: Trb. 1996, 152
In force since: 20 June 1996

212

Title: Protocol, drawn up on the basis of Article K.3 of the Treaty on European Union, on the interpretation, by way of preliminary rulings, by the Court of Justice of the European Communities of the Convention on the establishment of a European Police Office
Date and place: 24 July 1996, Brussels
Authentic texts: Danish, Dutch, English, Finnish, French, German, Greek, Irish, Italian, Portuguese, Spanish, Swedish
English text: Trb. 1996, 265
Dutch text: Trb. 1996, 265
Reservation: (Translation (Original Dutch))
The Kingdom of the Netherlands reserves the right to determine in their internal legislation that, whenever a question regarding the interpretation of the Europol Convention comes up in a case pending before a national judicial authority, of which the decisions under national law can not be appealed against, this authority shall

	be bound to submit the matter to the Court of Justice of the European Communities.
Declarations:	The Kingdom of the Netherlands will accept the competence of the Court of Justice of the European Communities in the manner as determined in Article 2, paragraph 2 sub b.
	The governments of the Netherlands, Belgium and Luxembourg call upon the need to find a satisfactory solution forthwith comparable to this Protocol in relation to the competence of the Court of Justice of the European Communities regarding the Convention on the use of information technology for customs purposes and the Convention the protection of the European Communities' financial interests.
Related to:	200

213

Title:	Convention, drawn up on the basis of Article K.3 of the Treaty on European Union, relating to extradition between the Member States of the European Union
Date and place:	27 September 1996, Dublin
Authentic texts:	Danish, Dutch, English, Finnish, French, German, Greek, Irish, Italian, Portuguese, Spanish, Swedish
English text:	Trb. 1996, 304
Dutch text:	Trb. 1996, 304
Declarations:	Joint Declaration on the right of asylum
	The Member States declare that this Convention is without prejudice either to the right of asylum to the extent to which it is recognized by their respective constitutions or to the application by the Member States of the provisions of the Convention relating to the Status of Refugees of 28 July 1951, as supplemented by the Convention relating to the Status of Stateless Persons of 28 September 1954 and by the Protocol relating to the Status of Refugees of 31 January 1967.
	Declaration on the concept of 'nationals'
	The Council takes note of the Member States' undertaking to apply the Council of Europe Convention of 21 March 1983 on the Transfer of Sentenced Persons in respect of the nationals of each Member State within the meaning of Article 3(4) of the said Convention.
	The Member States' undertaking mentioned in the first paragraph is without prejudice to the application of Article 7(2) of this Convention.

Council declaration on the follow-up to the Convention
The Council declares:
a) that it considers that there should be a periodic review, on the basis of information supplied by the Member States, of:
– the implementation of this Convention;
– the functioning of this Convention after its entry into force;
– the possibility for Member States to amend the reservations entered in the framework of this Convention with a view to easing the conditions for extradition or withdrawing its reservations;
– the general functioning of extradition procedures between the Member States;
b) that it will consider, one year after entry into force of the Convention, whether jurisdiction should be given to the Court of Justice of the European Communities.

Related to: 60, 69, 109, 161

214

Title: Protocol drawn up on the basis of Article K.3 of the Treaty on European Union to the Convention on the protection of the European Communities' financial interests
Date and place: 27 September 1996, Dublin
Authentic texts: Danish, Dutch, English, Finnish, French, German, Greek, Irish, Italian, Portuguese, Spanish, Swedish
English text: Trb. 1996, 330; 1996 OJ C 313/1
Dutch text: Trb. 1996, 330; 1996 PB C 313/1
Related to: 203

215

Title: Convention on the Transfer of Sentenced Persons between the Kingdom of the Netherlands and the Republic of Venezuela
Date and place: 8 October 1996, Caracas
Authentic texts: Dutch, Spanish
Dutch text: Trb. 1996, 297

216

Title: Agreement on mutual administrative assistance for the proper application of customs law and for the prevention, investigation and combating of customs offenses between the Kingdom of the Netherlands and the United States of America
Date and place: 28 October 1996, Washington
Authentic text: English
English text: Trb. 1996, 331

Contributors

Peter Baauw studied law at Utrecht University (1968). He became senior lecturer in criminal law and criminal procedure at Utrecht University. He has presented a dissertation on pre-trial detention (1978). He is a part-time practising criminal lawyer (1980), a part-time judge at Utrecht District Court (1985) and Amsterdam Court of Appeal (1992).

Rijnhard Haentjens studied law at Amsterdam University (1972). He has been a research associate at Amsterdam University (1976) and Leiden University (1980), then senior lecturer in (international) criminal law and procedure at Amsterdam University. His publications dealt, *inter alia*, with the Food Legislation (dissertation 1978) and Drugs Legislation in the Netherlands (1988), mutual assistance in criminal law (1992). In 1993 he became judge at the Rotterdam District Court, then at the Amsterdam Court of Appeal (1996).

André Klip graduated from Utrecht University (1989). He has been a researcher and teacher in (international) criminal law since 1989 at Utrecht University. His dissertation on Witnesses Abroad in Criminal Matters, a comparison of the law of the United States, Germany and the Netherlands, was published in 1994. In 1996 he became a part-time judge at the Utrecht District Court.

Coen Mulder studied law and Scandinavian languages at the University of Amsterdam. He became a research associate and later lecturer in international criminal law at the University of Amsterdam. He is writing a dissertation on the international criminal cooperation between the Nordic countries. Publication is expected in 1997.

Désirée Paridaens studied law at the University of Utrecht (1984). She became a research associate, and later lecturer in international criminal law at the University of Utrecht. Her dissertation was on the conditions governing the transfer of enforcement of criminal judgments (1994). Since 1994 she is senior policy adviser at the Office of International Legal Assistance of the Ministry of Justice.

Julian Schutte studied law at Leiden University. He was senior counsel to the Minister of Justice 1975-1995. From 1990 to 1995 he held the Van Hamel chair of international criminal law at the University of Amsterdam. Since 1995, he is a director of the Legal Service of the Council of the European Union in Brussels. He was the General Rapporteur of Section IV of the 1994 Congress of the International Association of Penal Law in Rio de Janeiro.

Bert Swart studied law at Nijmegen University and at the University of Poitiers (France). His dissertation was on the admission and expulsion of aliens in Dutch law (1978). Other books include a study on Dutch extradition law (1986). Since 1980, he has been professor of criminal law and criminal procedure at the University of Utrecht. In 1996, he became a member of the Amsterdam Court of Appeal. He now holds the Van Hamel chair of international criminal law at the University of Amsterdam. He is a member of the Royal Netherlands Academy of Arts and Sciences.

Marius Teengs Gerritsen studied law at the University of Amsterdam. He worked at the Seminarium van Hamel of the University of Amsterdam from 1991 to mid 1994 as a teacher and researcher. Since 1994 he is a judicial trainee. In that capacity he works at the Groningen District Court.

Bibliography

Books/Monographs

Baaijens-van Geloven, Y.G.M., Overdracht en overname van strafvervolging. Arnhem 1996.

Bassiouni, M. Cherif/Wise, Edward. M., Aut Dedere Aut Judicare; The Duty to Extradite or Prosecute in International Law. Dordrecht/Boston/London 1995.

Blankenburg, Erhard/Bruinsma, Freek, Dutch Legal Culture. Deventer-Boston 1991.

Buirma, J.J., Militair straf-, strafproces- en tuchtrecht. Derde druk. Zwolle 1991.

Cameron, Iain, The Protective Principle of International Criminal Jurisdiction. Aldershot 1994.

Corstens, G.J.M., Het Nederlands strafprocesrecht. Tweede druk. Arnhem 1995.

Dijk, P. van/Hoof, G.J.H. van, De europese conventie in theorie en praktijk. Derde druk. Nijmegen 1990.

Downes, David, Contrasts in Tolerance; Post-war Penal Policy in the Netherlands and England and Wales. Oxford 1988.

Guldenmund, R., Strafrechtelijke handhaving van gemeenschapsrecht. Arnhem 1992.

Haentjens, R.C.P., Schets van het Nederlandse kleine rechtshulprecht in strafzaken. Tweede druk. Arnhem 1992.

Hazewinkel-Suringa, D./Remmelink, J., *Inleiding* tot de studie van het Nederlandse strafrecht. Veertiende druk. Arnhem 1995.

Hofstee, E.J./Schalken, T.M., Strafrecht binnen het Koninkrijk, Beginselen van inter-regionaal en internationaal strafrecht. Arnhem 1991.

Hebenton, Bill/Thomas, Terry, Policing Europe, Co-operation, conflict and control. New York/London 1995.

Jörg, N./Kelk, C., Strafrecht met mate. Zevende druk. Alphen aan den Rijn 1992.

Joubert, Chantal/Bevers, Hans, Schengen Investigated. The Hague/London/Boston 1996.

Kalmthout, Anton M. van/Tak, Peter J.P., Sanction-Systems in the Member-States of the Council of Europe, Part II. Deventer-Boston 1992.

Keijzer, N., Het Europees verdrag tot bestrijding van terrorisme. Deventer 1979.

Keijzer, Nico, Military Obedience. Alphen aan den Rijn 1978.

Klip, André, Buitenlandse getuigen in strafzaken (Witnesses Abroad in Criminal Matters). Arnhem 1994.

Krabbe, H.G.M., De Opiumwet; Een strafrechtelijk commentaar. Alphen aan den Rijn 1989.

Kuyper, Pieter Jan, The Implementation of International Sanctions; The Netherlands and Rhodesia. Alphen aan den Rijn 1978.

Lensing, J.A.W., Amerikaans strafrecht; Een rechtsvergelijkende inleiding. Arnhem 1996.

Maathuis, H.H.M./Valkenburg, W.R.C.A., Bestuurlijke boeten in het fiscale recht. Deventer 1995.

Mok, M.R./Duk, R.A.A., Toepassing van Nederlands strafrecht op buiten Nederland begane delicten. Preadvies Nederlandse Juristen-Vereniging. Zwolle 1980.

Noyon, T.J./Langemeijer, G.E./Remmelink, J., Het Wetboek van Strafrecht. Zevende druk. Arnhem (looseleaf).

Oehler, D., Internationales Strafrecht. Zweite Auflage. Köln-Berlin-Bonn-München 1983.

Oppenheim, L./Lauterpacht, H., International Law, A Treatise. Eighth Edition. London 1955.

Orie, A.M.M./Meijs, J.G. van der/Smit, A.M.G., Internationaal strafrecht. Tweede druk. Zwolle 1991.

Paridaens, D.J.M.W., De overdracht van de tenuitvoerlegging van strafvonnissen. Arnhem 1994.

Pompe, W.P.J., Handboek van het Nederlandse strafrecht. Vijfde druk. Zwolle 1959.

Remmelink, J., Uitlevering. Vierde druk. Arnhem 1990.

Rüter, C.F., Enkele aspecten van de strafrechtelijke reactie op oorlogsmisdrijven en misdrijven tegen de menselijkheid. Amsterdam 1973.

Schutte, J.J.E., Volkenrechtelijke aspecten van het Nederlandse uitleveringsrecht. Volkenrechtelijke aspecten van uitleveringsrecht. Preadviezen Nederlandse Vereniging voor Internationaal Recht Nr. 85. Deventer 1982.

Siegrist, Dave, Hoheitsakte auf fremdem Staatsgebiet. Zürich 1987.

Siekmann, R.C.R., Juridische aspecten van de deelname met nationale contingenten aan VN-vredesmachten (Nederland en Unifil). Den Haag 1988.

Sjöcrona, Jan M., De kleine rechtshulp. Arnhem 1990.

Smidt, H.J., Geschiedenis van het Wetboek van Strafrecht. Haarlem 1881.

Strijards, G.A.M., Internationaal strafrecht, strafmachtsrecht. Arnhem 1984.

Strijards, G.A.M., Uitlevering. Zwolle 1988.

Swart, A.H.J., Goede rechtsbedeling en internationale rechtshulp in strafzaken. Deventer 1983.

Swart, A.H.J., Nederlands uitleveringsrecht. Zwolle 1986.

Swart, A.H.J., De berechting van internationale misdrijven. Arnhem 1996.

Tak, Peter J.P., Criminal Justice Systems in Europe: The Netherlands. Helsinki 1993.

Thomas, F., De Europese rechtshulpverdragen in strafzaken. Gent 1980.

Wattel, Peter Jacob, Fiscaal straf- en strafprocesrecht. Tweede druk. Deventer 1989.

Wisselink, M.A., Fiscale informatie-uitwisseling tussen Europese en andere landen. Deventer 1996.

Wortel, J., Vervolgen in belastingzaken. Deventer 1991.

Articles

Berghuis, Bert/Franke, Herman (Eds.), Foreign Views on Dutch Penal Policy. Tijdschrift voor Criminologie 34 (1992), pp. 189-268.

Doelder, H. de/Hulst, J.W. van der, EEG-sancties en ne bis in idem. Sociaal-Economische Wetgeving 41 (1993), pp. 722-733.

Egter van Wissekerke, F.A., De implementatie van het folteringsverdrag, internationaal versus nationaal strafrecht. Nederlands Juristenblad 63 (1988), pp. 113-117

Figge, Claus, The European Conventions on Mutual Assistance in Criminal Matters and on Extradition and the Exchange of Information in Tax Matters. Intertax 1980, pp. 86-96, 130-139.

Graaf, Frank G.B., Netherlands. In: Richard Parlour (Ed.), Butterworths International Guide to Money Laundering Law and Practice. London 1995, pp. 123-140.

Haentjens, R.C.P., Is de voorgestelde wijziging van de opiumwet een strafrechtelijk monstrum? Delikt en Delinkwent 14 (1984), pp. 32-49.

Haentjens, R.C.P., Perikelen in het kleine rechtshulprecht in strafzaken: de inbeslagneming. Delikt en Delinkwent 15 (1985), pp. 732-748.

Haentjens, R.C.P., Perikelen bij huiszoeking en inbeslagneming in het kader van de kleine rechtshulp. Delikt en Delinkwent 26 (1996), pp. 451-463.

Hendry, I.D., The Third Pillar of Maastricht: Cooperation in the Fields of Justice and Home Affairs. German Yearbook of International Law 36 (1993), pp. 295-327.

Heymann, Philip B., Two Models of National Attitudes toward International Cooperation in Law Enforcement. Harvard International Law Journal 31 (1990), pp. 99-107.

Heymann, Philip B./Heath Gershengorn, Ian, Pursuing Justice, Respecting the Law. In: Albin Eser/Otto Lagodny (Eds.), Principles and Procedures for a New Transnational Criminal Law. Freiburg im Breisgau 1992, pp. 101-147.

Hullu, J. de/Tillema, A.J.P., De verdragsverplichtingen en de wetgevingsgeschiedenis. In: H.G.M. Krabbe (Ed.), De Opiumwet; Een strafrechtelijk commentaar. Alphen aan den Rijn 1989, pp. 15-63.

Hulsman, L.H.C./Nijboer, J.F., Criminal justice system. In: Jeroen Chorus/Piet-Hein Gerver/Ewoud Hondius/Alis Koekkoek (Eds.), Introduction to Dutch Law for Foreign Lawyers. Deventer-Boston 1993, pp. 309-358.

Jung, Heike, Zur 'Internationalisierung' des Grundsatzes 'ne bis in idem'. In: Peter-Alexis Albrecht et al. (Hrsg.), Festschrift für Horst Schüler-Springorum zum 65. Geburtstag. Köln 1994, pp. 493-502.

Keijzer, Nico, Participation in Crime – Developments in Dutch Law. In: Raimo Lahti/Kimmo Nuotio (Eds.), Criminal Law Theory in Transition, Finnish and Comparative Perspectives. Helsinki 1992, pp. 491-502.

Keijzer, N., Het oorlogsstrafrecht. In: Th.J. Clarenbeek/G.L. Coolen/F.F. Langemeijer/N. Keijzer/W.H. Vermeer (Eds.), Het militaire straf- en tuchtrecht. Arnhem (looseleaf).

Klip, A., Extraterritoriale strafvordering. Delikt en Delinkwent 25 (1995), pp. 1056-1078.

Klip, A., Witnesses before the International Criminal Tribunal for the former Yugoslavia. Revue Internationale de Droit Pénal (International Review of Penal Law), 67 (1996), pp. 267-295.

Kommer, Max, Punitiveness in Europe – a comparison. European Journal of Criminal Policy and Research 2 (1994), pp. 29-44.

Krabbe, H.G.M./Poelman, H.M., Enkele aspecten van het *ne bis in idem*-beginsel in internationaal verband. In: Liber Amicorum Th.W. van Veen. Arnhem 1985, pp. 123-145.

Kuyper, J.R.H., The Netherlands Law of Extradition. In: H.F. van Panhuys/W.P. Heere/J.W. Josephus Jitta/Ko Swan Sik/A.M. Stuyt (Eds.), International Law in the Netherlands, Vol. II. Alphen aan den Rijn 1979, pp. 203-245.

Meyer, Jürgen, The Vicarious Administration of Justice: An Overlooked Basis of Jurisdiction. Harvard International Law Journal 31 (1990), pp. 108-116.

Mouton, M.W., De Wet Oorlogsstrafrecht en het internationale recht. Nederlands Tijdschrift voor Internationaal Recht 7 (1960), pp. 59-71.

O'Keeffe, David, The Schengen Convention: A Suitable Model for European Integration? Yearbook of European Law 11 (1991), pp. 185-219.

Orie, A.M.M./Rüter, C.F./Schutte, J.J.E./Swart, A.H.J., International Crimes and Domestic Criminal Law, Netherlands National Report. Revue Internationale de Droit Pénal 60 (1989), pp. 395-418.

Paridaens, D.J.M.W., The Extradition of Nationals According to Dutch Law. Revue Internationale de Droit Pénal/International Review of Penal Law 62 (1991), pp. 515-521.

Paridaens, D.J.M.W., De uitlevering van eigen onderdanen door Nederland. In: C.H. Brants/C. Kelk/M. Moerings (Eds.). Er is meer. Deventer 1996, pp. 107-117.

Paridaens, Désirée/Harding, Christopher, The Transfer of Prisoners with Special Reference to the Netherlands and the UK. In: Phil Fennell/Christopher Harding/ Nico Jörg/Bert Swart (Eds.), Criminal Justice in Europe; A Comparative Study. Oxford 1995, pp. 363-378.

Poelman, H.M., Wat aan de Wet Wapens en Munitie is voorafgegaan. In: D.M. de Jong/H.G.M. Krabbe (Eds.), De Wet Wapens en Munitie; Een strafrechtelijk commentaar. Alphen aan den Rijn 1989, pp. 17-25.

Röling, B.V.A.R., Enkele volkenrechtelijke aantekeningen bij de Wet Oorlogsstrafrecht. In: Varia Juris Gentium, Liber Amicorum J.P.A. François. Special Issue Nederlands Tijdschrift voor Internationaal Recht. 's-Gravenhage 1959, pp. 263-291.

Röling, B.V.A.R., The Law of War and the National Jurisdiction since 1945. Recueil des Cours 100 (1960 II), pp. 329-456.

Röling, B.V.A.R., Het volkenrechtelijk misdrijf van genocide en het Nederlandse strafrecht. Nederlands Juristenblad, 37 (1962), pp. 377-384.

Rüter, C.F./Helder, K./Swart, A.H.J., Immunity, Exterritoriality and the Right of Asylum. Revue Internationale de Droit Pénal 49 (1978), pp. 553-563.

Rüter, C.F./Swart, A.H.J., De toepasselijkheid van de Nederlandse strafwet; van locus delicti naar goede rechtsbedeling. In: Gedenkboek Honderd jaar Wetboek van Strafrecht. Arnhem 1986, pp. 243-274.

Rüter, Frits, Drugs and the Criminal Law in the Netherlands. In: Jan van Dijk/Charles Haffmans/Frits Rüter/Julian Schutte/Simon Stolwijk (Eds.), Criminal Law in Action; An overview of current issues in Western societies. Arnhem 1986, pp. 147-165.

Schutte, J.J.E., Overdracht en overname van strafvervolging, Ars Aequi, 35 (1986), pp. 31-37.

Schutte, J.J.E., Administrative and Judicial co-operation in the Fight against EC Fraud. In: M.S. Groenhuijsen/M.J. Veldt (Eds.), The Dutch Approach in Tackling EC Fraud. The Hague-London-Boston 1995, pp. 127-134.

Schutte, Julian, The European System. In: M. Cherif Bassiouni (Ed.), International Criminal Law, Vol. II Procedure. New York 1986, pp. 319-335.

Schutte, Julian J.E., Schengen: Its Meaning for the Free Movement of Persons in Europe. Common Market Law Review 28 (1991), pp. 549-570.

Schutte, Julian J.E., Administrative cooperation. In: Mireille Delmas-Marty (Ed.), What penal policy for Europe? The Hague/London/Boston 1996, pp. 191-204.

Schutter, Bart de, International Criminal Law in Evolution: Mutual Assistance between the Benelux Countries, Nederlands Tijdschrift voor Internationaal Recht 1967, pp. 382-410.

Serière, Victor de, The Netherlands. In: Gerhard Wegen/Heinz-Dieter Assmann, Insider Trading in Western Europe; Current Status. London 1994, pp. 109-133.

Silvis, Jos, Enforcing drug laws in the Netherlands. In: Ed Leuw/I. Haen Marshall (Eds.), Between Prohibition and Legalization; The Dutch Experiment in Drug Policy. Amsterdam/New York 1994, pp. 41-58.

Smid, H.A.C., Ervaringen vanuit politie en justitie met het meldpunt MOT. In: G.J.M. Corstens/E.J. Joubert/S.C.J.J. Kortmann (Eds.), Maatregelen tegen witwassen in het Koninkrijk. Arnhem 1996, pp. 185-200.

Strien, A.L.J. van, De rechtsmacht van Nederland ten aanzien van rechtspersonen. In: Grensoverschrijdend strafrecht. Arnhem 1990, pp. 65-83.

Strijards, G.A.M., Het primaat van het territorialiteitsbeginsel. Delikt en Delinkwent 18 (1988), pp. 121-136.

Strijards, G.A.M., Rechtsharmonie en wetsharmonie in het internationale strafrecht. Ars Aequi 45 (1996), pp. 378-385.

Swart, A.H.J., Die Auslieferung von Folkerts, Wackernagel und Schneider. Zeitschrift für die gesamte Strafrechtswissenschaft 91 (1979), pp. 773-797.

Swart, A.H.J., Police and security in the Schengen Agreement and Schengen Convention. In: H. Meijers (Ed.), Schengen, Internationalisation of central chapters of the law on aliens, refugees, security and the police. Deventer 1991, pp. 96-109.

Swart, A.H.J., Jurisdiction in Criminal Law: Some Reflections on the Finnish Code from a Comparative Perspective. In: Raimo Lahti/Kimmo Nuotio (Eds.), Criminal Law Theory in Transition, Finnish and Comparative Perspectives. Helsinki 1992, pp. 527-543.

Swart, A.H.J., Refusal of Extradition and the United Nations Model Treaty on Extradition. Netherlands Yearbook of International Law 23 (1992), pp. 175-222.

Swart, A.H.J., De Nederlandse strafrechtspleging in een internationaal krachtenveld. In: M. Moerings (Ed.), Hoe punitief is Nederland? Arnhem 1994.

Swart, A.H.J., Toelating, uitzetting en uitlevering in de herziene Grondwet. In: J.B.J.M. ten Berge/P.J. van Buuren/H.R.B.M. Kummeling/B.P. Vermeulen (Eds.), De Grondwet als voorwerp van aanhoudende zorg. Zwolle 1995, pp. 73-91.

Swart, Bert (A.H.J.), Human Rights and the Abolition of Traditional Principles. In: Albin Eser/Otto Lagodny (Eds.), Principles and Procedures for a New Transnational Criminal Law. Freiburg im Breisgau 1992, pp. 505-534.

Swart, Bert (A.H.J.), The Protection of Human Rights in International Cooperation in Criminal Proceedings. Revue Internationale de Droit Pénal/International Review of Penal Law 65 (1994), pp. 371-400.

Swart, Bert/Young, James, The European Convention on Human Rights and Criminal Justice in the Netherlands and the UK. In: Phil Fennell/Christopher Harding/Nico Jörg/Bert Swart (Eds.), Criminal Justice in Europe; A Comparative Study. Oxford 1995.

Trechsel, S., Grundrechtsschutz bei der internationalen Zusammenarbeit in Strafsachen. Europäische Grundrechte Zeitschrift 14 (1987), pp. 69-78.

Vermeulen, G., Het beginsel ne bis in idem in het internationaal strafrecht, Een evaluatie van de nationale en verdragsrechtelijke waarborgen in het strafrechtsverkeer met onze buurlanden. Panopticon 15 (1994), pp. 217-235.

Reports

Drugs Policy in the Netherlands; Continuity and change. Ministry of Health, Welfare and Sport, Rijswijk 1995.

Explanatory Report on the European Convention on the International Validity of Criminal Judgments. Council of Europe, Strasbourg 1970.

Explanatory Report on the Additional Protocol to the European Convention on Mutual Assistance in Criminal Matters. Council of Europe, Strasbourg 1978.

Explanatory Report on the Seventh Protocol to the European Convention. Council of Europe, Strasbourg 1984.

Extraterritorial Criminal Jurisdiction, European Committee on Crime Problems. Council of Europe, Strasbourg 1990.

First Commission's Report on the implementation of the Money Laundering Directive (91/308/EEC) to be submitted to the European Parliament and to the Council. Brussels 1994.

Gijsen, M.M.P., Evaluatie van de Wet overdracht tenuitvoerlegging strafvonnissen, onderzoeksperiode 1991-1994. Ministerie van Justitie, 's-Gravenhage 1996.

Individu en internationale rechtshulp in strafzaken, Rapport van de Commissie tot bestudering van de positie van verdachten en andere belanghebbenden in de internationale strafrechtelijke samenwerking. Ministerie van Justitie, 's-Gravenhage 1993.

Knaapen, M.H.F./Kallen, S.M. van der, Evaluatie van drie jaren Wet overdracht tenuitvoerlegging strafvonnissen. Ministerie van Justitie, 's-Gravenhage 1991.

Netherlands Report on co-operation in criminal matters. Netherlands Yearbook of International Law 19 (1988), pp. 298-308.

Voorontwerp van Rijkswet inzake de strafrechtelijke samenwerking tussen de landen van het Koninkrijk, Rapport van de Commissie artikel 40 Statuut. Amsterdam 1992.

Westerweel, J.C./Hillen, J.L.S.M., Measures to combat Money Laundering in the Netherlands. Ministry of Finance, The Hague 1995.

Index

Beiträge und Materialien aus dem Max-Planck-Institut

für ausländisches und internationales Strafrecht, Freiburg i.Br.

Herausgegeben von Professor Dr. Dr. h.c. Albin Eser, M.C.J.

INTERNATIONAL CRIMINAL LAW

**Max-Planck-Institut für ausländisches
und internationales Strafrecht Freiburg**

Beiträge und Materialien aus dem Max-Planck-Institut
für ausländisches und internationales Strafrecht, Freiburg i.Br.

Herausgegeben von Professor Dr. Dr. h.c. Albin Eser, M.C.J.

REPARATION IN CRIMINAL LAW

Band S 59   **Desmond Greer (ed.)**
COMPENSATING CRIME VICTIMS   ·
A European Survey
The countries covered by the Survey are Austria, Belgium,
Denmark, Finland, France, Germany, Greece, Ireland, Italy,
The Netherlands, Norway, Portugal, Spain, Sweden and the
United Kingdom (with separate reports on Great Britain and
Northern Ireland).
Freiburg 1996, 728 pages   DM 49,-

Band S 57/1   **Albin Eser/Susanne Walther (Hrsg.)**
WIEDERGUTMACHUNG IM KRIMINALRECHT
REPARATION IN CRIMINAL LAW
Internationale Perspektiven/International Perspectives

The reports of this volume examine both the framework for
reparation with regard to criminal law theory and the system
of sanctions as well as the forms and functions of reparation
in particular. In addition, they address reparation during imprisonment, state compensation of crime victims and settlement
of conflict outside the courtroom.
Vol. 1: National reports on England, Finland and Russia (in
English), on The Netherlands, Sweden and Poland (in German)
Freiburg 1996, 635 pages   DM 58,-

Band S 57/2   Vol. 2: National reports on the USA, Australia and Uganda
(in English), on Japan (in German)
Freiburg 1997, 465 pages   DM 54,-

Max-Planck-Institut für ausländisches
und internationales Strafrecht Freiburg